Contents

D1389162

Illustrations

All photographs are by the author

Maps and diagrams

(Those other abbeys whose plans are unknown appear alphabetically in the
  main text)

Introduction

Abbeys is a companion volume to my *Cathedrals* in this series, and some comparisons may be helpful. Only a few abbeys still have active religious life, whereas with cathedrals it is the reverse. With cathedrals the history and contents are dealt with up to the present day, even in the case of the minority which have gone to ruin or become ordinary churches. Many medieval abbeys, however, became the nuclei of great or lesser houses built out of their wrecks by the families to whom they were 'granted' at the Dissolution, and it would be inappropriate to attempt detailed descriptions of their subsequent histories or of their contents – some of which are nevertheless of the utmost architectural and historical importance. To keep the book within manageable size the emphasis has therefore to be on monastic remains and on subsequent work (buildings and fittings) of ecclesiastical but not secular character.

As with cathedrals, criteria for inclusion proved curiously elusive. Foremost was the problem of priories, and a decision had to be made either to eliminate them altogether or to include selected 'major' ones. Since many major priories only appear to be so through being fortuitous survivors of the hundreds that once flourished, and since a dividing line between 'major' and 'minor' would be impossible to draw satisfactorily, 'abbeys only' became the rule. Here it should perhaps be explained that abbeys, in general, have always been required to have thirteen monks at least, including an abbot, whereas priories are generally smaller; but whilst in some orders almost every establishment quickly became an independent abbey, in others (e.g. Augustinian and Cluniac) even quite large houses continued to be priories to the end. That is one reason why many small abbeys were smaller than some big priories and why important churches like Bridlington, Christchurch, Wenlock are excluded.

Priories which became abbeys are of course included. Conversely, abbeys which lost that status have had to be treated on their merits and included if their abbey remains are of sufficient extent and interest. Into this category fall half a dozen or so principal survivors of the innumerable pre-Conquest establishments (e.g. Monkwearmouth and Reculver) – of immense importance to the architectural historian though not primarily thought of as monastic (examples of the 'clas', the Celtic equivalent in Wales, have left little trace).

Abbeys which (either at the Reformation or later) became cathedrals are mentioned but not fully described, so as to avoid repeating what is in the book on cathedrals. Exceptions are Osney and Westminster, which quickly lost their cathedral status: they are here in full. Likewise cathedral priories (i.e. monastic cathedrals which had a bishop and a prior, but not an abbot) are excluded though they ranked as abbeys; an exception however is Bath which, although always known as an abbey, did in fact cease to be one when it became a cathedral priory linked with Wells in 1090.

Then there are the 'modern' abbeys like Ampleforth and Mount St Bernard, some of them (such as Buckfast) established in buildings of medieval origin and therefore especially interesting for their adaptation into the world of today of a way of life that goes back to the earliest days of Christianity. One or two are Anglican, not Roman Catholic.

Lastly there is a very large class of 'abbeys' which are not abbeys at all and never have been, though it is true that many of them were priories. Their honorary titles are usually due to nothing more than an innocent lack of appreciation of the meanings of the terms – especially during the eighteenth century when a gentleman's estate was incomplete without its romantic ruin. Possibly for the same reason there are instances of perfectly good abbeys (e.g. Norton and St Osyth) which have become irrevocably known as priories.

Monastic history

In a limited space it is impossible to sketch more than an outline of the history of monasteries, and the few pages that follow (based on the writings of one of the greatest experts in the field, the late A. Hamilton Thompson) are meant merely as a general background to the architectural descriptions of abbeys and should be supplemented by more detailed reading.

The earliest 'monks' were solitary hermits or anchorites in the East who gave themselves to religious contemplation. True monasteries began under the influence of St Benedict towards the end of the fifth century. His Rule, composed for his own community at Subiaco in Italy, has formed the basis for all others. Wars and strife throughout the so-called Dark Ages smothered the spread of his teachings and discouraged the revivals promoted from time to time by his successors.

The abbey of Cluny (Burgundy) founded in 910 by William, Duke of Aquitaine, was an exception in that it not only prospered under a succession of influential abbots but also had powerful influences in many parts of Western Europe. Many orders found it difficult to dissociate prosperity from a decline in observance of their original ideals, and there arose new, stricter ones such as the Carthusian whose monks lived in separate cells within a main enclosure and took their name (anglicised as Charterhouse) from La Grande Chartreuse in Dauphiné, and the Cistercian, founded in 1098 at Cîteaux (Burgundy).

The Cistercian order owed its spread to St Bernard, who went to Cîteaux in 1113 and two years later became abbot of its daughter house Clairvaux. By the time of his death in 1153 there were 330 Cistercian houses, mostly in Europe but some in the Near East, all loosely linked in allegiance to Cîteaux. In another century there were some 700. Their monks were distinguished by wearing white habits instead of black. The order of Savigny was a short-lived one amalgamated with the Cistercian in 1147.

In Britain St Augustine introduced the Rule of St Benedict in 597. After that, however (and even before, if we are to believe traditions and legends), the Celtic type of monastery, which was more akin to the Eastern, prevailed. The other great figure was St Dunstan, who did much to revive and promote Benedictinism in the south of England in the tenth century. An effect of the Norman Conquest was an even more powerful revival, many abbeys already

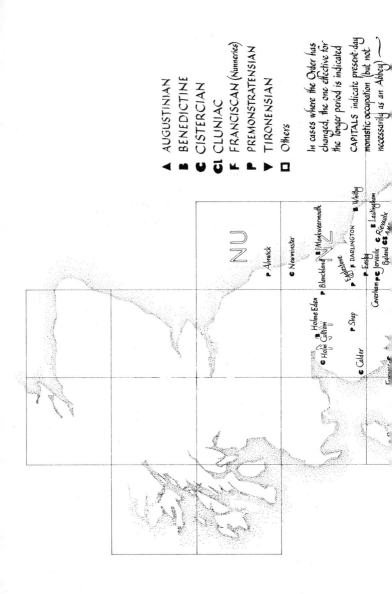

▲ AUGUSTINIAN

B BENEDICTINE

C CISTERCIAN

Cl CLUNIAC

F FRANCISCAN (Nunneries)

P PREMONSTRATENSIAN

▼ TIRONENSIAN

□ Others

In cases where the Order has changed, the one effective for the longer period is indicated

CAPITALS indicate present-day monastic occupation (but not necessarily as an Abbey)

N U

P Alnwick

C Newminster

C Holm   B Holme Eden
    Cultram
          P Blanchland   P Monkwearmouth

P Shap   P Egglestone

C Calder   P DARLINGTON   P Whitby

          P Easby
Coverham P C Jervaulx   C E Lashingham
                    C Rievaulx
              Byland C E A...

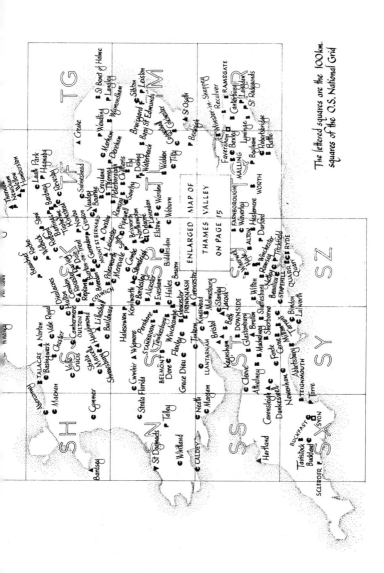

The lettered squares are the 100 km. squares of the O.S. National Grid

ENLARGED MAP OF
THAMES VALLEY
ON PAGE 15

existing being refounded, expanded and completely rebuilt in the more settled political climate.

The true Cluniacs, already mentioned, had some important houses in Britain but few abbeys; mostly they were priories directly or indirectly subservient to Cluny, until the French wars forced them to buy new 'nationality'. There was also the order of Tiron, with only a handful of houses.

About this time there arose too the orders of canons, as distinct from monks. Their aim was to combine the idea of community life with that of serving cathedrals and parish churches rather in the way that Benedictines do today, but eventually when most monks became priests the distinction became blurred. The first fully recognised order of canons was the Augustinian, founded on the Rule of St Augustine of Hippo (not the English Augustine), which came into prominence about the time of the Conquest. These were the Black or Austin Canons. There were sub-orders: the Victorine whose head was St Victor's abbey in Paris and the Arrouasian which originated near Arras. Augustinian houses were independent of higher authority and of each other, and the priories seem often not to have aspired to become abbeys.

In a similar relationship to the Augustinian canons as the Cistercian monks were to the Benedictine were the White or Premonstratensian canons, named after St Norbert's abbey of Prémontré near Laon in Picardy.

Numerous nunneries followed the rules of St Benedict or St Augustine, and a few of these ranked as abbeys; so did one or two of the Franciscan order of Poor Clares. There was also the curious Gilbertine order in which canons and nuns used a single church, but none of their houses became abbeys. Similarly needing in this context no more than a passing mention are the churches of the wandering friars – the black or Dominican, the grey or Franciscan, the white or Carmelite, and the Austin friars.

The monasteries' fate after the Dissolution varied. A few of their churches survived in use, wholly or in part, but as a general rule they and the monastic buildings passed into private hands. All materials of value were stripped out and sold. As that included lead the effect on roof timbers and walls was disastrous if somewhat delayed. But usually the walling stone was quarried away either by the owner for use in other buildings or by anyone else who had access. The more remote the abbey the less likely this was. Fountains and Tintern survived relatively complete.

One of the most interesting consequences was the conversion of

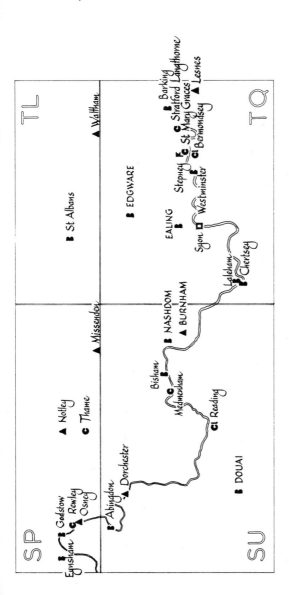

Enlarged map of the Thames Valley

some part or other to domestic use, and the ingenuity with which houses ranging from farmsteads to noblemen's mansions were produced is sometimes remarkable. Obvious choices for adaptation were the abbot's quarters, the cellarer's range, or the dorter range using the chapter house as a principal room. Often only one range was fully used, the rest being kept for stables or stores. Lacock and Delapré, where all three ranges were converted and only the church was done away with, are exceptional, though no doubt others like them have not survived. Very occasionally the church itself was converted, as at Buckland and Titchfield. In many cases the cloister garth survived; sometimes (as at Walden and Woburn) its plan is preserved even where successive rebuildings have obliterated all trace of actual monastic structures.

In Scotland, in spite of the violence of the Reformation, the Dissolution was a much more gradual process than that enforced in a space of three or four years in England and Wales by Henry VIII, but the end result was just the same.

In the eighteenth century abandoned ruins of monasteries and castles began to be appreciated for their picturesque qualities, and where real ones were lacking ambitious 'follies' were often set up instead to improve the landscape. As the nineteenth century progressed, genuine archaeological interest in ruins very gradually took the place of poetic and purely possessive mania and by the 1880s and 1890s 'digs' were more often than not being properly conducted and recorded by experts who were able to interpret what they found and, equally important, to preserve it.

The rebirth of monasticism in Britain was largely due to the gradual return of communities exiled to the Continent for over two centuries and then driven back by the French Revolution and its aftermath. Their resettlement was encouraged by the gradual emancipation of Catholics – the lifting of penal laws which had virtually put a stop to their form of worship – and by the munificence of a number of landowners. Sponsorship of this kind was not unlike the endowment of monasteries in the Middle Ages. It extended to the Anglo-Catholics, the 'high' branch of the Anglican church which grew up in the nineteenth century, and some flourishing Anglican abbeys will be found in this book. Most communities had one or more temporary homes before finding or building a permanent one; the fortunes of all are at the mercy of social and political climates, for it has never been possible for them to dissociate themselves from the world as completely as their ideals would require.

Abbey layouts

No two medieval abbey plans are quite alike; yet the resemblances are so strong that however scanty the remains it is usually a simple matter to identify the principal parts or to say where they are likely to have stood. The nucleus, strictly speaking, is not the church but the cloister, four covered walks around a square garth. Along its E side at first-floor level runs the monks' dorter or dormitory, terminating at one end with the reredorter or latrines. The reredorter was important enough to influence the entire layout. Which end it was put usually depended on the lie of the land, for a stream had to be diverted to cleanse it and to serve the kitchen, washplace and other parts. If possible it was placed to the S so that the church could be on the N side of the cloister and not overshadow it. Processional doorways from the corners of the cloister lead into the church nave. A night stair leads into the church transept from the dorter, while the quire and presbytery of the

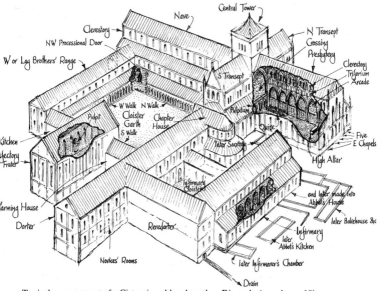

Typical arrangement of a Cistercian abbey based on Rievaulx (see also p. 18)

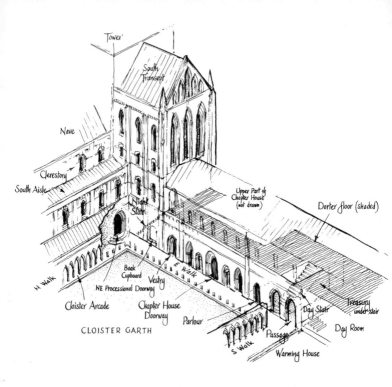

church, with high altar and probably a number of chapels, stretch further E.

Alongside the transept, usually accessible both from it and from the cloister, are a sacristy and/or library; book cupboards are often located nearby in the cloister. Near the centre of the E walk is the chapter house entrance, the meeting room itself being preceded in bigger abbeys by a lower vestibule which still allows the dorter to pass over the top. The remainder of the ground floor of the E range (the dorter undercroft) may contain a parlour, the day stair to the dorter, a treasury, a slype or passage (often towards the infirmary), a common room perhaps allocated to novices, and a lower storey of reredorter – possibly in that order.

The cloister range standing opposite the church (usually S, sometimes N) contains the refectory or frater. In Cistercian houses this was usually planned (in some cases replanned) at right angles to the cloister walk; in others it is parallel. Outside it are a washing trough and towel cupboards. On its E side so as to release some warmth into it is the warming room; on the W, usually with a food hatch between, is the kitchen.

The W range of Cistercian houses was occupied by lay brothers, manual workers who did not become fully professed monks. The first floor is their dormitory (with its own reredorter) and the ground floor is divided into stores, common room and refectory, the last being near the main kitchen. Separate access is provided into the W end of the church, which was screened off as virtually a separate building. In bigger Cistercian houses the lay brothers also had a 'lane', a separate long court isolating their range from the W walk of the cloister so that their mundane operations would not disturb its quiet. In non-Cistercian houses the W range is usually the cellarer's and mostly given over to stores.

The infirmary is a separate building, normally standing towards the SE and consisting of a hall or ward split in later years into separate cells. It often has its own chapel, kitchen and stores, garderobes and infirmarer's dwelling. The guest house, usually near the main gatehouse, is somewhat similar. The abbot, though enjoined in every Rule to sleep with his brethren, eventually had his own lodging – which in later years became in some instances a lavish, not to say grandiose, residence belying the original austerity of the community and attracting fierce criticism and greedy eyes from without.

Many other alterations occurred fairly generally over the years, resulting chiefly from changes in numbers – sometimes quite dramatically upwards or downwards. In Cistercian houses the lay brothers dwindled and disappeared. In all, the Black Death and other plagues, as well as wars and rebellions and social changes, caused reductions which were reflected in the buildings. Refectories and church naves were sometimes reduced in length. Churches, on the other hand, tended to blossom out at their E ends with ever more numerous and lavish chapels and shrines, towards which pilgrimages (and hence wealth) were directed.

In all this, nothing has been said about either the immediate or the more distant possessions: the abbey precinct with its wall, gatehouses, granary, mill, brewhouse, fishponds, stables, corrodiars' (pensioners') houses, cemetery, almonry, chapel outside the gate, etc.: the farms and granges with their produce, and the outlying parishes whose monies augmented the purely commercial revenue. Monasteries in their heyday were not only the principal centres of art and culture but they were also what would now be termed 'big business' and their customers (for wool in particular) could be found as far afield as Italy.

Nothing has been said about architectural style either. Quite simply, abbeys were built in the styles of their times. The only important thing to add is that early Cistercian buildings are distinguished by a characteristic austerity and refinement.

As for present-day abbeys, a large proportion were designed by or under the influence of the early Gothic Revivalist A.W.N. Pugin or one of his sons, and though their individual parts are markedly traditional their actual arrangement is usually less rigid and formal. Many are no more than adaptations or extensions of pre-existing mansions and very few are 'modern' in any accepted sense.

The drawn plans

An understanding of abbey remains is almost always aided by a plan, and one of the aims of this book is to provide one, wherever possible, which shows what *was* in a clear relationship to what *is*; for this reason I have used different conventions from those for cathedrals.

So far as possible, monastic walls (of whatever period) still visible are shown in full thick line; interrupted ('dotted') thick lines indicate walls proved by excavation but no longer uncovered. Later walls, i.e. post-Dissolution of whatever period, are in thinner line, and where they themselves have disappeared these thinner lines are dotted. Distinct script and block lettering will also help to separate monastic and non-monastic features. Very fine interrupted lines indicate conjectures (or in some cases earlier buildings lying beneath). Areas now roofed or vaulted (whatever their age) are shaded in half-tone; these, together with the arrow indicating the usual point of entry, will be found of considerable help in the often baffling task of getting one's bearings on arrival at a site. Existing roads and paths of significance are lightly dotted. All plans are to a scale of 1:2500.

The completeness of many of the plans is due to the enthusiasm of antiquaries and diggers since about the middle of the nineteenth century, and to the care with which their finds have usually been recorded. Here I must express my indebtedness to the library of the Society of Antiquaries and to its staff who almost always guided me to what I wanted amongst the proceedings of the numerous archaeological societies who sponsor and publish this kind of research. Much of the information available goes far beyond the scope of this book, so descriptions and plans have had of necessity to be simplified. For example one cannot in the space of a page or two dwell much if at all on hidden evidence of the layout of a previous monastery underlying a plan now exposed; however in a few significant cases such layouts are, as already mentioned, shown in thin dotted lines.

It is only right that at this point I should also record my thanks to very many others – abbots and abbesses, parsons, houseowners, librarians, museum curators, antiquarians – who have assisted with plans and checked my texts. Special gratitude is due to Mr G.K. Beaulah and Mr A.E. Kirkby for information on their own researches on Meaux and Humberston respectively; these few lines are however far too brief an acknowledgment of the immense amount of trouble everyone has taken, and I hope they will be accepted in lieu of separate letters of thanks. If I seem to have ignored some of the suggestions it is almost certainly either through lack of space or – occasionally – because there are differing schools of thought on dates or on the significance of points of detail.

Sometimes it is hard to know which lines on an antiquary's plan were based on actual sight of masonry and which on deduction or even conjecture. I have tended to give the benefit of doubt, for a reasonably complete reconstructed plan has a peculiar fascination when all that can be seen on the ground is a few jagged lumps or even a totally unrelated group of recent buildings. Where the plans have serious gaps (and there are many) or are not given at all, it may be because stonework has been robbed to the foundations by post-Dissolution owners (or by local townsfolk), because the evidence has been totally obscured by later building, or merely because no one has done any digging (in some cases for the good reason that private owners do not want the disturbance). Gaps in the plans of present-day abbeys are few, thanks to generous assistance for which I am immensely grateful. There are, however, some 'enclosed' houses where information is simply not available.

A further difficulty is that relics of ill-conducted digging, and even attempts at reconstruction work, by enthusiastic amateurs, may have distorted an already confused picture. Spoil heaps formed with the best of intentions by one generation become grassed and brambled long before the next arrives. Aerial photography, which has revealed much, loses its value after such disturbance, so it is more than ever important to conduct 'digs' properly or not at all. However much we may side with the advocates of 'romantic decay', there is not a shadow of doubt about the benefits of professionally controlled digging and conservation; the only alternative is 'leave alone'. After the depredations of previous centuries, it is good to know that protection has the force of law but disturbing to come across the rare instance where the law is flouted either through ignorance or from a selfish lack of appreciation of the irreplaceability of what remains. Each site, to those who have eyes to see, guards a unique and distinct facet of history; each has its *genius loci*, a powerful and often overwhelming individuality of which mere words and pictures can convey no more than an inkling.

Visiting abbeys

An attempt has been made in every case to indicate the possibilities of a visit. At State-owned sites and the bigger 'stately homes' this is usually a clear 'yes' or 'no', with stated hours and dates, but elsewhere things may be less straightforward and it may be necessary to ask specific permission. This is no place to discuss the law of trespass, but it is worth remembering that 'Private' signs can be (and are) put up beside legitimate public footpaths and that they are intended to warn off poachers, picnickers, persons with metal detectors, and other 'undesirables' – whereas genuine enquirers and amateur historians will almost always meet with a warm welcome once they have identified themselves. Of course such a welcome may simply not be possible if the site is very obviously either a private residence or the home of an active community of nuns or monks, but the guidance given here and there in the book may help to open a few doors. In cases of doubt a letter of enquiry a reasonable time in advance of a desired visit may well clear misunderstandings before they even arise.

The actual ownership of abbeys is a complex subject, and the indications given are meant as no more than a guide. There can be said to be five main categories: the State (or Crown Estates), local councils, private individuals (or trusts or companies), church parishes or dioceses, and religious communities. Those in State 'care' (Department of the Environment, Welsh Office or Scottish Development Department guardianship) are not necessarily State-owned, even if they have standard signposting and admission arrangements, but there would be no practical value in making differentiations. A further complication is that some sites are only partially 'in care', the rest being privately occupied. Again, some urban sites have become so fragmented that they can really only be labelled 'in multiple ownership'. In the cases of private ownership I give family names rather than individuals, partly to reduce the rate at which the information will inevitably become outdated and partly because family trusts and companies are often involved – a kind of detail hardly relevant to the scope of this book.

Where a charge is made for admission I have noted the fact – but without giving figures for they too are liable to change. Against sites in State care I have generally noted 'standard hours'. These are 9.30 a.m. to 6.30 p.m. (but to 4.0 p.m. from 15th March to 15th October). Except in some larger abbeys in the summer, Sunday opening is not till 2.0 p.m., and some may be found closed any day between 1.0 and 2.0 p.m. Some however (as noted in the text) are always open. At churches in use it may be assumed that no fixed charge is made, but since the size, and hence the cost of upkeep, of former monastic churches is greater than the average, visitors ought to contribute as generously as they can.

Each site is identified in the text heading by its Ordnance Survey National Grid 6-figure reference, which pin-points it within 100 metres on the map.

Summary

The following table summarises the main points of interest to visitors under various headings, the symbol ○ meaning 'good' and ● 'poor'.

architecture ○ moderately important ○○ of particular importance (including post-monastic)

setting ● poor ○ attractive ○○ specially fine

guide ○ leaflet available at site ○○ more lavish illustrated book available at site

restrictions ● limited times (or parts) of access ●● no public access ●●● exterior not visible to public

accessibility ● physically difficult

extent ○ considerable remains ○○ unusually complete ○○○ 'live' community ● little to be seen above ground ●● exact site uncertain

	archi-tecture	setting	guide	restric-tions	accessi-bility	extent
Abbotsbury	○	○		●		
Aberconwy		○	○			
Abingdon		○	○			
Alcester						●●
Alnwick		○		●		
Alton				●		○○○
Ampleforth	○	○	○○	●		○○○
Athelney		○				●●
Bardney						●
Bardsey		○			●	
Barking						○
Barlings						
Basingwerk			○			○
Bath	○○	○○	○○			
Battle	○	○	○○			○
Bayham		○				○
Beauchief		○	○			
Beaulieu	○	○○	○○			○
Beeleigh		○		●●		

	archi-tecture	setting	guide	restric-tions	accessi-bility	extent
Belmont	○	○	○	●		○○○
Bermondsey		●				●
Biddlesden		○		●●		●
Bindon		○		●		○
Bisham		○		●●		●
Blanchland	○	○	○			○
Bordesley				●		○
Bourne	○	○	○			○
Boxley				●●		
Breedon	○	○	○			
Bristol	○○	○	○○			○○
Brixworth	○○		○○			○
Bruern		○		●●		●●
Bruisyard				●●		●
Bruton			○			●●
Buckfast	○○		○○	●		○○○
Buckland	○	○○	○○			○
Buildwas	○	○○	○			○○
Burnham				●		○○○
Burton-on-Trent						
Bury St Edmunds	○○	○	○○			○○
Byland	○○	○	○			○○
Calder	○	○○		●●		○
Caldey		○	○	●	●	○○○
Canonsleigh						
Canterbury	○○	○	○○			○○
Cerne	○	○				
Chatteris						●
Chertsey				●		●
Chester	○○	○	○○			○○
Cirencester		○				
Cleeve	○	○	○○			○○
Cockersand						
Coggeshall		○				
Colchester						
Colwich				●		○○○

	architecture	setting	guide	restrictions	accessibility	extent
Combe		O				O
Combermere		OO		●●●		
Coverham			O			
Creake			OO	●		O
Croxden	O		O			O
Croxton		O		●●		●
Croyland	O		O			O
Cwmhir		O				
Cymmer		O	O			O
Dale		O				
Darley						●
Darlington	O			●		OOO
Delapré		O	OO	●		O
Denny	O		O			O
Dereham						●●
Dieulacres						
Dorchester	OO	O	OO			O
Dore	OO	O	O			O
Douai	O		OO	●		OOO
Downside	OO	O	O	●		OOO
Dunkeswell		O	O			
Durford						●
Ealing	O		O	●		OOO
Easby	O	O	OO			OO
Edgware			O	●		OOO
Egglestone		O	OO			O
Elstow						
Ely	OO	OO	OO			
Evesham	O	O	O			O
Eynsham			O			●
Farnborough	O		O	●		OOO
Faversham						●
Flaxley		O		●●		O
Forde	OO	OO	OO	●		O
Fountains	OO	OO	OO			OO
Furness	OO	OO	OO			OO

	archi-tecture	setting	guide	restric-tions	accessi-bility	extent
Garendon		○		●		●
Glastonbury	○○	○	○○			○
Gloucester	○○	○	○○			○○
Godstow		○				
Grace Dieu				●●		●●
Hagnaby					●	●●
Hailes	○	○	○○			○
Halesowen		○				
Hartland		○○		●		
Haslemere				●		○○
Haughmond	○	○	○			○
Holm Cultram			○			
Holme Eden		○		●		○○○
Hulton				●		
Humberston						●
Hyde						
Jervaulx	○	○	○			○○
Kenilworth						
Keynsham				●		
Kingswood						
Kirkstall	○○	○	○○			○○
Kirkstead						
Lacock	○○	○○	○○			○
Laleham	○			●		○○
Langdon			○			
Langley						
Lastingham	○	○	○			○
Lavendon						●●
Leicester						
Leiston						○
Lesnes		○				○
Lilleshall	○	○				○
Llantarnam		○		●		●
London (St Mary of Graces)		○		●●		●
Louth Park						●

	archi-tecture	setting	guide	restric-tions	accessi-bility	extent
Lulworth		O				●●
Lyminge			O			
Maenan						●
Malling	O	O	OO	●		OOO
Malmesbury	OO	O	OO			O
Margam	O	OO	O			O
Marham						
Meaux						●
Medmenham		O		●●		●
Merevale						
Milton	OO	OO	OO			O
Minster-in-Sheppey			O			
Missenden		O		●●		
Monkwearmouth	O		OO			
Mount St Bernard		O	O	●		OOO
Muchelney	O		O	●		O
Nashdom	OO	O	OO	●		OOO
Neath	O		OO			OO
Netley	O	OO	OO			O
Newbo						●●
Newenham						
Newminster					●	
Newsham						●●
Northampton		●				●●
Norton	O	O	OO			O
Notley		O		●●		
Osney		●				●
Oulton				●		OOO
Owston			O			O
Pershore	OO	O	OO			O
Peterborough	OO	O	OO			OO
Pipewell						●
Polesworth						O
Prinknash	O	OO	OO	●		OOO
Prinknash (old)		O	OO	●●		OO
Quarr	OO	O	OO	●		OOO

	archi-tecture	setting	guide	restric-tions	accessi-bility	extent
Quarr (old)			○○			○
Ramsey	○	○		●		○
Ramsgate	○○		○○	●		○○○
Reading						○
Reculver	○	○	○			
Repton	○	○	○○			
Revesby		○				●
Rewley						●
Rievaulx	○○	○○	○○			○○
Robertsbridge				●●		
Rocester						●●
Roche	○○	○○	○○			○○
Romsey	○○		○○			○
Rufford		○		●		●
Rushen			○○			
Ryde			○○	●		○○○
St Albans	○○	○	○○			○
St Benet of Holme		○			●	
St Dogmael's			○○			○
St Osyth	○	○	○○			
St Radegund's		○	○			
Salley						○
Sawtry						●
Sclerder				●		○○○
Selby	○○		○○			○
Shaftesbury		○	○			
Shap		○				○
Sherborne	○○	○	○○			○
Shrewsbury	○		○○	●		○
Sibton					●	
Stanbrook	○			●		○○○
Stanley						●
Stapehill				●		○○○
Stepney		●				●●
Stoneleigh	○○	○○	○○	●		○
Stow	○		○			

	archi-tecture	setting	guide	restric-tions	accessi-bility	extent
Strata Florida	O	O	O			
Strata Marcella						●
Stratford Langthorne		●				●●
Sulby						●●
Swineshead						●●
Syon		O	OO	●		OOO
Syon (old)		O	OO			●
Talacre		O	O	●		OOO
Talley		O	O			O
Tarrant		O				●●
Tavistock				●		
Teignmouth			O	●		OOO
Tewkesbury	OO	O	OO			O
Thame		O		●●		
Thorney			O			
Thornton	O		OO			O
Tilty						
Tintern	OO	OO	OO			OO
Titchfield	O		OO			O
Torre		OO	OO			O
Tupholme						
Vale Royal						●
Valle Crucis	O	O	OO			O
Vaudey		O		●●		●
Walden	OO	OO	OO			●
Waltham	OO		OO			O
Warden						
Waterbeach						●
Waverley	O	O		●		O
Welbeck	OO			●●●		
Wellow						●●
Wendling						●
Westminster	OO	O	OO			OO
Whalley		O	OO	●		O
Wherwell				●		
Whitby	OO	OO	OO			O

	archi-tecture	setting	guide	restric-tions	accessi-bility	extent
Whitland						●
Wigmore		○		●		○
Wilton	○○	○	○○			
Winchcombe						●
Winchester		○				●
Woburn	○○	○	○○			●
Worth	○	○	○○	●		○○○
Wymondham	○○	○	○○			○
York	○	○	○○			○

Alternative names

The names in the first column include historical and modern alternatives, while the second column indicates the names adopted in this book.

Axminster	Newenham
Bradsole	St Radegund's
Caerleon	Llantarnam
Chich	St Osyth
Conway	Aberconwy; also Maenan
Dene	Flaxley
Dover	St Radegund's
Enlli	Bardsey
Glyn y Groes	Valle Crucis
Grimsby	Wellow
Kemmer	Cymmer
Leek	Dieulacres
Ludham	St Benet of Holme
Maldon	Beeleigh
Medeshamstede	Peterborough
Modwennestow	Burton-on-Trent
Nedd	Neath
New Abbey	St Mary Graces, London
Newhouse	Newsham
Oxeney	Barlings
St Augustine's	Canterbury
Sawley	Salley
Stanley Park	Dale
Thurnham	Cockersand
Tyndryn	Tintern
Vallis Dei	Vaudey
Vallis Florida	Cleeve
Vanner	Cymmer
Welford	Sulby
Westwood	Lesnes
Ynys Byr	Caldey
Ystrad Fflur	Strata Florida
Ystrad Marchell	Strata Marcella

Abbotsbury: Abbey barn: *c.*1400

Abbotsbury Dorset: in village   SY 578852

Benedictine abbey of St Peter founded *c.*1026 by Orcus, steward of
King Cnut. Dissolved 1539 and sold to Sir Giles Strangways

Owned partly by parish, largely by Earl of Ilchester. Church site
accessible at all times without charge; remainder mostly private

What little is left of the buildings is variously 12th to 15th c. The
chief is the famous tithe barn of *c.*1400. There are also parts of two
14th c. gatehouses, some other outbuildings incorporated like them
into dwellings, a prominent fragment of an unidentified building, a
15th c. fragment of the church, and several lengths of precinct wall.
The well-known swannery is of medieval origin too.

Sir Giles Strangways made a house out of some of the buildings
but little of it survived a siege by Parliamentarians in the Civil War.
Excavations in 1871 revealed part of the church; since then the
parish churchyard has been extended into the site of the nave.

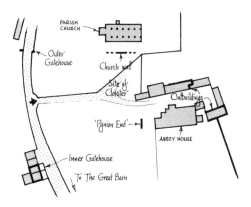

The remains lie close to the lane (Church Street and Abbey
Road) on the W side of the parish church. From this lane a driveway
to the S side of the churchyard starts at a Jacobean archway. The
15th c. fragment of abbey **church** will be found in the churchyard
close to the S wall of the parish church; there are remains of wall
shafts and wall seat, and a pile of carved stones nearby.

S of the churchyard gate is the tall shapeless mass called Pynion
End, dated *c.*1400 but of unknown purpose; remains of a fireplace

and doorway are evident. Beyond it in the valley can be seen the tithe barn. To the E of Pynion End is the 17th c. Abbey House, on the other side of which stands a small 14th c. outbuilding. These are private, and so is the group nearer the church (Abbot's Wind) of which the E part is 14th c. too.

Back now into Church Street. A little way up to the right (marked with a 'Give Way' sign) are two bits of the 14th c. **outer gatehouse**: on the E of the road just a pier, and on the W the beginnings of arches and various carved fragments built into the wall behind.

Turning now down the lane, on the right of the hill will be found the strongly buttressed **inner gatehouse**, turned into a house; the main arch at its lower end is filled with two storeys. Finally the great tithe barn, one of the largest in England even in its incomplete state, almost one half being now roofless. The hammer-beam roof is 17th c., but the almost cathedral-like porch (there were two) is original. It is worth walking further along the lane for a view of its noble W front with a niche on top of the central buttress. The pigeon house in the field behind almost certainly originated from the abbey too.

Aberconwy Gwynedd: in Conwy town centre   SH 782775

Cistercian abbey of St Mary and All Saints founded 1186 at
   Rhedynog-felen in Llanwnda parish near Caernarfon, a daughter
   house of Strata Florida; moved to Conwy by 1200. Dissolved 1283
   and moved to Maenan

Parish church. Open during normal hours

Aberconwy became important as a burial place of native princes and a repository of Welsh records. As an abbey it has to be imagined in the usual Cistercian isolation on an unfrequented river bank. But after a century Edward I ousted the monks to make space for his castle and fortified town, and their church passed to parish use. It subsequently underwent a typical sequence of alterations and rebuildings, so that now the only visible original (pre-1283) work is at the extreme W and E ends. The tower, nave, chancel and sacristy are of c.1300, the S transept early 14th c., the aisles mid-14th c. and the porches 16th or 17th c. Nothing is left of the monastic buildings; they lay to the N as at the rebuilt abbey, which is described under 'Maenan'.

Blackened ancient woodwork is one of the principal attractions of the church interior – a 15th c. screen and stall fronts, and some 17th c. balustrading. Numerous ledger stones and other memorials are of interest; also a small parish museum off the W end of the N aisle.

Outside, thin grey stones roughly coursed indicate work of before 1283, i.e. of the abbey. The N aisle wall and the tower are on abbey foundations; its S aisle seems to have extended W to match the N. The now very worn tower doorway may perhaps have been moved from the chapter house. The three lancets above are original, but the upper part of the tower is 15th c. The S side presents similar features, including a second timber-framed porch, and at the E end the present 'Perpendicular' window can readily be seen to be an insertion into the original wall.

Abingdon Oxfordshire: in town   SU 500972

Benedictine abbey of St Mary founded 675 in Bagley Wood near Sunningwell, by Hean. Moved to Abingdon 695. Dissolved 1538

Owned by Vale of White Horse District Council, the Friends of Abingdon, and others. Church site open at all times without charge. Checker etc. open every day 2.0 to 6.0 p.m. (admission charge)

Tradition tells of twin foundations for men and women by Hean and his sister Cilla. Only the former prospered. Sacked by Danes in the 10th c., the abbey was refounded by King Edred *c.*954 under St Ethelwold, pupil of St Dunstan, and rose to the forefront of Saxon culture. Under Norman rule it lost and recovered power and was rebuilt. The 14th c. saw constant friction with the town that had grown up beside it. In the 15th c. the church nave was rebuilt with W towers and a great central tower.

At the Dissolution everything disappeared but the gatehouse and a few minor buildings by the millstream. Partial excavation in 1922 established the church and cloister outlines in Abbey House gardens; the existence of Saxon foundations is still conjecture.

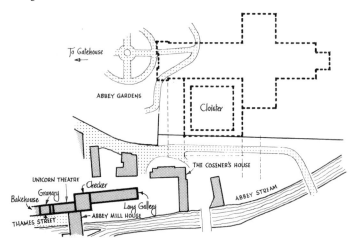

A sequence of checker ('exchequer'), church, gatehouse is convenient. The line of **checker** buildings now in the care of the Friends of Abingdon is entered at the end of the granary barn. From a small museum area one crosses a passage into another barn (Checker Hall) used as a small theatre and entered on the stage. Though much altered, it has a fine 14th c. timber roof. Behind the auditorium is the checker itself – with a similar roof, a specially good 13th c. fireplace, good window and doorway stonework, and a 14th c. dividing partition. Next is the Long Gallery (c.1500), built as a series of small rooms possibly for clerks but subsequently so altered by a brewery that its original layout is lost. The continuous windows were never glazed. The far end, with a fireplace and cellar, has been a house; steps here lead to a long undercroft and out to a rear yard which provides views of the N face and (through a passage) of part of the river front with inserted Elizabethan windows. The vaulted checker undercroft (with another 13th c. fireplace) can be entered; the exit leads into Checker Walk from which the gabled 13th c. chimney is visible, the finest of its date in England.

Ahead up the lane are the gardens of 18th c. Abbey House (now council offices). A 19th c. owner used medieval stones to build tracery patterns in the outer wall and an artificial ruin just inside; where they came from has been forgotten. The **church** extended

from the edge of the circular path across the park beyond, nearly to
the paddling pool; nothing of it can be seen.

The **Abbey Gate** lies to the W beside St Nicholas's church. Much
of it is 15th c.; the S arch of the three is a 19th c. addition. The
statue of St Mary facing Market Square is original, except the head.
The adjoining building to the S, mostly 15th c., was St John's
Hospital, its N wing being heightened in 1759 to provide a council
chamber. The former hall in its E range became a school in the 16th
c. and is now known as the Roysse Room.

Alcester Warwickshire: ¼ mile NW of town centre   SP 088578

Benedictine abbey of the Blessed Virgin Mary, St Anne, St Joseph,
St John the Baptist and St John the Evangelist founded 1140 by
Ralph le Boteler; became cell to Evesham 1466; passed to
Thomas Cromwell 1536. The partially explored site (Williams
family) lies in river meadows behind the schools in Priory Road.
Further N near the end of Ragley Mill Lane are a fishpond and
millstream and two lengths of precinct wall.

Alnwick Northumberland: NU 179141
in Hulne Park, ¾ mile W of town centre, close to Eglingham road
B6346

Premonstratensian abbey of St Mary founded 1147 by Eustace
fitzJohn, a daughter house of Newsham. Dissolved 1535,
refounded 1536, and again suppressed 1539. Granted to Sadler
and Winnington families

Owned by Duke of Northumberland. Exterior of gatehouse may be
seen on Saturdays and Sundays from 11.0 a.m. till dusk (i.e.
when Hulne Park is open). Entry passes available for other times,
on application to Estates Office, Alnwick Castle. No cars
allowed.

Only the 14th c. gatehouse remains above ground, though in the
18th c. one Thomas Doubleday had a house within the abbey ruins.
The entire plan of the remainder was found by excavation in 1884
and is marked out on the grass.

Gatehouse

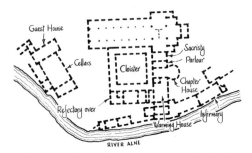

Guest House

Cellars

Cloister

Sacristy

Parlour

Chapter House

Refectory over

Warming House

Infirmary

RIVER ALNE

   Entry to Hulne Park (on foot only) is by Forest Lodge ½ mile due
W of the Castle. Visitors should follow paths down to the river and
walk upstream, over the footbridge and then back downstream (700
yards) to the abbey, (alternatively the gatehouse may be glimpsed
from Canongate Bridge over the Alne).

   The imposing fortified gatehouse retains a niche on the S side,
also a projecting garderobe on the W side near the top; the
carriageway has a simple tunnel vault. The ground plan markings of
the abbey itself lie between here and the river and are partly crossed
by horse-riding tracks. Any recommendation of an itinerary would
be pointless, but the chapter house of unique shape (part circular,
part rectangular) should be sought out. Another somewhat unusual
feature is the lack of any western range to the cloister.

Alton Hampshire: SU 676377
1½ miles ENE of Medstead on Alton Road

Abbey of Our Lady and St John, Anglican Benedictine, founded
   1895 by the Rev. Charles Hopkins

Church open during normal hours on application at main entrance

The community was founded in 1884 to promote charitable work
among seamen, its first priory being at Calcutta, the second at Barry
Docks (1893) and the third at Greenwich (1899); all are now closed.
The still incomplete church of this, the mother house, and a
detached gatehouse are mostly by Percy Green (1896–1907), and

much of the remainder (including an attached Seamen's Home) by Sir Charles Nicholson (1929–36); the latter was extended in 1955–6 under Henry Rushton, and completion of the monastery will at the time of writing shortly be in hand – so that what follows may be found to be out of date in certain respects.

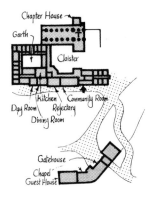

The entrance is through Nicholson's homely brick-arched portico, set back from the road. A passage between monastic (private) rooms leads informally to the **church**. Bare brick and flint inside and out, its design was based, it is said, on Jervaulx, and has an austere individuality. Even the pulpitum is flint-faced; it carries a simple Rood by Nicholson. On its right is a way to the S quire aisle and thence to the quire temporarily beneath the tower – with canopied altar also by Nicholson, and three old chests, probably 17th c. On the N, as though it were a transept, is the little chapter house with five stalls each side, and on the S the sacristy with a gallery over.

Outside a complete circuit can be made – turning right along the Georgianesque S front with its pleasant flush brick and flint and continuing round the church. On its N side a small undercroft is visible; on the E is 'toothing' for the unbuilt presbytery and aisles. The pyramidal tiled roof of the 'central' tower was added by Nicholson. Up by the road, the not-too-serious orieled gatehouse of 1903 suggests Green's very personal brick-and-flint idiom, though the design was, at least in part, the work of the Rev. J.C. Hawes.

Ampleforth North Yorkshire: SE 598788
1 mile E of village and 3 miles SSW of Helmsley

Benedictine priory of St Laurence the Martyr founded at
  Dieulouard, Lorraine, 1619; moved to England 1793 and to
  Ampleforth 1802; became abbey 1900

Church (only) open to the public during normal hours

The exiled community in France traced its lineage back to
Westminster Abbey through Sigebert Buckley, the latter's last
surviving monk. Driven out by the Revolution, it returned to
England and had temporary houses in Shropshire and then
Lancashire before going to Ampleforth Lodge, built in 1793 by
Lady Anne Fairfax for her chaplain. The monks added wings to it
and in 1857–61 built a church to its W under Charles Hansom. In
1894–8 the main monastery, further W, was built under Bernard
Smith; it was extended in 1929 under Sir Giles Gilbert Scott.
Hansom's church was replaced in two stages in 1922–61 by a much
bigger one by Scott. The school, now called Ampleforth College,
was established with the priory and its extensive buildings (mostly
to the E of the abbey) range in date from 1812 to 1983.

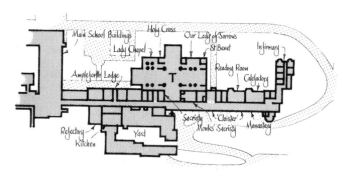

  The **church** orientation is the reverse of normal, but for
consistency (in spite of the compass points used above and in the
guide book) the following assumes the quire to be at the E end.
Entry, then, is to the S transept across a short 'public' section of the
long so-called cloister that links the school buildings on the left with
the monastery on the right. The crossing, with tall pointed arches
and a saucer-dome, is wide and rather austere with a rough plaster

finish. On every side a very short buttressing bay is followed by another arch – after which the transepts have broad barrel vaults with windows cut into their lower parts, and the nave and quire each a slightly lower saucer-dome. The nave, the longest of the four arms, finishes with a barrel vault like the transepts. The nave aisles have plain flat ceilings, and their arcades plain round columns with surprisingly naïve caps and bases. The quire, to be seen later, is of 1922–4, the remainder 1957–61 – both Scott but quite different in character from his work at Downside and Liverpool. The altar and grey stone Byzantine canopy (1930) are also his – a curious composition with kneeling and standing saints. The E window behind is by Herbert Hendrie. Looking now S, the organ is seen on a gallery extending back over the cloister passage. To its right is a small sacristy, then stairs to the **crypt**.

Like the church above, the crypt is of two dates. It has no fewer than 25 chapels. The first and biggest, that of SS John Fisher and Thomas More, has an 18th c. Spanish crucifix. In front of a chapel to the right is the large brass of Bishop Hedley (d. 1915) and in St Alban Roe's chapel (beneath the N transept) a slate slab to Abbot Matthews (d. 1939) and some 14th c. glass from the demolished house Moreton Paddox in Warwickshire. The Madonna at the W end of the ambulatory is by Jonah Jones, 1966, and by the third chapel from the end is a memorial to Abbot Oswald Smith (d. 1924). The glass in this group of chapels is by Geoffrey Webb.

Another stair leads back to the N quire aisle. Across the transept from there are the Holy Cross chapel, with a 14th c. Italian crucifix, and the Lady chapel with another of the 16th c. and a jolly 14th c. French Madonna. The Annunciation window is by Patrick Reyntiens.

Scott's **quire** is similar in form to his later nave but quite different in detail: arcades on clustered columns with Romanesque style caps, traditional arch mouldings, window dressings etc., all in 'Blue' Hornton stone. In the N ('Memorial') chapel is a rich stone and gilded wood reredos by Scott – also glass by James Powell & Son ('Eve'), Hendrie ('David') and Joseph Nuttgens (the remainder). St Benet's, the little chapel beyond, has relics of Byland in the altar slab and a 14th c. alabaster panel. The quire woodwork, by Robert Thompson, bears his 'mouse' symbol; only the dignitaries' stalls along the E wall have canopies, with a simplified Gothic coving right across. In the S quire aisle is more glass from Moreton Paddox – also the 19th c. gilt and enamel shrine of St Laurence.

The main cloister corridor, if followed to the right on leaving the church, leads into **Ampleforth Lodge**, passing the monks' refectory (unusual in being outside the monastic enclosure) on the left. The graceful curved stair and carved doorcase are earlier than the house and came from Ness Hall at Nunnington. **Outside**, the five-bay house of 1793 is distinct, and the three-bay extension on each side; the pedimented doorway came from Nunnington too. Beyond are school buildings. The church dominates the entire long range facing the valley; the junction between its own two phases is evident. The great tower has two bells, one of them cast in 1658 for the Newcastle Guildhall. Past the quire stands the five-storey monastic building of 1898, completed at the far end with the lower 'New Wing' of 1929.

Athelney Somerset: ST 346293
1 mile E of Lyng on Taunton-Street road A 361

Benedictine abbey of St Peter, St Paul and St Athelwine founded *c*.888 by King Alfred in gratitude for regaining his throne after defeat by the Danes; refounded *c*. 960 and dissolved 1539. An obelisk of 1801 marks the reputed site, at the end of a low ridge above the marshes. Leave to visit should be sought at the farmhouse (Morgan family).

Bardney Lincolnshire: ¾ mile NW of village   TF 113705

Benedictine abbey of St Peter and St Paul founded by 697 by King Ethelred; destroyed 870; refounded 1087 as priory of St Peter, St Paul and St Oswald by Gilbert de Gaunt, Earl of Lincoln, dependent on Charroux abbey; became abbey again 1115 or 1116. Dissolved 1538 and granted to Sir Robert Tirwhit

Owned by Bardney Parochial Church Council. Open to the public at all times without charge

Nothing is known of the first buildings; their founder Aethelred became abbot and was canonised. The Danes sacked them and an entirely new monastery was begun two centuries later. The church, begun *c*.1120 at the E end, was not completed with its W front till *c*.1270, though the chapter house and refectory were in use by *c*.1140 and the W range of the cloister by *c*.1200. The dorter was rebuilt in the 13th c. and the gatehouse in the 14th c.

   Six monks were executed in 1537 for their part in the Lincolnshire

Rising. The Tirwhits used the abbot's lodging as a house and the cloister as a garden; the rest went to ruin, and so later did the house. Excavations in 1909–14 revealed the plan and architectural treatment in great detail but little was done to preserve it, and so weather and vegetation have again gained the upper hand. The 65 medieval grave slabs discovered, many of them serving as paving, presumably lie beneath the grass. Even more unfortunate are the quantities of dislodged worked stones lying about.

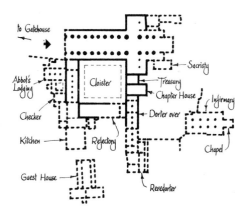

The site, signposted from the village, lies to the right of the lane, opposite and just beyond Abbey Farm. At the point where the lane turns sharply left is a big tree near where the gatehouse stood. 80 yards E of this is the line of the W front; twin lines of hillocks conceal the nave pier bases beyond. The outbuilding in the right foreground was probably the abbot's house. At the crossing, the NW main pier can be readily identified; the E end is now indeterminate but the transept outlines are clear. Now turning S, the fairly flat square cloister garth can be seen, with parts of the treasury and chapter house walls still exposed; to their S is the clear shape of the dorter undercroft and, on the S of the cloister, that of the refectory. Undulations still further S represent the guest house. Finally the W cloister range can be readily picked out, with the kitchen to its S and the various additions on its W side which were seen at the start.

In the parish church are the grave-slab of Abbot Horncastle (d.1508) and numerous carved stones, all brought from the abbey.

Bardsey Gwynedd: on Bardsey Island   SH 120222

Culdee community probably founded *c*.516 by Cadvan, king of
North Wales; became Augustinian abbey of St Mary *c*.1210.
Dissolved *c*.1537

Owned by Bardsey Island Trust. Site accessible at all times without
charge, but visitor's permit has to be bought. Irregular motor
boat service from Abersoch (Mr S. Thomas, Abersoch 2268),
allowing two hours on island

Or Enlli, one of the great centres of Celtic monasticism and the
reputed burial place of 20,000 saints. Of the abbey buildings little is
known and even less survives – merely the shell of a 13th c. tower,
in unknown relationship to the remainder.
   Ruin seems to have been a gradual process; the church ruin stood
in 1662 and the abbot's house was still occupied in 1814 but had
gone 30 years later.

The island now has only a handful of permanent residents.
Staying visitors travel on the Trust's boat from Pwllheli, but that
does not allow enough time for day trippers. The walk up the rough
track from landing to abbey takes about twenty minutes each way
and passes several farm and domestic buildings amongst which a
few bits of abbey stone have been identified. The tower stump, 20
feet or so in height, stands at one corner of the island churchyard
between two big crosses – one a war memorial and the other erected
by Lord Newborough in memory of the '20,000 saints'. There are
indications of former walls extending to the S and towards the road
on the W, and burials have been found on the other side of the road
(within the farm Ty Nesaf or Hen-dy). Also there are three lumps of
fallen masonry around the churchyard steps. Within the tower two
cross-slabs have been set up – the smaller of about the 8th c. and the
larger (inscribed) perhaps 10th c.
   Aberdaron, whence medieval pilgrims sailed (three pilgrimages
to Enlli were regarded as equal to one pilgrimage to Rome) has a
cottage reputed to have been their rest-house.

Barking London: in town centre   TQ 441839

Benedictine nunnery of St Mary and (later) St Ethelburga founded
c.666 by St Erkenwald, Bishop of London. Dissolved 1539 and
passed to Edward, Lord Clinton

Owned by London Borough of Barking. Open at all times without
charge

Destroyed by the Danes in 870, it was refounded c.965 under the
Benedictine order by King Edgar and St Dunstan. Becoming one of
the most important nunneries in England, it was William the
Conqueror's temporary seat of government following his
coronation at the end of 1066. In the 12th c. the church was rebuilt;
its apsed E end gave way to a Lady chapel in the 13th c. Of the
monastic buildings little but their general plan is known; the two-
storeyed 15th c. Fire Bell (curfew) Gate on the E side of the
precinct however survives.

The church was demolished in 1541. Many of the abbey materials
were used in the royal palaces at Deptford and Greenwich. The site
was acquired by the Urban District Council in 1910 and excavated
in 1911.

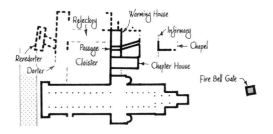

Fire Bell Gate forms the main entrance to what is now a public
open space N of the parish church. Its upper floor (not open to the
public) is the Holy Rood chapel, and contains a very worn 12th c.
stone Crucifixion formerly on the outside wall.

Not all the excavated remains lie exposed, and some walls are
indicated by obviously modern cappings. However the general
layout of the principal buildings is easily grasped. First seen past the
gate on the right are foundations of the infirmary chapel, and then,
below on the left, the entire N side of the church, the S side being
marked by the churchyard wall (much patched and heightened).

The path follows a clearly defined passageway and descends to the square lawn which was the cloister garth. Note the chapter house on the left of the steps; then cross the cloister to the W end of the church where a gate leads into Abbey Road, which was only formed in 1909. From here the great size of the church can be imagined. Unfortunately the columns are not marked, but on the S side the transept with its apse is obvious, and it is worth walking the length of the nave and quire and up into the square-ended Lady chapel at the extreme E.

Barlings Lincolnshire: TF 089735
7 miles E of Lincoln and 2½ miles SE of Langworth on A158

Premonstratensian abbey of St Mary founded 1154 by Ralph de
  Haya at Barlings Grange, a daughter house of Newsham; moved
  soon after to Oxeney, 1 mile to S. Surrendered 1537 after
  execution of abbot and four canons and given to Duke of Suffolk

Owned by Thomas family. Accessible at all times without charge

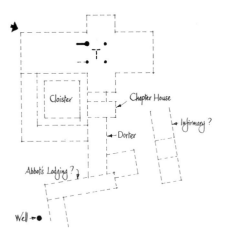

The church seems to have been lavishly rebuilt in the 14th c. Of the rest little is known; air photography shows only the barest outlines but the general plan evidently followed standard lines. Dissolution and dismantling came in the aftermath of the Lincolnshire Rising.

However parts of the E cloister range stood till at least 1730, the stately tower did not fall till 1757, and there is still a tall isolated fragment of nave wall – which a 19th c. farmer with a team of horses failed to topple.

The fragment is of the NE corner of the nave and survives through being a solid side wall of the canons' quire, forming in effect a buttress for the tower. It shows shafts of the crossing pier, the easternmost cap of the nave arcade, some good carved corbels, and springers of both nave and aisle vaults. The cloister to the S is far from clear, but some distance beyond is the abbey well virtually intact, fenced in and with a tree beside it. Still further and to the left are the abbey fishponds.

Carved pieces of abbey stone can easily be seen both in the adjoining Ferry House and in an older cottage by the turn at the end of the lane.

Basingwerk Clwyd: SJ 194773
¼ mile SW of Greenfield, on Holywell road B5121

Savigniac abbey of the Blessed Virgin Mary founded *c.*1132, probably by Ranulf, Earl of Chester, and probably at first at Hen Blas, 3 miles nearer Flint; became Cistercian 1147. Dissolved 1536 and granted to Henry ap Harry and Peter Mutton; briefly refounded in reign of Mary I

In care of Welsh Office. Open during standard hours without charge

The outer walls of the cloister survive in part from the 12th c. buildings, but nothing of the church, which is early 13th c. along with most of the E range. The refectory is only a little later, and there were few subsequent changes.

After the Dissolution all worthwhile materials were soon removed and the buildings went to ruin. Much of the lead seems to have gone to roof Dublin castle. The remains were given into the care of the Commissioners of Works in 1923 and consist mainly of the E and S cloister ranges and the shell of a range believed to occupy the site of the infirmary.

The approach is towards the cloister, the church being on the left. Only the bases of the cloister walks are visible, and the W range has gone altogether. The **church** ruin can be entered by the SW doorway. Though so little is left its plan, wholly 13th c., is readily

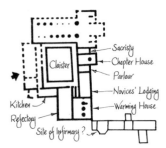

understood: nave column bases, arch into S transept (with roof line of S aisle showing), foundations of both transepts (each with two E chapels), foundations of presbytery, and slightly more of the S wall of the S transept and of the adjoining sacristy.

Next to the sacristy along the E **cloister** walk is the chapter house, still with two 13th c. arches across its E end and with the E part of its N wall high enough to show the base of the vault. Its W half is 12th c. The E range continues with the parlour, supposed novices' room (with the day stair to the dorter at the corner of the cloister), and warming house. The last is the room with round column bases, and higher end wall with 15th c. fireplace added.

In the usual Cistercian position at right angles to the S walk, the **refectory** is much the most impressive surviving room, though its ends have nearly gone. The long E wall, nearly of full height, is quite plain except for a cupboard recess near the entrance. The W wall has lancet windows; the twin ones lighted the pulpit stair, of which the bottom doorway is blocked. The pulpit itself had a cupboard below, also filled in. At the cloister end is the food hatch from the kitchen; little of that room survives, though the drain and fireplace can be traced. Past the back of the refectory, at the SE corner of the site, is the shell of a range of buildings long used for farm purposes which seem to contain medieval work and probably originated as the abbey infirmary.

Bath Avon: in city centre   ST 752648

Monastery of St Peter founded c.676 by Osric, probably at first for nuns as well as monks; refounded c.963 as Benedictine abbey by St Dunstan. Dissolved 1090 and became cathedral priory. Priory dissolved 1540 and granted to Mathew Colthurst

Parish church. Open during normal hours

Bath has less right to be described amongst abbeys than is popularly supposed, less indeed than almost any other in this book. The monastery's foundation story figures amongst legends of the dark period following the Romans' withdrawal. By 781 it was famous and, following St Dunstan's refoundation nearly two centuries later, it was important enough to see the crowning of King Edgar. Its change in status resulted from the Normans' decree that cathedrals must be in bigger towns; so the bishop moved from Wells, the abbey church became his cathedral and was rebuilt, and the abbot became prior.

But matters were less straightforward when the bishop moved back to Wells. The Bath chapter retained a share of the rights of election, and to this day the bishop is of Bath and Wells; moreover until the Dissolution he was nominally abbot of Bath too.

Of the Saxon abbey nothing is known. Of the Norman cathedral something is known from excavation but all that survives above ground is one arch, between its S nave aisle and S transept. It was totally rebuilt from 1499 onwards, much smaller in size, neither an abbey church nor a cathedral, and was not really completed till the 19th c. The mason designers, Robert and William Vertue, were also responsible for Henry VII's chapel at Westminster and for St George's chapel, Windsor, for which the fan vaults of Bath were in a sense trials. But the tower and transept vaults were not built till the later 16th and early 17th c. and that of the nave not till 1869–73. The monastic buildings had been dismantled after the Dissolution, but Edmund Colthurst gave the church to the city and, remarkably, building work continued intermittently under both royal and episcopal patronage. The church is notable for its very large collection of wall memorials, many of them dating from the city's 18th c. heyday as a fashionable resort under 'Beau' Nash. As the couplet says: 'These walls so full of monument and bust Show how Bath waters serve to lay the dust.'

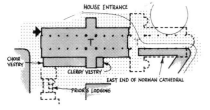

The whole church is remarkably uniform in detail, so from the back of the **nave** it is possible to take in almost the whole design: clustered columns and four-centred arches, the hood-moulds of which merge into the vaulting shafts descending through the clerestory; clerestory exceptionally tall (there is no triforium); nave and aisles all fan-vaulted, the aisles with a stone pendant in each bay. The quire is similar. The crossing too is fan-vaulted. Most of the glass is 19th c.; however an old coat of arms is in the second window from the W of the S clerestory.

Now a clockwise circuit, starting in bay 2 of the **N aisle** to the right of the lobby. Not only are the walls themselves encrusted with monuments, but even the face of the wall-seat. Only those of special size or merit or of interesting personages can be noted. In bay 2: Jonathan Henshaw (d. 1764) centrally. In bay 3: Robert Walsh (d. 1788) with broken Ionic column, and James Grieve, physician to the Empress of Russia (d. 1787) and (below with allegorical group) his wife (d. 1757). In bay 4: a tablet to Sir Isaac Pitman (d. 1897) and heraldic glass commemorating donors to the clerestory, reset in 1951; under the nave arcade the splendid tomb-chest of Bishop Montagu (d. 1618), a recumbent effigy and four black columns oddly connected by entablatures merely two and two at head and feet. In bay 5: centrally, General William Steuart (d. 1736) with medallion and coat of arms. Against the NW crossing pier is the pulpit, by Sir George Gilbert Scott, 1874.

The **N transept** contains the organ and has a delicate but curious wrought iron screen made from the two halves of the 1725 communion rail by William Edney fixed one on top of the other; it was rescued in 1959 from a balcony. The nearby oak statue of King David was on a previous organ (1702). The remarkable narrowness of the transepts results from the reuse of Norman foundations for the main arcades.

Next the **N quire aisle**. In bay 1: Henry Harington (d. 1816) with organ; above, Admiral Arthur Philip, first Governor of Australia (d. 1814) with a real Australian flag. In bay 2: Fletcher Partis (d. 1820) with Good Samaritan, also a Prophets window of c.1930. In bay 3: Andrew Barkley (d. 1790) a standard composition with urn and mourning woman. The E window (King Edgar) is of 1949. In the corner is a gadrooned font of 1710 with an ill-fitting cover of 1604; the nameless portrait tablet behind is of the actor James Quin (d. 1766). Floor gratings against the sanctuary screen enable parts of the column foundations of the Norman cathedral to be seen. The whole of the present church lies within its nave and aisles, with the exception of the transepts; the Norman central tower stood beyond the big square-headed E window.

The glass of this window – 817 square feet of it, containing 56 scenes in the life of Our Lord – is by Clayton & Bell, 1873, and was put in during Scott's restoration; after severe war damage in 1942 it was restored by M.C. Farrar-Bell. Most of the other furnishings and fittings date from that time too: the brass communion rail, oak stalls, oak screen to N aisle, and intricately traceried and coved reredos. The memorial to the left is by John Bacon to Lady Miller (d. 1781) and that on the right with kneeling figures to Bartholomew Barnes (d. 1605). A brass is to Sir George Ivy (d. 1639) and his wife. The stone screen on the right encloses the chantry of Prior Birde (1515), entered from the aisle. It has a bay and a half of miniature fan vaulting and at the end a panelled barrel vault – all much restored in 1930. Just outside the **S chapel** is a late 18th c. oak font. Inside, tucked behind the chantry, is a memorial by Sir Francis Chantrey to William Hoare (d. 1828); others, on the S wall, are to Granville Pyper (d. 1717), canopied and with coat of arms, Mary Frampton (d. 1698) and Dorothy Hobart (d. 1722), both with busts, and Elizabeth Winckley (d. 1756), tiny, postage-stamp-like. Of surpassing interest, however, is the Norman arch still to be seen around the E window. In the **S quire aisle** are several cartouches and then a big tablet to Sir Philip Frowde (d. 1674) with bust and trophy of arms. Then another by Chantrey, to Sir Richard Bickerton (d. 1632), and past the vestry doorway a quaint walking profile of Dr John Sibthorpe (d. 1796) by John Flaxman, showing the influence of his teacher Josiah Wedgwood. The vestry ceiling can be seen on request; its early 17th c. ribbed pattern resembles that of the nave before the present 19th c. vault.

Round the corner in the **S transept** are several memorials of around 1800. Among them may be noted Elizabeth Moffat (d. 1791), Mary Boyd (d. 1763), both with small standing female figures, and, further along, a similar one to James Sill (d. 1824). The much bigger one centrally under a window is to Jacob Bosanquet (d. 1767); it has a nice relief of the Good Samaritan. To its right, Josiah Thomas (d. 1820) by Sebastian Gahagan, and in the corner a small piscina indicating a former altar position. The big canopied monument beneath the very tall end window has recumbent and reclining figures of Lady Jane Walker (d. 1633) and her husband. The glass above in the form of a Jesse Tree was a thank-offering for Edward VII's recovery (as Prince of Wales) from typhoid. Of the many tablets on the W wall only that of Lady

Wentworth (d. 1706) need be singled out: two cherubs and a portrait in oval frame.

A diversion now into the **crossing** area; the fan vault here is late 16th c. The civic sword-rest on the SE pier dates only from 1916.

In the **S nave aisle** the first monument in bay 5 (numbering from the W again) is to Richard Nash, the renowned 'Beau' Nash (d. 1761 but the memorial somewhat later). To its right, William Baker (d. 1770) by J.F. Moore, with a separate allegorical relief above. In bay 3 an excellent large cartouche to Anne Finch (d. 1713); in bay 2 a big doorway to the 'cloister' (choir vestry) added in 1925–6 by Sir Thomas Jackson, and a large uninspired white marble monument to Charles Godfrey. Beside it are two quaint brass inscriptions. In the 'cloister' are several fragments of Saxon and Norman carving, to be seen on request. In bay 1 a much looked-at tablet by Flaxman to William Bingham, a US senator (d. 1804) and an odd flying cherub for John Balfour (d. 1791). Many more tablets line the ins and outs of the W wall and here too is the big 19th c. font.

In the nave on either side of the W doorway are bigger memorials to Herman Katencamp (d. 1808) by John Bacon junior and Col. Alexander Champion (d. 1793) by Joseph Nollekens. In the NW entrance lobby are none of particular importance.

Finally the **exterior**, starting at the W front with two unusual features: first the W doors of 1617 carved with three heraldic shields, and secondly the stone ladders on the two stair turrets, representing the dream which Bishop Oliver King had, prompting him to build the church. Angels climb up and down from heaven; those who are upside-down are, it is thought, correct representations of the original figures which otherwise could not be shown to be climbing downwards. On the outer left (N aisle) buttress is a renewed rebus of the builder: a mitre, olive tree and crown. Other carvings and figures abound, including Henry VII just above the main doorway and the Twelve Apostles, three each side of each ladder.

On the S side Jackson's 'cloister' should be noted, also the flying buttresses added to the nave by Scott when he replaced the wooden roof with a vault. Like the narrow transepts, the oblong shape of the tower results from the reuse of Norman foundations; in plan it matches one bay of the former nave. This irregularity is well disguised by the lightness of the stone framing and panelling. More remains of the Norman cathedral are at the SE corner: the base of the aisle-transept arch already seen inside the chapel. The main E window is worth another look from outside; its unusual square head with traceried spandrels seems unrelated to the vault inside. The equally odd round turrets unaccountably replaced square ones in 1833.

Battle Sussex: in centre of town   TQ 750157

Benedictine abbey of St Martin founded 1067 by William I, a
    daughter house of Marmoutier. Dissolved 1538 and passed to Sir
    Anthony Browne

In care of Department of the Environment and Battle Abbey
    School. Open (except school) during standard hours (entrance
    fee)

William the Conqueror decreed the siting to be such that the high altar stood exactly where King Harold fell. The E end of the church was much extended early in the 14th c. in the form of a chevet. The original chapter house was retained but probably extended; the cloister was rebuilt late in the 12th c., the rest of the monastic buildings in the 13th c., and parts again in the 14th and 15th. The precinct was fortified in the 14th c. and the gatehouse enlarged.

The church seems to have been demolished quickly after the Dissolution. Sir Anthony Browne, an executor of Henry VIII's will, used the abbot's house and began converting the guest house into a mansion for the then Princess Elizabeth; but she never lived there. His son became Viscount Montague, and from his successors the estate was sold in 1719 to the Webster family. The abbot's house was extended in 1857 under Henry Clutton and is now used as a girls' school.

The arrowed itinerary from the ticket office is somewhat puzzling since it starts by passing right round the W side of the school precinct and the first ruins one sees have nothing to do with the abbey – two slender polygonal 16th c. turrets at the beginning of **Princess Elizabeth's Lodging**. The terrace path runs the whole length of its buttressed wall, of which the first third is due to Browne and the remainder formed part of the 13th c. abbey guest house. Behind is a barrel-vaulted basement, and on top was a 16th c. mansion, its appearance known from old engravings.

Suddenly at the end of the terrace the full-height walls and gable end of the 13th c. abbey **dorter** tower up dramatically; beyond it is the reredorter, much less well preserved. The upper part of the

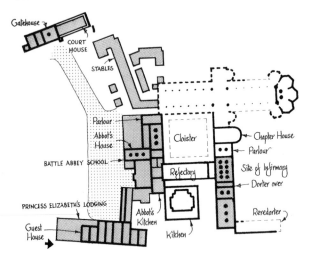

dorter is a roofless shell, but its undercroft (here at the bottom of the slope a very tall apartment with a fireplace, thought to have been the novices' room) is still entirely vaulted and can be entered. These are impressive rooms with simple ribbed vaults and round columns. The second is reached by a flight of steps; then comes a cross-passage; then another big room built as a common-room and now containing a great number of carved stones.

From this a doorway leads back to the outside path which takes one up to the lawn, identifiable at once with the **cloister**. On its far (W) side, set into what is now the school building, is the mostly 15th c. wall-arcading of the W walk. Behind and above it lay the abbot's house, remodelled by Browne in the 16th c. and again by the Websters in the 19th c., and still retaining many medieval features. It is not open to the public.

Without going on to the lawn one can glimpse (to the left) the foundations of the refectory which closed the S side of the cloister, and beyond it the kitchen. The end wall of the refectory is embedded in the house. On the E side, though also little more than foundations, the parlour and original apsidal chapter house can be identified. On the N, the S aisle of the **church** is represented by the line of the garden wall and by a considerable amount of masonry at the point where it abutted the house. Nothing is to be seen on the other side of the wall, which is private, so turn E into the garden where a small monument marks the place of Harold's fall and the site of the high altar. Beyond, hidden till one gets close, the early 14th c. crypt of the three polygonal E chapels has been fully excavated, and two still have their piscinae.

The parish church is prominent, separated by the street and precinct wall. Follow the wall, either at ground level or along its upper walk (the latter is not specially rewarding) to the **gatehouse**. Historically this building is more complex than it appears. Both ends contain 11th and 13th c. walling. The first (E) part was rebuilt in the 16th c. as a town court house, but it forms a shell for a much later brick building within. The turreted gatehouse itself, with separate vaulted footway and carriageway, is fine Decorated work of *c.*1340.

From **outside**, the gatehouse dominating the triangular market place is even more impressive, giving as much the idea of a castle entrance as an abbey's. The precinct wall, once enclosing 20 acres, has however gone except on this side.

Bayham Sussex: TQ 651366
4 miles ESE of Tunbridge Wells and ¼ mile N of Lamberhurst road B2169

Premonstratensian abbey of the Blessed Virgin Mary founded *c.*1208 largely by Robert of Thornham, a daughter house of Prémontré. Suppressed by armed force 1525 and given to Cardinal Wolsey to provide for his new colleges

In care of Department of the Environment. Open during standard hours without charge

The foundation was an amalgamation of the abbeys of Brockley and Otham, both founded several years previously and both unsuccessful. Much of the original early 13th c. monastery survives, at least in plan. The cruciform church was extended eastwards later in the 13th c., the first transepts being kept and much bigger ones built, with a polygonal apse beyond. In the 15th c. the nave (which never had aisles) was heightened.

After Wolsey's fall the property passed to Lord Montagu. In 1714 it was bought by Sir John Pratt. About 1750 Pratt's grandson, later the 1st Marquess Camden, built the 'villa' now called the Dower House to the W of the ruin. At the end of the century that was enlarged and Humphrey Repton used the abbey ruin as a landscape

feature of the estate. The house some distance to the NW, called
Bayham Abbey, was not built till 1870. The then Ministry of Public
Building and Works took over the ruin and the Dower House in
1961.

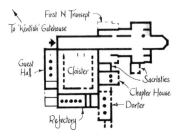

Entry is towards the SW corner of the monastic buildings but it is
best to go on past the W range (with the 'Gothick' Dower House on
one's left) and to enter the **church** by its W doorway. It is complete
enough to be readily understood. Parts of the W end stand high,
with attached wall shafts once supporting the vault, and with big
windows; these are Perpendicular on an earlier base. As one moves
E the early transepts are easily identified. Turn left through a
doorway into the N one, which in the second phase of building was
curtailed and walled off as a side passage leading parallel to the
nave. It continues with two well defined bays, one with a niche, the
other with a tomb recess, and then through a full arch into the later
N transept.

The **crossing** and transepts are excellent Early English work on a
modest scale, without triforium. The richness of the crossing piers
was originally increased by clusters of detached shafts, though not
of Purbeck marble. On the N side the two E chapels are still vaulted
and each has its piscina. There are also many astonishingly well
preserved corbels – heads and foliage of a full-blown character not
known elsewhere. Some of the openings here and elsewhere have
been blocked with stonework to improve stability. The E end is
unusual in England in being polygonal; pictorially it is enhanced by
the splendid beech whose roots clutch the walls. On the N side of
the presbytery is a curious blank sexfoil high up, and on the S some
remnants of sedilia. The Sackville monument on the N side is not
medieval.

Now turn W to see the S transept, virtually identical with the N

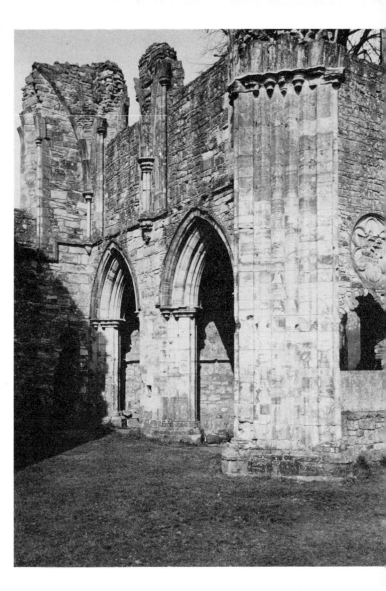

Bayham: Late 13th c. N transept

but less complete. The small structure outside its SW corner was a
sacristy. As on the N side, an ambulatory or closed aisle leads
alongside the nave into the old transept, which here more nearly
retains its original shape. Like the 'new' transepts, these each had
two E chapels; the outer has gone and the inner became part of the
passage. The big double recess in the S wall of the transept proper
suggests that it may have become a library. Another cupboard is in
its N wall, and a niche in its W one. On the S are the remains of the
earlier sacristy (or parlour?).

Next the **cloister**, well defined, especially on the N side where the
high nave wall is dramatically strengthened by comparatively
modern buttresses. Off the E walk, the chapter house retains one of
the two three-bay arcades that divided it laterally. S of this is the
slype, then the dorter undercroft with little to show but foundations
except at the far corners. Along the S walk are two smaller rooms,
then the refectory undercroft, with leaning stumpy columns only
uncovered in recent years, some remains of vaulting, and on the
other side a single lancet window in a higher lump of walling.
Towards the end of the walk the ornamented washplace and the
steps and doorway to the refectory can be identified. The W range,
also recently unearthed, is no more than wall-bases, probably of the
guest house or the abbot's hall.

The picturesque 'Kentish' gatehouse, some distance to the NW, is
early 14th c. but was altered in the 18th c. so as to form a garden
feature with a bridge over the Teise. The loggia on its W side
contains two 13th c. arches that almost certainly formed part of the
missing second arcade of the chapter house.

Finally one can walk round the outside of the church and back
across the cloister, though there is nothing else of significance to
see. The main, 'Sussex', gatehouse has long disappeared, and so
have other 'domestic' buildings of the abbey which probably lay
around the Dower House.

Beauchief South Yorkshire: SK 334819
3½ miles SSW of Sheffield city centre, near B6068

Premonstratensian abbey of St Mary and St Thomas of Canterbury
    founded c.1173 by Robert fitzRanulph, a daughter house of
    Welbeck. Dissolved 1537 and granted to Sir Nicholas Strelley

Owned by Sheffield Corporation (including chapel). Chapel

accessible during normal hours on application to nearest cottage; remainder accessible at all times

Founded in expiation for complicity in the murder of Thomas à Becket, it was never of great size; probably the 14th c. tower was the only substantial addition. Unlike most monastic estates, it passed for centuries in line through one family, till 1923. Edward Pegge, married to a Strelley, built Beauchief Hall of abbey stone in 1671, having made a chapel in the W part of the church – keeping the tower at a reduced height. The abbey site was partly excavated in 1923–5 and re-covered, and in 1943 the estate was ceded to the local authority.

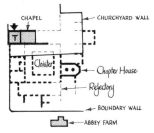

The **W front** has a plain window put in in 1967, the filigree edge of the 14th c. tracery being left. The once rich Early English doorway below has lost all its five shafts each side. The side arches (N 12th c., S 14th c.) are not *in situ*, though the ogee-headed (14th c.) N doorway into the tower is. Inside is a 19th c. font. The **chapel** is entered beneath a kind of gallery and is notable for its 17th c. furnishings: box pews, squire's pew on the S side, pulpit beside the altar, and reading-desk with clerk's seat below. The four carved coats of arms are of the Strelley and Pegge families and there are two tablets to Pegges and one to Elizabeth Burnell (d. 1844) by Henry Weeks. Other features include a medieval cupboard and an early 19th c. psalm board of unique design, with Pegge Burnell arms on the back.

Outside, the E face of the tower exhibits the former nave roof line, and the S face that of the W cloister range. The round-headed doorway (now a window) in the church S wall led into the cloister. The field to the S roughly represents the S half of the cloister; E of it the horseshoe-shaped chapter house is traceable, with two round columns inside and two grave slabs in the walk outside. The flat area S of the cloister was the refectory, with two fragments of kitchen wall beyond that. The church extended to just outside the present burial ground; a mound marks the E wall.

Beaulieu Hampshire: in village, on B3054   SU 388026

Cistercian abbey of the Blessed Virgin Mary founded at Faringdon (now Oxfordshire) 1203 by King John, a daughter house of Cîteaux; moved here 1204. Dissolved 1538 and granted to Thomas Wriothesley, later Earl of Southampton

Refectory parochial; remainder owned by Lord Montagu. Refectory open during normal hours; remainder (with admission fee) 10.0 a.m. to 5.0 p.m. (Easter to September 6.0 p.m.) daily

Beau lieu = beautiful place. The main buildings were almost wholly 13th c., but the gatehouse was built or rebuilt in the 14th c. The general plan, typically Cistercian, had the refectory placed N to S, and the church had a continuous ring of radiating chapels round the ambulatory (the final type of Cistercian E end).

After the Dissolution the church was abandoned and the parish took over the refectory as a church; its preservation in such a way is most unusual. The gatehouse was adapted to domestic use and eventually enlarged in 1872 under Sir Arthur Blomfield to form Palace House. The W (lay brothers') cloister range continued as storehouses but most of the remainder went to ruin, the stone being used in Calshot, Cowes and Hurst castles. Excavations in 1901–2 revealed the plan, much of which has been laid out in the grass. The Montagu Motor Museum was set up in the grounds in the 1950s, and it is through its entrance that visitors arrive – except at advertised times when the refectory (church) only may be entered normally from the public road.

The first monastic building seen across the car trial area is the shell of a monastic outbuilding that later became a wine-press house. Further down the road the W front of the **church** is represented by concrete blockwork indicating the main doorway and buttresses. The main columns are marked out on the grass, also the N wall – but the S wall still stands with its two doorways to the cloister, and at its W end the end of the lay brothers' range.

Under glass within the N aisle is a stone coffin. The E end of the

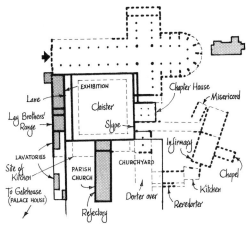

church is also marked out, but the apse with its peripheral chapels disappears into the shrubbery. Of the S transept the W wall and part of the S wall stand, with the night stair to the dorter quite recognisable.

The **cloister** is reached from the S aisle through a 13th c. doorway of which the shafts are missing; it will be taken clockwise, with first a book recess on the left containing a memorial of 1969 to European Resistance members trained at Beaulieu. Then the sacristy, with some old tiles, and one vault bay rebuilt, followed by the three arches of the chapter house – themselves remarkably complete but with only low walls behind. Past that is a slype which leads towards the infirmary; of this the misericord, main hall and chapel are marked by yew hedges. The last opening of the E walk goes into the dorter undercroft, but most of the site of that is now walled off as part of the churchyard. The curved steps at the corner began the day stair to the dorter.

From the S walk is a view across the cloister to the shallow blank arches of the S aisle wall. Remains of a washing trough adjoin the **refectory** entrance. Doors with medieval ironwork lead into this impressive room which is now the parish church. Its best-known feature is the pulpit, the original reading place in the side wall, with its own arcaded stairs lit by windows which break the otherwise even rhythm of lancets. The pulpit itself is 19th c., but the carved conical supporting bracket is original and so is the vault of the little passage. The conspicuously blocked lancet behind the altar is due to a big buttress added in the 18th c. Another above it indicates that the original ceiling was higher; the present segmental one painted red and with heraldic bosses is mostly 15th c. The low iron screen is 19th c. and the canopied monument in the chancel commemorates Mary Do (d. 1651).

Now back to the cloister and a blocked doorway to the destroyed kitchen. Nothing is left of the cloister arcades; but the W walk is double, a Cistercian arrangement occasionally found, providing a separate 'lane' for the lay brothers. Here quite high walls survive, and the actual W range is practically complete, with only minor alterations. In its vaulted ground storey is an 'abbey exhibition' which includes a font and a fine carved niche. The outer face of the range is reached by returning to the road. The porch at its N end is entirely modern; at the other end an opening leads into a court from which the side of the refectory-church can be seen.

Palace House, to the SW, was built around the main **gatehouse**. The present entrance leads into its side. The dining hall, seen first, is the inner half, and the lower drawing room the outer, both having tierceron vaults of 14th c. type (but without bosses), the authenticity of which is in doubt. The carriageway ran where the drawing room fireplace now is, and across the dining hall and fountain court. Upstairs both rooms, unusually, were chapels and still have piscinae to prove it. Big traceried windows and flat timber ceilings preserve their Gothic character. They also are a drawing and a dining room now. An added floor above is not shown but its windows can be seen from the gardens, as well as a niche which was over the outer entrance. The rest of the house is by Blomfield (1872); the round towers in front are of 1722 and were meant to be defensive. Further S, the much simpler outer gatehouse also stands, late 13th c. (the clock turret is of course modern), and one wall of the abbey mill close by. There are other remains of precinct walling, as well as some of the medieval fishponds.

Beeleigh Essex: ¾ mile NW of Maldon   TL 840077

Premonstratensian abbey of St Mary and St Nicholas founded 1172 at Great Parndon, Essex by Roger de Perendune, a daughter house of Newsham; refounded on present site 1180 by Robert Mantell. Dissolved 1536 and given to Sir John Gate

Owned by Foyle family. Not open to the public

Called Maldon abbey when first on this site. The SE parts of the main monastic buildings survive and are early 13th c. The remainder, and the church, have entirely gone; it is evident where they must have stood but nothing of their architecture seems to be known. The picturesque existing house embodies the chapter house, dorter and undercroft, and parlour between them (all vaulted and little altered), as well as an end wall of the refectory with passage and day stair walls on its E. The chapter house has slender octagonal Purbeck marble columns, and a twin doorway. The dorter (now library) has a 15th c. open timber roof, and its undercroft round columns and a medieval fireplace.

Timber-framed additions comprise a modern projection into the SE corner of the cloister and a 16th c. westward extension from the reredorter. Rooms over the chapter house are also mostly modern.

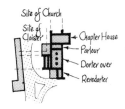

The grounds are private but two picturesque views are possible. The first, from the main gate, looks NE diagonally at two gables, the creepered left one being above the end of the refectory and the right the 16th c. continuation of the reredorter. The second, more informative sighting is to be had by following the footpath eastward to the far end of the garden and turning left. From here the dorter and its undercroft appear comfortably spread, with three big Perpendicular windows below and smaller ones above. To the right is the chapter house block, three-storeyed, and to the left (but not projecting) the other end of the reredorter.

Traces of the former buildings at Great Parndon are visible just E of Great Canons, 1 mile N of the church (TL 433103).

Belmont Hereford and Worcester:　　　　　　　　　　SO 483381
2 miles SW of Hereford and 300 yards N of Abergavenny road A465

Benedictine abbey of St Michael and All Angels founded 1853 by

F.R. Wegg-Prosser; church became cathedral 1855, but see removed to Cardiff 1920

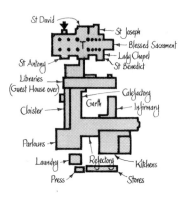

Church (only) open during normal hours

For a full description see *A Guide to the Cathedrals of Britain*, p.27.

Bermondsey Greater London: TQ 333794
On A100, ½ mile of S of Tower Bridge

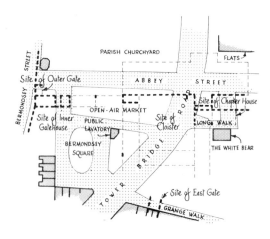

Cluniac priory of St Saviour founded 1082 by Alwin Child, a
    daughter house of La Charité-sur-Loire; became abbey 1399.
    Dissolved 1538 and given to Sir Robert Southwell

Owned by the London Borough of Southwark. Virtually no remains

The first church, apparently already standing at the Domesday
Survey, seems to have been largely rebuilt in the 14th c. The scanty
evidence of its size and position is based on old documents and on
drawings made early in the 19th c. when not only the inner and
outer gatehouses still stood, but also the decrepit walls of
Bermondsey House, built in the 16th c. by Sir Thomas Pope on the
site of the monastic buildings.
    The whole area is now criss-crossed by roads. The only visible
relic is a part of the wall of the eastern gatehouse, forming part of
the front of a house on the S side of Grange Walk. Two big hinge
pivots, said to have supported one of the abbey gates, are
embedded in it.

Biddlesden Buckinghamshire: close to parish church   SP 633399

Cistercian abbey of the Blessed Virgin Mary founded 1147 by
    Ernald de Bosco, seneschal of the Earl of Leicester, a daughter
    house of Garendon; dissolved 1538 and passed to Thomas Lord
    Wriothesley. The buildings then went to the Peckhams, the
    parish being allocated a chapel, perhaps of the infirmary. The
    Sayers family rebuilt house and church *c.* 1731–5, making the
    latter look like part of its stables. It lies at the end of a drive
    (public right of way, key at lodge). The house grounds are private
    (Seton Gordon family) and no definite abbey remains are known.

Bindon Dorset: SY 853868
½ mile E of Wool and 4¼ miles W of Wareham

Cistercian abbey of the Blessed Virgin Mary founded at West
    Lulworth 1149 by William of Glastonia, a daughter house of
    Forde; moved to Wool 1172. Dissolved 1539 and given to
    Thomas, Lord Poynings

Owned by the Trustees of the Weld Estate. Accessible to the public
    only by permission from the Estate Office, Lulworth Castle

On its new site the abbey was built in the late 12th to mid-13th c. The ruins, which are fairly complete in layout but mostly of no great height, suggest little if any work of later date.

As so often happened, a mansion was built out of the wreck of the monastery in the 16th c. This was improved c.1608, sold in 1641 to the Weld family, and burnt down in the Civil War. Thomas Weld allowed much of the stone to be used at Lulworth Castle in the 1770s and in 1794–8 built a Gothick 'summer' house and gatehouse just W of the abbey. The family was one of those chiefly concerned in the Roman Catholic revival at that period.

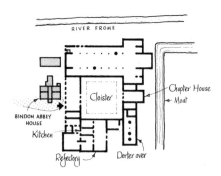

From the gatehouse the approach passes the 1794 house on the left and leads towards the W range of the cloister. The foundations of this can be crossed and one can then walk up the site of the W walk (all the actual walks have gone) to the W end of the **church**. Here the S wall is a few feet high, but the N has gone except further E. What does survive is the masonry of both arcades – on the N side practically to full height. There are clear remains of the pulpitum which divided the nave. In the N transept the two E chapels are just decipherable but much overgrown. The presbytery likewise has low wall bases only; on its N side is a stone coffin. The S transept walls stand somewhat higher; in its left-hand chapel is the matrix of a big brass, with a marginal inscription to Abbot de Maners, c.1310, and on the S side a two-arched recess containing an unusual miniature effigy, probably of another abbot. Beside it is a doorway to the sacristy, and through this another to the **chapter house** where three 13th c. and some later grave slabs are visible. The walls here are rather higher and in the chapter house are vaulting shafts recessed into the wall like those at Forde. The doorway has quite gone, but next along the S walk is that of a passage and then an opening into the dorter undercroft which still has some column bases; the purpose of the small compartment at its N end seems to be unknown.

Of the S range very little is left, but the general layout of refectory and kitchen is traceable and parts of the drains are visible. From here it is worth doubling back behind the E range, following a path along the bank of the big square placid moat lying immediately E of the abbey, then turning left between the N side of the church and a branch of the river Frome, and coming back to the remnant of high masonry at the W end.

The house, used by Downside Abbey as a retreat house and not open to the public, is an excellent example of late 18th c. 'Gothick' and has a chapel on the upper floor. Pieces of worked stone from the ruins (many with dog-tooth) are ranged along the front. On the river just to the N is Bindon Mill, which is of monastic origin.

Bisham Berkshire: in village   SU 846850

House of the Knights Templars founded by 1139 by Robert Ferrers, Earl of Derby; dissolved 1307. Augustinian priory founded 1337 by William Montacute, Earl of Salisbury; dissolved 1536. Benedictine abbey of Jesus Christ and St Mary founded 1537 by Henry VIII for monks from Chertsey to pray for soul of Queen Jane Seymour; finally dissolved 1538. The house now called Bisham Abbey, used by the Central Council of Physical Recreation, was a manor house originating with the Knights Templars. Nothing is left of the abbey, which lay beside it to the NE. The river path from Marlow provides a picturesque view across the Thames.

Blanchland Northumberland: in village   NY 967504

Premonstratensian priory founded 1165, a daughter house of Croxton; became abbey late in 13th c. Dissolved 1539 and passed to Bellow and Broxholm families

Church used by parish. Other buildings owned by Lord Crewe Trustees. Church open during normal hours. Remainder privately occupied

The now very incomplete church is 13th to early 14th c. and the only other substantial relic of the monastery is the gatehouse of *c*.1500.

After two centuries of decay, extensive remodelling of the remaining buildings was done in the 1750s by the trustees of Lord Crewe, Bishop of Durham, who had bought them and bequeathed them for charitable purposes. Part of the church was converted in 1753 for use as a chapel in Shotley parish and it later became an ordinary parish church.

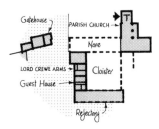

It is not the S front of the church which faces the road but the two-bay W side of the N transept with, on its left, a transeptal tower (a usual position in Premonstratensian churches) and, on its right, two matching bays (making four in all) erected in 1753 to enclose the W end of the quire, the nave (which extended forwards to the road) having gone to ruin.

Transept and tower, including its outer doorway, are of *c*.1300. To the left of the latter, outside, is a holy water stoup; inside is a collection of carved stones. The transept has an E aisle which was rebuilt in 1854, but its arcade with circular pier is 13th c.; the two clerestory windows were left blocked. The arch at the S end, to the former crossing, is also 13th c., but the thin trussed roof of the transept is probably of 1815.

Moving S, on the left are three medieval ledger stones, the first two attributed to abbots and the third to an abbey forester. A walkway formed between two lengths of 17th or 18th c. communion rail leads through a 20th c. screen into the carpeted chapel of St Gabriel. The modern 'Northumbrian' patterned cames of its N window are attractive; so is the similar glazing of the two Y-traceried main W windows opposite the chapel. Further along, against the screen, are three more tomb slabs: another abbot, a huntsman named Robert Eglestone, and a woman named Cecilia Hapbun (a woman's burial in a monks' church is unusual).

The **chancel**, which formed the abbey presbytery, is of *c*.1200 but its E end was rebuilt in 1884. The flat panelled ceiling and the oak screen, pews, pulpit and choir stalls are all of 1884. Some fragments of 15th c. glass can be seen in the first and second E windows and the second on the E side, and on the right (hidden behind the stall-backs and screen) are very much restored 13th c. triple sedilia. The 19th c. reredos, containing a 16th c. embroidered Crucifixion, no doubt displaced the four 18th c. panels of the Creed, Decalogue and Lord's Prayer now on the S wall.

The W wall of the present **nave** was built in 1752–3 to cut it off from the former monastic nave. Part of the S wall was rebuilt too, though it seems there was never a S transept. The big font at the W end is probably 12th c.; close to it is an iron fireback bearing the arms of James I which was at one time in the Vicarage. Returning through the transept, note again the tall tower arch with its three orders of shafts. On the left are reproductions of the medieval glass and a chair containing an early 16th c. panel said to have formed part of the abbot's throne.

Outside, turn right, passing round the tower to the N transept aisle, where the blocked clerestory is again visible above the 19th c. roof, as well as the line of the original transept roof on the S face of the tower. The chancel is ordinary Early English (except for the rebuilt E end) but it is worth going round it as far as one can, to look over the wall into the square garden of the Lord Crewe Arms, for this represents the abbey cloister. The range of buildings on the left is on the site of the refectory, over which was the dormitory; the main hotel building stands where the kitchen and abbot's guest house were, and incorporates much of their walling. It became the manor house of the Jacobite Forster family and figures in Walter Besant's novel *Dorothy Forster*. On its left end a wide arched recess can be seen; this was the washplace.

Return now to the road, past the 13th c. churchyard cross. The S part of the churchyard is the site of the nave, a lancet window of which can be seen by the rear corner of the hotel. Turn left towards the village square. The Lord Crewe Arms is on the left; the arched building on the right was the abbey gatehouse and guest house (*c*.1500). At the end of the hotel a trefoil-headed doorway led to the monastic kitchen. The informal L-shaped village square is a specially attractive example of small-scale planning; that it follows the layout of the outer court of the monastery seems likely but can only be conjecture.

Bordesley Hereford & Worcester: SP 046687
¾ mile NNE of Redditch and ¼ mile E of A441

Cistercian abbey of the Blessed Virgin Mary founded *c.*1138 by
   Waleran de Beaumont, a daughter house of Garendon;
   refounded 1141 by Matilda. Dissolved 1538 and leased to Thomas
   Evans

Owned by Redditch District Council. Not open to the public but
   near access possible at all times

Unusually detailed studies of the structure and its surroundings
have been done, in the 1860s and more particularly since 1967, and
the plan appears to have been fairly typical save for an apparent
intrusion by the S transept into the cloister walk. The mid-12th c.
buildings evidently underwent several subsequent improvements,
mostly minor, up to *c.*1300. Though a 'royal' abbey it suffered great
hardship and diminution of numbers over a long period in the 14th
c. but afterwards revived. Extensive traces have been found nearby
of a metal industry apparently conducted by the monks – a
forerunner of those of modern Redditch. Tiles were made too.
   The buildings were quickly demolished, but the gatehouse was
kept for many years, and St Stephen's chapel adjoining it stood till
1807. From the 16th till the 20th c. the site was owned by the Lords
Windsor who became Earls of Plymouth; its earthworks and
waterworks are better preserved than most, and quite extensive.

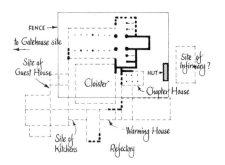

   The entrance is by a short lane from near the crematorium gates.
The field gate at the end marks the gatehouse site, and the trees on
the right that of St Stephen's chapel. The abbey site lies in the open

field almost straight ahead, with a high steel fence around it which allows a fairly good view from all sides of the excavated SE parts of the church; it is easy to identify the wall bases of the presbytery, S transept with its chapels, and crossing piers. The base of the night stair is also exposed. The nave, of which the W doorway and some column bases have been found, has been covered in again. The cloister area, a clear square depression, is partly outside the fence and the general layout can be traced from ground irregularities, particularly two rectangular hollows that were probably undercrofts.

Many excavated relics are in the County Museum at Hartlebury Castle. A large stone boss is in the grounds of Redditch church, and a patch of old tiles under a table in the vestry.

Bourne Lincolnshire: in town   TF 097200

Arrouasian (Augustinian) abbey of St Peter founded 1138 by
    Baldwin fitzGilbert. Dissolved 1536 and passed to Sir Richard
    Cotton; nave remained parochial and assumed dedication to St
    Peter and St Paul

Owned by parish. Church open during normal hours

Little is known of the abbey's history, and nothing at all of the monastic buildings. The 13th c. church had transepts and chancel and a small aisled nave. Twin W towers were prepared for but only the SW one was built and that not finished till much later. The subsequent sequence is obscure in many details but the chancel seems to have been left to ruin after the Dissolution, then patched up, and in 1807 rebuilt. The aisles, clerestory and porch are largely 15th c.

All but the church must have been quickly demolished and quarried away; carved stones have been found in many parts of the town. Abbey House, which occupied part of the site, has also gone, though parts of it were incorporated into the present vicarage.

From the centre of the W end the church layout is easily

appreciated, and in particular the 12th c. **nave** arcades on round columns with scalloped capitals, plain 15th c. clerestory, and high-pitched 19th c. roof with big gilded bosses. The font is 15th c. and bears an abbreviated inscription in Latin: 'Jesus is the name which is above every name.' Two old tables and a chest stand nearby; to the left of the W doorway is a wooden medieval carved group of six saints, and on the N jamb of the arch to the nave two other small carvings.

The nearer (W) ends of the arcades differ. On the N are remains of the original W end, cut away c.1200 to accommodate the new tower base and no doubt intended (with the arcades) themselves to be replaced. The tower was never finished, but the sill-level walkway gives a hint of its intended scale and there are springers for a vault. On the S side the tower was eventually completed c.1400; the end of the arcade had to be rebuilt to carry its weight, resulting in the wide end arch and big octagonal pier.

Widening of the **N aisle** in the 19th c. has obliterated any evidence which may have remained of a transept or of an adjoining cloister. The roof, vestry enclosure, twin E arches and organ chamber are likewise 19th c., as well as the mock-Norman pulpit and the **chancel** roof. Close to the pulpit, as well as on the opposite side, are the piers of the original chancel arch. The monastic chancel was presumably much bigger. The present one is largely of 1807 but its 15th c. E window was transferred in 1883 from the W end and lancets of Early English type reinstated there. Before the organ chamber was built there were remains of a staircase. Some minor wall monuments are worth noticing, but the most memorable feature of the building, best seen from here, is the magnificent brass chandelier of 1742. The brass lectern is of 1902.

The **S transept** (shortened, as will be seen outside) has a piscina, and the aisle has an aumbry. Near the S doorway are two piles of stone with dog-tooth carving, evidently only a little later than the Norman building and perhaps salvaged from Abbey House.

Outside, the W front is a patchwork but mostly of c.1200. The earliest work is in the interlaced arches at the base of the tower, the top of which is Perpendicular. So also are the main W doorway and the stoup beside it. Another stoup is on the S porch. The S side as a whole looks 15th c., but the transept is earlier and half a doorway in its W wall shows that it was once longer. Well-carved tombs and headstones, from 17th to 19th c. in date, abound in the churchyard. On the N, the bowling green occupies roughly the site of the cloister and surrounding buildings.

Boxley Kent: 2 miles N of Maidstone   TQ 761587

Cistercian abbey of the Blessed Virgin Mary founded 1143 (or 1146)
  by William Ypres, Earl of Kent and colonised from Clairvaux.
  Dissolved 1538 and passed to Sir Thomas Wyatt

Owned by Best-Shaw family. Not open to the public

Called also S. Crucis de Gratiis on account of the 'Rood of Grace'
which was an object of pilgrimage. The evidence suggests a late 12th
c. building layout conforming with standard Cistercian practice but
with the refectory retained parallel to the cloister walk. The cloister
is known to have been partly if not wholly rebuilt late in the 14th c.;
the W porch was of similar date. After the Dissolution the W range
was altered to form a house, and the remainder mostly demolished.
In the 19th c. the house was itself much reduced in size.

  The visible remains are mostly in the garden and comprise parts
of the nave and aisle walls (a water garden existed where the nave
and N aisle were and the S aisle is covered by a terrace), a marking
out of the presbytery by clipped yews, the drain from the
reredorter, and much of the W and N walls of the refectory. Parts of
a late medieval canopied tomb are preserved in a small enclosure at
the W end of the S aisle. Excavations in 1971–2 established the
general layout.

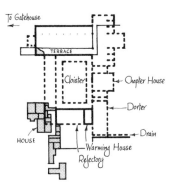

  Though none of the above can be visited by the public, the brick
jambs of the outer gatehouse still stand at the W entrance from
Abbey Gate and from this point much of the precinct wall can be
seen continuing in a wide sweep to the N. The N wall of the church –

or rather the field wall built on it – lies straight ahead. To its right amongst trees is the house, and to the right of that the great late 13th c. abbey barn.

Breedon Leicestershire: SK 405233
5 miles NE of Ashby-de-la-Zouch and ¼ mile N of Breedon-on-the-Hill on A453

Benedictine abbey of St Mary and St Hardulf founded *c*.675 by King Aethelred, a daughter house of Peterborough; dissolved (probably sacked by Danes) 874; refounded *c*.1120 as Augustinian cell to Nostell, Yorkshire. Dissolved 1539 and sold to Francis Shirley

Parish church. Open during normal hours

The early history of the spectacular hill on which Breedon church stands is lost in antiquity and legend, but certainly included earthwork defences in the 1st c. BC and a period in the 8th c. when it seems to have been one of the cultural centres of Mercia. An astonishing series of Saxon carvings (probably the most extensive anywhere), believed to have been in the then abbey church, was somehow saved from the abbey buildings and incorporated into the fabric of the 13th c. priory church, the E part of which was in its turn saved at the Dissolution to serve as the parish church, instead of the W part which was demolished.

The tower was central and is of the period of the priory foundation, early 12th c. Because the nave and aisles have gone it now appears as an ordinary W tower and its S transept acts as a porch. This and the remainder are 13th c., with arcades on columns of quatrefoil section, rib-vaulted N aisle (the S aisle was vaulted too) and 15th c. clerestory and main roof.

In the present context the Saxon sculpture is all-important. However there are other notable features: 18th c. box pews; the Shirley family pew of 1627 in the N aisle; the tall compartmented monument of Sir George Shirley (d. 1588); tomb-chests of Francis Shirley (d. 1571) and his wife, and John Shirley (d. 1585) and his

Breedon: Early Saxon saint, E wall of S aisle

wife; the heavy iron grille around the Shirley tombs; 18th c. pulpit
and reading desk and organ gallery; and 15th c. font.

The **sculpture** turns up in many more places than is at first evident
– so deftly has it been fitted into the medieval walls. Most of it
consists of running friezes, for a start along the E wall of the N
chapel (a single piece) and chancel. In the E wall of the S chapel are
groups of saints, in its S wall more groups and a lion-like beast, and
in the S aisle wall a long frieze of knots, animals and birds, as well as
other carvings. In the spandrels above the main arcades are ten
more lengths of frieze (one partly hidden by the organ), including a
splendid horseman charging for ever into the E wall. Beneath the
tower two lengths of frieze are on the N wall and two longer ones on
the S wall. Finally, one of the finest surviving examples of Saxon
figure sculpture and perhaps the earliest carved angel in England is
in the ringing chamber of the tower, only accessible by prior
arrangement. This, like the figures at the end of the S aisle, is
almost pure Byzantine in character, whereas the friezes show Celtic
influences too. A Danish character is apparent in a collection of
cross fragments in the N aisle.

Bristol Avon: in city centre   ST 578727

Augustinian (Victorine) abbey of St Augustine founded *c.*1140 by
    Robert fitzHarding, later Lord Berkeley, and colonised from
    Shobdon priory, Herefordshire. Dissolved 1540 and became
    cathedral (except from 1836 to 1896)

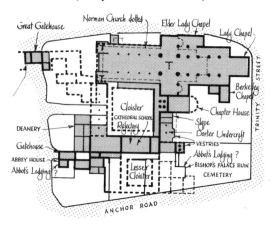

Cathedral church (only) open during normal hours: remainder
  private

For a full description see *A Guide to the Cathedrals of Britain*,
pp.50–6.

Brixworth Northamptonshire: SP 747712
in village on A508, 6 miles N of Northampton

Benedictine abbey founded *c*.680 by Cuthbald, abbot of
  Peterborough, a daughter house of Peterborough. Dissolved
  c.870 (?)

Parish church of All Saints. Open during normal hours

Though its dating is still subject to investigation, the church is
undoubtedly the most important and astonishing of the early Saxon
period in England and has been called by Sir Alfred Clapham
'perhaps the most imposing architectural memorial of the seventh
century surviving north of the Alps'. More recent and more
scientific archaeology however ascribes the aisled and clerestoried
nave to the 8th c. It had an E apse and triple chancel arch like
Reculver, and a five-cell W narthex with probably an upper floor.
The aisles were divided into porticūs or chapels, and there was a
vaulted semicircular crypt outside the apse. Nothing of the
monastery buildings is known, and everything else is later, i.e. after
the church is believed to have become parochial. The tower, over
the surviving central compartment of the W narthex, was begun
about the 11th c. and finished in the 14th. The apse was rebuilt in
the 10th or 11th c., and again in 1865 on old foundations. The aisles
and crypt disappeared and a 12th c. S doorway was put in – followed
by a 13th c. S chapel.

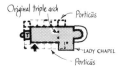

The wide **nave** is dominated by the big flat two-ring arches of
Roman tile-like bricks on each side, in irregular (not all radiating)
patterns. These are now thought more likely to be 10th c.
insertions, and so are the similar clerestory window openings – the

nave walls themselves being 8th c. except of course the blocking masonry in the main arches. The wide 14th or 15th c. chancel arch replaced a triple one (perhaps original, perhaps 10th c.), a springer of which survives on the N side. The roof is 19th c. Also in the nave are the small round font, probably 17th c., and near the pulpit a 14th c. reliquary and part of a Saxon cross.

The **quire** was aisleless. On its N side is a small blocked original doorway to a porticus. The S side is changed by the insertion of the 13th c. chapel arcade, but over that is a blocked early window. The 'tiled' narrow sanctuary arch is like the nave arcades; on either side is a small window, and below those are low doorways which led to the 'ring-crypt' around the apse.

The 15th c. former chancel screen has been moved to the S or **Lady chapel** and repainted. There are minor wall-tablets, also a tomb recess with a knight's effigy contemporary with the chapel. Back in the nave, the S windows of 1888 (artist unknown) are noteworthy. The W wall has another original 'tile'-arched doorway, a blocked window above, and then a later Saxon (11th c.?) triple opening with fat balusters. The doorway leads into the **tower**; ahead, the W opening, once an imposing main entrance, is blocked by the later Saxon stair. To the left, in the S wall, is a doorway that led to the side chambers of the narthex.

Beside the way out, lit by a window in the lobby, is a bold little carved eagle said to be of *c*.800. **Outside**, the big 'tile' arches faced into the vanished aisles, the roofs of which rested on the offsets just below the clerestory; the parapets are largely 14th c. Beyond the 13th c. Lady chapel the sunken area around the apse represents the former semicircular crypt; in spite of much reconstruction it is easy to see how it linked the low doorways on each side of the sanctuary arch. On the N side (opposite the Lady chapel) the quire wall is still the original in its W half, but otherwise all is similar to the S side. On both sides of the tower the start of the narthex can be seen, also the 11th c. stair turret with bands of herring-bone masonry.

Bruern Oxfordshire: SP 266204
1¾ miles NW of Shipton under Wychwood

Cistercian abbey of the Blessed Virgin Mary founded 1147 by Nicholas Basset, a daughter house of Waverley; dissolved 1536 and granted to Sir Anthony Cope. The basically 18th c. big house may perpetuate the cloister layout – or may not even be on the site at all. Nearly 100 yards to the E the Georgian cottage (Astor family, not open to the public) contains a three-bay groin-vaulted chamber ascribed to the abbey.

Bruisyard Suffolk: TM 335661
½ mile E of Bruisyard church and 1¼ miles N of Framlingham–Saxmundham road B1119

Franciscan nunnery of the Annunciation of St Mary founded c.1364–7 by Lionel, Duke of Clarence on the site of a secular college; dissolved 1539 and given to Nicholas Hare. Early 17th c. Bruisyard Hall (Rous family, empty at time of writing) incorporates abbey walling and an arch at base of SW corner.

Bruton Somerset: in town on A359   ST 685347

Benedictine priory founded c.1005 by Algar, Earl of Cornwall; refounded c.1135 as Augustinian priory of St Mary by William de Mohun, later Earl of Somerset; became abbey 1511. Dissolved 1539 and granted to Sir Maurice Berkeley

Owned by King's School, Bruton. Site accessible at all times without charge

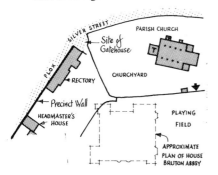

The scanty knowledge of the buildings relies mostly on documents. The adjoining parish church may have served the monastery, but a separate church is more likely. The Berkeleys' house on the abbey site was demolished in 1786; King's School playing field now covers

the whole area. Town and family gave their names to Bruton Street
and Berkeley Square in London.

The giant buttressed wall along the street called Plox was probably
the Berkeleys', not the abbey's; so, it is thought, was the Pigeon
Tower on the hill to the S.

Buckfast Devon: SX 742674
¾ mile N of Buckfastleigh and ¼ mile W of Exeter road A38

Benedictine abbey of Our Lady founded 1018 by Duke Aylward;
  became Savigniac and a daughter house of Savigny 1136; became
  Cistercian 1147; dissolved 1539 and granted to Sir Thomas
  Dennis; reoccupied as priory 1882 by Benedictines from La
  Pierre-qui-Vire; became abbey again 1902

Church (only) open during normal hours

Buckfast for nearly 350 years suffered the same fate as most other
medieval abbeys – its stones quarried away, such buildings as still
stood being put to farm uses, and a gentleman's mansion built
amongst the remains. But its subsequent history is unique, a
completely new monastery having risen on the old foundations.

Of the original Benedictine buildings nothing is known, but the
12th c. Cistercian plan was uncovered after the French exiles took
possession, broken into only by the Gothic-style house built c.1800
by Samuel Berry on the site of the W range. That with its octagonal
turrets still stands. A small piece of undercroft (now a chapel of St
Anne) and further S the 14th c. Abbot's Tower are the only whole
medieval buildings to survive. Almost the whole of the remainder
was designed by Frederick Walters and built during the period
1907–32 by the monks themselves, never more than six at one time.
All but the nave was complete by 1922. Some buildings near the
Abbot's Tower, including the library, were begun earlier, and there
have been later additions in the tower belfry (1938), the 'New' or
Blessed Sacrament chapel (1966) and an extension of the E claustral
range (1970s). The French community gave way to a German one in
1902, and that to a British one in 1920. To tourists the tonic wine
and honey prepared by the monks are well known.

It is unlikely that the design of the **church** resembles the
Cistercian at all closely. Certainly the plan is practically the same,
but the fresh white Bath stone with dark joints dispels any illusion

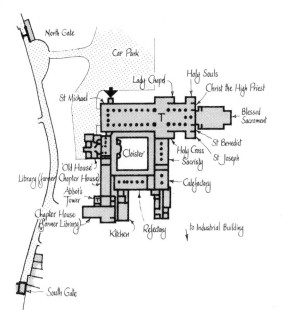

of antiquity, and there is altogether something of a French character. The infilling of the quadripartite vaults is of local red sandstone; the clerestory beneath is three-arched with the central arch dominant, the triforium has two twin pointed openings under round arches, and the main arcades are of early Gothic type on tall clustered piers. The presbytery is similar, even in its E wall. There is a small W gallery.

At the W end of the **N aisle** is St Michael's altar, and others stand against the arcade piers. The aisle vault system follows that of Fountains, with transverse barrel vaults. The seventeen enamelled Stations of the Cross round the church are copied from a 13th c. Austrian altarpiece. The quire, W of the crossing, has rich Gothic-style stalls and a mosaic floor of Cosmatesque pattern. The N transept, approached behind the organ, is similar in design to the nave, but has a corbelled balcony. In its NE corner is the **Lady chapel**, with a particularly fine stone reredos; the mosaic floor here is of 1958 and the Madonna incorporates a medieval fragment found nearby.

The **crossing** has another fine mosaic floor and a high flat ceiling painted and gilded in Byzantine style by Dom Charles Norris. Above the four big arches is another corbelled walkway. The **presbytery** is dominated by the big sexfoil-shaped copper gilt corona with its 48 lights and by the gilded high altar and reredos, a copy of the Golden Altar of Stavelot in the Cluny Museum in Paris. The abbot's throne contains 16th c. panelling from a house at Kingsbridge which belonged to the medieval abbots of Buckfast.

At the far end of the N aisle are two more chapels and a double stair. The downward flight leads to an exhibition crypt, and the upward to the **Blessed Sacrament chapel**, contrasting vividly with the Gothic of the rest of the church. The windows, including the giant Christus behind the altar, are by Dom Charles Norris, and the timber mural occupying the S wall is by David Weeks.

To the left on re-entering the main church are two more chapels, and in the first bay of the S presbytery aisle a bronze bas-relief of Abbot Vonier, under whom the church was rebuilt (d. 1938). In the **S transept** is the Holy Cross chapel, balancing the Lady chapel opposite. The S wall of the transept contains a 'watching' window and on the W side is a full-length portrait of Abbot Vonier. Generally the S side of the church matches the N; its doorways however lead into the cloister (private), and at its W end is the exceptionally ornate bronze font, a slightly modified copy of the famous Romanesque one at Hildesheim in Germany. The supporting kneeling figures represent the four rivers of Paradise.

The **exterior** of grey and brown stone is dominated by the 158-foot high pinnacled tower, somewhat later in historical style than the late Romanesque of the remainder, and containing fifteen bells. Beyond the N transept is private ground, but the angular Blessed Sacrament chapel may be seen from the far side of the extensive car park, and in the opposite direction it is possible to walk past the W front with its Norman-style portal and preponderance of brown stone to the monks' main entrance which stands in front of the so-called Old House, the turreted Berry mansion of c.1800. Next is the chapter room, built under Walters on the site of the W range, and then the four-storeyed 14th c. Abbot's Tower, the only substantial survival from the original complex. Some remains of two gatehouses may however be found a short distance up and down the lane.

Buckland Devon: SX 488668
4½ miles S of Tavistock and 1½ miles W of Plymouth road A386

Cistercian abbey of the Blessed Virgin Mary and St Benedict
    founded 1278 by Amicia, Countess of Devon, a daughter house
    of Quarr. Dissolved 1539 and leased to George Pollard

Owned by National Trust. Open Good Friday to end of September
    11.0 a.m. (Sundays 2.0 p.m.) to 6.0 p.m. Remainder of year
    Wednesdays, Saturdays and Sundays only, 3.0 to 5.0 p.m.
    Admission charge

Almost the last Cistercian abbey to be founded in England, as well
as the most westerly, it is also unusual in the preservation of its
church as a dwelling whilst its monastic buildings have almost totally
disappeared. The church, cruciform and aisleless, tallies in style
with the decades following its foundation. The tithe barn, preserved
complete, is of *c.*1320.

From the first lessee the abbey passed quickly to Sir Richard
Grenville, then to his grandson of *Revenge* fame, and in 1581 to Sir
Francis Drake. It remained with Drake's descendants till the 1940s,
passed to the National Trust in 1949, and is now used by Plymouth
City Museum and Art Gallery. It was the Grenvilles who put
intermediate floors into the church and added a domestic wing S of
the chancel. The present staircase at the junction was inserted
*c.*1770, at which time some of the cloister buildings to the N were
still standing. Relics of the Drakes were saved when the building
was severely burnt in 1938.

The form of the church (far from elegant in its guise as a house) is
readily grasped from the S approach: nave, squat central tower, and
chancel beyond. What looks like a transept but is actually one bay
further W is a 16th c. staircase wing; both transepts have in fact
gone, but it is evident where they were. The entrance, round the
other side past the N transept site, is into a vaulted passage which
was one of the transept chapels. This continues as a 16th c. cross-
passage dividing the crossing space (now Great Hall) from the
chancel (now domestic **chapel**). This chapel (now only room-height)
was formed in the 1920s, when the sedilia, piscina and aumbry,
parts of columns, and other stonework were re-exposed, and the
high altar rebuilt from fragments.

The **Great Hall**, extending a few feet into the nave, has elaborate
plaster and woodwork of 1576. Drake's drum and other relics are

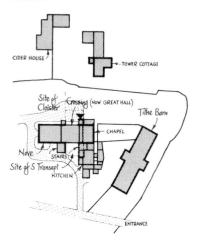

here. The main stair, a modern replacement, leads to a mezzanine museum gallery and on to three first floor rooms. Alongside the eastern one (the 'Georgian Room') is a passage to the 'Georgian Stair', a complex arrangement of stairs and landings with the chancel arch incongruously soaring above.

Continuing up the main stair, the topmost ('Naval') gallery is reached. This is within the roof space and provides odd views of the tops of all four **crossing** arches: the W strengthened with concrete, the N with a fireplace inside it, the S with a window, and the E with a giant panel of Geometric tracery in the crown. The Georgian stair leads up to the tower roof (private), passes (on the floor below) a part of the circular stair in the SE pier of the crossing, and leads at ground level to the 16th c. kitchens added by the Grenvilles, where there is now a tea-room.

Outside, the N front shows clearly the blocked transept arch and the line of its roof – also the added windows of the nave and the blocked arches of the original ones. The porch is 16th c. The E wall is mostly rebuilt. A stepped path leads to the 14th c. **tithe barn**, 160 feet long and 40 feet high. The abbey had a licence to crenellate in 1336, and this barn seems to have been regarded as defensive. In it now is a display of carts and farm implements.

The S side of the house is similar to the N, but for the added kitchen wing; on the W side of that can be seen the two arches of the S transeptal chapels, while a stone head inserted over a doorway further S is thought to portray the foundress. In the W wall of the church are more traces of old window and door openings; the present doorway there leads into a National Trust shop.

The Cider House and Tower Cottage to the N (private) probably incorporate parts of the dorter and abbot's lodging respectively, while the farm to the E may well represent the infirmary.

Buildwas Shropshire: SJ 643043
close to village, but on S side of river Severn

Savigniac abbey of St Mary and St Chad founded 1135 by Roger, Bishop of Coventry and Lichfield, a daughter house of Furness; became Cistercian 1147. Dissolved 1536 and granted to Edward Grey, Lord Powis

In care of Department of the Environment (but part-owned by Central Electricity Generating Board). Open during standard hours (admission charge); N and NE ranges not open to the public

The mid-12th c. buildings continued almost without alteration throughout the abbey's life, and their ruin is a modest and reasonably complete example of the Transitional Norman style. A chapel added on the S side in the 14th c. but now reduced to its foundation is the only exception.

Parts of the infirmary and abbot's house became incorporated in a private house, now a sports club house; the refectory site also lies in its garden. The remainder passed to the Commissioners of Works in 1925.

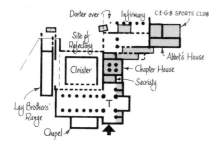

From the SE approach the **nave** arcades are seen particularly well as a result of the aisle walls having gone. The round piers combined with scalloped capitals and obtusely pointed arches are typical of the middle of the 12th c., though rather severe in character. The clerestory had simple shafted windows and there was no triforium.

Enter by the **S transept**, noticing the two E chapels, each with a piscina and quite rough groined vaults. At the SE corner is the base of a spiral stair. Go next through the **crossing** space beneath the former tower into the presbytery with its three tall windows (Gothic in proportions, yet round-headed). 13th c. triple sedilia survive, and traces of the former rib-vaulting.

Looking now W, the extent of the monks' quire is marked by a step across the nave and by the remains of low walls closing off the aisles; these walls continued westwards. The **N transept** retains two chapels like the S, as well as the stone part of the night stair to the dorter. The patch of floor tiles is a reconstruction.

Only the outline of the **cloister** walks is visible, though the lower part of the E range is fairly complete. First on the right is a groin-vaulted crypt under the N end of the N transept; its use is unknown. Then the sacristy with another vault (its ribs have fallen off), and next to it the chapter house. This has rib-vaulting carried on round and octagonal columns with varied capitals, and another area of old floor tiles. The doorway and the windows on either side of it are much eroded. Last is the parlour.

At the W end of the N walk is the refectory end wall base. The refectory site is private but looking across it one can see some arches of the dorter undercroft, and on their left an outbuilding on the infirmary site. Continue along the W walk towards the church; on the right is the cellar of the lay brothers' range.

From inside the **church** the crossing arches are seen to advantage, and the high-pitched roof lines on the W face of the tower; the W and E arches are on corbels because of the quire stalls. There being no W doorway, the outside of the W front is reached by crossing the S chapel site; the two round-arched windows, originally shafted, add to its simple dignity.

Burnham Buckinghamshire: SU 930804
1¼ miles S of village and 600 yards S of A4

Augustinian nunnery of St Mary founded 1266 by Richard, King of the Romans. Dissolved 1539 and leased to William Tyldesley.

Anglican Augustinian Society of the Precious Blood founded in
Birmingham 1905 and moved here 1916

Owned by the Society of the Precious Blood. Limited public visits
by written application to Mother Superior (not Fridays or
Sundays)

The buildings were modest in scale, with the cloister N of the
church. A 14th c. column base suggests a rebuilding of the cloister,
but there is no other evidence of work after the end of the 13th c.

The church was demolished *c.*1570 by Paul Wentworth who made
a house in the N and E cloister ranges. By 1719 the property had
become a farm, the nuns' dorter being used as a hay loft. The barns
were added in the 1830s, by which time the N range had nearly
gone. In 1913 the property was bought by Lawrence Bissley, who
began restoration and made a chapel of the chapter house; three
years later there came a community of nuns bearing, as it chanced,
the name of the relic originally given to Hailes Abbey by Burnham's
own founder. They made the E range habitable again, built a
refectory on the site of the abbey chancel and, in the 1960s, erected
a new 'gatehouse' and kitchen to the S of the cloister, the original
outline of which is partially preserved.

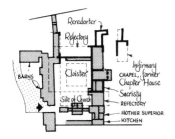

Past the barn at the entrance, the visitor encounters the
uncompromising concrete 'gatehouse' by Francis Pym standing
within the S end of the **cloister** court – which extends further S than
in medieval times and takes in part of the original church site. Its N
end (behind the lean-to roof) is formed by the S wall of the 13th c.
refectory, while to the right is another old chalk and flint wall
fronting the former parlour, chapter house and sacristy; over these
ran the first floor dorter. The chapter house, behind the bigger of
the 13th c. doorways, is now the nuns' chapel; its E wall was rebuilt

further out in 1951 to give more space. Inside the smaller doorway visitors cross a passage which may have contained the dorter stair, into the **sacristy**. A blocked doorway from this led into the church; a much more elaborate gabled opening beside it, facing into what is now the refectory and therefore not seen by visitors, has never been satisfactorily explained; it may be part of a shrine. A glimpse into the former chapter house is allowed; its furnishings as a chapel are of course comparatively modern.

In the far corner of the cloister is a block of masonry marking the junction of the N and W ranges. Through the arch lies the nuns' private garden, with remains of the refectory (and of the Tudor house adapted from it) just on the other side, and, to the right and also out of sight, walling of the reredorter and of a small infirmary.

The ancient cob wall with tiled top along Huntercombe Lane formed the E boundary of the precinct.

Burton-on-Trent Staffordshire: in town centre   SK 251227

Monastery founded in 9th c. by Modwena; refounded as
    Benedictine abbey of St Mary and St Modwen c.1003 by Wulfric
    Spott. Dissolved 1539; refounded 1541 as college for dean (the
    last abbot) and four prebendaries; dissolved 1545 and granted to
    Sir William Paget

In multiple ownership. Remains of chapter house accessible during
    market hours; infirmary (part only) during licensing hours

Anciently Modwennestow. Knowledge of the abbey buildings relies mostly on a plan made shortly after the Dissolution, and on limited 19th c. excavations. Though never large it seems to have been quite wealthy. The surviving fragments, mostly of the infirmary and chapter house, show work of several periods.

Part of the abbey church evidently passed to parish use; it was rebuilt in 1719–26, slightly towards the N. The market that (as was often the case in the Middle Ages) had sprung up at the abbey gate developed into an extensive (19th c.) market hall covering much of the site of the cloister and the entrance court, while the infirmary hall and chapel became the nucleus of a 19th c. house and now form the Abbey Inn.

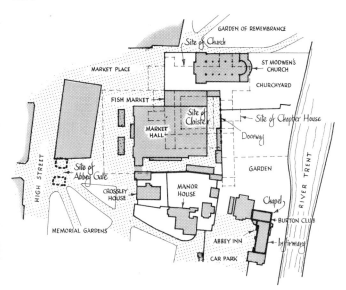

An inspection can only be fragmented. From the High Street one sees, left to right, the church, market hall and a lane that leads past the Manor House (on its left) to the car park of the Abbey Inn. Where the lane meets the High Street, parts of the gatehouse stood till 1927. Between the Manor House (now solicitors' offices) and the Market Hall is a stretch of boundary wall of the inner precinct. In the Abbey Inn the medieval work is much overlaid. Some can be detected in the bar in the S wing (the supposed infirmary hall) but the best is in private areas: a 14th c. timber roof to the hall, and in the Burton Club parts of the 13th c. lancet windows at E and W ends. The external niche is 19th c. but many bits of older carved stonework have been built into the car park wall.

The remains at the back of the market hall are reached either by the service road on the S side or through a door at the end of the fish market. They are the bases of a 15th c. doorway to the chapter house, of two blocked 13th c. openings at the side, and of a 12th c. arch to the parlour.

At the SE corner of the churchyard, on the river bank, is a late medieval doorway re-erected – but facing the private garden of the inn. For a more complete view of the infirmary (inn) it is necessary to cross the river by the park footbridge; if nothing else, it emphasizes the extent of 19th c. work added to the medieval.

Bury St Edmunds Suffolk: in centre of town   TL 857642

Monastery founded *c*.633; became Benedictine 1020 and recolonised from St Benet of Holme. Dissolved 1539 and sold to John Eyer

In care of Department of the Environment, Suffolk County Council, Bury St Edmunds District Council, the Provost and Chapter of St Edmundsbury and others. Open from about 7.30 a.m. (weekdays) or 9.0 a.m. (Sundays) till about dusk, without charge

Siegbert, first Christian king of East Anglia, founded a monastery to which in 903 the body of King Edmund, d. 870, was brought. His shrine attracted pilgrims, encouraging King Canute to enlarge both the community and its church *c*.1020. William the Conqueror promoted its rebuilding on the grandest scale which began *c*.1090 and was completed *c*.1210 with W front (longer than any other in Britain) and magnificent W tower both rivalling Ely. A NE Lady chapel was added *c*.1275. Bad relations with the town erupted at times into riots, with consequent damage and partial rebuildings. The W steeple also suffered two collapses and a fire in the 15th c.

The abbot's palace continued in use as a house till 1720; parts of the precinct wall, with the Abbot's Bridge, Great Gate and St James's Gate have survived, together with the charnel chapel and the churches of St James (now the cathedral) and St Mary. The remainder became a quarry for the town, though several little houses built into the W front of the church have ensured its partial preservation. Excavations begun in 1957 have revealed the church crypt and other foundations.

The defensive **Great Gate**, the larger and newer of the two surviving, is of *c*.1330–80 and typically Decorated. In passing through, note the remains of vaults and the portcullis. Preferably make first for the church ruin. So bear diagonally right; on the right is a stretch of wall that bounded the Palace Yard. Pass between the bowling green (left) and the kiosk (right), which is on the site of the cellarer's gate, and turn left (E) between the yew hedge and rose

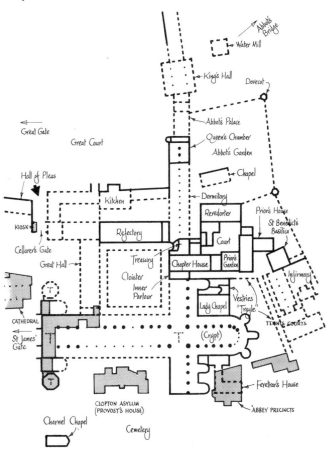

garden. The grassed area with a copper beech was the **cloister**; the long enclosure on the left with a line of Irish yews was the refectory. Ahead, near the centre of the S walk, is a gate to the fenced-off area under the Department of the Environment. Here the main parts of the ruins are clearly labelled.

To the right, the highest mass is the N wall of the N transept. The rectangle to its N, separated by the slype which at Bury was called

Trayle, is the **chapter house** with (modern) tomb-slabs of abbots
along the centre. Next to the N is the treasury, set behind a shafted
segmental entrance. N again from this (with a misleading bank
across) runs the long dormitory block with, at the end and over the
fence, the Queen's Chamber.

Now follow the fence the opposite way, around the whole E end.
It passes between the remains of a detached chapel (left) and the
buttresses of the reredorter (right), and then turns right and passes
the infirmary. Just before it turns right again is the square
foundation of the Saxon chapel of St Benedict, built c.1030. Much
of the infirmary now lies beneath the tennis courts; so does
Bradfield Hall, probably the original manor house and later the
infirmarer's. Next, the great **crypt** of c.1090 – as impressive in its
way as Canterbury or Winchester crypts, though leaving the
columns, the vaults and the presbytery above entirely to the
imagination. The plain rectangle to its N was the Lady chapel, built
c.1275 in place of Canute's round church. Around the crypt
perimeter are the apsed sub-chapels of the chevet. Some plaster
remains, and even some minute fragments of wall-paintings.

Continue round the outside; then step down into the transept at
its SW corner. To the right are steps into the crypt. Ahead,
however, the tallest masonry of all is the NE crossing-pier, on which
a tablet of 1847 commemorates the Magna Carta Oath of 1214. The
central tower was rebuilt in the 14th c. Moulded bases indicate the
beginning of the presbytery arcades, and here from the site of the
quire altar one can look again into the crypt.

Turn about and go up the double bank into the **nave**. At its W end
a great deal remains, but inextricably entangled with the private
houses built into it and more picturesque than informative. So
return to the gate, recross the cloister, and turn left (S) at the kiosk.
On the right is St James's church, since 1913 the cathedral, and on
the left the **W front**, its extraordinary embedded houses giving it the
air of a stage set. The octagonal NW tower has gone; just beyond it
an opening into the Courtyard (on the site of an apsed chapel)
provides a peep behind the scenes. Then come three big decayed
arches, once rather like Peterborough or Lincoln. Next, another
chapel, and finally the substantial SW tower, reduced probably by
one storey and visible also from the rear garden. The small isolated
ruin in the cemetery (towards St Mary's church) is the late 13th c.
charnel chapel, chiefly interesting for its 18th c. moral epitaphs.

Exploration towards the E from here is less profitable. Beyond
the brick Clopton Asylum of 1730 is another glimpse of the E end of

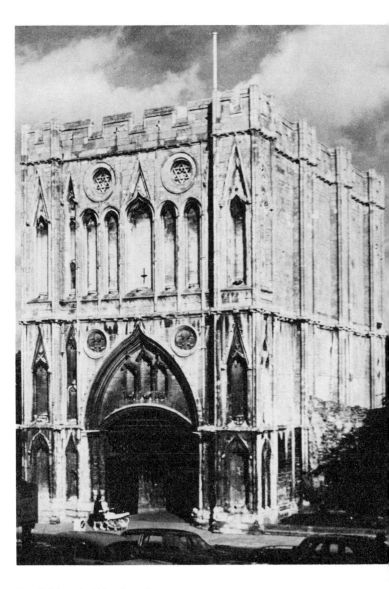

Bury St Edmunds: 14th c. Great Gate

the church, and in the County Council car park some bits of precinct wall can be found.

Walk now around the S and W sides of the cathedral (passing the grand Norman gatehouse which serves as its tower) and into the precinct through the Great Gate a second time. Straight ahead is the ruined Queen's Chamber and, beyond, a stretch of the abbot's garden wall with a hexagonal dovecote. Past that again is the early 13th c. Abbot's Bridge over the Lark, with pieces of precinct wall conspicuous on both sides; at the bridge was All Souls' Gate, a town gate controlled by the abbey. Bearing left, however, one can leave the precinct at the site of the small Abbot's Gate into Mustow Street.

Byland North Yorkshire: SE 549789
1½ miles NE of Coxwold and 2 miles S of A 170

Savigniac abbey of St Mary founded at Calder 1135, a daughter house of Furness; plundered by Scots and moved to Hood (near Thirsk) 1188; refounded at Old Byland 1143 by Roger de Mowbray; moved to Stocking 1147 and became Cistercian; moved finally to Byland 1177. Dissolved 1539 and granted to Sir William Pickering

In care of Department of the Environment. Open during standard hours (admission charge)

After so many temporary homes the monks were able at once so to plan their buildings that no later changes were needed; the church plan is of late Cistercian type with square end and ambulatory, and the style early Gothic with round-arched windows but pointed vaults. However construction must have occupied over 50 years, so it was a later generation who enjoyed them to the full. The S transept of the church, the wall between church and cloister, and the lay brothers' wing were probably ready when the monks moved in, and the remainder of the monastic buildings as well as the church (excepting the W two-thirds of the nave) by c.1200. The nave was finished by c.1225 and the only subsequent work was in minor alterations and additions.

Nothing of the post-Dissolution history seems to be recorded; the buildings must have gone gradually to ruin, aided no doubt by persistent quarrying of stone for other uses.

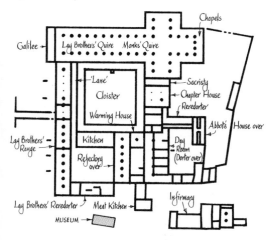

Byland is remembered for its **W front**, with the lower half of a once splendid wheel window of *c*.1220 flanked by one precarious pinnacle and the stump of another. The three lancets beneath are intact, and the trefoil-headed main doorway. In front of this (and of the plainer aisle openings) stood a porch of which the wall and roof lines are visible. In the **nave** only bases remain of the piers, and a few bits to show what the rest was like. The N aisle wall is almost complete, with lancet windows not yet Gothic-arched, vault springers, and the capitals and corbels of wall shafts; subtle changes in the capitals mark the pause at the fourth bay. The nave altar step is defined, but not the line of the pulpitum which stood two bays beyond the altar. In the S aisle are several areas of the tiled paving which is a special feature of Byland, though the same intricate patterns are met elsewhere. In the monks' quire further E the ornamental stone plinth behind the stalls has been partly re-erected. Through a gap in this the **N transept** is reached, with its two chapel divisions visible. Here too the narrow round-arched windows and vault springers remain but the main columns are gone.

The N quire aisle and the **presbytery** have more tile patterns – for instance a complex 'wheel' at the end of the aisle. Against the E wall (with lower vaults) were five little chapels, each with a single tall window. Past them, a doorway from the S quire aisle leads into the monks' cemetery where a railed-in length of drain is visible. The ruin beyond has not been identified.

Byland: 13th c. church interior looking W

Back in the church, on the N side of the presbytery stands a reconstructed length of the low trefoil-headed arcade at the back of the stalls. The **S transept** has wonderfully preserved floor patterns in both its E chapels. It also has more walling to show than the N transept (which was a decade or two later). Indeed its SE corner gives the best clue to the church's general arrangement of triforium and clerestory and suggests that the main spans were never vaulted. Below is a double piscina. From here steps lead down to the plain sacristy-library and thence to the **cloister**, the wall-bases of which largely remain; the original open arches on twin columns gave way in the 15th c. to solid walls and windows. Curved steps lead up to the S aisle, and to their right are book cupboards. Turning S, however, the chapter house is next, with little to show of its doorway – but clear remains of its stone seats. Then a parlour, and next a slype which should be followed into the undercroft of the reredorter where the drain is exposed. At the end, in an apparently insalubrious position, was the abbot's house; another drain runs right under it. S of this are footings of various outbuildings, and at the far corner the infirmary (long used as a cottage and much altered).

Back now to the abbot's house, noting the doorway on its W (cloister) side. Between it and the cloister is the dorter undercroft, cut up with later (ruined) partitions. By the cloister doorway is the start of the day stair to the dorter. Next, the S walk. At once on the left is the warming house with very large fireplace in its W wall. Then the **refectory**, lying N–S in true Cistercian style, with steps both up to it and down to the cellars below; all along, springers of the cloister vaults remain. Then a big kitchen parallel to the walk, with central fireplaces at two levels, and at the corner the day stair to the lay brothers' dorter.

Parallel to the W walk is the lay brothers' 'lane'. Alongside it, the undercroft of the lay brothers' range has a long line of column bases, occasional cross-walls, and many corbels of the vaulting – with scallop ornament and therefore as early as any of the abbey structure. Southwards the lane goes to a grassed court behind the kitchen. On the further side was the lay brothers' reredorter, with a drain through it; beyond is the modern **museum** building with a display mostly of carved capitals and corbels and including the remarkable stone base of the abbey lectern. Going now E, the low detached ruin with four distinct fireplaces was the 15th c. meat kitchen. Beyond, also detached, is the **infirmary** – first a portico foundation, then the main hall, a transverse hall with tile-backed fireplace, a double room up steps, and finally an undercroft with its columns re-erected.

Return now past the museum and along the outside of the lay brothers' range with its flying buttress bases. Near the church end, it is worth going through into the 'lane' again to see the stone seat recesses – no fewer than 35 of them. If time allows, a walk round the N side of the church is also worth while, seeing the W front again, the N side of the nave, the N transept, and the E end.

All that is left of the gatehouse, some distance to the W, is a large round 13th c. arch which spanned the roadway inside, and a wall with a trefoil-headed doorway.

Calder Cumbria: NY 050064
½ mile NE of A595 at Calder Bridge

Savigniac abbey of St Mary founded 1135 by Ranulph Meschines, a
daughter house of Furness; moved to Hood ¹¹˙ ˌnd to Old

Byland 1143; refounded from Furness 1142 and became
Cistercian 1148. Dissolved 1536 and given to Thomas Leigh

Owned by Burns-Lindow family. Not open to the public

Scots raids (particularly one in 1137) were responsible for the
abbey's uncertain beginnings and, no doubt, for its unambitious
size. Building of the church seems to have proceeded normally from
E to W – after which the E end was built afresh, so that the nave of
c.1175 is oldest and the chancel and transepts a decade or two later.
It is likely however that further work was done to the nave in the
13th c. and after a raid *c*.1332. The monastic buildings were entirely
reconstructed during the 14th c.

The monastic ranges were adapted to domestic use, while the
church seems to have been allowed to decay gently. The W cloister
range has disappeared, the E has to some extent survived (including
one bay of the chapter house vault), and the S was absorbed by
stages into the present house, where the undercrofts of the refectory
and of rooms to its E are preserved in the basement.

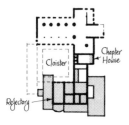

The drive to the abbey may be followed past the 'Private' notice
but only as far as the field gate marked 'No Visitors' – where a
public footpath crosses it. Fortunately this is a good vantage point
for the whole group, with the late 12th c. N nave arcade prominent
(alternate octagonal and quatrefoil columns) and the round-headed
W doorway just visible. The S arcade has gone, but all four crossing
arches stand, and to their left the N and W walls of the N transept.
Through the crossing the unusual sedilia can be glimpsed – three
oddly trefoiled heads grouped beside an opening to the S transept.
That is more complete but rather hidden; it has big blank plate-
traceried arcading at triforium level.

Further to the right the late 13th c. chapter house doorway can be
picked out, and the former cloister. Right of that is the house, of

Calder: Church interior of *c*.1200

which the W wing is of *c*.1800. The curved bay on its S front represents a prolongation of the refectory.

Up the valley to the left of the ruin, a mound is visible. This covers an abbey oven, near which was a mill. From it a watercourse still runs to and under the main building. Much nearer, and in the opposite direction, an apparently more modern group contains the 14th c. abbey gatehouse.

An alternative (in fact the original) approach is by the often very muddy public footpath from Calder Bridge. This leads to the S end of the gatehouse (two-storeyed and much altered) and through a garden to the gate and viewpoint described above.

Caldey Dyfed: SS 143966
on Caldy Island, 2½ miles S of Tenby

Anglican Benedictine community of Our Lady and St Peter
    founded 1896 by Benjamin Carlyle (Abbot Aelred) in the Isle of
    Dogs, London; moved to Caldy 1906; became Roman Catholic
    1913, abbey 1914; moved to Prinknash, Gloucestershire 1928.
    Refounded as Cistercian abbey of Our Lady and St Samson 1929,
    a daughter house of Chimay, Belgium

Accessible Monday to Friday from Whitsun till about 20th
    September by frequent boat service from Tenby. Church open at
    all times. Guided tours of parts of abbey (men only) advertised
    outside nearby post office

A Tironensian priory of St Illtud was founded on Ynys Byr or Caldey in 1113 as a cell of St Dogmael's abbey, on the site of a cell reputedly founded in the 5th or 6th c. Its modest remains, including the complete church and gatehouse, have no historical connection with the present abbey, which was built by a community of different character and is now used by one that is different again. By its founder it was meant to become part of a complex comparable with great medieval monasteries. Little more was realised (in 1910–13) than a chapel, three ranges around a cloister (intended to become a boys' school when the rest had been built) and an imposing abbot's house – all in a somewhat Italianate style with white roughcast walls and red arches and pantiled roofs. Changes from Anglican to Roman Catholic and then from Benedictine to Cistercian have little visible effect except in the church interior, redone more austerely in 1951 after a fire. Perfume-making from gorse and lavender is a thriving industry.

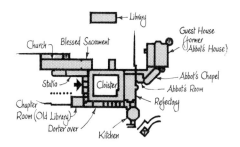

The main public concourse around the tea gardens looks up at the four-storey S wing (actually N, for the church orientation is reversed), which has chapter room and offices on its ground floor and sleeping rooms above. The octagonal building to the right is the kitchen (inspired by that of Glastonbury), while to the left is the three-storey W wing fronting an outer court from which the guided tours commence. The tile-arched main doorway has chequerwork at the sides and a statue of Our Lady over; it leads into a **cloister** walk with plain open roof, big round-arched windows and quarry tiled floor. The way leads past the day stair, along the S walk past the offices and into the refectory in the E range. Like a baronial banqueting hall, this has a huge fireplace at one end, open timber roof, and oak panelling and reading pulpit. Unfortunately sheet glass has been substituted for the original leaded patterns.

Passing the Stations of the Cross painted on slate panels by a Belgian artist, parties are led out into a grassed court, facing the library (a prefabricated building) and with the turreted guest house (former abbot's house) on the right. Hidden behind that is the abbot's chapel, apsed at both ends and panelled like the refectory. The way out however passes the splayed base of the **church** tower. Through the gate and to the left is the church entrance, a simple doorway of Romanesque type with wheel window over. Visitors are allowed up the steep stair to the gallery to see the white interior: simple hammer-beam roof, small 'Norman' windows, plain stone altar W of the former chancel arch, stalls of wenge wood W of that (1951), a Belgian Madonna over the arch, and an openwork iron hanging Rood. At the further end is the Blessed Sacrament chapel with its own altar.

Canonsleigh Devon: ST 067174
5 miles WSW of Wellington and 1¼ miles NW of A38

Augustinian canons' priory of the Blessed Virgin Mary and St John
the Evangelist founded *c*.1161 by William de Clarville; refounded
as nuns' abbey (additionally dedicated to St Etheldreda) 1285 by
Maud, Countess of Devon; dissolved 1539. The surviving, half-
explained buildings comprise a massive 15th c. gatehouse in
Canonsleigh Barton farmyard (Godberford family) and – much
further E – high walls thought to be of the abbey mill.

Canterbury (St Augustine's) Kent: TR 154579
300 yards E of cathedral

Benedictine abbey of St Peter and St Paul founded 598 by St
Augustine; rededicated 978 by St Dunstan to St Peter, St Paul
and St Augustine. Dissolved 1538 and became Crown property

In care of Department of the Environment and St Augustine's
College. College buildings not open to the public; remainder
open during standard hours (admission charge)

The Romans forbade burials within city walls, so St Augustine set
up a monastery outside to receive the bodies of archbishops and
kings. The tombs of archbishops have been found where
documented, six of them in the original N porticus and two outside.
King Edbald *c*.613 founded a second church, St Mary's, 50 feet to
the E, to be a royal mausoleum instead of the N porticus. A church
of St Pancras, 260 feet further E still, was also of St Augustine's
time. The monastery church was extended westward *c*.1000, and
c.1050 it was linked to St Mary's by an octagonal structure known as
Abbot Wulfric's rotunda. There may even have been a fourth
church just W of St Peter and St Paul's – like the rotunda probably
never finished, for a complete new abbey was begun in 1070 and all
but St Pancras's was swept away. This was substantially complete by
early in the 12th c. but badly damaged by fire in 1168. Dates of
numerous additions are known: charnel chapel on S side 1288; great
gatehouse 1300–5; chapter house 1325; St Anne's chapel 1360;
cemetery gatehouse 1360–75; Lady chapel early 16th c. There was
also a detached bell-tower of unknown date.
    After the Dissolution a royal palace was built N of the nave,
incorporating the N wall and NW tower, and the W cloister range

with the abbot's house, and using the two gatehouses. It survived until late in the 17th c.; what was left of the splendid Norman tower did not fall till 1822. The rest of the abbey was dismantled and the stone sent for use elsewhere – to as far even as the fortifications of Calais. In 1844 St Augustine's College was founded, with buildings by William Butterfield incorporating still-surviving bits of the abbot's house; the college estate was gradually extended to include virtually the entire abbey site, which was systematically excavated in 1900–27. Except for the library, the college buildings are now largely occupied by King's School; the remainder of the site was taken over by the Office of Works in 1939–40.

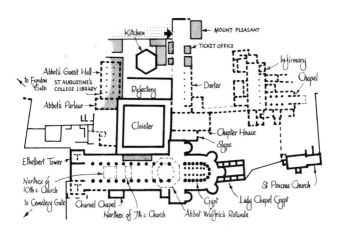

The cloister buildings lay N of the church, and the present-day approach is via the N end of the dorter, past the ticket office, to the NE corner of the garth. The big Victorian building to the NW is Butterfield's college library of 1844, standing on the partly medieval undercroft of the abbot's guest hall. The **church** is entered via the E cloister walk (to the left of which the chapter house site now lies beneath the high bank). Ahead, right in the centre, is Abbot Wulfric's rotunda, reduced to eight impressive square piers within a circle. It is of c.1050 and linked the two pre-existing churches; the design was based on St Benigne at Dijon. Of St Mary's to the E, only a trace of the W wall is left; the rest was displaced by the Norman quire of which the **crypt** (c.1070–90) can next be seen by going through the N transept to the crossing and looking E. The enclosing wall is complete to about 10 feet in height, and the bases survive of slenderer columns down the centre. Modern steps lead into it on the S side. Off its outer ambulatory is a series of apsidal chapels, remarkably complete (but that at the E end is a partial reconstruction) separated by plain walling – with pilasters and carrying clear indications of the former vaulting.

Back next up the steps into the N transept, which has the base of another (upper-level) apse on its E side, and along the N **nave** aisle – with the cloister on the right and the now shapeless nave pier bases on the left. The modern pantiled roof protects the Roman brick foundations of the early 7th c. porticus of St Gregory which was part of St Augustine's own first monastery church. Within, the tombs of three archbishops who succeeded him are clearly labelled, found exactly as was chronicled four centuries later (St Augustine's own tomb was later displaced by the third pier base of the Norman nave arcade and replaced by a shrine in the easternmost apse). Lines across the Norman nave indicate the W front and narthex of that first church, the floor of which was 3 feet lower; others further W show the extent of its enlargement, c.1000.

The preservation of the pilastered N aisle wall is due to its incorporation into Henry VIII's palace; the brickwork added on top is of that time. Only the base is now left of the once splendid early 12th c. NW 'Ethelbert' tower. Where the main W doorway stood is a gateway to the college. Of the SW tower very little remains; the boulder and broken monolith now on its site were found whilst the Saxon nave was being excavated and may be Roman. Just to the S some more Saxon foundations have been exposed.

Next the S side of the nave. Under the first arch of the arcade the patch of sand protects a small area of ancient tiles. Outside the aisle wall are foundations of the charnel chapel, late 13th c., and further on (clearly labelled) is the site of the 7th c. St Martin's porticus balancing St Gregory's opposite, with the foundation of the 14th c. chapel of St Anne just beyond.

The S transept is also reduced to foundations. The four tombs along its S end are of 7th and 8th c. kings reburied in the 12th c., and have been repaired with modern brick. On the E side the start of a spiral stair can be seen, and part of another apsidal chapel.

Now go back across the crossing, turn right outside the transept and follow the outside of the crypt. Beyond it is the crypt of the early 16th c. Lady chapel. Further on, within the precinct, is the 7th c. church of **St Pancras** – much more complete than the 7th c. work swallowed up in the abbey church but no doubt once similar. Its W porticus still stands quite high in parts. The apsed chancel, which once had a triple arch to the nave, was replaced in the 14th c.

There remain the other monastic parts, and first the **cloister** – beneath which many traces of a somewhat random series of Saxon monastic buildings have been found. The shafted doorway of *c.*1200 in the SW corner (close to the church) now looks into the college court, and above are traces of the chapel window of the abbot's lodging, which occupied much of the W range. Projecting into the garth on its N side is the outline of a polygonal lavatory; steps opposite this led into the 13th c. refectory. Of that and the slightly later hexagonal kitchen beyond, only low walls remain. Of the long dorter range nothing much stands at all except the far end wall. The infirmary, further E, has been reburied after excavation.

The exhibits in the **museum** should certainly be looked at before leaving the site; there is also a model of a reconstruction.

Finally the **gatehouses**. Fyndon Gate, vaulted and richly embellished, is of 1300–9 and now forms the entrance to St Augustine's College which is not open to the public – so the abbey survivals within cannot normally be seen. Further along Monastery Street is Cemetery Gate, later and much less spectacular and made into a house.

St Mildred's church, Canterbury (at TR 144575) has been identified with a recorded early Saxon abbey of St Mary, but the evidence is tenuous.

Cerne Dorset: ST 665015
in town, 300 yards E of Sherborne–Dorchester road A352

Abbey founded at least by 9th c., refounded for Benedictines by
     Ethelmar, Earl of Cornwall *c.*987 and dedicated to St Mary, St
     Peter and either St Edwold or St Benedict. Dissolved 1539

Mainly owned by parish. Open to the public at all times (voluntary
     admission charge)

Practically nothing is known of the main buildings. The church is believed to have been 12th c. and may have stood in such a position that the still existing well or spring of St Augustine occupied the angle between nave and S transept. If that is so, the cloister and monastic buildings would have been to its N; but all traces have disappeared, probably largely concealed beneath the parish

churchyard (a detached one some 150 yards N of the parish church).
The main survivals are the abbot's hall porch of *c*.1500, a supposed
guest house of *c*.1460, and two barns. Abbey Farm house is thought
to have been built around remains of the main gatehouse.

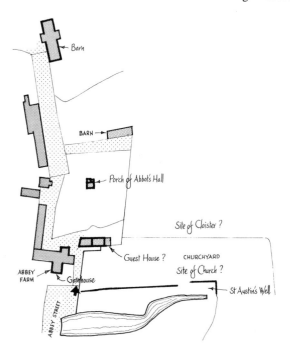

The remains have to be picked out piece by piece. Abbey Street
led straight to the **gatehouse**, now represented by Abbey Farm
house (private). Though refaced in the late 18th c. after a fire, its
central gabled part is 15th c. in origin and has angle buttresses and
traces of the outer arch. The path on the right leads (past a payment
box) to a rear courtyard on the right of which is the two-storeyed
'**guest house**', faced with bands of flint and stone and with a pretty
oriel on its N side. It may have been built as the **abbot's house**, the
successor of which stood where the lawn above is now, just E of its
surviving porch amongst the trees. This is so grand that one
wonders what the hall itself was like. Inside is a fan vault, and on

the W or outer side a splendid oriel rising through two upper floors.

From the courtyard the lane leads up, through a gateway, to a small but altered 15th c. **barn**. In the S wall of this is a 13th c. piece of foliage carving.

Back now past the house to the churchyard, entered through an early 17th c. gateway with obelisk ornaments. St Augustine's well or spring, enclosed by an L-shaped wall, is about 50 yards along on the right, and feeds the pond at the top of Abbey Street. The wall may possibly have been part of the abbey church, as mentioned above.

Numerous fragments of abbey stonework are to be found built into walls about the little town. In addition there is the splendid 14th c. flint-faced **tithe barn** which stands about ¼ mile SW of the parish church close to the street called The Folly.

Chatteris Cambridgeshire: in town centre   TL 393858

Benedictine nunnery of St Mary founded by 1016 by Ednoth,
  Bishop of Dorchester. Dissolved 1538

In multiple ownership. Precinct wall only, accessible at all times

The last of nine pre-Conquest nunneries in England, it was probably refounded and rebuilt early in the 12th c. About 1308 the buildings were practically destroyed by fire. The church was reconsecrated in 1352; though it became parochial, it was not kept after the Dissolution. What did survive was the W range of the cloister containing the guest house and perhaps the abbess's lodging. This became Park House, was much altered by the Gascoyne family in the 17th c., and was pulled down in 1847. The former precinct, bounded by Park Street and West, South and East Park Streets, was then cut across by Victoria Street and carved up.

Pieces of the precinct wall still exist along South Park Street and at its junction with East Park Street, and small bits of carved stone can be observed there and in one or two buildings in the town. The church plan is very largely conjectural.

Chertsey Surrey: 200 yards NE of town centre   TQ 044672

Benedictine abbey of St Peter founded 666 by St Erkenwald; ravaged by Danes late in 9th c. and refounded 964 from Abingdon by King Edgar; became mitred. Dissolved 1537 and given to Sir William Fitzwilliam, but community moved to Bisham

In multiple ownership. Church site not open to the public

Much is known of the abbey's history but little of its buildings. They were begun in 1110 and work continued on them till the 13th c. The church plan had an apsed E end, the apses being attached, not in the usual way to a semicircular ambulatory, but to a rectangular one, rather like Romsey.

Instead of a straightforward dissolution, the establishment was moved – for a brief period – to Bisham 'by favour of the King', who thereupon took much of the building material to further his schemes at Hampton Court. Amongst the ruins Sir Nicholas Carew built a house in the 17th c., which was demolished *c.*1810. The site was further divided and villas built. Excavation in the 1850s and 60s revealed the church plan (confirmed by more recent digs) and produced mainly 13th c. fragments including many tiles of patterns and workmanship unexcelled at any other abbeys.

N of the parish church (reputed to stand on the gatehouse chapel site and still possessing an abbey bell) is the little irregular Abbey Green. There the old barn on the E side is probably not earlier than the 17th c. A little further N the modern road Abbey Gardens leads to the E with recent houses one side and bigger 19th c. ones on the other. The abbey church site is mostly in the private grounds of the latter, close to the road and visible from it.

From Abbey Green a straight lane leads further N. In the wall on the left at the first bend are the remains of a stone doorway of unknown purpose. The barn opposite, though much patched and altered, is partly medieval and must have been an abbey

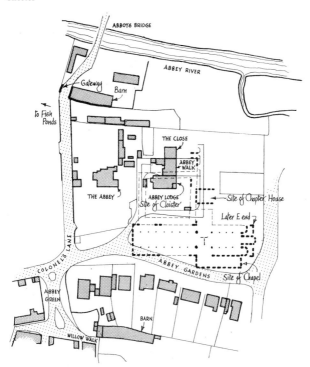

outbuilding. Further W, but only accessible from the Staines Road, the abbey fishponds can still be identified.

Chester Cheshire: in city centre   SJ 406665

Monastery of St Werburgh founded *c*.907 by Ethelflaed, daughter of King Alfred, for secular clerks; refounded as Benedictine abbey 1092–3, a daughter house of Bec-Helllouin, Normandy. Dissolved 1540; became cathedral of Christ and St Mary 1541

Cathedral church, refectory, etc. open during normal hours; St Anselm's chapel on request

For a full description see *A Guide to the Cathedrals of Britain*, pp.81–9.

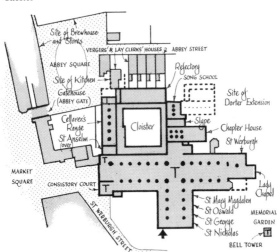

Site of Brewhouse and Stores

VERGERS' & LAY CLERKS' HOUSES 2 ABBEY STREET

ABBEY SQUARE

Refectory

SONG SCHOOL

Site of Kitchen

Gatehouse (ABBEY GATE)

Site of Dorter Extension

Cellarer's Range

Cloister

Slype

St Anselm (over)

Chapter House

St Werburgh

MARKET SQUARE

T

T

Lady Chapel

CONSISTORY COURT

T

ST WERBURGH STREET

St Mary Magdalen

St Oswald

St George

St Nicholas

MEMORIAL GARDEN

BELL TOWER

Chester: Abbey gate

Cirencester Gloucestershire: in town centre   SP 023022

Augustinian abbey of St Mary founded 1117 on site of earlier
    church; became mitred 1416. Dissolved 1539 and given to Roger
    Bassinge

Owned by Cotswold District Council. Site accessible at all times
    without charge

The story of a 'minster' founded in the 9th c. by one Alwin has been
discredited as probably medieval invention. But excavations in
1964–5 to reconstruct the abbey plan revealed lower-level
foundations of a perhaps 8th c. aisled and apsed church 175 feet
long (the longest known Saxon one in England) stretching from the
centre of the abbey nave to a point 80 feet further than the W front.
Beneath this again are Roman wall-bases. The abbey church was
consecrated in 1176, but much extended in the 14th c. with an
eastern ambulatory.

A house (Abbey House) was built on the site of the monastic
buildings by Richard Master late in the 16th c. Rebuilt *c.*1780 and
subsequently altered, it was demolished in 1964 and replaced by a
block of flats set back further from the abbey area, which is now
part of a public park. The excavated remains are reburied, the only
building above ground being the gatehouse known as Spital Gate.

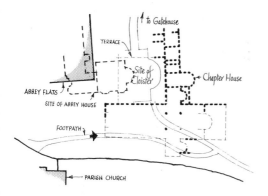

The plan shows the position of the abbey buildings but nothing of
them is now to be seen. A few bits of carved stone are in the parish
churchyard wall along the S side of the park; parts of the precinct

wall also survive on the W along Gosditch Street. Spital Gate, at the N end of the park and separated from the by-pass by the little river Churn and a bridge, is familiarly called the Saxon Arch but is actually Norman, with a massive vehicular arch of three orders and a smaller pedestrian one. The gates themselves are ancient; so are parts of the adjacent cottages.

Abbey stone was evidently reused throughout the town, notably in nos 33–35 Gloucester Street where parts of the cloister washplace have been recognised.

Cleeve Somerset: ST 047405
2 miles SW of Watchet, and ¼ mile S of A39 at Washford

Cistercian abbey of the Blessed Virgin Mary founded *c*.1190 by
    William de Romare, Earl of Lincoln, a daughter house of
    Revesby. Dissolved 1537 and granted to Robert, Earl of Sussex

In care of Department of the Environment. Open during standard
    hours (admission charge)

In its charters Vallis Florida, but always known as Cleeve. The basic plan and earliest surviving walls are of *c*.1200. The E or dorter range, nearly complete, is mostly mid-13th c., and the S range probably of *c*.1280–90; the church nave was not finished till about that time. Late in the 15th c. the dorter was altered and the S range completely replanned so as to include an abbot's house at its W corner. The last has mostly gone (except for part of an even later two-storey remodelling of the W cloister walk) but the first-floor refectory (planned E–W again contrary to Cistercian traditions) remains as a splendid hall.

The church was soon demolished except for parts of its S side, kept by the lessee Anthony Busterd to enclose the cloister garth as the courtyard of a house. So the claustral ranges and gatehouses were preserved; they went to farm uses, later belonged to the Luttrell family, and became state property in 1950.

The **gatehouse** has 14th and 16th c. additions to the original 13th c. structure, and more modern strengthenings. Two-storeyed and now open to the roof, it was vaulted in two long bays and had no separate pedestrian opening. The inscribed panels, niches and other high-level details are 16th c. Through it lies the outer court, still

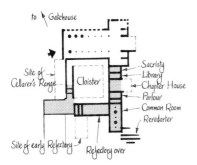

with substantial lengths of its bounding walls, and with a leat running through it from the Abbey Mill; one of the later farm buildings on the far side now contains the ticket office.

To the left of that is the outer wall of the W cloister walk (the W range itself has gone), and to the left again is the **church** site. Apart from the high S wall, little of this survives but the foundations are clearly set out. A few of the round pier bases are original. An area of floor tiles in the S aisle should be noted, also an abbot's grave in the centre of the nave, a tomb-slab with shield in the N transept, the foundations of the quire stalls, and the two chapels to each transept. The S transept gable stands entire, with the upper opening for the night stair.

Off the transept is the sacristy, barrel-vaulted and with a big round window, much old tiling (mostly collected from elsewhere on the site), piscina, double cupboard and simple painted wall patterns. The **cloister** can only be reached through the church. Except on the W where changes were begun in the 16th c., nothing is left of the walks, but against the church is a rare 'collation' seat, where the abbot sat for ceremonial readings. However the E range is remarkably complete, with a long line of lancets lighting the dorter, and the S range is two-storeyed too, with big Perpendicular windows to the refectory, and a little bellcote.

Next to the sacristy but entered from the cloister is the separate barrel-vaulted library, an unusual refinement; then the chapter house with low quadripartite vault (its E bay has gone), more old tiles (reset), some patterned wall-painting, and plate-traceried windows each side of the doorway; then the late 15th c. day stair to the **dorter**, an impressive long room with reconstructed roof. The further end is of a later 13th c. date than the rest, and the fireplaces are post-Dissolution. An opening at the NE corner seems to have led to a treasury over the S transept, and one at the SE to the reredorter; by the latter is a lamp niche.

Returning to ground level, the parlour and slype have barrel vaults too. The **common room** vault (forming the dorter floor above) is rebuilt in concrete; the fireplace is damaged, but at the far end are two fine two-light windows of *c*.1280, with inner tracery. Along the S range are first another passage, then a series of small rooms with wooden ceilings. These were private chambers and studies used in the abbey's later years by senior monks and scholars; two have garderobes. The 13th c. washing recess in the cloister was kept when they were formed. So was the doorway to the **refectory** when it was rebuilt at first-floor level, and a curving stair now leads to this superb white-walled room. Stone angel corbels support an unusual roof that is neither a true waggon roof nor a hammer-beam, embellished with big bosses and angels and rich carving on the beams and wall-plates – but never ceiled. The glazing is modern except for a few fragments, and unluckily the pulpit and stair have been spoilt by a post-Dissolution fireplace. At the same level, beyond the head of the stair, are a gallery and two smaller rooms, one with a big 15th c. wall-painting. There is a second-floor room too, only reachable through a trapdoor.

The W cloister walk survives in a muddled form. The window wall to the garth is early 16th c., but that behind is 13th c. A 17th c. farm building occupies the S end, and a carved timber partition defines a post-monastic cross-passage.

Back now to the SE corner passage, and through it to the outer side of the refectory, very similar to the cloister side. Below it is a remarkable relic of the 13th c. refectory, which in proper Cistercian style stood at right angles to the S range: no walls left, but a splendid area of patterned paving.

Cockersand Lancashire: SD 428537
2 miles WSW of Thurnham, on seashore

Hospital of St Mary founded by 1184 on land belonging to Leicester abbey; refounded as Premonstratensian priory (a daughter house of Croxton) by 1190; became abbey *c*.1192 but continued also as hospital. Dissolved 1539 and passed to John Kitchen

Owned by Dalton family. Accessible at all times, except interior of chapter house.

Or Thurnham abbey. The remains are practically confined to the
early 13th c. octagonal chapter house, used for centuries as a
mausoleum by the Daltons of Thurnham Hall. Excavations in 1923
disclosed the abbey's general layout, but most of it is grassed over
again.

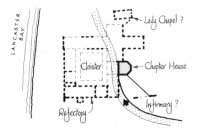

From the disused farmhouse a gated track towards the foreshore
leads over the site, passing the chapter house whose stunted
appearance is due to the rise of several feet in ground level. Inside
(but not possible to see) it has a curiously asymmetrical ribbed
vault, with a central clustered column. Apart from a disjointed
fragment of the N transept and traces of the extreme SE corner of
the dorter block, little else is visible but vague outlines.

By tradition, the splendid late Gothic stalls in Lancaster church
came either from here or from Furness.

Coggeshall Essex: 700 yards SE of town centre   TL 855222

Savigniac abbey of the Blessed Virgin Mary founded 1140 by
   Stephen and Matilda; became Cistercian 1147. Dissolved 1538
   and passed to Sir Thomas Seymour

Owned by Brew family. Monastic parts accessible without charge
   subject to specific permission from house

The principal structures were late 12th c. and have mostly
disappeared. But there is 13th c. work in the surviving SE buildings,
and remains have been found of 15th c. cloister arcading. Also 13th
c. is the former gate chapel, restored in 1896 by Bodley & Garner
after degradation as a barn, and regarded till recent years as
containing the earliest brickwork in England.

After the Dissolution a house (dated 1581) was built on the site of the reredorter, and the parts beyond were left as outbuildings; a nearby detached building also survived as a barn. The remainder was probably rapidly taken down for the building materials, and the general plan has mostly been deduced from grass markings in dry weather.

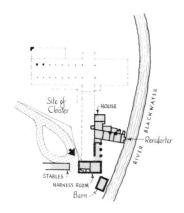

The early 13th c. gate chapel of St Nicholas, now Little Coggeshall church, stands on the left of the lane. The abbey church was 100 yards or so further on, its site starting in the field on the left but extending into the garden of the house. Further down the lane and straight ahead is a two-storeyed stable building (possibly the infirmary) with open stairs on the end, and behind it to the right stands the separate brick barn. Both were monastic but their purpose is very uncertain. To the left of the stable an open passage leads to an enclosed court by the river – the passage being one bay of a 13th c. brick and flint vaulted range running back towards the house. Its purpose is unknown too; it must have stood beyond the reredorter and its upper part may have formed an annexe to the main dorter. Its lower storey shows a variety of blocked arches on the side away from the river and connects by a single-storey link to the largely 16th c. house, part brick, part plastered; two Norman piers inside must be part of the reredorter undercroft. From all sides it is a highly picturesque group.

Colchester Essex: ¼ mile S of town centre   TL 998247

Benedictine abbey of St John the Baptist founded 1096 by Eudo,
   seneschal of William Rufus; became mitred. Dissolved 1539 and
   passed to the Crown

Owned by Ministry of Defence. Gatehouse only (not its interior)
   open to the public without charge

Very little is known of the abbey buildings, except for the precinct
wall and the splendid 15th c. gatehouse. They were preceded by a
little apsed church of St John the Evangelist (called Sigeric's after its
priest), partly excavated in recent years. It is believed to have been
superseded by St Giles's and taken down and buried early in the
12th c., when levels were drastically changed to enable the abbey's
domestic buildings to be resited to the S of its church and away from
the town. Subsequent history was punctuated by dissensions, and a
sequestration by the Crown occurred in 1404 because the abbot was
a conspirator for the restoration of Richard II. The last abbot was
hanged for alleged treason and as a result the lands were again
seized by the King. Later they were leased to Sir Thomas Darcy;
what was left of the buildings was destroyed in the siege of 1648.
The precinct is now part of the garrison lands.

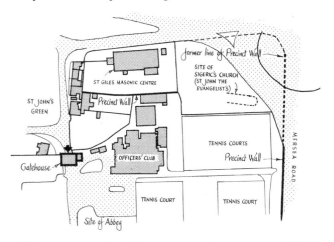

The two-storeyed **gatehouse** commands one corner of St John's
Green, a picturesque group cut off from the town centre by the

relief road. The outer side has excellent flint flushwork panelling all over, with three niches and the usual large and small openings, while the inner side is plainer, with single big arch and rebuilt parapet. The lierne vault within has lost its central boss but has carved corbels at the corners.

The **precinct wall**, much patched and altered, can be found next to St Giles's church (originally within the wall and now a masonic hall) just to the NE and followed up one side of Mersea Road. At the top of the hill is The Mount, perhaps a 'prehistoric' earthwork and probably used for a windmill. The wall then turns right parallel to Napier Road along the crest, but peters out. Another right turn leads back to St John's Green via Flagstaff Road, beside which a few more pieces remain.

Colwich Staffordshire: SK 008214
between villages of Colwich and Little Haywood on former A51 (now by-passed)

Benedictine nunnery of Our Lady of Good Hope founded in Paris 1651, a daughter house of Cambrai; moved to Marnhull, Dorset 1795, to Cannington, Somerset 1807, and to St Benedict's Priory, Colwich 1836; became abbey 1928 and resumed original dedication

Church (only) open at service times as advertised

Mount Pleasant (later Mount Pavilion) was built *c*.1730 by Charles Trubshaw around an older farmhouse of which three rooms still exist. It was extended (but not completed) *c*.1825 by Viscount Tamworth as a hunting lodge in the so-called Gothick style; the architect was probably Robert Chaplin. This part became the S range. A W range of dormitories was added in 1836, and the unfinished hall (which was in two levels across its width) became the chapel, to which the sanctuary was added in 1928 under Arnold Crush. In 1977 the N range was demolished and the W range rebuilt in brick in a more compact form; the architects were George Grey & Partners.

The drive leads past the side of the newer part of the church to the grey stone E end of Lord Tamworth's building. The prettiest part, a bay with three two-light windows on the left of the entrance, lights the sacristy (built as a library) but has been rather spoilt by

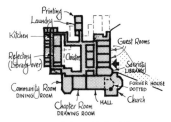

Crush's addition of the N transept. Above it, three round-arched windows with ogee hood moulds serve what is now a guest room. The embattled block to the right is of 1836.

Entry into the church is by the N or secular chapel, from which most of the interior can be seen. The original rectangular hall, now the nuns' quire, ended at the flat roof beam. E of that is a bay with elaborate panelled roof in Tudor form, and a delicate oriel with plaster vault; these are by one of the Pugins. The stalls came from Atherstone priory (now closed) and have carvings by a monk of Mount St Bernard. The central E window is by Christopher Webb and those on either side by Hardman & Co. A niche on the garden front (not visible to visitors) has a figure of Virgin and Child, substituted for one of Bacchus but still retaining his grapes!

Combe Warwickshire: SP 403798
4 miles E of Coventry and ½ mile N of Lutterworth road A427

Cistercian abbey of the Blessed Virgin Mary founded 1150 by
    Richard de Camvilla, a daughter house of Waverley. Dissolved
    1539 and granted to Earl of Warwick

Owned by City of Coventry. Exterior accessible at all times

The Norman chapter house entrance and other survivals of the E range confirm a mid-12th c. origin, and remains of the N and W sides of the cloister indicate a 15th c. rebuilding there. The church has completely gone; it stood to the S.

John, Lord Harrington formed the three cloister ranges into a house in 1581, and in 1667 Isaac Gibson made an extension westward from the S end of the W wing. That was continued in 1680-90 under William Winde to form a grand W range. Capability Brown later landscaped the grounds, but it was Eden Nesfield in 1861-4 who designed the picturesque 'moat' on the church site and a complete new E range in medieval style built around the Norman remains. That in its turn was nearly all cleared away in 1925, since when the house has become the centrepiece of a public pleasure park.

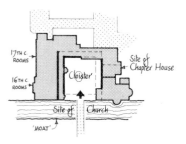

The **cloister** garth is approached across the moat by a 19th c. bridge. To the left is the two-storeyed W range of 1581, built over the cloister walk and retaining a row of Perpendicular windows. These continue along half the N side at the base of a three-storey range; the remainder, and the whole E side, are single-storeyed and what is seen now is a mostly 12th c. façade screening some mock-Norman compartments saved from the Nesfield house. The 'show' part is the red chapter house doorway with its flanking windows. Another opening to its right was to a sacristy, while one to the left probably led to a parlour. Round the corner, actually at the end of the N range, is a doorway which seems to have been moved, for it would have crossed the E walk. The church stood where the moat now is, its N transept occupying the place of the surviving corner of Nesfield's building which projects on big columns into the cloister and with a sort of bastion into the water.

The interiors (including a grand plaster ceiling in the saloon) cannot normally be seen; nothing else however is visibly medieval though some monastic remains must certainly be embedded in the W and N ranges. A walk to the further side of the W range (via the exit at the NE corner of the cloister) is rewarding in showing the façades of the 1580s and 1680s as well as Nesfield's gardens and the lake; the latter is linked with the monastic fishponds further N.

Combermere Cheshire: SJ 587441
3 miles NE of Whitchurch and 1 mile NW of Newcastle road A525

Savigniac abbey of St Mary and St Michael founded 1133 by Hugo
    de Malbanc; became Cistercian 1147. Dissolved 1538 and passed
    to George Cotton

Owned by Viscount Garnock. Not open to the public

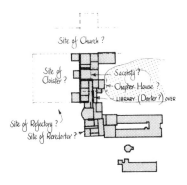

The abbey's chief claim to fame seems to have been an incessant
series of quarrels and disputes, both personal and communal.
Almost nothing is known of its buildings on the picturesque lakeside
site, though a certain amount of evidence must certainly be
preserved in the existing two-storeyed house formed (probably out
of the E range of cloister buildings) soon after the Dissolution. In an
early painting it is shown decorated with half-timbering. But *c*.1828
it was drastically remodelled inside and out in the prevalent early
Gothic Revival manner. Traditionally its first-floor library (a 16th
and 17th c. room beneath a 15th c. timber roof) was the refectory.
Really however it seems likely to have been part of the monks'
dorter and, in spite of successive alterations, the resemblance of the
whole main house plan to the standard monastic E range of S
transept, sacristy, chapter house, parlour and day stair is strong
though not irrefutable. Such a theory would place the church where
now is lawn to the N, and the cloister in the exact position of the
vanished walled garden shown on the painting.
    There is no public access, nor any point from which the buildings
may be seen.

Coverham North Yorkshire: SE 106864
2½ miles S of Leyburn and A684

Premonstratensian abbey of St Mary of Charity founded at Swainby 1190 by Helewisia, daughter of Lord Chief Justice Ranulf de Glanville, probably a daughter house of Durford; refounded at Coverham *c.*1212 by her son Ranulf fitzRalph. Dissolved 1536 and sold to Humphrey Orme

Owned by Aylmer Johnson family. Open during normal hours (admission charge)

The fairly modest 13th c. church was reconstructed with new arcades after Scottish raids of 1331–2. The only other surviving work is early 16th c., in remains of the guest house and gatehouse.

The buildings seem mostly to have gone quickly to ruin, but a house was built amongst them in 1674, succeeded in the 18th c. by the present one called Coverham Abbey. The adjoining garden and farm layout preserve much of the abbey plan and some of the sculpture, while most of the W cloister range still stands, having been rescued from former farm use.

The approach lane goes beneath the gatehouse arch towards a nursery garden where the entry fee is paid. An iron gate nearby leads into the main flower garden. Visitors may walk across this, through the beech hedge, past the front of the house and (passing numerous stone fragments built into walls) round the further side to the back where the **church** was. The two standing arches on quatrefoil columns with moulded caps were part of the 14th c. S nave arcade. The base of one pier is exposed 3 feet below the present ground, and much more could obviously be found by digging. The N half of the **cloister** garth is unbuilt on; on its E side, against the S transept, are remains of a book cupboard and at its opposite end the W range (now Garth Cottage) with an elaborate 16th c. doorway, moved from another position and topped by an

IHS monogram. Some other similar decorative panels will be noticed, but the best one has gone to a private house, Bear Park near Aysgarth. Further N, the W wall of the church survives only at the end of the N aisle. From the lane behind, the W side of Garth Cottage can be seen, modern at the near end with old bits built in, but 16th c. further along with an unusual nine-light window which lit the guest hall.

Going back now along the lane, a right turn at the 'cross roads' leads through a gate back towards the house. Here stood the N transept, and two lancet windows of its 13th c. W wall survive on the right. On the left, at the back of a small garden, are remains of the main E wall; some coffin lids can be seen, and the bases of the aisle arcade responds.

On the way out, to the right of the gateway into the forecourt of the house, are two splendid effigies of knights, originally recumbent, of *c*.1300.

Lastly the **gatehouse**, of which the inner arch is complete; the outer has its responds only, and the structures both sides are altered for farm use.

The original site at Swainby (in Pickhill parish at SE 336856) has nothing to show but some unexplained earthworks.

Creake Norfolk: TF 856395
1 mile N of North Creake and ¼ mile E of Burnham Market road B1355

Augustinian priory of St Mary of the Meadows founded 1227 by Sir Robert de Nerford; became abbey 1231. Dissolved 1506 and given to Christ's College, Cambridge

Owned by Thursfield family; church in care of Department of the Environment. Church open at all times without charge; remainder not open to the public

The founder and his wife built a chapel in 1206, and in 1217 a hospital of St Bartholomew, which later became fully monastic. The E end of the church is of that period, side chapels being quickly added to the presbytery, followed by an aisled nave and transepts of standard design but only moderate size. In the 14th c. the twin N transept chapels were extended to form a single big one. After a fire in 1378 the buildings were restored, but another *c*.1480 spelt disaster: the nave was abandoned and the transepts blocked off,

leaving only the inner and outer N chapels and the inner S one.
Barely a decade later, all the canons and lastly the abbot died of an
epidemic and the property reverted to the Crown.

Parts were converted to domestic and farm use; in 1950 the
church passed to Ministry of Works care, but the monastic site is a
private house and garden preserving a number of medieval features.

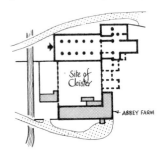

The 13th c. **nave** as seen from the W entrance probably looks
much as it was left c.1490, with column stumps only, the base of the
N aisle wall, and the S aisle wall which was kept to enclose the
cloister. All the crossing-piers stand, and the arches from both aisles
into the transepts are complete; the 15th c. scheme of reduction
involved blocking these, the two-light 13th c. window on the S being
transferred from elsewhere; the blocking on the N side has since
disappeared.

The **crossing** became merely an ante-chapel to a quire
compressed towards the E end, so its arches were filled in too and
parts of the transepts enclosed to form parallel passages on either
side. Some of these blocking walls remain; probably they were the
same both sides. The side walls of the **presbytery**, the earliest part
of the church, have impressive mid-13th c. wall-arcading, with high
window openings surviving on the S side. The arches into the side
chapels were late 13th c. insertions; beyond the N one is a well
preserved early 14th c. arcade to the wide outer chapel, and in its
far left corner the base of a spiral stair – originally reached from the
transept but, when that was abandoned, made to open to the chapel
instead. The arches from transept to chapels are a 14th c. pair (one
fallen) to the outer chapel, and an earlier single one to the inner,
aligned with the N nave aisle. The outer chapel has a tomb recess
and piscina, and the inner an aumbry and another piscina.

On the S side the chapel (rebuilt smaller in the 15th c.) has

remains of another piscina. The blocking wall across this transept
has what is now a gateway through which the chapter house site may
be glimpsed. The private house beyond incorporates parts of the
dorter block and its walled garden represents the cloister. Another
doorway to it, towards the W end of the S aisle, has been reset in
reverse.

Croxden Staffordshire: SK 067397
in village of Croxden 4 miles NW of Uttoxeter

Cistercian abbey of the Blessed Virgin Mary founded at Alton (2
    miles N) 1176, a daughter house of Aunay, Normandy; moved to
    Croxden 1179. Dissolved 1538 and granted to Francis Bassett

In care of Department of the Environment. Open at all times
    without charge

Part of the church was in use by 1181, but it was not complete till
1254. Its chevet of five radiating chapels is unusual for the
Cistercians but was copied from Aunay. The chapter house,
refectory and gatehouse were finished about the same time, the
kitchen and infirmary rather later, and the W range *c*.1290. A new
abbot's house was built in the 14th c.
    Destruction of the church after the Dissolution was so thorough
that a public way, now a metalled road, grew up across it. The other
buildings went to domestic and farm uses, and the ruins were in
1936 made over to HM Office of Works by W.G. Vickers.

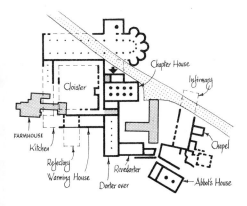

An odd effect of the road is that at the entrance gate one is already within the church facing the inner S wall of the **S transept**. On the left is one of two E chapels, with its piscina, and high in the S wall is the doorway at the head of the night stair (which was of wood) formerly leading to the dorter.

First, then, one passes out of the church into a sacristy, leading on the right through a still-vaulted room (probably library) into the **cloister**. The E range is partly preserved and should be viewed first from the centre of the garth: high on the left are the W and S walls of the transept with their tall lancet windows; below is the library doorway; then the window, doorway, window of the chapter house; then doorways to the parlour and lastly to the slype. In the chapter house the clustered column bases and the start of the vault on the N side can be seen. The purpose of the cloister bay projecting into the garth outside this room is unknown.

The slype still has its pointed ribbed barrel vault. It leads on the right into the **dorter**, with undercroft vault springers still visible, and through that into the reredorter. Along the lower side of the reredorter the stone drain has been revealed, and this can be traced past the bottom end of the infirmary which lay towards (and partly under) the road. The clearly defined rectangular building with a big window arch, furthest from the road, was the abbot's house of 1335–6.

Return now to the cloister through the dorter undercroft again. The dorter above, as often the case, was eventually extended right over the chapter house to the transept, connecting with the night stair doorway already seen. In the S range the first main room, with a fireplace (altered after the Dissolution), was the warming room. Then the refectory, also with a fireplace: but this too is misleading because it was a transverse room running N–S, and the fireplace wall was built before or possibly after the Dissolution to cut off the further part. The rest of the range has gone, and the picturesque farm stable juts right out into the garth. Beyond it and N of the house can be seen what is left of the late 13th c. W range, with vaulting springers and a curious small opening into the church.

To reach the **church** one has to return to the once splendid doorway of four orders at the NE corner of the cloister. No column bases remain, but two bays of the S aisle wall indicate their spacing and show that the aisles were vaulted. The W wall is a fine specimen of Early English work and is best seen from outside its rich doorway. The three big lancet windows are unusual in having sills of unequal height. From here look towards the E end where the only upstanding masonry is a piece of the northernmost chapel. This has to be reached by crossing the road to the other part of the site. Here the impressive foundation of the chevet and apse can also be seen, as well as three stone coffins, some small areas of tiled paving and a collection of moulded stones.

Croxton Leicestershire: SK 823276
1¼ miles SW of Croxton Kerrial and ½ mile S of Melton Mowbray–
Grantham road A607

Premonstratensian abbey of St John the Evangelist founded by 1160
by William, Count of Boulogne, a daughter house of Newsham.
Dissolved 1538

Owned by Duke of Rutland. Site not open to the public

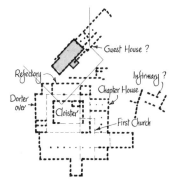

Nothing of the main buildings remains above ground, but the plan was recovered by digging c.1926. Apparently the first church was aisleless and in the 13th c. it was much enlarged and the cloister extended to rectangular form, so leaving the 12th c. N range with refectory undisturbed. Probably because of the steeply sloping site the dorter seems to have been transferred – very unusually – to the W side. A fire in 1326 may have necessitated some rebuilding such as the W part of the S arcade. More extensive improvement of the aisle and presbytery went on right up to the Dissolution. The occupied house close to the N end is one half of a larger building which may have been a guest house; but it now contains little that is old. Along the valley below are extensive fishponds.

Croyland Lincolnshire: in town of Crowland   TF 242103

Benedictine abbey of St Mary, St Bartholomew and St Guthlac
    founded *c*.716 by King Ethelbald. Dissolved 1539 and given to
    Clinton family; part of church retained for parish use

Owned by parish. Open during normal hours

The abbey rose around the cell of St Guthlac, part of which survives
against the foundation of the W front. A Danish raid in 870 and a
fire in 1091 necessitated rebuildings, of which the latter took from
1114 to 1195. The W front and the E parts were altered after the
middle of the 13th c. The nave with its arcades and aisles was
reconstructed in the 15th c. when the NW tower was added and the
W front again altered.
    At the Dissolution the nave and aisles were left for the parish and
the rest demolished. Cromwell's men are said to have bombarded
them in the Civil War and eventually in 1720 the nave roof
collapsed. In 1743 the S aisle was demolished and the materials used
to enclose and repair the N aisle and tower.

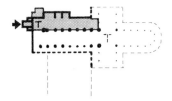

First the **W front**: the N end with big tower and porch of *c*.1450,
the low S end Norman of perhaps *c*.1140 with zigzagged arches in its
four surviving tiers, and between them the proud nave end of *c*.1260
with saints' statues in panels. The quatrefoil in the tympanum of the
main (double) doorway contains scenes from St Guthlac's life. The
main window gave way to a bigger one in the 15th c.; that in its turn
has gone but the two upper tiers of saints belonging to it survive.
    The two-storeyed **porch** was vaulted. Inside on the right is the
so-called Canarie chapel, now used to store carved stones. On the
left a stair (private) leads to the upper room which has a window
into the tower. The **tower** has a remarkably high flat ceiling and a
'lantern' window over the roof of what was the N aisle but is now
the parish nave. The panelled arches (that on the S is blocked)
should be noted, also: some minor wall-tablets; various old prints

etc.; the 15th c. 'tub' font; on the S wall an incised 15th c. memorial slab to William of Wermington, master mason of the 15th c. work, and the small stone lid of a heart burial; and in the S jamb of the arch to the aisle a big holy water stoup made out of an earlier font. What appears to be a tomb-chest beneath the war memorial was made up in 1923 from a medieval coffin lid and other fragments.

The **N aisle** (parish nave) has a 15th c. tierceron vault, not springing from the usual capitals but from shafts adapted (on the N side at least) from the Norman work. The six big bosses are well preserved. Of the three outer chapels, also once vaulted, the centre one is restored to use and contains four old paintings, a three-locked chest, and a stoup and a boss from elsewhere in the church. The others serve as a vestry and organ chamber. Continuing E, on the left is a quaint wooden memorial to Abraham Baily (d. 1704). The brass lectern is of 1927, and the screen largely 15th c.; it was probably the side screen of a chapel, and traces of its original paint remain. The sanctuary was extended into the transept aisle late in the 19th c., and the arch built. The three-sided communion rail with slender balusters is 18th c.; so are the paintings of Moses and Aaron on the S wall. Beneath them is another old chest, and further along are royal arms of 1775. The pulpit is 18th c. too, on a newer base. The big window on the S side contains glass by A.K. Nicholson, with a few medieval fragments at the top.

Return to the W front and enter the abbey **nave**. The 15th c. arcades largely remain, and on the N side the passage above. But the clerestory and roof have gone, and on the S only three arches are left; springers of the high vault can however be seen at the W end. One pier base on the S has been cut away to expose a miscellany of 13th c. column stones sacrificed and thrown in as hardcore. The Norman W arch of the crossing survives through having been filled in (on top of the pulpitum) when the nave was walled off for the parish. Equally interesting at this end are the ends of the Norman arcades and gallery, left by the 15th c. rebuilders. The pulpitum is 15th c. too. On its other face is elaborate but very worn stone panelling.

Continue around the NE end, looking up at what is left of the big N and S crossing arches. Beside the parish chancel are the beginnings of two entirely distinct arches from N aisle into N transept, the one 12th c., the other 15th c. On the N side the three little chapels fit inconspicuously between great buttresses and the tower dominates – though its stunted stone spire is an anti-climax. Back once more at the W front, note the marked position of St

Guthlac's cell, found in 1908 and covered again. The monastic buildings lay to the S beneath the churchyard and hardly anything is known of them.

Cwmhir Powys: SO 056711
in village of Abbey-Cwmhir, 6½ miles N of Llandrindod Wells

Cistercian abbey of the Blessed Virgin Mary founded *c.*1143 by
 Maredudd ap Idwerth at Ty-faenor, a daughter house of
 Whitland; refounded at Cwmhir 1176. Dissolved 1536

Owned by Hamer family. Accessible at all times, with public right
 of way

Cwmhir = long valley. Only the nave and the start of the transepts
of the very large early 13th c. church were built; ambitions of
completing the remainder were probably finally dashed by Owain
Glyndwr's raid of 1401. Of the monastic buildings, lying to the S
towards the river, hardly anything is known.

   At the Dissolution parts of the nave arcading were reused at
Llanidloes church. The remainder went to ruin and nothing now
remains above ground except the lower parts of the aisle walls and
those of the adjoining transepts.

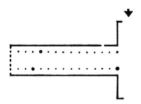

   The approach is through a field gate at the top of the hill just E of
the village and Home Farm house. From the downhill path the ruin
is soon visible – the base of the walls of an aisled nave comparable in
length with Ely's. Inside, two column bases are easily discovered,
and the much bigger base of one of the crossing piers. The remains
of attached shafts occur at intervals inside the S wall, and others
inside the N transept. But the former splendour is reduced almost to
nothing; the W end is indefinite and there is no evidence of the
cloister or other buildings except an unexplained mound where the
cellarer's range would have been.

A modern slate slab near the crossing piers commemorates
Llewelyn ap Gruffydd, the last native-born Prince of Wales (d.
1282) who was buried here.

The arcade re-erected at Llanidloes in 1542 is of the finest
clustered Early English type, with eight triplets of attached shafts to
each column, and a variety of capitals typical of the development of
foliage carving in the period c.1190–1215 but reassembled in
somewhat random order. Though only five bays of the twice
fourteen that there were, their survival is something of a miracle.
The 13th c. S doorway also came from Cwmhir, and some other
carved stones are at Llanbister church.

Cwmhir: 13th c. arches re-erected in Llanidloes church

Cymmer Gwynedd: SH 722195
1 mile NW of Dolgellau and 300 yards E of Ffestiniog road A487

Cistercian abbey of the Blessed Virgin Mary founded 1198 by
   Gruffydd and Maredudd ap Cynan, a daughter house of Cwmhir.
   Dissolved 1536

In care of Welsh Office. Open during standard hours (admission
   charge)

Cymmer = meeting, i.e. of the waters. The names Kemmer and
Vanner are also used. The buildings erected in the decades
following the abbey's foundation seem never to have been finished,
and the 14th c. W tower was the only addition of any consequence,
built after hopes of a central tower had been given up. There seems
never to have been a W range to the cloister, nor did the church
ever receive transepts or a presbytery.
   The buildings fell to ruin and only the church walls now stand to
any height. However the picturesque little farmhouse to their W
almost certainly incorporates parts of the monastic guest house.

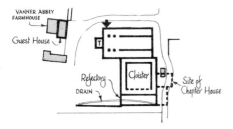

   Tickets are obtained at the farmhouse. The much truncated **tower**
facing it, an evident addition to the W end of the church, is mid-14th
c. and has the remains of a circular stair. Passing to the left of it, one
enters the **church** on the N side. There were arcades both sides,
with octagonal columns and a clerestory over, but the S one has
gone; beyond them are solid walls and at the E end three lancets
(with signs of three more above) in a wall meant to be temporary
but in fact permanent, for no more was built beyond. The outer
walls have both gone, that of the N aisle now standing being fairly
modern. In the sanctuary are two tomb recesses and part of a third,
also piscina and sedilia, the latter with one foliage capital surviving.
   The **cloister** has little to show. The chapter house entrance is
identifiable (just S of the yew) by a lower piece of foundation, and

the doorway into the church from the W walk can just be traced.
The prominent drain channel running along the refectory site is not
medieval.

Dale Derbyshire: in village of Dale Abbey   SK 438387

Augustinian priory founded *c*.1155; refounded as
   Premonstratensian abbey of St Mary *c*.1198, a daughter house of
   Tupholme. Dissolved 1538 and passed to Francis Pole

Owned by British Steel Corporation. Open without charge at all
   times, subject to permission from Abbey House adjoining

Also known as Depedale or Stanley Park. The first, Augustinian
monastery was associated with a pre-existing hermitage, perhaps of
the early 12th c. It was refounded by Premonstratensians from
Tupholme, again from Welbeck, and again, after a third failure,
from Newsham. The building sequence is somewhat obscure, but
the 12th c. quire was probably rebuilt *c*.1270 and the crossing in the
14th c. A N nave aisle was added in the 13th c., an outer S chapel in
the 14th c., and the clerestory throughout probably in the 15th c.
   The buildings seem to have gone quickly to ruin, only the E wall
of the presbytery surviving as a landmark. The glass of several 15th
c. windows, believed to be from the cloister, is now in Morley
church. The font is in the quaint nearby church of Dale Abbey, and
its cover and some screen and stall woodwork in Radbourne church.
The abbey site was excavated in 1878–9 as far W as the crossing.

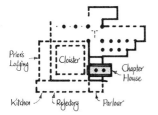

   Abbey House, a cottage with massive chimney, is supposed to
have been part of the abbey kitchen. Accessible through its garden
with permission is a hut on the chapter house site, covering column
bases and shafted entrance doorway and containing a fine canon's
effigy of *c*.1400 amd other memorial and moulded stones and tiles.

Outside the hut, the side walls of the chapter house are traceable. The stone field wall represents the eastward extent of the cloister; over it on the right is the base of an outer doorway to the S transept, and on the left a part of the SW crossing pier. The remains of splendid Geometric tracery can be clearly seen in the E window, contemporary with that of Lincoln. The lines of the inner and outer S arcades can also be easily identified. The mound to the N is excavated soil. Just W of it is the polygonal base of the spiral stair at the NW corner of the quire; this almost certainly led upwards to the belfry of a central tower. A look back at the E window from this point gives an impressive idea of the scale of the quire. Near the base of the bank the N walls of the transept and of the supposed Lady chapel on its E side can be made out.

The W boundary of the orchard defines the extent of the nave, and the shed outside the S wall contains traces of vaulting from the vicinity of the refectory.

Further away to the NW, some walling at the entrance to Abbey Farm may be part of the gatehouse, while behind the Methodist church on the other side of the road is another ancient building known as the 'Prison'. The quaint and tiny church of All Saints may have been used as an infirmary chapel following alterations made to it in the 15th c.; but its original structure antedates anything in the abbey itself.

Darley Derbyshire: SK 352383
1 mile N of Derby and ¼ mile E of A6

Augustinian abbey of St Mary founded *c.*1146 by Robert Ferrers, Earl of Derby, a daughter house of St Helen's priory, Derby; dissolved 1538 and given to Sir William West. The 18th c. house called Darley Park (Derby Corporation) was demolished in 1962. A 14th c. or 15th c. building, now a public house called The Abbey, may have had some connection; so may no. 7 Abbey Lane, a partly 15th c. cottage.

Darlington Durham: 1 mile W of town centre   NZ 272145

Franciscan nunnery of St Clare founded at Rouen 1644, a daughter house of Gravelines; moved to London 1793, to Haggerston Castle, Northumberland 1795, to Scorton Hall, Yorkshire 1807, and to Darlington 1857

Church (part only) and entrance garden court opened on request

Persecution in England led to the 17th c. foundation in France, whence the community was later driven back by the Revolution. Its eventual home was built under Joseph Hansom in 1855–7 on land bought from the Carmelites, and has been little altered since. Built around three garden courts, variously in one, two and three storeys, it is of red brick with Gothic windows and stone dressings, and slate roofs. The former chaplain's house N of the church is now used by the Cross and Passion Sisters.

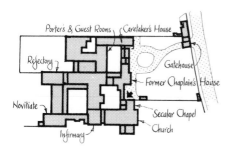

The high brick wall along the road is broken by a little gatehouse and lodge, with a drive up to a niched porch. To the right is the caretaker's lodging where enquiry may be made and it may be possible to see the court behind where the actual convent entrance is.

The **church** is at the other end of the road front. Only the secular N chapel may be visited. A single stone screen to the sanctuary and a double one facing the 'nave' (nuns' quire) mean that the latter can hardly be seen; changes are however planned. But the fine E window is visible, and the stone reredos with intricate statuary, considered in its day to be one of the finest in the north. The timber ceilings are painted blue. There is a W organ gallery (out of sight), and at the NW corner is a small pinnacled turret.

Delapré Northamptonshire: SP 759591
1 mile S of Northampton town centre and ¼ mile E of A508

Cluniac nunnery founded *c.*1145 by Simon de St Liz (Senlis), a dependency of Cluny abbey, Burgundy. Dissolved 1538 and granted to John Mershe

Owned by Northampton Corporation. Grounds open May to
September during daylight hours without charge. House open
Thursdays only 2.30 to 5.0 p.m. (May to September) or 4.30 p.m.
(October to April) without charge. Guide accompanies

Delapré = 'of the meadow'. This was one of the few Cluniac
nunneries in Britain and little is known of its history. The nearby
Eleanor Cross commemorates the resting of the body of Edward I's
Queen in its church for one night in 1290. In 1460 the battle of
Northampton took place just outside its precincts.

   The plan of the church and little cloister is well preserved. The
little original walling that survives (late 12th and early 13th c.) is
principally in the church nave, subdivided by Bartholomew Tate
into smaller rooms in two storeys in the 16th c. Zouch Tate early in
the 17th c. demolished the chancel and extensively altered the
remainder, the W range being completely rebuilt with a new porch.
Admiral Charles Hardy c.1750–60 rebuilt the S range and added an
orangery and separate stable block. Edward Bouverie built a library
at the SW corner c.1830, and John Bouverie made some internal
changes c.1871. The whole estate was sold to Northampton
Corporation in 1946; the house has been used since 1958 by the
Northamptonshire Record Office and Northamptonshire Record
Society.

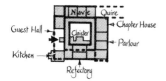

   The drive leads past the turreted stable block of c.1750 to the 17th
c. porch (instructions for visitors are here). The clockwise tour
follows a passage which probably exactly represents the **cloister**
walk, the outer rooms being now mostly used for archives and the
passage itself for paintings and other exhibits. The only specifically
monastic remains are the stone lantern recesses on the inner angles
of the N walk, one at each end. The church stood beside the N walk;
the two Tudor doorways, however, are Bartholomew Tate's, one of
them leading to a spiral stair. At the beginning of the E walk was
the chapter house, replaced by the present 17th c. kitchen with a big
fireplace.

   The S range, probably always at a higher level and built over

cellars, originally formed the refectory. The present rooms are 18th
c., occupied now as reading rooms and libraries. The furthest one is
Edward Bouverie's library of *c*.1830. The stair, projecting into the
courtyard, is John Bouverie's, and so is most of the internal
decoration.

   Outside, turn left, pass the library and orangery and then cross the
walled garden (on the site of the nuns' cemetery). Beyond this, and
past the 18th c. stable block, is the N front. Substantially this is the
N wall of the church **nave**, though any detail is hard to pick out
amongst the later openings; towards its left end a vertical straight
joint may represent a Norman window jamb, whilst a break near
the right end marks the NW corner (the internal partition at this
point is quite thick and is probably the original W wall). At the
further end, where the yard is marked 'Private', stood the chancel.

Denny Cambridgeshire: TL 492685
close to A10, 6½ miles NNE of Cambridge

Benedictine priory of St James and St Leonard founded by 1159 by
   Robert, Chamberlain of Duke Conan IV of Brittany, dependent
   on Ely; transferred 1170 to Knights Templars and suppressed
   1308; re-established as Franciscan nunnery of St Mary and St
   Clare 1342 by Mary de St Pol, Countess of Pembroke, to replace
   Waterbeach. Dissolved 1539 and granted to Edward Elrington

In care of Department of the Environment. Open during standard
   hours (admission charge)

Denny is doubly unique. Nowhere else in Britain are there
considerable remains of a monastery of the Minoresses or 'Poor
Clares', and nowhere else an instance of Franciscans taking over
buildings of another Order. The result takes some disentangling,
but careful removal of parts of the 18th c. farmhouse which had
grown in and around it has clarified first the cruciform Benedictine
church, then the Templars' completion of its nave and S aisle, and
finally the nuns' extensive changes. They made the nave and
transepts into apartments for the abbess and/or the countess,
demolished the chancel, and in its place built a new abbey church
(itself now disappeared).

   The monastic buildings have almost wholly gone, except the
nuns' refectory. The property passed to Pembroke College,
Cambridge, and in 1947 to the Ministry of Works.

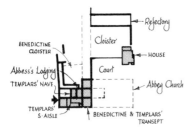

On the left of the approach is the Templars' Norman W doorway
– the first indication that this is really a church and not the
farmhouse it seemed. The next doorway leads into a series of rooms
added by both Templars and nuns to the original S aisle – now
enclosed by Georgian walls on much older foundations. On the left
are Norman arcade arches – the first, with volute and scallop
capitals, being blocked. Through the second the old nave can be
seen, its W crossing arch blocked by the nuns and then pierced with
domestic openings.

At the end of the aisle the S transept is revealed, with a patch of
14th c. floor tiles, part of a corner stair, and a collection of carved
stones. Next, the crossing, its four Norman arches blocked, and all
with 14th c. openings. From the N transept a modern wooden stair
leads to rooms in the upper part of the crossing and in the S
transept. Much of the Norman work now carefully uncovered had
been hidden since the nuns' arrival. The upper rooms over the S
aisle (left as a wooden skeleton) are visible, and similarly one at
second-floor level over the S transept. Their exact uses are
unknown; probably there were suites both for the abbess and for
the Countess of Pembroke. The upper room over the nave exhibits
the Templars' clerestory windows; in the further bay is a farmhouse
fireplace.

Back now to ground level, and out through the E doorway to the
site of the nuns' church. The beginnings of its arcades can be traced
but its eastward extent is undiscovered. An opening beyond the N
transept leads into a garth, marked only by low foundations and
affording a view of the N side of the church. The 14th c. refectory
shell stands some way to the NE beyond a bigger, vanished cloister
and has few features of interest. Finally, and much more
fascinating, the main S front should be examined – a Georgian
façade built into a medieval one. The big brick gable of the S

transept, for example, retains on its left side the original 12th c. stair turret.

A dole gate from the abbey is at Coughton Court, Worcestershire, whither the last abbess retired.

Dereham Norfolk: 1 mile SSW of West Dereham church   TF 662006

Premonstratensian abbey of the Blessed Virgin Mary founded 1188 by Humbert Walker, Dean of York; dissolved 1539 and given to Francis Derham. Owned by Shropshire family. Sir Thomas Derham used the four-storey gatehouse as the centrepiece of a great house. By the 19th c. this had become reduced to the size and status of a farmhouse, now a solitary ruin in the middle of a field. A series of farm buildings 200 yards to the S at the far corner of the field may also have monastic origins.

Dieulacres Staffordshire: SJ 983578
1 mile N of Leek at Abbey Green

Cistercian abbey of St Mary and St Benedict founded at Poulton, Cheshire by Ranulf, Earl of Chester, a daughter house of Combermere; moved to new site 1214. Dissolved 1538 and granted to Sir Ralph Bagenall

Owned by Docksey family. Accessible at all times subject to permission from farmhouse

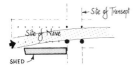

Dieulacres = Dieu l'acreisse = may God increase it – and is still approximately so pronounced. Clearly the buildings were 13th and 14th c., for many bits survive. The only part evident on the site is the crossing of the church: bases of two big clustered piers and evidence of the others. The rest of the ruin was tidied away in 1818–20 and the stone extensively used for a series of farm

outbuildings – with innumerable carved and moulded pieces built in
in nightmarish patterns.

The timber-framed farmhouse is of 1627. Just before it on the left
is a fantastic gateway made up of all kinds of abbey bits. Straight
ahead in the farmyard is a boss depicting two birds, built into a barn
end. All around are other fragments – pieces of tracery, niches,
vault springers etc. A left and a right turn lead past the farm along a
track where the surviving piers can be found in the right-hand verge
just past a long shed; between them lies a small stone coffin.

Dorchester Oxfordshire: in village on A423   SU 579942

Augustinian abbey of St Peter, St Paul and St Birinus founded
    c.1140, probably by Bishop Alexander of Lincoln, on site of
    Saxon cathedral. Dissolved 1536 and granted to Edmund
    Ashfield

Parish church. Open during normal hours

By the former Roman town, about 635, St Birinus founded a
bishopric which after the Conquest was transferred to Lincoln. The
cathedral became a collegiate church till the monastery was set up.
It was rebuilt to a cruciform plan late in the 12th c., but its N wall
may still preserve some earlier masonry. The N quire aisle and
transept chapel were added early in the 13th c. and altered c.1300.
The S quire aisle is of c.1320; soon after that the S nave aisle was
added for parish use and then the quire itself extended in a rich
version of Decorated with several unique features.

After the Dissolution Richard Beauforest bought the church and
gave it to the parish. The rest of the abbey was so thoroughly
destroyed that very little is now known except the extent of the
cloister. The W tower was rebuilt c.1602 and the N transept later
demolished. 19th c. restorations were done by Sir George Gilbert
Scott and William Butterfield.

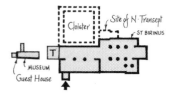

The S porch, 15th c. with wooden traceried sides, covers a 14th c. main doorway with rosette ornament. The **nave** and S aisle, now rather bare, give little hint of the quire's elaboration, though on one column of the tall 14th c. arcade is a curious carved stone bracket apparently depicting monks asleep, probably once a base for statues. Nave and aisle roofs are by Scott, c.1865. The late 12th c. font is not only one of the finest of the 30 or so in England made of lead, but also probably the only monastic one to have survived; its decoration depicts the seated Apostles.

The tower, rebuilt after the Dissolution, has only a small doorway to the nave. Looking now E, one sees the great 14th c. E window with its net tracery, splendid glass and unusual central buttress. On the left, the nave N wall is 12th c., but in part perhaps older; the blocked doorway at the end led to the cloister. The wide E arch, too slender to have supported a crossing-tower, is late 12th c. The very rough N and S crossing-arches beyond are thought to have been rebuilt in 1633; their piers are much older. That was when the **N transept** was truncated and its E chapel demolished.

Now across into the **quire**. The roofs here are Butterfield's and the arcades again 14th c., but earlier (c.1320) than the nave and more richly moulded, and not quite alike. Through the screen beside the organ is **St Birinus's chapel** (reserved for private prayer), begun in the 13th c. (witness the fine shafted Geometric windows and beautiful Early English arch with stiff-leaf capitals). Shafts on the N wall indicate an intention to vault it, made impracticable when the arcade was re-formed so much higher. Near the doorway is a flue, possibly used for baking wafers; a triple aumbry further along has big 19th c. oak doors. The E window has a 13th c. glass roundel of St Birinus; the big piscina is of the same date.

The **chancel** has not only the superb E window, rich with original glass and (as becomes evident at close quarters) carved on its mullions with scenes from Christ's life – but also the unique N window in the form of a Jesse Tree, with much original glass too and with the stone 'tree' springing from the figure of Jesse on the sill and then branching into columns of little statues. The S window, less ambitious, has a sculpture of a funeral (variously interpreted) on its transom, as well as 14th c. shields in its present glass. Originally the glass in each of the three windows combined with their stone carving to portray single themes – a rare concept. It should be added that the top part of the E window was restored under Butterfield in 1847.

The sedilia and double piscina, as lavish as the window

Dorchester: Church interior, looking E

stonework, have four most unusual little windows inside, with ball-flower ornament and glass of *c*.1300. Another double piscina further W served before the presbytery was extended. A brass to Abbot Bewfforeste (*c*.1510) lies just outside the 18th c. balustered altar rail on the N side, and there are indents of several others. The stalls, though much repaired in the 19th c., are essentially early 16th c. and one poppy-head end bears a crozier with Bewfforeste's name on a scroll.

The S **quire aisle** is unusual in having two vaulted E chapels, each of two bays. They are earlier than the chancel E end. Their vaults, though always intended, had to wait till 1872 to be completed: together with the curious gallery above they are due to Scott. Against the back of the stalls are a 14th c. bishop's effigy and two more brass indents, while the three effigies on tomb chests, from N to S, are said to be of a Segrave, *c*.1400 (alabaster), Sir John

Holcombe, *c*.1270 (a most lively knight), and (more certainly) John de Stonor (d. 1354). Between the two last are three fragmentary brasses, the part figure being Sir John Drayton (d. 1417), while close to the wall is another to Margaret Beauforest(d. 1524) and two husbands – but one of them only is left. In the little chapels (both with John Hardman glass of *c*.1840) are: first (Lady chapel) a memorial to Bishop Wilberforce (d. 1873) and reredos by F.E. Howard, and second (All Souls), another fine double piscina and a matching doorway to a stair. On the S side the glass with rich browns and purples is by Mayer & Co., 1899. The gabled shrine of St Birinus is a simplified reconstruction of 1964 incorporating 14th c. fragments. The nearby 'brass' on a wooden chest is a replica of that of Abbot Bewfforeste (see above). The pulpit is by Butterfield. At the W end of the aisle is a framed vestment of *c*.1500.

The **S nave aisle**, added for parish use in the 14th c., is entered through a small doorway in what had hitherto been an outside wall. On the right is an aumbry, on the left the altar, raised over a burial vault. The Crucifixion painting on the wall behind is 14th c., a good deal restored; the coloured areas close to the blocked window may be parts of a *Doom*. Now a glance at the floors, pleasantly varied throughout – a patch of medieval tiles beside the low screen, several more brass indents, and several nicely lettered 18th c. ledger stones including a quaint one to Sarah Fletcher (d. 1799, 'a martyr to excessive sensibility') and one to an archdeacon of Dol, Brittany (d. 1798). Against the S wall are two stone coffins and at the W end an interesting old chest and several modern paintings. The choir vestry screen at the W end of the nave is formed with old, probably 17th c. panelling.

Outside much of the interest lies in seeing the window patterns again. Near the porch stands a fine churchyard cross of *c*.1400 with somewhat renewed head. The big niched corner buttress may have been moved westwards when the aisle was extended; its pinnacle is recent. Then the 17th c. tower, of a type with corner turrets common in the Thames valley but unusual in its date and in the curious omission of a turret in the corner that actually contains the stair. Of the bells, the two largest are 14th c., one 16th c., three 17th c. and two 19th c. On the N a garden occupies the site of the monastic buildings. Variations in the character of the nave walling have given rise to theories that parts may be Saxon and therefore survivals of the early cathedral. The former 12th c. N transept is identifiable by the Norman doorway and by the curiously mullioned 17th c. window inserted when its end was cut off. Next, round the E end with its varied 13th and then 14th c. windows (including the four little ones of the sedilia) and a curious 14th c. buttress with dog-tooth ornament of much older character, and then along the S side where the junction of early and later 14th c. work is evident.

What is now partly a museum to the W of the tower was probably once the abbey guest house, 14th and 15th cc., and became the village school. The lychgate is by Butterfield.

Dore Hereford & Worcester: SO 387303
in Abbeydore village 9½ miles SW of Hereford on B4347

Cistercian abbey of the Blessed Virgin Mary founded 1147 by Robert de Ewyas, a daughter house of Morimond, Burgundy. Dissolved 1536 and passed to John Scudamore; E end of church restored 1634 and became parochial

Parish church. Open during normal hours

The buildings that are left – comprising little more than the E parts of the church – are considerably later than the foundation date, being of c.1175–1215. Probably the lay brothers' quarters, now totally gone, were earlier. The church, developed as it was built, started with a simple two-bay presbytery and transeptal chapels and finished fully aisled and with an E ambulatory of great beauty. This was completed after a pause and consecrated c.1280. The nave was was extended too, to ten bays from the original nine. The chapter house was twelve-sided, like that of Margam.

All the buildings fell quickly to ruin after the Dissolution, but Viscount Scudamore, great-great-grandson of the grantee, blocked off the nave and aisles, rescued and reroofed the presbytery, crossing and transepts, blocked off the remainder, built a new tower over one of the S transept chapels, and refurnished the interior under the influence of Archbishop Laud. This is the only Cistercian E end still in use in Britain. A restoration was done in 1902–3 under Roland Paul, who also reconstructed the general plan of the abbey.

Entrance is by a little informal 17th c. timber porch into the **S transept**. The great crossing arches on shafted piers belong to the earliest part of the church and give a good idea of the scale when it was whole; the W piers may have been altered when the nave was blocked off. Pointed arches pierce the E walls of both transepts; they are on Corinthianesque capitals of before 1200 and the two on each side led to chapels. The replanning of c.1210 however

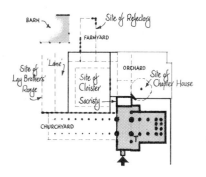

converted the inner chapel on each side into the first bay of the presbytery aisle. Around the arches are hood moulds with prominent rosettes, and above them a clerestory of lancets but no triforium. The roofs of both transepts are part of the 1633 reconstruction done by one John Abel for Lord Scudamore, plain and flat with wooden scrolls and wall shafts resting on the medieval piers. Originally there were vaults. Numerous painted texts and patterns survive on the walls, one of them dated 1701; David with his harp and Time with his scythe can be picked out. In the S wall near the entrance is an unusual square aumbry with dog-tooth ornament all round. Nearby are a poor-box dated 1639, and the octagonal font, quite plain, which must be 17th c. too.

At the **crossing** is an oak choir gallery on four classical columns, again 17th c. A heavy screen, similar in date and style, separates the presbytery. The strapwork ornament and uninhibited mixture of Gothic and classical detail are typical of its date; flanking the central royal arms are those of Lord Scudamore and Archbishop Laud. The **presbytery** is much like the transepts in design, but with less intrusive hood moulds on the arches. The first arch each side is much narrower and earlier than the rest for at first it opened merely into a transept chapel. As already seen, these inner chapels were absorbed into the aisles, linked in their turn around the E end by the retro-quire which is Dore's special glory. As seen from the W this displays three deeply moulded arches and piers, with three lancet windows over. The glass in these is, surprisingly, of 1634; so are the roof and ceiling, again matching the transepts. The altar is the Cistercian stone one, restored in 1633; the altar rail with stout balusters, the canopied pulpit, and most of the seating and the

panelling behind it are early 17th c., but the lectern is by Roland
Paul. Above the N end of the altar rail is a miniature effigy of
Bishop le Breton of Hereford (d. 1275).

Back now through the crossing into the **N transept**. More painted
wall decoration survives, mostly texts but with a fine royal arms
dominating the N wall. Close to that is the dorter doorway which
was at the head of the night stair. The doorway below led to the
sacristy. On the floor are numerous ledger stones from the 17th c.
onwards, with excellent lettering. The vaulted outer N chapel is
now a vestry. The **N presbytery aisle** is fully vaulted (the first bay
again was a chapel originally) with heavy transverse arches and
foliage capitals of early type. Under the arch next to the sanctuary is
the torso of a stone knight in chain mail, late 13th c., and in the end
bay a big trefoil-headed aumbry.

The splendid **E ambulatory**, a forest of vaults and clustered
columns, had five altars separated by screen walls. Now it is a
repository for sculptured fragments including superb roof bosses
and pieces of a monument or shrine. The E window glass is mostly
late 19th c. but at the S end is some of c.1600 and on the S side some
medieval bits. Nearby, in the SE corner chapel, two more lengths of
17th c. communion rail are reused. As on the N side, a 13th c.
knight's effigy lies beneath the arch by the main altar; this one is
better preserved. In the next bay of the aisle are an unidentified
stone coffin and some roundels of old glass. The end bay, which
began as a chapel, became part of the aisle and finally formed the
base of the tower. The outer chapel, entered off the S transept, has
a double-bowl piscina, an aumbry, the tomb chest of John Hoskyns
(d. 1638) and a screen of 1899 by Roland Paul.

Outside it is best to start with the oldest work, what is left of the
nave. One arch of the S arcade survives (with modern buttress), and
one column of the N arcade. The scallop and similar decorations
confirm a late 12th c. date, but the rest of the nave may well have
been rather later. The aisle roof lines are evident, and the big
crossing piers. Westward, the churchyard wall follows the outer line
of the N aisle, and at the end are 18th c. gates. N of the N transept
stands the shell of the sacristy, and one ivy-clad corner of the
chapter house just beyond. The rest stood in what is now an
orchard. There is nothing to see of it, nor of the other monastic
buildings; their site, which is glebe land, may be reached through
the gate by the NE corner of the church but the few bits of wall
found are no longer visible. The exterior of the aisles and
ambulatory is noteworthy for the string course with billet moulding

rising and falling over the lancet windows; originally there must have been little gables but the eaves were altered in the 17th c. Lastly the tower, wholly 17th c. and distinctly odd in the way it rises from the aisle roof and blocks the clerestories of both transept and presbytery.

Douai Berkshire: 1 mile N of A4 at Woolhampton   SU 577681

English Benedictine abbey of St Edmund, re-established 1903 after
   suppression at Douai, Artois

Church open to the public during normal hours

The English Benedictine community in Paris, founded in 1615, was suppressed in the French Revolution, refounded at Douai *c*.1818 in buildings vacated by St Gregory's (see Downside) and transferred here in 1903, to a Catholic Diocesan College which had been set up in 1838.

The original chapel, serving the school and as a parish church, is of 1848. School and monastery have been gradually extended N and E and the school now uses the original college. The gatehouse and other additions are by Frederick Walters (1893–5), the school and monastic refectories by S. Pugin Powell, and the library block by J.D. Kendall; the school was further extended in the 1960s and 1970s. The abbey church, designed by Arnold Crush, was begun in 1928 but only the Lady chapel and quire have been built. The monks' and novices' building and the common room and offices are by Sir Frederick Gibberd, 1965; his own proposals for completing the church are in abeyance.

Though brick outside, the church is of clean white Bath stone inside, and all vaulted. The lean-to 'nave' stands in place of the crossing tower and the quire occupies the intended Lady chapel. Reordering, with a new brown marble floor in the quire, has been done under Desmond Heuvel, with hanging Rood and Blessed Sacrament chapel glass and grille by David John. The triptych in the N aisle, though labelled 'Ghirlandaio', is more likely to be north German; that in the S aisle is an early 16th c. Flemish Adoration.

Outside, the temporary W wall does not entirely hide the concrete roof frame. On the N side the careful brickwork with flint and stone chequered parapets and well-mannered flowing Decorated window tracery make one regret that no more could be

Douai: Monastery building of 1965

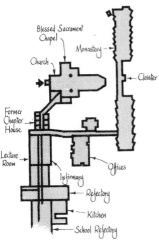

Blessed Sacrament
Chapel

Church

Former
Chapter
House

Lecture
Room

Monastery

Cloister

Offices

Infirmary

Refectory

Kitchen

School Refectory

built. Past the little cemetery are the two monastery buildings by
Gibberd (1965) connected by a 'cloister', and round to the S a
grassed court beyond which (also by Gibberd) are the adminstrative
buildings of abbey and school. Past here is private, so one must turn
back to the W end. In the irregular façades from here to the school
chapel the sash-windowed parts were designed to be temporary and
those with stone surrounds permanent.

Downside Somerset: ST 655507
in village of Stratton-on-the-Fosse, on Shepton Mallet–Bath road
A367

Benedictine priory of St Gregory the Great founded 1607 at Douai,
    Flanders; moved to Acton Burnell, Shropshire, 1795 and to
    Downside 1814; became abbey 1899

Church (only) open to public during normal hours

To the original Downside House (*c*.1700) a chapel and other rooms
were added in 1823 by H.E. Goodridge, and a further extension in
1853–4 by Charles Hansom. A complete new complex on a much
bigger scale was designed by Dunn & (Edward) Hansom in 1872.
The monastery was begun first, but the church transepts, crossing
and one bay each of the quire and nave, as well as most of the S

tower, had been built by 1884. A curiously disconnected string of chevet chapels followed, actually starting in 1883 with the Lady chapel crypt. Of these St Isidore's and St Benedict's at the SE are rectangular in plan and Perpendicular in style, distinct from the Decorated elsewhere.

Sir Ninian Comper undertook the Lady chapel decoration in 1898. Thomas Garner built the quire and St Sebastian's chapel (thus linking the chevet and transepts) in 1902–5; he also completed the N cloister and the line of upper-level chapels over it. The sacristies were added by Frederick Walters in 1913–15. The nave, which is still incomplete at the W end, was built in 1922–5 and the top of the tower in 1938, both under Sir Giles Gilbert Scott. The E range of the cloister, including the refectory, guest house and offices, was completed in 1975 and the nearly detached library in 1970, all under Francis Pollen. The school buildings, merging with the monastic, include the original priory nucleus, extensively added to by Leonard Stokes, Scott and others.

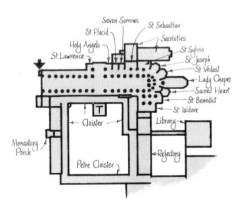

In view of the odd sequence of building, the unity of the church interior is surprising. Entry by the temporary NW porch brings one into the noble Scott **nave**, entirely traditional in general form and showing in its crisp lines his mastery of detail. The furthest bay, next the crossing, was built by Hansom at the same time as the crossing arches – with true medieval concern for their stability – but Scott altered it a little to match his own work. The blue and gold quire E window is by Comper, 1936. Looking the other way, the temporary W wall with its three great lancets was intended to come down when two more bays were built, but may be used as the basis for a permanent W front; on it are school war memorial plaques.

A clockwise tour starts in the **N aisle** with Scott's canopied tomb of Abbot Ramsay (d. 1929). The upper chapels on the opposite side (actually over the cloister walk and not open to the public) can be glimpsed. On the left of the aisle, St Lawrence's chapel has a relic cupboard painted by Nathaniel Westlake and shows in its vault the striped stone effect which Hansom originally intended throughout. His **N transept** design obviously influenced Scott's nave; the corbelled gallery is perhaps its least happy feature. The pinnacled reredos below once served the high altar when (until Garner built the quire) the church consisted of little more than the transepts and crossing. Near it is a 17th c. chest, and on the right four plain stone pillars support the shrine of St Oliver Plunkett by Ephraem Seddon, 1936.

Look across to the **S transept**. Behind it is the tower, so the lower windows look into the cloister and the five upper lancets are blank. The rich pinnacled organ screen by Scott (1931) was carved at Ortisei in the Tyrol under Ferdinand Stüflesser.

Next the N quire aisle and a view into Garner's **quire** with its clustered columns and luxuriant foliage capitals. Here too the bay nearest the crossing was Hansom's but in this case Garner removed Hansom's triforium and clerestory – having decided to dispense with a triforium altogether. A further departure from Hansom's intention was the square E end. The device of bringing the vaulting shafts down to angel corbels is another which Scott took up later in the nave. The stalls (originally further W), closely modelled on those of Chester, were made at Ortisei in 1932–3; the front rows were added in 1951.

The first small chapel off the N quire aisle or **ambulatory** is that of Holy Angels. It is by Hansom. The altar triptych is 15th c. Flemish, and the screen by F.C. Eden, c.1930; the tomb of Bishop Morris (d. 1872) is by Frederick Walters, c.1910. Here the aisle narrows. The next chapels, those of St Placid and of the Seven Sorrows of Our Lady, both have rich Gothic altarpieces, the former by Geoffrey Webb and the latter carved by Wall of Cheltenham and containing an early Crucifixion of Flemish or Rhenish origin. Nearby is another chest, probably 16th c.

St Sebastian's chapel, which is bigger, is by Garner (1902) and has a Comper reredos and stone side screen (1929), the latter completed in 1972 with statues by Peter Watts and marvellously delicate screenwork by Gilbert Sumsion. The side doorway leads to

Downside: Library of 1975 as seen from church tower

the sacristies and the central tomb-chest is of the van Cutsem family. On the N wall is a brilliantly fresh painting of a bishop enthroned, attributed to Francesco Botticini (15th c.). At this point a closer look at the quire stalls is possible: against their back are a memorial (by Scott) to Vicar Apostolic Peter Collingridge (d. 1829), and the canopied tomb of Bishop Baines (d. 1846) by Wall, 1913. Opposite is the priests' sacristy doorway; the pretty oriel above it lights a chapel of St Conrad. Then on the right is the tomb of Thomas Garner (d. 1906) and his wife.

The next three chapels are St Sylvia's (by Walters), with a medieval altar stone from Cannington, a painting of St John the Baptist (probably by Lazzaro Bastiani) and a bas-relief Christ by Hubert van Zeller, 1957 – then St Joseph's with a 16th c. chest, and St Vedast's with wall-arcading and a mosaic floor. Behind the quire altar, in the unusual semicircle left between Hansom's apse and Garner's square end, is that of the Blessed Sacrament. Steps lead up to the **Lady chapel**. Hansom built it, but Comper adorned it with the gates (1929), glass (1899–1927), 'English' altar with riddel-posts and tester (1898), and rich Gothic reredos with miniature, exquisitely detailed relic chests on top.

The chapels to the SE, all Hansom's, do not in the least match the NE ones. That of the Sacred Heart is on the level of the Lady chapel and contains Comper glass (1915), ceramic panels by Adam Kossowski (1956), another 16th c. chest, and a painting of St Francis, possibly by Ribera. From the ambulatory, past the standing Christ, steps lead down to the vaulted chapel of St Peter in Chains in the **crypt**. At the foot of the steps stands an old statue of St Benedict. The central floor brass in the chapel is to Edmund Pereira (d. 1872) and the Madonna at the W end came from Goodridge's old chapel.

Now Hansom's two rectangular lierne-vaulted chapels. The first, St Benedict's, has roof bosses representing the chief medieval Benedictine monasteries, as well as an elaborate painted triptych by Westlake, E and S windows by Lavers & Westlake (1896–7), a 14th c. chest, and a floor brass to the Rev. Francis New (d. 1896). The ivory figure on the Crucifix is ascribed to Andreas Faistenberger, *c*.1700. Under the arcade the tomb with richly crested canopy is of Cardinal Gasquet (d. 1929) – the design by Scott and the formalised effigy by E. Carter Preston. The outer chapel, St Isidore's, with elongated chequered floor, has windows also by Lavers & Westlake (1895–6); the altars in both these chapels, as well as the dividing screen, are by Walters (1897). Another 17th c. chest stands close by.

Next, follow the **S ambulatory** westwards. Against the back of the stalls are three canopied tombs, of: Monsignor Joseph Weld (d. 1898); Bishop Walmesley (d. 1797), erected 1911; and Abbot Ford (d. 1930), first abbot, by Scott. The N transept rose window glass, well seen from here, is by Hardman. Past Garner's plain doorway to the cloister (private) is the tomb of Arthur Stuckey-Lean (d. 1901), followed by stairs to the upper chapels (also private) and a 15th c. wood Madonna possibly by Nicolaus Gerhaert and possibly from Konstanz cathedral. Another doorway to the cloister is a typical Scott design and at the end is a 15th c. St Peter statue.

Outside, the grounds to the W and SW are private. Thus the temporary W wall can only be seen obliquely, and examination of the remainder of the church is mostly confined to the N side, starting with Scott's nave and aisles. Then come Hansom's transept, Garner's quire (to which Scott added flying buttresses in 1936), Walters's sacristies, and Hansom's Lady chapel, with Scott's 166-foot tower top visible over them all. Past the E end one can see Pollen's almost-detached library (1978) and the school beyond.

Further round, the E range of the monastery, also by Pollen, can be glimpsed.

Dunkeswell Devon: ST 143107
2 miles N of village and 6 miles N of A30 at Honiton

Cistercian abbey of the Blessed Virgin Mary founded 1201 by
   William de Briwere, a daughter house of Forde. Dissolved 1539
   and granted to John, Lord Russell

Parish chapel; remainder in multiple ownership. Ruin accessible at
   all times.

Hardly anything is known of the abbey buildings, except some
fragments of the W range and gatehouse which still stand. They
were quickly quarried away after the Dissolution, though parts of
the claustral ranges seem to have been inhabited till the 19th c., and
stone from them contributed in 1842 to building Holy Trinity church
in the middle of the abbey church site.

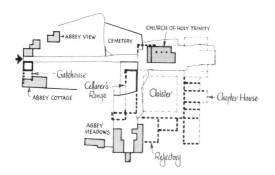

   The ruin by the churchyard entrance is the left side of the
gatehouse (not the right, as is proved by the arch jamb on the side
away from the gate). To the right of the box-lined path to the
Victorian church is a high lump of the NE corner of the W or
cellarer's range. Inside the **church** the sanctuary is paved with 13th
c. abbey tiles in varied patterns. Other ancient features include a
stone coffin and lid, an octagonal 'tub' font on four square legs, and
some 16th c. pieces in the pulpit.

Undulations around the church suggest some other features of the abbey plan, partially revealed by digs in 1841 and 1913.

Durford Sussex: SU 778234
2 miles E of Petersfield and ¼ mile S of Midhurst road A272

Premonstratensian abbey of St Mary and St John the Baptist founded 1161 by Henry Husey II, a daughter house of Welbeck; dissolved 1536 and granted to Sir William Fitzwilliam. Disasters included a plundering in 1317, a fire in 1335, loss of the bells by lightning in 1417, and the death of all but the abbot and three canons by plague in 1482. The modest farmhouse on the site (Manley family) is of 1784. At the back are worked stones and a coffin lid, to be seen with permission.

The cloister may have occupied part of the big farmyard – at the lower end of which is a medieval barn. Slight remains of a water-mill further down are likely to be monastic.

Ealing Greater London: TQ 174815
in Charlbury Grove, ½ mile NW of Ealing Broadway station

Benedictine monastery of St Benedict founded 1897, a daughter house of Downside; became priory 1916, abbey 1955

Church (only) open to public during normal hours

Building began in 1897, two bays of the church (by Frederick and Edward Walters) being complete by 1899. Two storeys of the monastery were built by 1905 and the third soon after. The church was extended in 1915 with a new sanctuary and NE Lady chapel. In the 1920s and 30s the SE War Memorial chapel was added and the four western bays of the nave with its W front built; these bays escaped the destruction of the older part by bombs in 1940. When it was rebuilt in 1960–2 under Stanley Kerr Bate the chapels were enlarged into full transepts and the base of a future central tower formed. In 1975 the monastery was extended with new refectory, calefactory, parlours and monks' rooms, thus freeing more accommodation for guests; the architects were the Hellberg-Harris Partnership. The abbey school was founded in 1902.

Behind the W front is a transverse narthex with gallery over.

Double doors lead into the aisles and into the very broad **nave**
which is spanned by graceful painted hammer-beam trusses, two to
each bay, resting on shafts alternately merging with the clustered
white stone piers and standing on the arcade hood-moulds (there is
no clerestory). The fairly narrow aisles are normally kept free of
seating. Except in the eastern bay the 1960 work exactly copies the
older; there however each aisle contains a small gallery on
additional arches, one of which supports the organ.

In the **N transept** the unfinished state of the E end becomes
apparent in the blind openings at triforium level and in the
ornamental but blocked N doorway. This is the Lady chapel and
contains a Madonna of Fatima by Thedim. The big N window is of
clear glass. That of the S transept forms a war memorial and is by
Sir Ninian Comper. It and the flat red ceiling of the crossing can be
seen from beside the monks' stalls.

Back now into the nave. From the quire entrance one can look
back at the colourful great W window ('Coronation of the Virgin')
by Burlison & Grylls, and the other way to the newer work of 1960,
the fairly simple oak stalls and the clustered piers of the crossing. A
windowless wall hides the site of the future quire; this temporary
end can be glimpsed from outside by going through a secondary
lobby off the E end of the S aisle – which gives access also to a series
of parish rooms all along the side of the church.

The **S aisle** itself has a series of small chapels, beginning with that
of St Boniface which contains a brilliant mosaic by David
Woodford-Robinson given by Germans in recompense for war
damage. The chapel of St Benedict has a statue by Ferdinand
Stüflesser.

Outside, twin copper-spiked turrets dominate the W end and mask the ends of the narrow aisles. The general style is Perpendicular, using white and yellowish stone. Areas of flint checkerwork however appear rather incongruously in the battlements. The original monastery building adjoining the N side is of red brick with Tudor-style windows – except on the first floor where the lintels display a curious embattled pattern. Beyond it is the plainer extension of 1975, making a feature of the jutting windows of the monks' rooms.

Easby North Yorkshire: NZ 185003
in village, 1 mile SE of Richmond and ¼ mile S of Brompton road

Premonstratensian abbey of St Agatha founded 1151 by Roald, constable of Richmond castle, a daughter house of Newsham. Suppressed 1537

In care of Department of the Environment. Open during standard hours (admission charge)

Of the church, built first, little survives; it was completed *c*.1310, and enlarged to the E in the 14th c. The cloister buildings to the S, largely early 13th c., are unusually arranged owing to the fall of the ground, the dorter being in the W range, where ingenious planning on three storeys provided separately for monks and guests. To the N, the infirmary and abbot's house, also planned together, were begun early in the 13th c. and altered and extended over a long period. War damage, particularly in 1346, led to rebuilding work.

After suppression, which had been resisted in 1536, the early 14th c. gatehouse was made into a granary and thus survived. Apart from the church, the main buildings also seem to have been spared wholesale destruction. The nearby parish church was founded long before the abbey.

The entrance is towards the SW corner of the claustral buildings which are basically early 13th c. First is the guest hall: two of its walls remain, with relics of vaulting and, above, a fireplace of the first floor prior's solar or living room. Broken steps lead up to the cloister, and others on their right to the **refectory** undercroft, an impressively long compartment once with a low vault but now open to the high refectory hall above. This upper part was rebuilt *c*.1300

with fine Geometric windows (the E five-light), some of whose tracery is left. Outside to the S lay the kitchen, which seems to have had a gallery from which there exist two hatches into the refectory. From here it is worth looking again at what is left of the three-light side windows and at the pulpit projection towards the E end (with a doorway under).

Now go up into the cloister and along its S walk. Here one can look across the refectory to the pulpit again. At the end of the walk is a vaulted parlour, made unusable by the spiral stair inserted in the 15th c. to serve a suite of upper rooms. Off the E walk, the chapter house retains the base of its own vault, as well as stone benching at the sides and telling evidence of enlargement of the main E window in the 15th c. At higher level is a fireplace in one of the added living rooms, the exact purpose of which is not known. Next (but entered from the church) is the sacristy, the further half of which was an afterthought and contains a stair added later still to serve the treasury and sacrist's lodging above. The base of the church doorway remains, with a medieval grave slab just outside.

From the centre of the **church** its general form is clear though so little is left. Its plan, more typically Cistercian, had three E chapels to each transept (as is clear on the S side). The quire, extended in the 14th c., also received a new sacristy on its S side. The two recesses in its N wall and one in its S probably contained tombs of the Scrope family; some fragments of sedilia remain too. Back at the crossing, note the nave paving, with incised circles as markers for processions, and that of the N transept with numerous memorial crosses. From here a 13th c. doorway leads to the **infirmary**, above

Easby: Early 13th c. refectory

which (unusually) was the abbot's lodging. His gallery lay over the long wide passage: its fireplace and chimney stack survive.

The big room on the left is believed to have been the misericord, where meat eating was permitted; above was the abbot's solar. Steps ahead lead down to the 13th c. infirmary hall, various small added rooms at the end of which include a 15th c. chapel still with its stone altar and (with an arched garderobe) the infirmarer's lodging. Further N, through a pantry and buttery, is the infirmary kitchen, an eloquent ruin with big fireplaces. Above the pantry (with a three-light window) was the abbot's chapel. The return to the N transept can be via the storeroom at the W end of the hall (over this store was the abbot's hall) and the misericord.

Beside the transept stands an almost separate early 14th c. chapel, traditionally the Scrope chantry chapel, with three broken N windows. To the N of the nave site are foundations of several unidentified outbuildings. To its SW the **W monastic range** begins with the warming house (its fireplace is on the cloister side) and a series of column bases and cross-walls beyond. Above was the canons' dorter. Parallel and to the W is a three-storey guest wing (as is supposed): the top floor a dorter, the middle a solar, and at ground level storerooms. On its further side is a well preserved reredorter which will be seen later. The ingenious inter-relation of canons' and guests' sleeping, living and eating arrangements and their access to church, cloister and kitchens is analysed in the official handbook; unfortunately the disappearance of floors precludes thorough exploration.

In the cloister W walk an unexpected Norman door arch with beak-head ornament has been reset on later shafts; the broken steps here lead to the canons' dorter, and close by are the remains of a washplace. The fine refectory doorway is worth another look before going back down to the guest hall seen at the start.

To its N is a series of little rooms and passages leading on the left first to a long groin-vaulted cellar between the guest wing and the dorter range and then to the guest wing itself, an impressive shell with two levels of vault springers on all four sides. A way out at the far end leads round to the drain; the imposing reredorter above served all three floors. Up the path is a display of carved stones; from here is a good view of the end of the guest wing, with its plate-traceried first-floor window. Back now down its W side, where the flank wall of the reredorter, inadequately tied to the main block, has a spectacular lean. The external circuit can then be continued around the refectory and chapter house (looking through this into the cloister) and the E end of the church and thence perhaps back across the cloister again.

This leaves the **gatehouse**, up the lane – c.1300, rib-vaulted and with a division two-thirds of the way through to separate pedestrians from other traffic. The outer (S) end is, as usual, the richer. A large monastic barn, nearer the river, is now partly a house.

The rich, early 16th c. stalls in Richmond church came from the abbey; so, it is said, did some screenwork in Wensley church.

Edgware (St Mary at the Cross) Greater London: TQ 200927
in Hale Lane, ½ mile NE of Edgware Station

Nunnery of St Mary at the Cross, of an Anglican Order, founded
    1866 in Shoreditch by Hannah Skinner and the Rev. Henry
    Nihill; first abbess elected 1926; moved to Edgware 1931; became
    Benedictine 1935

Church and some other rooms may be seen on request

An abbey in all but name, for it has both an abbess and an abbey church. The community's work is in the care of the sick, and extensive wards adjoin the convent. The predecessor of these buildings was a children's hospital built in Shoreditch in 1870–80. Building at Edgware, at first a convalescent home dedicated to St Mary of Nazareth, began in 1874. The church, intended as the Lady chapel of a much bigger building, was commenced in 1889 under James Brooks, the connecting cloister being added in 1893. In 1931 the community was united when the Shoreditch hospital was closed and the name St Mary at the Cross transferred to Edgware. The wards were extended in 1937 and given their own chapel (St Michael's); further extensions were made in 1955–62, and a permanent narthex in contrasting style was added to the chapel in 1965 under Norman Davey.

The main buildings are of red brick with Bath stone dressings, their windows being mostly wide lancets with transoms; picturesquely irregular in layout, they have been much built on to at various times. From the main entrance visitors are conducted to a parlour and thence past the impressive little brick-vaulted refectory and down the cloister walk (one side of an uncompleted square) to

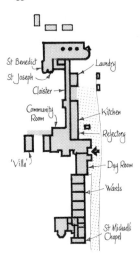

the steeply copper-roofed church. Norman Davey's low flat timber-ceilinged narthex, brilliantly lit with big random rectilinear patterned windows by Goddard & Gibbs, includes twin apsidal chapels – all lined with grey brick. It lies low against the end of the stone-vaulted quire, itself in a rather idiosyncratic version of Early English. Heavy columns divide off a brick N aisle that was meant only to be temporary. On the outside, where the main building should have joined on, is more blanked-off arcading and an unfinished turret.

Egglestone Durham: NZ 062151
1½ miles SE of Barnard Castle and 1 mile N of A66

Premonstratensian abbey of St Mary and St John the Baptist founded *c*.1190, probably by Ralph de Moulton, a daughter house of Easby. Refounded 1537 to avoid suppression as lesser monastery, but dissolved 1540 and granted to Robert Strelly

In care of Department of the Environment. Open at all times without charge

Never large or important, Egglestone began with few endowments, and apart from modest enlargements to its aisleless church hardly any building was done after the 13th c. It suffered moreover both in the Scottish invasion of 1315 and in subsequent counter-measures. The cloister of *c*.1195 survives in little more than plan. The church, of which much more is left, was extended southwards and eastwards – with a new presbytery *c*.1250, transept chapels a little later, and *c*.1300 a widening of the nave to match the presbytery. The cloister, which from the start extended rather oddly beyond the W front, only received a W range late in the 13th c.

Robert Strelly is believed to have converted the cloister buildings into a house; in doing so he rebuilt the outer wall of the E range. They eventually became cottages. Stone was taken away (even as late as *c*.1900) to Rokeby Hall but some, including the Bowes tomb, has been returned. In 1925 the ruins passed into state guardianship.

The **church**, standing high at both ends, is approached from the S and is readily understood. The transept W wall is part of the late 13th c. enlargement; the plan of the first (simple cruciform) church is laid out on the ground. The prominent tomb, referred to above, is of Sir Ralph Bowes (d. 1482); its top slab is missing. Further W are several medieval slabs, only one of which – to a Rokeby – is inscribed. Another shows a hand and crozier. The nave N wall is late 12th c. at the base where it bounded the original cloister, and a little later above, with lancets. The W window is off-centre through the nave being widened to the S, although its Geometric tracery is apparently of the same date as the S wall; signs of the original lancets can still be seen.

Of the N transept little is left, but the mid-13th c. chancel with its lancet windows and shafted jambs is much more complete. The E window, divided by four mullions carried right up to the arch without tracery, puzzles antiquaries; if original, its design is unique for its period. Beneath are two aumbries and two piscinae, one very big.

Now the **cloister**; nothing much is left though preserved stones show that the outer arcade was 13th c. Because the church is so short the doorway at the W end of the S walk led not into it but into its forecourt. Of the late 13th c. W range only foundations remain; the N part has been a kitchen but probably only in the Strellys' time. The N range comprised refectory (at upper level) and warming room. The massive fireplace on the N side is due to Strelly who made the refectory his hall; deep reveals of the original windows remain in front of it. The warming room fireplace is small by comparison. The little room beyond this, and the cramped passage to it, are difficult to explain.

The **E range** clearly shows Strelly's domestic outer wall and windows. Little survives of the chapter house at its S end, but it seems to have projected into the church transept; near the junction is an abbot's tomb slab. At its N end is one of the most interesting parts of the abbey, original work of *c.*1200 but with a later 13th c. vault that supported the reredorter above. Two small privies opening off the further corners of the lower chamber (which has a fireplace) are served by a drain which from the outside can be seen to have run beneath a set of upper latrines. Nearby is a pile of 13th c. stones, many of them recovered from Rokeby Hall.

Finally it is worth looking from the **outside** at the W wall of the nave, and the S wall with its broken buttresses and three-light windows. The stair turret at the transept junction was clearly a late addition, but there is evidence too of earlier preparations to add a S aisle, opening into the transept.

In the Abbey Mill on the Tees below, a very little monastic stonework survives; there is rather more – mostly reused stones – in the farmhouse W of the abbey.

Elstow Bedfordshire: TL 048474
in village 600 yards E of A6, 1½ miles S of Bedford

Benedictine nunnery of St Mary and St Helen founded *c.*1075;
    refounded *c.*1178 by Judith, Countess of Huntingdon. Dissolved
    1539 and estate passed to Edmund Harvey

Part parish church. Remainder owned by Whitbread family. Church
    open during normal hours

The early history as known incompletely from excavations is
complex but probably no more so than many sites less intensively

probed. Not only the 11th/12th c. monastery foundation has been
found, intermingled with that of its replanned successor of the 14th
c., but also probable Bronze Age works, and burials of the 5th/6th
c. and of the Saxon period. The abbey church of c.1100 onwards
was extended westwards in the 13th c. by rebuilding one bay and
adding another; a detached tower was also built. Next the cloister
was enlarged and the monastic buildings completely rebuilt. The
upper parts of the tower were added or rebuilt in the 15th c.

The nave, excepting its two E bays, reverted after the Dissolution
to use by the parish, with the outer parlour as a vestry (from the
14th c. there had been a separate parochial chapel). A new E wall
was built in 1580, and the rest of the church demolished. In 1616 Sir
Thomas Hillersdon bought the remains of the monastery and built a
house incorporating its W range. This in its turn is a ruin. The
church was much restored in 1880 under Sir Thomas Jackson, the S
aisle and much of the N being rebuilt.

The foliage-ornamented W doorway of c.1220 prepares one for
the two W bays of the **nave**, with massive octagonal piers and
stiff-leaf capitals, and a clerestory of shafted lancets. The remainder
(including what is now the chancel) is of c.1100; very plain arches on
piers cross-shaped on plan, and a simple round-headed clerestory.
The roof is Jackson's. Behind, the much reduced W window is
probably of 1580, the fine royal arms of 1775.

Along the N aisle are three hatchments, an oval memorial to
Robert Crompton, d. 1681, and the large 15th c. font with curious
animals and heads at its base; here John Bunyan was baptised in
1628. Past the doorway is a cartouche to Lovet Crompton, d. 1684.
The oak pulpit with dog-tooth is 19th c. The organ almost blocks the
way to the **N chapel**, whose E window has glass in honour of Bunyan.

The three-windowed E wall of the **chancel** is also of 1580; beyond stood two more bays of nave. On it are set two carved stone brackets and, strangely above the altar, a monument to Sir Humphrey Radclif, d. 1566, and his wife. On the last full column of the S arcade a small stone box, probably for a lantern, has been reset.

The **S chapel** has another Bunyan window and preserves the tall communion rail of his time from the chancel. There is a large piscina with a fluted drain; also two 17th c. tablets to the Hillersdons, builders of the adjoining mansion. In the aisle floor, protected by the red carpet, are fine brasses to Margery Argentine, d. 1427, and her granddaughter Abbess Elizabeth Herwy, d. 1524.

A door on the left leads to the **vestry** or so-called 'chapter house', really the 13th c. outer parlour of the abbey. This has a fluted octagonal column and an unparalleled vault with ribs straying from quadripartite into a kind of scissor pattern. The aisle stair turret and the transverse arches buttressing the main arcade are additions by Jackson.

Outside, note the unfinished state of the NW doorway. That on the N side is a Jackson 'restoration' but supports a genuine Norman Majestas of *c*.1140; the figures to left and right are St Peter and St John. The tower is 13th c. at the base but 15th c. for the most part.

The rest of the church exterior has little of interest, thanks to Jackson. Nor is there much evidence of the excavations of 1968 onwards – only some mounds in the adjoining field that roughly indicate the chapter house and the E range of monastic rooms. The ruined outer walls of Hillersdon Hall show clearly where the S and W ranges stood; its once three-storeyed Jacobean porch bay is in the centre of the former W walk. Returning through the gate beside the vestry, notice its masonry pattern, as wayward as that of the vault inside.

Ely Cambridgeshire: in town   TL 541803

Monastery of monks and nuns founded 673 by its first abbess St Etheldreda; destroyed by Danes 870, but eight priests returned to found college; Benedictine abbey refounded 970. Became cathedral priory 1109

Cathedral church open during normal hours. Stained Glass Museum in triforium open 11.0 a.m. to 4.0 p.m. (Sundays 12 noon to 3.30 p.m.)

For a full description see *A Guide to the Cathedrals of Britain*, pp.148–157.

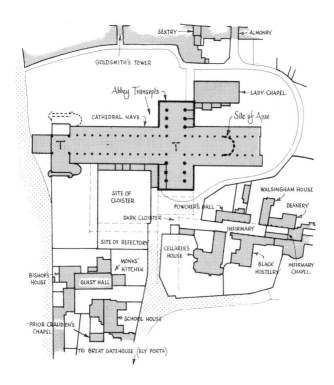

Evesham Hereford & Worcester: in town centre SP 037436

Benedictine abbey founded 701 by St Egwin, Bishop of Worcester and later dedicated to St Mary and St Egwin; became collegiate 941, monastic again *c*.970, collegiate again *c*.975 and monastic again *c*.995; became mitred. Dissolved 1540 and sold to Philip Hobby

Mostly owned by Rudge Estate, except parish churchyard. Most of the remains accessible to public at all times without charge

Evesham: Early 16th c. bell tower

Recorded dates include 960 when the church fell down and 1054 when there was a reconsecration. It was again ambitiously rebuilt *c.*1080–1175, the quire once more after storm damage in 1207, and a Lady chapel begun *c.*1275. Thus the nave finally was late Norman, the crossing and transepts early Norman and the E end Gothic (rebuilt *c.*1400) – all very much as at Pershore. Of the monastic buildings only the chapter house is architecturally datable (late 13th c.) from its surviving doorway, but other dates are documented.

The splendid detached bell-tower is of *c.*1530, unusually late and lavish. A remarkable event was the colonising in 1086 of a daughter house at Odense in Denmark.

After the Dissolution the two churches within the precinct and to the N of the abbey church sufficed for the town's needs. The great church and almost all the monastic buildings were taken down, leaving two gatehouses and some adjacent structures for domestic use and the bell-tower for parish and civic pride. The ground lying E of the sites of nave and cloister is leased to the council as a public park; the remainder (apart from the churchyard) is used as a market garden – merely an extension of the area given over to cultivation by the monks.

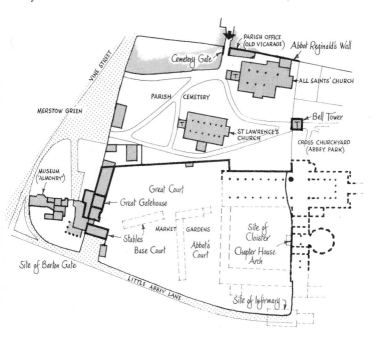

Entry from the Market Place to the churchyard is through the so-called **Norman Gateway**, half-timbered in its 15th c. upper storey but of stone with original 12th c. wall-arcading in its lower; the present pavement level is obviously much above the original.

Evesham: 14th c. chapter house doorway

Alongside to the left is the one-time vicarage, also timber-framed.
Beyond, behind All Saints' church, the precinct wall ('Abbot
Reginald's wall') continues. More of it can be seen at the other end
of the church.

The **bell-tower** stands 110 feet high, guarding the way from the
parish churchyard to the former Cross Churchyard which is now a
park sloping down to the Avon. The overall panelling of the
stonework is typically late Perpendicular but unusual on this scale.
Apart from the ground stage vaulting, which may never have been
completed, it is entire.

Immediately to the S and visible from the park is a small mass of
masonry, all that is left of the abbey **church**. It consists of part of the
junction of the N transept with the N nave aisle, and part of a pier of
the crossing tower. Further along, railed round on the cloister side
for public viewing, is the late 13th c. **chapter house** doorway – rather
French in character with its two orders containing little statues in
niches, one set standing and the other seated. The wall continues
more or less to follow the W side of the former dorter undercroft
and ends at the supposed infirmary site but has no further features
so it is best to go back beneath the tower and to turn left in the
churchyard. The garden wall running W from the transept stump
follows the line of the outer wall of the N nave aisle. The part
further forward alongside St Lawrence's bounded the Great Court
W of the abbey church.

The path leads on to the open space called Merstow Green with a
picturesque L-shaped group in the near corner. The nearest house
on the left is of 1711 but is built around remnants (mostly inside and
not visible by the public) of the great gatehouse. The further arm of
the L is called the **Almonry** but is in fact probably not; in any case it
is a highly picturesque mixture of stone and timber framing, 14th
and 15th cc., and now a museum, with much of interest concerning
abbey and town. If it is closed, its back and various abbey fragments
can still be seen from the side. From Little Abbey Lane at the rear
(which follows the outside of the wall back to the riverside park) the
stables behind the gatehouse are visible; these too contain medieval
bits.

Eynsham Oxfordshire: in village, SE of church   SP 433091

Benedictine abbey of St Mary (also St Benedict and All Saints
and/or possibly St Andrew and St Eadburgh) founded 1005 by

Ethelmar, Earl of Cornwall; dispersed at Conquest but
refounded by 1086 by Bishop Remigius of Lincoln; moved to
Stow 1091 but re-established c.1109; dissolved 1539 and given to
Earl of Derby. The site, inconclusively excavated, stretched from
the parish churchyard across to the Catholic church grounds. A
small arch is re-erected by the vicarage in Mill Street and other
fragments can be found around the village.

Farnborough Hampshire: SU 873560
in village, 300 yards E of A325

Premonstratensian cell of St Michael the Archangel founded 1887
by the Empress Eugénie of France, colonised from Storrington.
Became French Benedictine 1895; abbey 1903. Became English
Benedictine cell to Prinknash 1947; priory 1969 and independent
community 1980

Guided visits to church only, 2.45 and 3.30 p.m. daily from 1st
August to 15th September; otherwise Wednesdays, Saturdays
and Sundays only; additionally Sundays at 4.15. Admission
charge to crypt

The curious history commences with the building of a 'prieuré' and
mausoleum-church on Coombe Hill by ex-Empress Eugénie in
1883, in Flamboyant style under Gabriel Destailleur, in memory of
her husband Napoleon III (Bonaparte) and their son the Prince
Imperial. The first, Premonstratensian, canons were succeeded
after eight years by Benedictines from Solesmes, Maine; they began
extending the house in 1900–12 under W.E. (later Father Benedict)
Williamson to a design based on Solesmes, but did not complete it.
In 1947 they in their turn gave way to English monks from
Prinknash. The present community is engaged in pastoral and
teaching work and the operation of a bookbindery and press.

The domed **upper church**, cruciform and aisleless, is spanned by
heavy arches without capitals, and pendant vaults between.
Additional richness is given by 'bottle glass' throughout the
windows and by the panels beneath, 'Way of the Cross' lithographs
by Sir Frank Brangwyn. At the crossing, the pendentives of the
octagonal dome carry the arms and emblems of Napoleon III; his
'bees' symbol may be found in a number of places in the church.

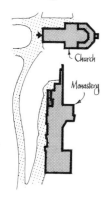

The apse has an even more complex pendant vault and a Corsican marble floor in memory of Napoleon I. The noted organ, behind the altar, is by the French builders Cavaillé-Coll (1902). The paintings behind the choir stalls in the transepts, copied from the Rubens *Deposition* in Antwerp cathedral, came from the Tuileries palace.

The crypt, separately entered at the E end, is in a heavy Romanesque style with Corinthian-type capitals and quite high vault. Behind St Louis's altar at the W end is the simple sarcophagus of Eugénie (d. 1920), while on the right (N) side is the tomb of Napoleon III (d. 1873) (given by Queen Victoria); his Garter banner hangs above, and at the foot is a head of the Madonna copied from Michelangelo's *Pietà*. The Prince Imperial's tomb (d. 1879) stands on the opposite side; the head of Christ is by Jean Clesinger. Furniture and other objects in the crypt have further associations with the Bonapartes. The teak staircase leading from an inconspicuous corner to the sacristy above is remarkable for its craftmanship.

Externally the church's French character is emphasised by its great gargoyles, Flamboyant window tracery, traceried parapets and flying buttresses. The dome is said to have been inspired by that of Les Invalides, burial place of Napoleon I.

The **abbey**, down the hill, has a brick centre part (including the slated spire) by Destailleur, the theatrical-looking stone additions either side being by Williamson. It is not open to the public, and only the façade can be seen.

Faversham Kent: at NE corner of town TR 020618

Independent abbey of the Holy Saviour founded 1147 by King
   Stephen. Dissolved 1538 and granted to Sir Thomas Cheyne

Owned by Kent County Council (church site); remainder in several
   ownerships. Church site accessible to public without charge;
   remainder private

In several ways Faversham abbey was most unusual, and not least
through having been founded and built around a royal mausoleum.
Though colonised from the Cluniac abbey of Bermondsey it does
not seem to have had definite affiliations with any order. The great
length of the original church, with its eastern arm longer than the
western, is explained by the fact that the royal chapel took up six
whole bays. This, with the consequent displacement of the crossing
and transepts two bays westwards, seems to have been decided
upon after the monastic buildings were begun; the cloister as a
result had to be in a very odd position.
   Most unusual of all was the reduction in overall size of the abbey
a century or less after its foundation and almost certainly before it
was complete. Much of the E end and part of the W end of the
church were abandoned, the cloister was made substantially
smaller, the W and refectory ranges were brought further in, and
the dorter was shortened.
   Abbey stone went to the walls of Calais after the Dissolution. The
inner gatehouse stood till 1771; the outer partly survives in Arden's
House. The general plan was revealed by a 'rescue' dig in 1964–65
and now lies partly under Queen Elizabeth's school playing field
and partly under orchard. The royal burial vaults (minus the coffins
of Stephen and Matilda whose reputed tombs are in the parish
church) were found, also a Roman villa just E of the abbey.

   The site is approached through Abbey Close and lies behind
Fighting Cocks Cottages. Turn behind them into the left corner of
the field, where a detailed plan is exhibited and the base of the W
front forms the rear wall of gardens. Further N (reached by Abbey
Road) are two timber barns of the abbey and a stretch of precinct
wall. Arden's House, on the corner of Abbey Street and Abbey
Close, was built by Thomas Arden *c*.1540; his murder inspired a
play of the period.

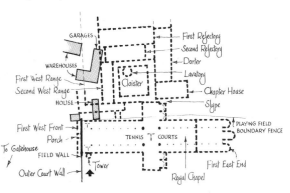

Flaxley Gloucestershire: SO 690154
in village, 1 mile N of Cinderford–Westbury road A4151

Cistercian abbey of the Blessed Virgin Mary founded 1151 by
  Roger, Earl of Hereford, a daughter house of Bordesley.
  Dissolved 1536 and given to Sir William Kingston

Owned by Watkins family. Not open to the public except on
  occasional advertised days (admission charge for charity)

The abbey (also known as Dene) is said to mark the spot where the
founder's father was killed whilst hunting in the Forest of Dean. It
was unusual in being under the special protection of the Crown and
seems to have been used from Henry II's reign onwards as a royal
hunting lodge, the lay brothers' refectory being turned into a guest
hall. About 1355 Edward III had the abbot's guest chamber
improved and embellished for his own occasional use. That,
together with most of the remainder of the W range (otherwise
largely 12th c.) still stands.
  By the time of the Dissolution many of the buildings were already
pronounced ruinous and the church had been burnt. However the
Kingstons made a house of the S and W ranges, and it was sold to
the Boeveys in 1647. Much of the W range (which had already been
altered in the 17th c. and c.1751) survived a fire in 1777. Its N end
was then tidied up and a new S wing built under Anthony Keck.
Some Gothic dressing-up occurred early in the 19th c., and a good

Flaxley: Abbey W range, now a house

deal of classical remodelling was done under Oliver Messel in 1961–2. Traces of the S transept and apse-ended chapter house (including three tomb slabs) have been found beneath the present garden and ponds, and an 18th c. orangery preserves not only the line of the cloister N walk but also part of its NE doorway into the church. But much of the plan is conjectural.

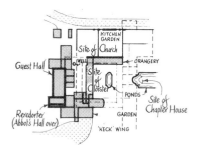

Though the public are not normally admitted, enough of the important parts of the house can be seen from the road to justify a description, particularly of the impressive W façade. The centre

part of the upper storey (originally lay brothers' dorter but later
devoted to hunting guests) now has four 17th c. windows, but below
is the rib-vaulted 12th c. refectory. At ground level the right-hand
gabled projection contained a reredorter, but above is a 'secret
chamber' and above that the 14th c. abbot's or guest chamber which
has a fine arch-braced roof with carved detail as well as a restored
(reticulated) window and, on its return side, four tiny arrow-slits
which indicate an earlier defensive use; the balancing gable on the
left is an 18th c. invention. At the outer ends are three-bay 18th c.
extensions; the church site returns behind the left-hand one; the
other is the end of Keck's S wing of *c*.1780.

Forde Dorset: ST 359052
3 miles SE of Chard and 2 miles S of A30

Cistercian abbey of the Blessed Virgin Mary founded at Brightley,
    Devon by Richard fitzBaldwin, a daughter house of Waverley;
    moved to Forde (itself formerly in Devon) 1141. Dissolved 1539
    and granted to Richard Pollard

Owned by Roper family. Open Sundays and Wednesdays from May
    to September inclusive, 2.0 to 6.0 p.m.; also Easter Sunday and
    Bank holidays. Admission charge

The monastery is or was of two main periods: the 12th and 13th cc.,
of which the chapter house and dorter range respectively are the
chief survivals, and the early 16th c. when Abbot Chard built
himself a new 'lodging' with hall and porch of uncommon
magnificence and began in the N walk the rebuilding of the cloister
(which was N of the church). The 13th c. refectory, altered in the
15th c., remains too.
    More than a century after the Dissolution the abbot's house and
N and E ranges were remodelled as a mansion by Edmund
Prideaux. Anything left of the church was completely removed, the
E and W ranges were curtailed, and the chapter house made into a
chapel. The abbot's hall was kept, and the rooms around, at two
and three levels, altered and adapted with lavish woodwork and
plasterwork in the mid-17th c. fashion. The entire dorter range was
kept for servants' rooms and stores, and the refectory became a
library. The Gwyn family made minor changes during their tenure
from 1734 to 1846.

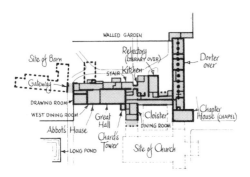

Coming from the E, the approach is past the chapter house (now chapel with bell cupola) – severed from the sacristy and from the church, which stood where now is lawn. Facing the lawn is the N walk of the cloister, early 16th c.; the other three walks have to be imagined, and the end bays where they abutted have been parapeted and filled with tracery to match the rest (that on the right is actually a pair of wooden doors).

The W range has given way to Prideaux's dining room (now office) and saloon over, and a late 18th c. portico. In the further angle stands Abbot **Chard's Tower**, his stately three-storeyed oriel porch, fan-vaulted inside and rich with carving above.

It leads directly into the **Great Hall**, mostly Chard's too, though the delicately panelled ceiling is later 16th c. and the wall panelling 17th c. From it the main stair rises directly to the first-floor saloon; both are of the 1650s (so cannot be fully described here) and are noted for their superb wood carving, panelling and plasterwork. The roof above the saloon ceiling is in fact medieval, but a series of 'State Rooms' opening out of it over the cloister is wholly of the 1650s, though redecorated in the 18th c. Behind them is the library, occupying the **refectory** which in the 15th c. was re-formed at this level within the hitherto longer and higher 13th c. one. It retains a splendid 15th c. arch-braced timber roof and the pulpit recess in the NE corner.

In the E range beyond the State Rooms is the **dorter**, also still complete but ceiled in below the timber roof and partitioned to form small bedrooms. A 17th c. stair leads down to the vaulted 13th c. undercroft, the S end of which is open to visitors, and to the inside of the N cloister walk. That has been seen from outside; the windowed arcade and the traceried rear wall are Chard's, but the

Forde: Abbey N and E ranges, looking across site of church

plaster vault (beneath the State Rooms) is late 18th c. In one bay
are 13th c. arches of the monks' washplace, and behind are the
kitchen and the lower part of the refectory, both much altered in the
17th c.

The **chapter house**, now chapel, is reached internally by an 18th c.
opening in its side wall. The two-bay rib vault, now supporting a
floor above, is 12th c., and so is the pillar piscina. The gilded
wooden screen is of c.1650, and the pulpit and 'Gothick' organ 18th
c. The principal memorials are to Edmund Prideaux and family
(erected 1704), Francis Prideaux (d. 1678) and Mrs Gwyn (d. 1808).
Outside, Norman buttresses survive, but the E window is 15th c.
and the W doorway and windows were 'classicised' by Prideaux.
The bell is 15th c.

Lastly an **outside** circuit, passing again the cloister and Chard's
Tower. Next are the four big windows of Chard's Great Hall, and
then his domestic rooms, provided in the 17th c. with classical
windows and interiors. To the SW are ornamental ponds and water
garden, originating from abbey fishponds. Against the end of the

house is a 15th c. gateway, showing on its side the roof line of a
vanished barn. The N side of the house is more informal and even
more irregular, and has some later structures against it. A line of
blocked high-level windows marks the back of the Great Hall. Then
come the 17th c. stair wing (with octagonal patterned windows), a
recessed early 16th c. porch, the porch with a tall 17th c. chimney,
and the refectory (now library above). The arches of the original
end windows of the last are just detectable; its E side, mostly 16th
c. in appearance, faces the site of the warming house. Finally there
is the long dorter block with lancets all along the upper floor and a
drain arch towards the end; its ground-floor windows are 16th c. A
transverse passage back to the E side of the house is vaulted like the
portion of undercroft already seen.

The former stable block beyond the dorter is early 17th c. and
contains a reused medieval roof.

Fountains North Yorkshire: SE 275683
3 miles SW of Ripon and 1 mile S of Pateley Bridge road B6265

Abbey of the Blessed Virgin Mary founded 1132 by Archbishop
    Thurstan; became a Cistercian daughter house of Clairvaux 1133;
    became mitred in 15th c. Dissolved 1539 and sold to Sir Richard
    Gresham

Owned by National Trust and in care of Department of the
    Environment. Open during standard hours (admission charge)

Fountains had a curious beginning, being founded by rebel
Benedictines of St Mary's abbey, York who, dissatisfied with
increasing laxity there, received the archbishop's support for setting
up an independent community in wild isolation. In a few months it
adopted Cistercian rule; after two years of extreme poverty it
received help from local landowners and could begin permanent
buildings. Thenceforward it prospered, and was to become the
premier Cistercian house in Britain. By 1170 it had colonised eight
daughter houses, including one in Norway.

Building, around a great cloister of the size existing today, was
cut short by a fire in 1147. By then the E part of the church, shorter
than now, was built; also five bays of the nave. In the second half of
the century the church was finished, the refectory rebuilt N–S in
Cistercian manner, the chapter house much enlarged, the dorter
lengthened and a new reredorter built, and the lay brothers' range

widened and lengthened and provided with its own infirmary. The church was greatly extended eastwards *c.*1210–40 and the eastern transeptal chapel of Nine Altars added; the cloister was also rebuilt and a big monks' infirmary added. Numerous alterations continued right up to the early 16th c. and culminated in the building of the great transeptal N tower.

At the Dissolution a scheme existed to make the abbey a cathedral, but Chester was chosen instead. Though ransacked by subsequent owners (for example by Sir Stephen Proctor who built Fountains Hall, 300 yards to the W, out of abbey stone), it remained more complete than most and in the 18th c. was 'landscaped' by William Aislaby as part of his Studley Royal estate. Exploratory digging and conservation went on throughout the 19th c. The West Riding County Council bought it as part of the estate in 1966 and passed it into state care; subsequently it became National Trust property.

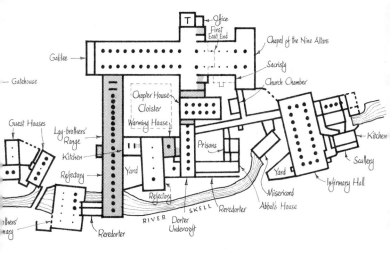

Past Fountains Hall, the early 17th c. house of the Proctors, stands the 13th c. **gatehouse**, of which only the walls of the actual carriageway stand. Now a museum, it contains a model of the abbey, as well as many carved stones and similar items.

Fountains has so much that many visitors will like to divide their tour. So the following sequence takes the **church** first, returns to the greensward at the W end (the site of the great court), and resumes there with the monastic buildings.

The church **galilee** has an open arcade partly re-erected, and is mid-12th c. like the W part of the nave. The elaborate W doorway is original, but the great window above, crowned with a niche and statue of the Virgin and Child, is of 1494; the original smaller windows can be traced from inside.

The 12th c. **nave** arcades, marvellously complete on both sides, have round columns, very weatherworn, with attached shafts towards the aisles only. The slightly pointed arches spring from scalloped capitals; there is no triforium – just a plain round-arched clerestory. The aisles still have transverse arches on corbels with similar capitals. These supported transverse pointed barrel vaults – a rare feature of Burgundian type like those of Rievaulx. The nave and transept roofs were of timber.

Towards the end of the N aisle the windows began (c.1500) to be converted to Perpendicular. At that time the N transept was opened into the new **tower** by a gigantic arch, and the two E chapel arches were blocked to strengthen it. With the transept roof gone, this 160-foot tower is all the more impressive. Its top stage, looking now rather an afterthought, was meant to finish with a system of pinnacles. Latin inscriptions appear on the string courses and several of the many niches still have their statues of saints. Building of this tower followed attempts to heighten the central one – abandoned when its piers began to give way.

The **presbytery** arcades have all gone. Here the 13th c. work begins – marked for instance by trefoil-headed wall-arcading which continues all round the E end, but marred by the robbing of all the Nidderdale 'marble' shafts, North of England equivalent of Purbeck. The aisle windows are lancets, with awkward blind arches at the sides to fit the vaults. At the presbytery entrance is the indent of a large brass of a 15th c. abbot, and on the N side a stone coffin. Patterned tiles at two levels (probably a restoration) mark the high altar site.

The E transept, the **chapel of Nine Altars,** was the model for that at Durham. Its astonishingly high arcades rest on columns nearly 50 feet high, originally also with attached shafts. Here the window system is of tall lancets with blanks between, and above them a clerestory passageway lit by single lancets under big arches. Fascinating details survive, like the angel flying through a window head (E end of N side) and remains of the altars and their piscinae and aumbries. The bigger windows are of course late 15th c.

Fountains: 12th c. W entrance to church

improvements; then too the vaults gave way to a timber roof.

As on the N, the **S transept** originally had three vaulted chapels. The outer one is remarkably complete. The second has a 15th c. extension and contains a 14th c. knight's effigy (not in its original place), while the arch to the third became the opening into the 13th c. presbytery aisle. The dorter doorway is high in the S wall of the transept, and remains of an earlier one can be seen lower down. The night stair below has gone.

Near the W end of the **S aisle** is another night stair doorway, that of the lay brothers whose quire occupied most of the nave. In their time the aisles were almost entirely walled off as passages, the subdivision into chapels being later.

Now the second and major part of the tour, commencing S of the gatehouse with the two-arched 13th c. mill bridge over the Skell. The water-mill itself, a little way upstream behind the modern restaurant and largely medieval too, is not open to visitors.

Along the river bank were **guest houses**, and ruins of two remain. The nearer is L-shaped, the wing by the river being late 12th c. and the rest 13th; fireplaces and traces of vaults can be seen. The further one, better preserved, is mostly late 12th c. and has clustered column bases as well as corbels and vault springers; a circular window at the N end is blocked by a later flue. At the S a privy and drain connect to the river near another bridge – reached only by going out of the guest house and round it. It leads to the dug-out foundations of the bakehouse and behind that the malthouse – difficult to interpret but with traces of kneading troughs and ovens.

Back now to the river and the late 12th c. **lay brothers' infirmary** which stood over the four-arched tunnel seen from the bridge. Its late Romanesque front stands high, with central doorway and round-arched windows. The contemporary two-bay facing block, also built over the river, is the lay brothers' reredorter. At the N end (towards the church) the infirmary hall can be entered, but it has little to show but a few column bases.

The long W-facing **lay brothers' range**, which is such a prominent feature of the abbey, is next. Near the middle is a doorway into its marvellous vaulted undercroft, no fewer than 22 bays on low piers with the rib-vault mouldings carried right down to their bases. It is the largest such building in Europe and although so consistent in design is actually of three periods. The oldest part (early 12th c.) is that alongside the cloister and extends for thirteen bays. First it was nearly doubled in width by rebuilding the W wall further out, and then (c.1190) it was lengthened by nine bays, which involved

carrying it across the river. This last part has pointed windows. The
lay brothers' dorter occupied the entire upper floor and only lacks
its roof; it is not open to visitors. Here the windows are uniformly
round-headed, an interesting instance of deliberate copying of
detail by then out of fashion. The day stair passes above the
cellarer's office projecting from the W face, while the night stair led
straight into the church, supported on cross-walls at that end. Other
cross-walls formerly divided off the refectory, parlour and other
rooms.

Into the **cloister** now – impressively large, the more so through
the entire loss of its walkways, which had open arcades on twin
colonettes. The octagonal basin in the centre is not in its original
position and its purpose is unknown. On the further side are the
three arches of the chapter house (c.1170) and that of the parlour
adjoining. On the right (S) is the refectory entrance, similarly
round-headed though rather later, with washing troughs each side,
and near the SW corner an arch to the kitchen. The lay brothers'
range forms the W side, broken up by piers and with upper (dorter)
windows only. On the N is the church nave (c.1140), plain too with
flat piers. Aisle windows and vault have almost gone, but the plain
clerestory is visible, a contrast with the ambitious tower beyond. To
the right of that the S transept comes forward, its gable indicating
how the first floor dorter was heightened.

The cloister buildings can now be examined in detail, starting
with the **kitchen** at the SW. Traces are visible of its vaults, central
hearths and drainage channel. More interesting is the opening into
the refectory which seems to have been a service hatch not unlike a
modern revolving door. The **refectory** itself was – and still is – a
magnificent hall built over the river at its far end and so wide that it
had a central arcade and twin gables. Shafted lancet windows
confirm its date as c.1200. The pulpit stair is complete, and the big
bracket on which the pulpit stood. Openings allowed heat to enter
from the **warming room**. That, still vaulted like the lay brothers'
undercroft, has two giant fireplaces (one blocked, the other with
modern wooden supports) with extraordinarily wide flat stone
arches with joggle joints. Behind on the left is a fuel store.

Back in the cloister, there is a towel recess; then the wide shallow
day stair to the dorter on its left. On the right at the top of this (but
not open to the public) is the muniment room, also still vaulted,
used up to the 19th c. as the court room of the Liberty of Fountains.
The E range begins at the church end with a vaulted slype. The
chapter house interior is disappointing after the splendid triple-

arched façade: there only remain column bases of the two former arcades, round-headed windows, springers of the vaulting, the stepped seating platforms, and graves of some of the nineteen abbots buried in the room. Then the parlour, also still vaulted, is followed by the usual continuation of the undercroft beneath the **dorter**, which extended at first-floor level from the church almost to the river. At the far end on the left is the undercroft of the reredorter; the drain beside it is spanned by a big free-standing arch where it enters the river. The **abbot's house** stood on the obviously insalubrious bankside area between this and the next bridge, part of it being formed out of the original reredorter which stood further N than the final one (the three square holes in the floor were part of it). Three small rooms to the left were prison cells.

Beyond, a broad path marks the infirmary passage, which once had a gallery on top. Pieces of wall-arcading survive here and there. A branch went to the E arm of the church, with a private gallery above for the abbot's use.

The main passage passes on the right the conduit house (with an uneven stone floor) and leads across a flatter area to what was the broad aisled hall of the **infirmary** (c.1230); an extra column centrally at each end shows that this had an ambulatory all round. Near the S end some columns have been re-erected – circular with four attached 'marble' shafts. Against the E end in sequence are: a group of complex chambers of uncertain use (one may have been a dispensary), chapel with raised dais, a yard, and a kitchen with drain holes into the river and two big hearths. The entire infirmary block was built over the river, after it had first been canalised into four stone tunnels.

Back now across the infirmary, noting the many old floor tiles. On the W side at an angle to other structures is the foundation of the misericord. From here it is worth going a short way up the wooded track to the S to enjoy the general view towards the chapter house and tower.

Walk next around the E and N sides of the church, past the E chapels and the great 15th c. nine-light E window, and notice again the tall slender columns just inside. In the grass below the E wall are the few surviving grave slabs of the cemetery, which was reached by the fine doorway at the N end of the E transept (balancing that to the infirmary passage). The way leads on round the tower, past the N aisle with its blocked doorway, and back to the W front.

At this point, with the layout freshly in one's mind, it is very rewarding to look again at the model in the gatehouse.

The **precinct** comprised about 70 acres. Much of its wall survives along the S side of the valley, and the W part, facing the car park and along the road towards Markington, can be seen for over ¼ mile.

Furness Cumbria: SD 218717
between Barrow and Dalton, close to E side of A590

Savigniac abbey of St Mary founded 1124 at Tulketh near Preston
  by King Stephen when Count of Boulogne; moved to Furness
  1126; became Cistercian 1147. Dissolved 1537 and granted to
  Thomas Cromwell

In care of Department of the Environment. Open during standard
  hours (admission charge)

Amongst the Cistercian abbeys, Furness was second in wealth to Fountains, and in precedence second to Waverley (for, though founded first, it had begun as Savigniac). By 1200 the Cistercians had greatly extended the Savigniac buildings, rebuilding the church, the W range (for lay brothers), the refectory (in a N–S direction instead of E–W) and the great gatehouse. During the 13th c. the E cloister range was mostly rebuilt with a big new chapter house and much extended dorter, the refectory enlarged, and the lay brothers' quarters extended. A detached infirmary was also erected to the SE, with a separate octagonal kitchen; this was fairly soon replaced by a much bigger one and itself converted into an abbot's house. About 1500 a very large W tower was begun, following an unsuccessful attempt to build a central one; it was almost certainly never finished.

A 16th c. owner, John Preston, built a manor house on the site of the abbey outbuildings near the gatehouse. This gave way to a 19th c. hotel, itself now mostly replaced by the Abbey Tavern. Large parts of the main buildings, in what was a fairly isolated spot before Barrow was developed, survived with the exception of the S monastic range; they were passed to the Office of Works by Lord Richard Cavendish in 1923.

The shape of the rocky hollow in which the abbey stands dictated its general layout and endowed the red ruin with a setting hardly equalled in Britain. The ticket hut, a splendid vantage point, looks

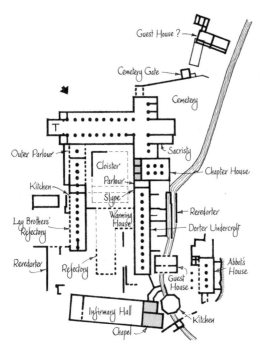

down on the enormous unfinished tower, the nave (column bases
only), the crossing piers and nearby complete transepts, and the
cloister with its unusually long E range.

Down in the **nave**, the late 12th c. columns can be seen to have
been alternately round and clustered. The gigantic tower arch piers
(*c.* 1500) stand complete, and the start of the arch itself. It was built
within the nave, curtailing the aisles by a bay. An upper doorway
near the W end of the fairly complete S aisle wall led to the lay
brothers' dormitory, but the recess below is unexplained; at the E
end of the aisle parts of the vault survive. The late 12th c. **crossing**
piers stand high too, its pointed E arch being still complete; the SW
pier has 15th c. stone panels, associated with the strengthening done
when a central bell-tower was attempted.

The **N transept** gives a fuller idea of the design of the whole:
Transitional arcades on clustered columns, triforium with plate
tracery, and altered (15th c.) clerestory and other windows. Little is

left of the three E chapels, but the right one has a pillar piscina. The **presbytery** was lavishly rebuilt in the 15th c. but blocked arches in the side walls indicate Norman work retained in its W part. The high altar base stands, and on the S are a superb group of piscina and four sedilia, amongst the finest anywhere and wonderfully preserved. The piscina has a triple canopy, its side recesses being for towels. Through the ogee-headed doorway nearby is the sacristy – in effect an extended chapel of the **S transept** with its own piscina. This transept, unlike the N, has no triforium and its S window is high to clear the dorter roof beyond. The night stair position can be readily seen. The arch to the S nave aisle was affected by the tower strengthening work of the 15th c.

Now through a 12th c. doorway into the **cloister**, the roof levels of which are evident. On the left of the E walk are, first, a former doorway to the original slype, absorbed into the S transept when it was extended; then a grand series of Norman arches, three and two, of which the actual chapter house is second and flanked by vaulted book cupboards. Above, a very long line of lancet windows lit the dorter. The **chapter house** behind the arches is itself 13th c. and so is its outer lobby with wall-arcading. Some lengths of delicate clustered columns have been re-erected, and the E end is noteworthy for its pairs of lancets with 'blind' plate tracery. Next past the chapter house is a parlour; then a slype which leads to two channels of running water which passed beneath the reredorter. The dorter undercroft continues beyond the slype for an astonishing twelve more bays, at the end of which can be seen the infirmary.

The S range is very incomplete. Continuing S, on the right the refectory plan is marked out; beyond it with two mounds is the 14th c. infirmary hall, only the E end of which stands high. To its left are the foundations of its octagonal 13th c. kitchen, with water flowing beneath. Cross this and go up to the 13th c. abbot's house under the cliff. This was the original infirmary, and evidently had a vaulted hall. Now pass round the lower side of the kitchen (with an impressive culvert arch) and turn W alongside the 14th c. infirmary chapel which is still vaulted and serves as a museum, chiefly for medieval effigies.

Past the W end of the infirmary another watercourse (now dry) ran at the bottom of a bank. The retaining wall formed the flank of the lay brothers' reredorter. From this point is an excellent view across the claustral remains; the low foundations in the foreground are of the lay brothers' quarters in the W range, at the far end of which against the church are the two-bay remains of 12th c.

vaulting. The three wall-lines marked out at the S end of the cloister indicate its original square shape with E–W refectory, the site of which was absorbed into the cloister in the 13th c.

Now make for the **tower** and walk round its W side. Low walls, the original aisle-ends, show how it was inserted into the earlier structure but never finished and tidied up. The sheer size, too, suggests that no more was built than now exists, for the difficulties of dismantling would have been considerable. Space prevented its being built further W, and precluded a W doorway, but the W window was once magnificent. Along the N side of the church the principal feature yet to be noted is the splendid round-headed doorway to the N transept. This had a porch outside. To the NE stands the arch of the cemetery gate, and a complex set of foundations thought to have belonged to a guest house.

It need hardly be added that fine views of the ruins are to be had from the high ground all round the W side. There are several outlying structures: a small 14th c. gateway to the S on the Barrow road, the 12th c. Great Gatehouse to the N (foundation only), and a smaller one (reconstructed) spanning the road beyond, with a late 13th c. gate chapel beside it (roofless walls).

Garendon Leicestershire: SK 501199
2 miles W of Loughborough and 1 mile N of A512

Cistercian abbey of the Blessed Virgin Mary founded 1133 by
    Robert, Earl of Leicester, probably a daughter house of
    Waverley. Dissolved 1536 and passed to Earl of Rutland

Owned by March Phillipps de Lisle family. Site accessible with prior
    permission from the Squire de Lisle, Quenby Hall, Hungarton,
    Leicestershire

Very little is known of the buildings but evidence exists of 12th and 14th c. work. Parts were incorporated into a mansion (Garendon Hall) after the Dissolution; this was bought in 1684 by the Phillipps family from the Duke of Buckingham. Subsequent rebuilding in 1742 and remodelling in 1864 by E.W. Pugin disguised the fact that medieval work had survived, and when the house was demolished in 1964 and the material used as hardcore for the M1 motorway it was recognised too late. Excavations have since revealed the chapter house plan and other fragments.

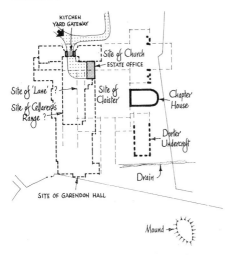

Apart from the stuccoed clock turreted archway of the kitchen yard and an isolated section of the rear buildings, the Hall site is grassed and mown. A mostly modern retaining wall defines the chapter house, about 3 feet below the present ground level. To the S, large stone slabs indicate the main drain, but the other excavated bits (of dorter and church transepts) are covered again. To the SE is a mound (like Pipewell), perhaps 'prehistoric' and probably used for an abbey windmill. To the NW is an extensive fishpond made into an ornamental lake, while to the N stands a long low barn of which the whole S wall is medieval and was the N wall of a monastic outbuilding. E of it is another, smaller; also a big square dovehouse of which the base was probably monastic.

Glastonbury Somerset: in centre of town   ST 500388

Monastery of St Peter and St Paul of unknown foundation date; became Benedictine 940. Dissolved 1539 and sold to Duke of Somerset

Owned by the Glastonbury Abbey Trust. Open from 9.0 or 9.30 a.m. till 4.30 to 7.30 p.m. according to season (entrance fee)

The fairly reliable tradition of foundation *c*.705 by King Ine became overlaid in the Middle Ages by stories of 5th and 6th c. connections with St Patrick and St David, later by legends of St Joseph of Arimathea having brought holy relics at the bidding of the Apostle Philip, and later still by the tale of the Christ Child Himself alluded to in William Blake's 'Jerusalem'. However there is ample evidence of pre-Christian occupation in the neighbourhood and of Christian burials at least as early as the 5th c.

St Dunstan introduced Benedictine rule and was buried here as abbot in 975. He had enlarged the church of King Ine, the plan of which has been traced deep below the later nave floor, and recovered. A complete rebuilding took place c.1080–1120, leaving only the 'old church' attributed to St David. Even that was destroyed in an all-enveloping fire in 1184. It was rebuilt first, in the form of a detached W Lady chapel. A new big quire and transepts were complete by c.1220, but the nave not till c.1330, all on the grandest scale. A galilee was built to join the Lady chapel and the nave. Soon afterwards the quire was lengthened, and after 1500 the Edgar chapel was added in the position of a normal Lady chapel. Of the sequence of the monastic buildings less is known and, apart from some important ancillary buildings, even less survives.

At the Dissolution the abbot and two monks were executed on Glastonbury Tor. The usual sorry story of division and destruction, quarrying and dispersal ensued. Some of the lead is even said to have been used on Mont Orgueil castle in Jersey. In 1907 a Church of England trust was set up to conserve what was left and to use Abbey House (c.1840) in the E part of the precinct. Excavations in 1908–22 and again intermittently from 1928 to 1964 enabled most of the layout to be reconstructed, at the same time providing evidence of St Dunstan's layout which it superseded.

The W end, with the Lady chapel, is approached first. Around it have been found extensive remains of burials of the 5th and 6th cc. Some way beyond is the octagonal abbot's kitchen. The **Lady chapel** is of 1184–6, very late for a Norman building but possibly so designed out of sentiment for the 'old church' it replaced. But closer examination shows Gothic detail creeping in – for example in the buttresses and the accompanying foliage carving. In the case of the gabled and many-arched N doorway it seems likely that much of the ornament was added later. It includes a number of still recognisable Nativity and similar scenes. All this, with the interlaced wall-arcades, the rich upper windows and the rectangular corner turrets, is surprisingly undamaged by contrast with the main church. In the

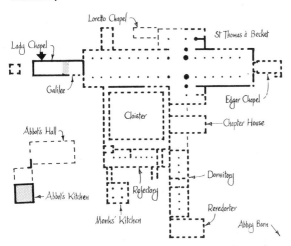

15th c. a vaulted undercroft was formed or re-formed within the chapel; it can be entered by descending the steps beside the doorway. Its floor and altar are of course modern. More interlaced Norman arches decorate the upper walls but the beginnings of the vault ribs indicate Gothic pointed forms. The arch between chapel and galilee was inserted in 1909 to stabilise the walls. In a big opening on the S side is a well which came to be associated with the cult of St Joseph; steep steps (not ancient) in the curious and uncommon 'zigzag' pattern lead outside. The wooden steps and platform however provide easier access to the upper level, from which one can look back at the triple W window, and forward through the galilee and a big 13th c. arch into the site of the nave – and then leave by the S doorway, which resembles the N but which was never fully carved. Many of the little shaft capitals here and elsewhere have been replaced by shapeless lumps of cement.

To the right of the doorway (looking from outside) the clearly incised words IESVS MARIA probably mark a prayer station. Walk now up the S side and go into the galilee, which is largely 13th c. but later in some of its upper detail. Its E arch into the nave probably contained a double doorway with a carved tympanum over.

Steps lead up to the **nave**, where the column bases are marked out in the grass and part of the S aisle wall still stands; its windows, a typical Glastonbury amalgam of Norman and Gothic, are round-arched inside but pointed outside. From the springer stones, the vault is deduced to have been 14th c. Traces of a doorway to the cloister can be seen at its W end; on the opposite (N) side the outline of the great N porch is marked out. Continue to the crossing, where both E piers stand to triforium level and connect with fragments of the **transept** E walls substantial enough to provide much evidence of the church design as a whole. As in the somewhat earlier examples of Oxford and Romsey, the main arcades and the triforium were enclosed in bigger arches – the arches themselves being pointed but the mouldings still with a lot of zigzag. The nave design is believed to have been similar, though later in the character of its details; the quire, which was earlier, was provided in the late 14th c. with a Perpendicular 'veneer' and new vault, much as was done at Gloucester.

On the W side of the N transept a trapdoor can be lifted to reveal some original floor tiles, while on the bank to its W is the supposed outline of the nearly separate Loretto chapel of c.1500. The chapel at the junction of the N transept and quire is believed to have been that of St Thomas à Becket; apart from the actual vault it is remarkably complete, even to its piscina.

Of the **quire**, much of the S aisle wall remains, as well as part of the N aisle wall (at its W end), and some fragments of the E wall of the retro-quire, which was lower. In the centre is the supposed grave of King Arthur and Queen Guinevere, with a descriptive plaque. Of the early 16th c. Edgar chapel at the extreme E, only parts of the E and S wall footings can be seen.

Next, follow the gravel path outside the S quire aisle (passing on the right a complete archway) to the S transept and down the slope to the NE corner of the cloister. The steps here led up to another door to the S aisle.

Of the monastic buildings little walling is exposed, but the square cloister can be used to establish one's bearings. If its E walk is followed towards the S (away from the church) a hollow will be seen on the left with a marker post; this is the chapter house site. From the SE corner the refectory, occupying the S range, can be identified by the column bases of its undercroft. Continuing in the same direction, one passes along the dormitory undercroft (more column bases) to the base of the reredorter with its splendidly clear polygonal drain system. Now turn W, towards the abbot's kitchen, passing on the right the site of the similar-sized monks' kitchen. Here one can turn N, towards the SW corner of the cloister, to see the other end of the refectory, before going to the **abbot's kitchen**.

The ruined wall beside it is part of the abbot's hall. The kitchen itself, late 14th c., is square with fireplaces at the corners surrounding an octagonal roof and lantern. Inside, the eight-ribbed roof is remarkably well preserved and there is an early 13th c. abbot's effigy (brought from the church). Other relics formerly here have mostly been moved to the museum.

Go now N again, past the Lady chapel, past a great oak Cross given by Queen Elizabeth II in 1965, past on the left a Glastonbury thorn tree (*Crataegus praecox*) to the tiny 15th c. St Patrick's chapel in its own sheltered corner. This can be visited; and so can the **museum** in the rambling 14th c. gatehouse (reached by continuing past the chapel by a path parallel to the entrance drive). Quantities of tiles and worked stones are displayed, culminating in a magnificent scale model by Nicholas Gaffney of the abbey as it was at its dissolution.

A tour right round the abbey **precinct** is well worth while. Outside the gatehouse (the bow windows of which are of *c*.1500) turn left along Magdalene Street, and at the end turn left. On the right after a few minutes' walk is the fine abbey barn of *c*.1500, used as the Somerset Rural Life Museum and usually open from 10.0 a.m. to 5.0 p.m. Turn left along Chilkwell Street as far as the High Street corner. In Bove Town, the lane to the right, no.7 was a

Glastonbury: 14th c. abbot's kitchen

'slipper' or pilgrimage chapel. Back towards the Market Place down High Street, on the right are first the 15th and early 16th c. George and Pilgrims Hotel (used by the wealthier pilgrims in the abbey's heyday) and then the smaller Tribunal or court house of similar date.

St Michael's tower on the **Tor** has less direct associations, but it probably marks a pre-Christian worship site and a climb to it in clear weather is thoroughly recommended. Below is the Chalice well, legends of which go back into the mists of time.

Gloucester

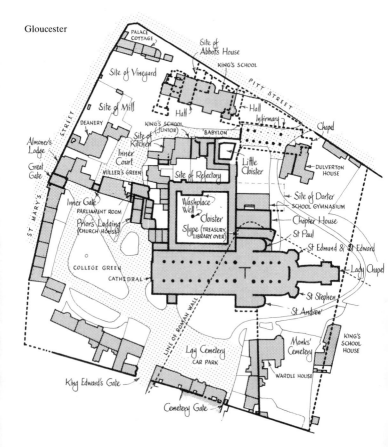

Gloucester Gloucestershire: in city centre   SO 831188

Abbey of St Peter and St Paul with abbess founded *c*.681;
  refounded for secular canons by 823; refounded as Benedictine
  c.1022; rebuilt after fire as St Peter's only *c*.1058; became mitred
  c.1400. Dissolved 1540; became cathedral 1541

Cathedral church, cloister etc. open during normal hours

For a full description see *A Guide to the Cathedrals of Britain*,
pp.175–83.

Godstow Oxfordshire: SP 483092
2½ miles NW of Oxford city centre, between Wolvercote and
Wytham

Benedictine nunnery of St Mary and St John the Baptist founded
  1133 by Edith Launceline. Dissolved 1539 and granted to Dr
  George Owen

Open at all times without charge

The abbey's immediate importance is shown by the presence of
King Stephen and Queen Matilda, the Archbishop of Canterbury
and four other bishops at the church's consecration in 1139.
Building works *c*.1180 are recorded; otherwise the building history
is obscure; what little remains is mostly 15th c. and suggests a quite
minor establishment.
  From Dr Owen the buildings passed to the Walter family and
were partly lived in. They were burnt in the Civil War and
subsequently fell to complete ruin excepting the precinct wall and a
supposed chapel at one corner.

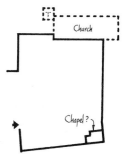

Little more than the walled enclosure is apparent, and that by no means in its original state. Walk first along the E (river) side; at the furthest corner is the roofless chapel, with several late Perpendicular windows. Entry can be gained at the W end of the S side – but there is little to be seen. A small high-level opening in the chapel shows that another building adjoined it on the N. The actual church, probably in some way double (the other half being used by the parish), seems to have been outside the present enclosure, the N side of which thus represents its S wall; the cloister adjoined it just inside.

The stretch of river alongside is in fact a new cut formed in 1780 to ease a sharp bend; this operation must have destroyed some evidence of the building layout, so making reconstruction of the plan even harder.

Grace Dieu Gwent: SO 4513 approx.
3½ miles W of Monmouth and 1 mile S of Abergavenny road B4233

Cistercian abbey of the Blessed Virgin Mary founded 1226 by John of Monmouth, a daughter house of Dore; dissolved 1536 and leased to John Vaughan. The name survives in the extra-parochial tract called Parc Grace Dieu (corrupted to Parker's Dew). The site may have been the farmstead of that name (barn with medieval fragments), or E of the Troddi brook as marked on the OS map or, most likely, near Abbey Bridge over the stream.

Hagnaby Lincolnshire: 3 miles SSW of Mablethorpe   TF 485807

Premonstratensian priory of St Thomas of Canterbury founded 1176 by Agnes of Orby, a daughter house of Welbeck; became abbey 1250; dissolved 1536 and given to Freeman family. The site, including an impossibly overgrown moated area amongst beet and potato fields, is reached by a farm track from the same point on the highway as the drive to Abbey Farm house (Willoughby Farms Ltd), and is completely unrewarding. A few carved stones have been found.

Hailes Gloucestershire: SP 050300
2 miles NE of Winchcombe and ¾ mile E of Cheltenham–

Broadway road A46

Cistercian abbey of the Blessed Virgin Mary founded 1246 by
    Richard, Earl of Cornwall and later King of the Romans, a
    daughter house of Beaulieu; became mitred. Dissolved 1539 and
    sold to Richard Andrews

Owned by National Trust and in care of Department of the
    Environment. Open during standard hours (admission charge)

Founded by a son of King John as a thank-offering following
shipwreck in the Scillies, the abbey was dedicated in 1252 in the
presence of his brother Henry III and Queen Eleanor. After a
reputed relic of the Holy Blood was given in 1270 by a son of the
founder it became a pilgrimage centre and the E end of the church
was rebuilt in the form, rare in England, of a chevet. The refectory
and much of the cloister were lavishly redesigned in the 15th c.
when the abbey's fortunes revived after a decline.

    After the Dissolution the Tracy family used the W and part of the
S monastic range as a mansion and the rest was demolished. By
1729 the buildings were farmhouses and a few years later even those
had gone to ruin. At the end of the 19th c. the plan was revealed by
digging, and in 1948 the site went to the National Trust. In recent
years numerous trees put in to mark the columns etc. have been
removed and the wall bases re-excavated.

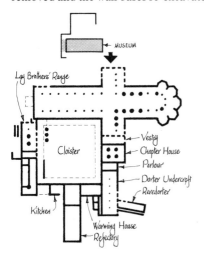

Entry is past the museum and ticket office towards the N transept of the **church**, of which only foundations are visible except for the S aisle wall. To the left is the complex chevet or half-ring of polygonal chapels formed c.1275. A central hump marks the main altar and a block of masonry further E was the base of the shrine of the Holy Blood. The chapel wall bases are much renewed but two on the S have old ashlar.

The **cloister** is reached across the S transept site. Its walks (rebuilt in the 15th c.) have mostly gone, though three arches of the W walk still stand, and so do the doorways of the 13th c. E range. The latter (the upper floor of which was, as usual, the dorter) starts with the wall bases of a vestry, entered by a doorway once double with central column and pierced quatrefoil head. The three big arches of the **chapter house** are now blank; inside are the bases of four columns which held up its nine-bay vault. Next is the parlour doorway, rather curiously showing work of both 13th c. phases as well as of the 15th c. At the end is an undercroft of unknown use, once vaulted and with the W wall standing high; towards the end, over the main drain and within the wall, is a double-sided latrine. This drain (with running water) continues beneath the reredorter which formed the usual L projection at the far end, and in the other direction can be seen in the court behind the warming room. There the hearth with its heat-reddened stone survives, also the N wall to full height with remains of vaulting.

Next is the **refectory**, impressively long but with low walls only. A set of cupboards at the cloister end includes a supposed cutlery cupboard – four little recesses formed out of one block of stone. The cross-wall may be post-Dissolution, or may represent a shortening when latterly the number of monks dwindled. On the further side are slight remains of the kitchen and its yard paving, then an opening into the lay brothers' range – low wall and column bases again, and a paved area across the centre leading to a porch. This was the nucleus of the Tracys' house; their overlaid work has been removed, leaving only the monastic. Nearer the church, on the W side, the lay brothers' reredorter stood over a continuation of the same drain as before.

The W wall of the church is reduced to a foundation, but inside the S wall are the bases of vaulting shafts. A doorway near its W end leads back into the cloister, close to the lay brothers' night stair. The three additional column bases at the N end of the W walk suggest that there was originally an open lane (as for example at Beaulieu) between cloister and W range. The big arched recesses

Hailes: 13th c. vault boss: Christ rending the jaws of Satan

along the N walk probably served as book cupboards; here too can be seen the complete disregard of the bay spacing of the 15th c. cloister for the earlier work.

In the museum some superb late 15th c. bosses are displayed, as well as other carved stones and tiles. Parts of the ambulatory were

incorporated in 1567 into the tower arch and W window of
Teddington church (5½ miles to the WNW).

Halesowen West Midlands: SO 976828
¾ mile SE of town centre and ¼ mile S of Kidderminster–
Birmingham road A456

Premonstratensian abbey of St Mary and St John the Evangelist
   founded 1215 by Peter des Roches, Bishop of Winchester, a
   daughter house of Welbeck. Dissolved 1538 and given to Sir John
   Dudley

Owned by Viscount Cobham. Open at all times subject to
   permission from farmhouse

What little remains indicates building dates immediately following
the foundation, with the exception of the abbot's house or guest
house which is later 13th c.
   Ever since the Dissolution the remains have gently decayed and
been quarried away and adapted to farm uses and they still present
the kind of wonderfully unconcerned workaday appearance once
possessed by so many ruins before being disentangled, mummified,
lawned and catalogued. Yet they are only 6 miles from the middle
of Birmingham.

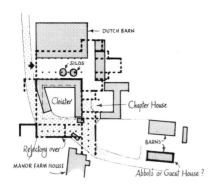

The lane to Manor Farm, just before the gate into the farmyard,
passes on the left a hay-yard with two round silos. This is the **church**
site. On the left a big barn overlaps into what was the N aisle. The

wall on the right stood between S aisle and cloister. Part of the S aisle/transept arch survives, and in the transept itself much of the W wall with two complete lancet windows, the base of the former vault, and the upper doorway (extended downwards) of the night stair. The N wall of the presbytery is also visible but not accessible from here.

Back in the lane, the stone wall on the left is part of the W monastic range, and the small byre ahead a part of the S range probably connected with the kitchen. Now through the gate into the farmyard, where three single-storey brick ranges approximately represent the **cloister**. The fourth side, with two and a half pairs of lancets, is the S wall (the inside) of the refectory. The pulpit can still just be traced.

The far wall at the end of the farmyard is of the dorter undercroft. Behind is another yard, enclosed on its N side by the S transept wall already seen.

Continue now up the lane, sometimes almost impassable with mud. The two-storey building ahead, now a pig-house, has variously been considered to have been the **abbot's house** or guest house and may well have been both. The end wall and many of the side openings are of later brickwork but essentially it is late 13th c. There are or were two small carved memorials set into the S wall inside: a 14th c. knight's miniature effigy and a 13th c. coffin lid.

Finally the broken N wall of the presbytery can be reached from here through a gate. With its bay and a half of lancets and the start of a vault it says little beyond proving an early 13th c. date.

Hartland Devon: SS 240249
1¼ miles W of town and 3 miles NW of A39

Arrouasian (Augustinian) abbey of St Mary and St Nectan founded
   *c.*1169 by Jeffrey de Dinham. Dissolved 1539 and granted to
   William Abbott

Owned by Stucley family. Open by written appointment only;
   grounds occasionally opened on advertised days (admission
   charge for charity)

Traditionally St Nectan is supposed to have set up a monastery in Hartland in the 6th c., probably at what is now the parish church. The abbey in the fertile valley below came much later. Little is known of its buildings except for a period of reconstruction in the

14th c.; this included the cloister, of which some stonework and an inscription survive.

The church fell to ruin, its last remains not being removed till the late 18th c. Meanwhile the refectory range, as well as the W one with the abbot's or guest house, had been turned to domestic use, a stable wing (since demolished) added to the NW, and in 1705 the so-called Queen Anne or SW wing adapted from an older building at the SW corner. Paul Orchard, the owner in 1779, demolished the S range and proceeded to make the E and W fronts classically symmetrical but largely 'Gothick' in style, incorporating 14th c. cloister stonework in the basement storey of both. The N end was heavy-handedly altered in 1860 under Sir George Gilbert Scott.

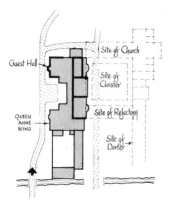

The W front, picturesquely irregular, has a contrived symmetry. The higher and recessed centre part contains reused 14th c. trefoil headed arcading in its lowest stage; the left-hand wing with its projecting bay is probably the abbot's or guest house adapted, whilst the right-hand is the 1705 wing provided with battlements and a matching bay in 1779. The E front, almost wholly late 18th c., has more cloister arcading at lower level, with an original Latin inscription along a string course referring to the work of Abbot John.

Inside, the fine suite of rooms on the main floor is evidently set between medieval cross-walls, and in the basement is the springing of an arch that probably led from the cloister walk into the W range; that, widened on both sides, forms the core of the present house.

An elaborate table-tomb from the abbey, possibly of Lady Muriel

Dynham (d. 1369), is at the parish church.

Haslemere Surrey: SU 878332
1½ miles W of town and ½ mile SE of A3

Benedictine nunnery founded at Brussels 1597 by Lady Mary Percy;
   moved to Winchester 1794, East Bergholt (Suffolk) 1857, and
   Haslemere 1947. Dissolved 1976

In multiple ownership. Not open to the public, but parts of grounds
   accessible

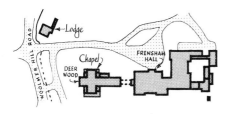

This was one of the English communities founded on the Continent
during the repression and later driven back by the French
Revolution. Its final home, Frensham Hall, Haslemere, is a large
and rambling two- and three-storey brick house of the 1890s
standing back from Woolmer Hill Road. Beside it the nuns added a
prefabricated concrete chapel. Reduced numbers forced them to
disperse to Oulton, Stanbrook, Teignmouth and elsewhere.
   The chapel, converted into a house called Deer Wood, faces the
road. Close to it is a white lodge cottage. The house stands behind
and its show front with a tall classical porch feature in gauged
brickwork can be seen from the drive. House and grounds are
divided into separate units and are private.

Haughmond Shropshire: SJ 542152
3½ miles ENE of Shrewsbury on Newport road B5062

Augustinian priory of St John the Evangelist founded c.1130 by
   William fitzAlan; became abbey c.1155. Dissolved 1539 and
   given to Sir Edward Littleton

In care of Department of the Environment. Open during standard
  hours

Something of the earliest (early 12th c.) buildings on the sharply
sloping site has been discovered by excavation. Most of the existing
ruins are later 12th c., with a N aisle and porch added to the church
in the 13th c. The abbot's hall and adjoining buildings are 14th c.,
and numerous alterations were made c.1500.

After the Dissolution the abbot's apartments became a private
house and passed to the Baker family; the church, dorter and other
parts were demolished. The house was burnt in the Civil War, but
some buildings continued in farm and domestic use until 1933 when
the Ministry of Works took the site over.

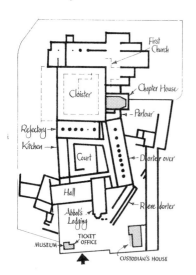

The approach from the S, through a 17th c. gateway, suggests
domestic buildings rather than monastic, an impression not entirely
dispelled until one reaches the church site beyond two more courts.
First seen, from near the ticket office, is the roofless early 14th c.
abbot's hall (attributed by some to the infirmary) and, to the right,
the abbot's lodging with a bay window of c.1500. Inside is a brick-
backed fireplace, doorways either side of which open on to the hall
dais. Inside, the hall is not unlike a church, with twin W doorways

and pointed corner turrets. The tracery of the big W window has gone. Outside, beneath this window, are the excavated foundations of an earlier hall.

Remaining outside the buildings, continue N, past the end of the hall and past the big bases of the kitchen chimneys (behind which lies the kitchen court) to the W front of the **refectory**. A small doorway leads into its 12th c. undercroft; the big window above was a 15th c. improvement to light the refectory itself. Bases of round columns remain, and on the left a wall and steep bank up to the cloister. At the SW corner are two Norman windows and some partly renewed wall-arcading. Below is a former serving hatch through which one can now pass into the kitchen to see the remains of three fireplaces.

Now up the hill on the left (N) side of the court. Across the top runs the dorter range, continuing to the left as the E range of the cloister and leading to the **chapter house** with the three rich Norman arches which are Haughmond's glory. Most unusually the spaces between the shafts were filled in the 14th c. with figures in niches. On the opposite side, also 12th c., are the two arches of the monks' washplace and the processional doorway into the SW corner of the church, the last being similarly embellished with niches. The inside of the chapter house is transformed into a 16th c. domestic hall, with richly panelled wooden ceiling (probably pre-Dissolution and brought from another building) and bay window. Many carved stone fragments are collected here. Outside, the line of the original end is exposed beneath the bay.

The **church** lay on the considerable W–E slope towards the end of the site. Little is left above ground, but once the main axis has been identified its various parts are readily recognised: the N aisle with one once-shafted 14th c. column base *in situ*, the transepts each with two chapels, the presbytery at high level, and evidence at the W end of a reduction in length at some late date. Wall bases in the S transept and within the cloister indicate the outline of earlier buildings. Near the E end two modern paving stones protect 13th c. grave slabs of John fitzAlan and Isabel de Mortimer; lower down, also covered, is that of another lady, Ankeret Leighton (d. 1528).

It is possible to return along the flat ground at the bottom along the site of the W cloister range (its former existence indicated only by an outward-facing fireplace from the post-Dissolution domestic occupation) – but more interesting to go along one of the upper terraces and look down on the outside of the E range and the drain emerging from the rocky hillside and running the length of the diagonally planned reredorter. The contours of the slope were the reason for many such irregularities of planning, and in their lower parts some of the buildings were even hewn out of the solid rock.

Holm Cultram Cumbria: in village of Abbey Town   NY 177508

Cistercian abbey of the Blessed Virgin Mary founded 1150 by Henry, son of David I, a daughter house of Melrose. Dissolved 1538 and became parochial

Parish church. Open during normal hours

At its foundation the abbey was in Scotland. It suffered in Scots raids in 1216 and in the 14th c. What is left confirms a late 12th c. date, but of the monastic buildings hardly anything is known.

The central tower collapsed in 1600, bringing down the chancel, so a wall was built across the E end of the nave. A century of neglect followed a fire in 1604; eventually the three end bays were abandoned too, the aisles removed, the roof lowered, and galleries inserted. This surviving fragment was 'restored' in 1883 and 1913, and in recent years linked by an ambulatory to two former cottages of monastic origin, so forming a small social centre.

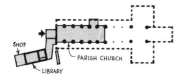

The W **porch** of 1507 covers a splendid Norman doorway of five orders, four of them with shafts and waterleaf capitals. Numerous stone fragments include tomb slabs to Abbot de Rawbankes (d. 1365) and Abbot de Rydekar, c.1434. The **nave** has six bays of Transitional arcades on clustered columns, again with waterleaf caps. The blocking walls, N and S, are of 1730, but the E window is considered to be that of c.1600, moved back three bays. Triforium (if there was one) and clerestory have gone, but the lowered roof of 1730 retains medieval timbers; its carved corbels are of 1913. The W gallery seems original, though the upper part of the wall is 18th c. Worth notice too are the Victorian royal arms, two medieval chests, some 18th c. engravings of the abbey, and the possibly 17th c. font.

The pulpit is part of an 18th c. 'three-decker'. What is now the chancel has an interesting variety of capitals on the N side; the last visible pier is cut away where the pulpitum was.

Next, the **ambulatory**, leading off the SW corner. In its walls built in the 1970s several interesting stones are preserved: three medieval cross slabs, and a long frieze of monks kneeling before the little enthroned figure of Abbot Chamber, from his early 16th c. memorial.

Finally the **outside**. On top of the 16th c. porch, a vestry was added in 1730, as an inscription says. Its windows are typical 18th c. 'Gothick'. The double bellcote is 18th c. too, but one of the bells is of 1465. The building to the SW, probably once part of the cellarer's range, has been converted into a shop, information centre and library. On its further side is a way into the churchyard, and there from the S aisle site one can look down on that of the cloisters, its W side marked by rough earthworks and its E approximately by a hedge. The present E wall of the church, with its belated Perpendicular window of *c*.1600, shows another pair of arcade piers. Further E, the crossing piers, excavated in the 19th c., can still be partly traced.

Holme Eden Cumbria: NY 472570
200 yards N of A69 at Warwick Bridge

Benedictine priory of St Scholastica founded for nuns at Fort
    Augustus 1891; became abbey 1918; moved to Holme Eden 1921.
    Dissolved 1983

Not open to the public

The red sandstone house, formerly Holme Eden Hall, was designed by John Dobson in 1837 for Peter Dixon, a Carlisle cotton manufacturer. Pseudo-Tudor at its most lavish, it has square-headed mullioned windows and stands at the end of a long drive from the village.

The vaulted entrance hall forms the ground stage of a low tower. The former ballroom, with Tudor arches and a low panelled ceiling, served as the nuns' church; its polychrome marble altar, which came from Fort Augustus, is now in a new church at Grange-over-Sands.

At the time of writing the house is being altered for use as a nursing home.

Hulton Staffordshire: SJ 905492
1½ miles NE of Hanley on Leek New Road A5009

Cistercian abbey of the Blessed Virgin Mary, St Benedict and All
    Saints founded 1219 by Henry de Audley, a daughter house of
    Combermere. Dissolved 1538 and given to Sir Edward Aston

Owned by Staffordshire County Council. Accessible at all times
    subject to permission from school

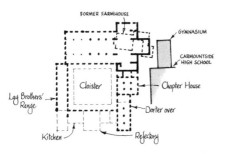

Of this abbey's building history little seems to be known. A farmhouse on the site was rebuilt at various times and in 1884 its then owner discovered the foundation plan by excavation. Several partial digs have since been done but at present only the presbytery and transepts of the church are exposed. Meanwhile the farm has given way to Carmountside High School and the abbey site is clear of other buildings. To reach it from the main school entrance it is necessary to walk right round to the other side of the sprawling classrooms. From there the ground slopes steeply down to Leek New Road and the Trent. A swift hill-stream just to the S served the abbey and its system of fishponds – which are still traceable between the road and the river.

Humberston Humberside: in village   TA 312052

Tironensian abbey of the Blessed Virgin Mary and St Peter founded
  c.1160 by William fitzRalph, a daughter house of Hambye,
  Normandy. Dissolved 1536 and given to John Cheke

Parish church, but S part of site owned by Horner family. Church
  open on request to vicar or caretaker. Monastic site accessible at
  all times

Never large, this was the only Tironensian house established in
England as an abbey. Fires in 1226 and 1305 necessitated
rebuilding, and the known remains point to 13th and early 14th c.
dates. After the Dissolution nearly all was soon demolished but
evidently part of the church remained parochial and in 1720–2 was
rebuilt. The abbey's position was forgotten until revealed by a dig in
1965–70, following trenching for a sewer across the site of the
presbytery. The area has since reverted to its former state.

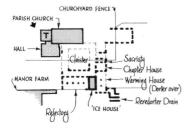

The church (now St Peter's only), classical brick with round-
headed windows and a deep gallery, should perhaps be seen first.
Architecturally nothing special, it has a memorial to its rebuilder
Matthewe Humberston (d. 1709), and within the tower the arms of
Queen Anne. The tower itself is 15th c. and therefore of the abbey:
the church rooms on its S side c.1970.
  Bearings thus established, one can go through the gate into the
small field at the back. The so-called 'ice-house', apparently a
grassy mound, was a vaulted passage from the SE corner of the
cloister. Tumbled bits of stonework beyond were part of the
reredorter drain. So the cloister lay between 'ice-house' and church,
half in the churchyard, half in the field; the chapter house was
wholly in the field. The E end of the abbey church was found (with
two stone coffins) well to the E of the present one, behind the

cottage gardens. Though of stone up to about 4 feet, the base of the present church is not medieval; a pre-Conquest stone with interlaced work towards the E end suggests however that one existed here long before the abbey.

Several carved abbey stones are in the Manor House garden and may be seen on request. Pottery and other relics are in the nearby public library.

Hyde Hampshire: SU 484302
½ mile N of Winchester city centre

Founded as New Minster for secular canons on site immediately N of cathedral 901 by Edward the Elder, son of King Alfred; became Benedictine abbey of the Holy Trinity, St Mary and St Peter 964; moved to Hyde 1110. Dissolved 1539 and passed to Thomas Wriothesley, Earl of Southampton

In multiple ownership. Gatehouse open to the public at all times

Parts of the original 10th c. buildings have been found (but re-covered) just N of the site of the Old Minster (Saxon cathedral) (see Nuns' Minster, Winchester). Their successors at Hyde, rebuilt after destruction in 1141 in the Civil War, have almost totally disappeared with the exception of the 15th c. gatehouse, though some 12th c. carved capitals (from the cloister?) are preserved in St Bartholomew's church nearby.

The abbey church site was finally cleared in 1788 for a gaol, and again in the 19th c. for small houses.

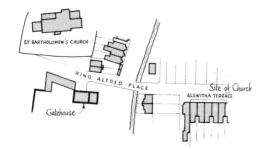

King Alfred's Place, off Hyde Street, leads to the church of St
Bartholomew Hyde on the left. On the right and facing it is the
abbey gatehouse, plain 15th c., lacking an upper storey and with a
low hipped roof. The adjacent barn (converted into a house) and
some boundary walling beyond it are medieval too. The road
crosses the mill stream; the W front of the abbey church lay 30 yards
or so beyond. The abbey mill stood a similar distance down the
stream, which is still spanned at intervals by little arches.

Jervaulx North Yorkshire: SE 172858
5 miles NW of Masham on Leyburn road A6108

Savigniac abbey of the Blessed Virgin Mary founded at Fors near
    Aysgarth 1145 by Akarius fitzBardolf, a daughter house of
    Byland; became Cistercian 1147; moved to Jervaulx 1156;
    became mitred 1409. Dissolved 1537

Owned by Burdon family. Open at all times (admission charge)

Jervaulx = Ure vale. The first abbey was further up the valley. The
second, probably begun before 1156 with the lay brothers' range
and completed by c.1220, is thus Transitional Norman to Early
English. But the infirmary is late 13th c. and there were additions
amongst the ancillary buildings to the SE up to the 15th c.

At the Dissolution the abbot and one monk were executed and
the church blown up. The buildings were mostly quarried away and
although nothing survives intact the ruins are remarkable for the
completeness and refinement of their plan, coupled with a
refreshing lack of over-tidiness.

Close to the entrance gate (reached by a field path from the road)
are octagonal 13th c. column bases laid out in the grass. These
represent the lay brothers' infirmary. To its right and parallel are
the remains of the undercroft of the main W or lay brothers' range,
not high enough to show anything of the vaulting. A path up its left
side goes under an arch that supported a link to the lay brothers'
reredorter, the drain from which runs off to the left. Through an
opening into the undercroft it can be seen again, railed round.
Continuing up the same path, on the left is a fragment of precinct
wall, and on the right glimpses through the undercroft to the
cloister. Ahead, next to the stair that led to the lay brothers' dorter,
is a delicate round-headed doorway with dog-tooth ornament,
leading into the **church**.

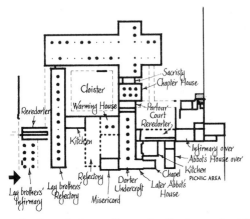

Again, only low walls survive (just enough at the SW corner to
show that the aisles were vaulted) and bases of clustered columns.
A great collection of worked stones forms the N side, and more line
the way past the W end up to a garden gateway made up of
fragments. In the turf are several cross-slabs, the best, centrally in
front of the pulpitum but originally in the cloister, bearing the name
Askarth. The mutilated effigy below the steps to the altar may be
that of Randolph fitzHenry (d. 1262).

In the transepts the stone altar in each outer chapel can be
identified. In the ambulatory E of the high altar are taller column
bases which give a little more idea of the general design. Six stone
coffins are ranged against the E wall. Part of the night stair remains
in the S transept and a shorter flight leads down into the sacristy
(once vaulted) and thence into the **cloister**. To the right is seen the
base of the processional church doorway, also a re-erected fragment
of cloister arcade. To the left is first the **chapter house**, early 13th c.:
doorway with fairly complete shafted window each side, re-erected
main columns (four of them with capitals), shafted corbels on both
side walls, step and wall seat all round, and nine grave slabs, many
of them of identified abbots. Next, with shafted corbels like the
chapter house, is a parlour which formed a passage towards the
infirmary; then another passage that originally contained the dorter
day stair and has a weatherworn doorway and various stone
fragments collected into its S wall. It leads (originally by a covered
way) across to a dwelling – either of the infirmarer or of visiting
abbots – still partly roofed and used as a store. S of this is a two- and

three-storey building, much ruined, most of which was the
infirmary. On its further side, against what is now a picnic area, is
the impressive undercroft of the infirmary hall, once vaulted. Two
of the upper two-light windows still contain Geometric tracery of
c.1280. In the SW corner the main drain is visible where it emerges
from the reredorter.

On the W of the picnic area stands the first **abbot's lodging**, much
of it to full height, with an external stair. Joist holes show that the
bottom storey was not vaulted. A trefoil-headed recess in the upper
storey marks a washplace. Another stair starts with curved treads in
the small court behind, and beyond that is the tall square meat
kitchen, with two enormous fireplaces complete with flues – that on
the N obviously built against an older wall. Round behind it is in
fact the main **reredorter** with a stone-lined drain connecting the
lengths already seen. An archway at the W end of this leads into the
dorter undercroft, at the far end of which (i.e. to the left) is the
ground storey of a later abbot's house with clear remains of a 14th c.
chapel opening off one end (alongside the meat kitchen). Altar and
steps and piscina bowl all survive. Looking the opposite way, there
is the 15th c. misericord where meat was eaten, and beyond it a big
open area from which the **refectory** has almost totally disappeared.
Where the doorway from the cloister was has been built up. From
here the line of lancet windows in the W wall of the first-floor dorter
(the tallest part of the ruins) is well seen; between is the roof line of
the warming house. Of the kitchen beyond the refectory are low
walls only, and traces of the hearth, and an opening into the SW
angle of the cloister. From here it is worth going up the W walk and
back to the church for a final look at what is left of the W front and
of a once fine five-arched doorway.

On the left on the way back to the road is the **gatehouse**, now part
of a private house. The right-hand portion is largely medieval but
entangled with later work.

Part of a screen in Aysgarth church probably came from the
abbey.

Kenilworth Warwickshire: in town, ½ mile NE of castle   SP 285723

Augustinian abbey of the Blessed Virgin Mary founded as priory
  c.1125 by Geoffrey de Clinton, treasurer of Henry I; became
  abbey after 1439. Dissolved 1539 and given to Sir Andrew
  Flamock

Owned by Warwick District Council and Kenilworth Parish
  Church. Accessible at all times

The Norman church was altered in the 13th c., the crossing being
then rebuilt and chancel aisles added. In the 14th c. the E end was
enlarged, the W front of the unusual aisleless nave altered, and a
detached octagonal tower built. Of the monastic buildings the
chapter house remained 12th c. but later additions were made
elsewhere. The guest house and gatehouse, which are substantially
preserved, are 14th c.

The property was sold to the Earl of Leicester and passed to the
Earls of Clarendon, and ultimately to the local authority who have
laid it out as a public park (except the part within the parish
churchyard). The extensive foundations revealed in an
archaeological dig have mostly been covered up.

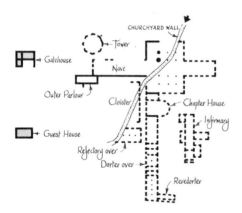

From the churchyard, the featureless mass of wall representing
the SW part of the S transept is prominent. Follow the churchyard
path and turn right towards it. The flat sunken area over the wall to
the right is the N transept, with some 13th c. column bases exposed.
The nave beyond is well defined, bounded along its N side by the
retaining wall and on its S by a much rebuilt wall incorporating
numerous worked stones in its outer face.

To the E a flattish area in the grass marks the presbytery site. Of
the monastic buildings down the slope nothing remains above
ground, so there is no point in descending further. Instead, follow

the outside of the churchyard wall, roughly along the line of the refectory, to the two-storeyed former guest house. This is late 14th c., but with the E gable rebuilt in brick and the W one half-timbered. The interior cannot be visited. Just beyond it, turn right to the 14th c. gatehouse, the most impressive part of the ruins and still vaulted. Walk through it and turn right again, back towards the cedar. Below on the right is the W end of the nave with remains of the 14th c. main doorway; the foundations beyond that are of a 13th c. outer parlour. Above on the left a squarish hole in the ground displays the outer face of one side of the unusual octagonal detached campanile added in the 14th c., and from there one can return past the outside of the N transept to the parish church.

Keynsham Avon: on A4, 100 yards E of parish church   ST 655688

Augustinian (Victorine) abbey of St Mary, St Peter and St Paul founded 1167–72 by William Earl of Gloucester. Dissolved 1539 and leased to John Panter

Owned mostly by Wansdyke District Council. Accessible to the public with permission from Folk House Archaeological Society

From what is left the buildings seem to have been mostly late 12th c., but the E parts of the church were enlarged early in the 14th c. and a N chapel added later.

Partial demolition c.1560 and c.1633 is recorded, for the purposes of restoring first the bridge and then the parish church (rebuilding the tower after lightning damage); other parts standing alongside a large house called Chandos House were demolished with it in 1776. Partial excavation was done in 1865–75; another is in progress at the time of writing, but not before the entire SW part including almost all the cloister site had been cruelly cut away in building the by-pass road. The Great Western Railway had already been cut through the precinct N and E of the abbey church.

From the old town centre Station Road leads E over the by-pass. Just beyond on the right is a 17th c. archway to Park House, into the back of which numerous 12th c. and later stones are built. A little further on is a road called Abbey Park; at the end of this on the right are, first, a large private garden in which part of a 15th c. pier can be seen, and then the fenced-in excavated area.

The remains bear no relationship to existing boundaries. The best point of reference is the triangular remnant of cloister against the

by-pass fence. NW of this, in the far corner of the compound, are remains of the nave and S aisle, while in the other direction the S transept and chapter house can be distinguished. Part of the base of the aisle-cloister doorway survives, and slightly more of the aisle-transept arch and of a cloister book cupboard in the transept wall.

Kingswood Gloucestershire: ST 747910
in village 1 mile SW of Wotton-under-Edge, on Wickwar road B4060

Cistercian abbey of the Blessed Virgin Mary founded 1139 by William of Berkeley, a daughter house of Tintern; moved to Hazleton, near Rodmarton, c.1149–50 and then back; some monks to Hazleton again and then to Tetbury c.1150–4. Recolonised from Waverley c.1164–70 on new site at Kingswood; dissolved 1538 and given to Sir John Thynne. The 16th c. gatehouse (Department of the Environment) is one of the last medieval English monastic buildings and one of the few to show Renaissance detail – notably a two-light window with mullion in the form of a baluster sprouting an Annunciation lily. The lierne vault over the road has good bosses; slight remains of precinct wall and other buildings adjoin. The key is at the next-door cottage (no charge). The abbey site, now fragmented, extended down to the stream. Its layout is unrecorded, but the parish church by the gatehouse is said to incorporate stone from the Lady chapel, which it superseded in 1721, and some walling near the bridge could well be monastic. The earlier abbey stood about 1 mile to the SW and has left no traces.

Kirkstall West Yorkshire: SE 259362
2½ miles W of Leeds city centre on Skipton road A65

Cistercian abbey of the Blessed Virgin Mary founded at
  Barnoldswick 1147 by Henry de Lacy, a daughter house of
  Fountains; moved 1152 to the site of a hermitage at Kirkstall.
  Dissolved 1540 and given to Archbishop Cranmer

Owned by Leeds City Council. Open during daylight hours without
  charge; museum (gatehouse) open 10.0 a.m. (Sundays 2.0 p.m.)
  to 6.0 p.m. (5.0 p.m. October to March) (admission charge)

Almost the whole of the main buildings are of 1152 to *c*.1175, in a
late and on the whole austere version of Romanesque with flat
buttresses, round-arched openings (but pointed constructional
arches) and rib vaults. The crossing tower was heightened in the
16th c. The E half of the chapter house is 13th c., and the complex
of buildings to the SE (including infirmary and abbot's house) 14th
and 15th cc. The separate guest house block to the W of the church
and the gatehouse to the NW are both 12th c. in origin.
  The extensive remains are as complete as those of any Cistercian
abbey in Britain. After Cranmer's martyrdom they reverted to the
Crown and passed to the Saviles and then to the Brudenells, earls of
Cardigan. The gatehouse became a farmhouse and the outer
monastic buildings were quarried away, but the remainder survived
through farm usage. For many years the lane up the valley actually
ran through the length of the church, the wall below the E window
having been knocked out for that purpose. Like Netley, the abbey
became in the 18th c. an epitome of the romantic ruin, a resort of
artists and poets. In 1889 it passed to civic ownership and was
repaired under J.T. Micklethwaite. Even now public access is
limited for safety reasons, so detailed inspection has to be confined
to buildings around the cloister and to a circuit of the railed-in
perimeter.

  The blackened W front of the **church** is the natural starting point.
Its great five-ringed Norman doorway is crowned by a gable with
intersecting arcading. The two windows above were later filled with
Perpendicular tracery, now broken, and the twin square turrets
have tops of the same period. The small aisle windows and flat
buttresses are typical of the building as a whole. The church
interior, visible only through this and other doorways, is amazingly

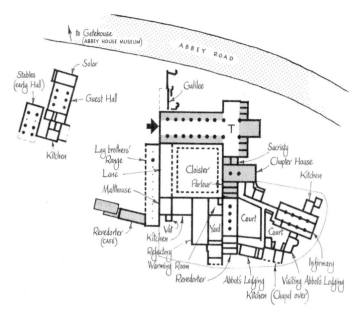

well preserved: complex clustered piers with scalloped caps, slightly pointed arches, single big round-headed clerestory windows, and rib vaults to the aisles. The nave was never vaulted and its roof has gone. At the crossing the W arch fell in 1779 but its S side is shored up with a column to prevent further collapse of the tower – which on the S and E sides survives almost to the full height of its 16th c. belfry.

Beyond the W front is the monastic **W range**, similar in general character. Its N and E walls stand (the latter with vaulting corbels and upper floor windows of the lay brothers' dorter) but the rest have nearly gone. What is now a café at the bottom end was the reredorter. A doorway in the centre of the range leads to the **cloisters** – the walls now marked out with tarmac but the arcades gone (though fragments of waterleaf capitals exist). The heavy buttressing of the W range is not original; in front of it ran the separate 'lane' or alley of the lay brothers. On the N is the church wall with joist holes of the cloister roof, a doorway at each end, and round-headed windows to aisle and clerestory all along. The S transept gable stands high, and the wall of the first floor dorter

Kirkstall: Late 12th c. church with remains of 16th c. tower top, seen from SW above the E range, two of its windows at the S end altered in the 15th c. (the ground-floor openings to the chapter house etc. will be taken later). The S range wall similarly stands to about 20 feet in height.

The church interior can be glimpsed again through its two S doorways. Opposite the SW is an unusual NW one (to be seen later), while the SE one unluckily looks into the main arcade where it is now blocked by a strengthening wall.

Now the E side of the cloister, starting with a book recess and a stair turret projection. Next is the small vaulted library, equipped in 1800 with a fireplace and a complete lining of iron slag, to form a rustic summer-house! The **chapter house** is remarkably complete. The square vestibule with double outer doorway and four-compartment rib vault is original, but the main room beyond is 13th c. and has narrower vault bays spanning its full width. Some stone coffins remain. Then the parlour, rib vaulted in two bays, with a small 15th c. window and doorway within the original arch, and beyond that the original day stair and a passage to the infirmary, both tunnel vaulted. Just past the S corner is a pointed arch which led to a later (13th c.) day stair formed out of a corner of the warming house. The arched recesses which follow are all that survive of a 13th c. washplace. The **refectory** behind may not be entered; it was drastically altered twice – first in the late 12th c. from an E–W position to the customary Cistercian N–S arrangement and then in the 15th c. by horizontal subdivision to form a misericord at lower level. A patch of 13th c. floor tiling lies across the centre.

Other round-arched openings along the S walk were associated with the first refectory, the W part of which became the kitchen. W of that, visible through the kitchen doorway, are two big Norman arches which formed a kind of gatehouse at the S end of the lay brothers' lane; this space was later made into a malthouse, which can be seen again by returning outside to the W range and looking in a side opening.

Now the S side of the abbey, beginning with the much altered lay brothers' reredorter, with upper slit windows and heavy buttresses. By the outer arch of the malthouse is the overgrown square base of the vat. The refectory is followed by a second kitchen with a court behind, and then the prominent remains of the monks' **reredorter** with part of a tunnel vault, continuing the line of the dorter range instead of projecting sideways from it as was more usual. The more complex **abbot's lodging** comes next. A 13th c. three-storey building with subsequent alterations such as quite elaborate fireplaces, it is one of the earliest and best of such houses that survive. The further part, more ruined except for its E wall, was a kitchen with chapel over, and the lower building round the corner with remains of a 15th c. polygonal oriel on an earlier base is believed to have been used by visiting abbots.

From this point is a good general view with the S transept gable, tower and presbytery. The **infirmary**, originally 13th c., clearly shows both the open aisled plan and the walls that later blocked the arcades to form smaller rooms. The kitchens projecting on the N were 15th c. A walk towards the two triple lancet windows of the chapter house reveals a view to the left into the court between infirmary and dorter, divided by the foundation of a covered way leading straight to a long flight of steps within the abbot's house. Around the E end of the church the three chapels of each transept are marked by windows enlarged in the 15th c. and by the sombre tunnel vaults visible through them. Likewise the great E window, bereft of its Perpendicular tracery, provides a view of the still-standing rib vault of the presbytery. Norman corbel tables survive at the tops of the walls, and the impressive N transept gable is complete and unaltered save for a 15th c. top window replacing a vesica. Past this, the severity of the N aisle wall is broken by one window enlarged in the 15th c. and by the Norman N doorway with its extraordinarily bold key ornament. In front of it are foundations of what may have been a galilee porch.

Of the **guest house**, 70 yards W of the church, only one upstanding piece at the NW corner remains, part of the solar or great chamber. Excavations still in hand at the time of writing suggest evidence of a timber-framed hall pre-dating the 13th c. one identified on previous plans.

The **gatehouse**, a black stone building with extensive 19th c. additions, now forms part of the Abbey Museum on the other side of the main road. The part that matters can be seen without going into the museum itself (which is not primarily concerned with the abbey) – three rib vaulted bays separated by a single big arch on the outer side and by pedestrian and wheeled vehicle arches on the inner.

Kirkstead Lincolnshire: 1 mile S of Woodhall Spa   TF 189617

Cistercian abbey of the Blessed Virgin Mary founded 1139 by Hugo

Brito, Lord of Tattershall, a daughter house of Fountains; moved
to new site nearby 1187; destroyed 1537 after execution of abbot
and three monks, and given to Duke of Suffolk; a big field
(owned by University of Nottingham) probably represents the
precinct. A track across it leads to the beautiful little 13th c.
gate-chapel of St Leonard, passing the curiously isolated
fragment of abbey church, the late 12th c. SE angle of the S
transept. Other parts are roughly traceable; undulations to SW
and N probably represent fishponds.

Lacock Wiltshire: ST 919684
in village, ½ mile E of Melksham–Chippenham road A350

Augustinian nunnery of St Bernard and St Anne founded 1232 by
Ela, Countess of Salisbury; became abbey 1241. Dissolved 1539
and granted to Sir William Sharington

Owned by National Trust. Open to the public April to October 2.0
to 6.0 p.m., but not Tuesdays (admission charge)

Ela's foundation was in memory of her husband William
Longespée, a witness of Magna Carta – a fair copy of which made in
1225 remained with the abbey till 1946. Husband and wife did much
towards building Salisbury Cathedral; he was buried there and she
at Lacock where she had become the first abbess. Most of the abbey
was completed by the middle of the 13th c. To the otherwise
aisleless church a Lady chapel S of the quire was added in the 14th
c.; numerous minor details are of this period too. The cloister walks
were rebuilt, mainly in the 15th c.
    Sharington demolished the church (leaving only its N wall),
adapted the remainder as his house, and used the church materials
to add the big Stable Court to the N. He and his successors retained
the monastic ground storey with few alterations, and its surviving
parts are as evocative as any similar remains in Britain (except
perhaps those of Inchcolm). He built an octagonal tower within the
former chancel, subdivided the first-floor refectory and dorter and
altered the South Gallery over the cloister walk. In 1754–6 John
Ivory Talbot remodelled the W range (hall and dining room), the
latter being classical, the former a 'Gothick' design by Sanderson
Miller. William Henry Fox Talbot made minor alterations c.1830,
and it was in this house that he did his early experiments and in 1835
made the first photographic negative ever. The estate passed to the

National Trust in 1944.

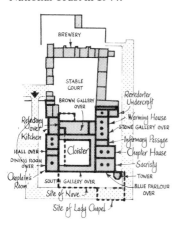

The show front seen from the drive is the façade of Miller's 'Gothick' hall, with the classical dining room on its right and monastic kitchen on the left. It is best to go past these first and round the corner to the S front. This is the actual N wall of the **church** – but punctuated by oriel windows of *c.*1830, the lawn below being the site of the church itself; Sharington's octagonal tower at the end juts into the sanctuary area. The smallest of the oriels was the subject of Fox Talbot's first successful photograph. A doorway beneath it (also inserted *c.*1830) leads into the **cloister**.

Entered thus from the spacious lawns and meadowland, the cloister (though its wide Perpendicular windows are no longer glazed) holds a fascinating medieval atmosphere. The 15th c. lierne vault (almost a fan vault) runs past 13th c. doorways in happy disregard for spacing and alignments and its bosses have a wealth of carvings. A turn to the left, past a small spiral stair that went to the abbess's rooms above, leads to a vaulted undercroft (labelled 'Chaplain's Room') with a fireplace on the far side. On this side of the square the cloister walk has gone, and in the corner nearest the chaplain's room it is 14th, not 15th c. The railed-in tombstone is supposed to be that of the foundress Ela but its actual date is uncertain.

Back now past the way in, to the SE corner. Here are a blocked doorway to the church, and the dorter stair. Off the E walk is first

Lacock: Abbey from W, with 'Gothick' additions 1754–56

the **sacristy**, a magnificent vaulted room (once tile-floored) with
one octagonal and one clustered column, a double book recess, and
a trefoil-headed doorway to the church with a stoup beside it. The
outer walls and windows all along this range were taken down in the
18th c. and conjecturally restored in 1894–1903. Next is the **chapter
house**, similarly vaulted but with a 19th c. tiled roof set rather too
high. There are some older tiles collected here, and the remains of a
fireplace put in by Sharington.

Then the infirmary passage, with pointed barrel vault (the
infirmary itself has gone), followed by a book recess and a blocked
doorway to the **warming room**, the last being now reached instead
by a doorway on the right of the vaulted parlour ahead. It is
remarkable not only for its big hooded fireplace but also for the
great cauldron of bell metal made at Malines in 1500 and for the
enormous stone tank of unknown purpose brought in from outside.
Beyond is the reredorter undercroft, barrel-vaulted again and
probably used as a fuel store. All these rooms have rough stone
paving; the stone coffins in the parlour come from various places in
the abbey.

The third remaining (N) cloister walk has little but the arched
remains of the washplace, altered when the 15th c. cloister was built
and with faint traces of paintings. The refectory stair began just
beyond.

Back now to the church site. Continuing round the outside, the
chapter house and other rooms (with their rebuilt outer walls) will

be recognised. Beyond the projecting reredorter is the post-Dissolution work of Stable Court, which can be followed round till one comes to the entrance archway. Looking through this, on the right side is the refectory range again and in the far right corner a curious single Ionic column attached to the reredorter, which ended just to the left of it. Around the court were the stables, dairy, brewery etc. built in the 16th c.

Finally the main first-floor rooms of the **house**. The hall, entered by the branching outside stair, is ornamented with wild 18th c. terracotta statues by Victor Sederbach, and by old glass of various periods. A passage from its N end leads into the subdivided monastic kitchen and then, turning right, into the Brown Gallery which occupies one side of the refectory (the rest is divided into private rooms). At the near end an original wooden wall-plate and a stone corbel head are visible. The windows overlooking the cloister are insertions by Sharington. Across the end runs the Stone Gallery, which is the E side of the nuns' dorter above the warming room and chapter house; here the windows are 18th c. The big square Blue Parlour at the end is over the sacristy and was an adjunct to the dorter, but the smaller rooms were added by Sharington outside the monastic upper wall and lead to his corner tower. Next, down into the South Gallery on top of the S cloister walk. Formed out of the abbess's chapel and a linking corridor, this was heightened by Fox Talbot c.1830 and provided with the oriel windows one of which he was to photograph. A few related exhibits are here but the majority are in a specially adapted barn by the abbey gate.

The route leads now through the spacious 18th c. dining room (over the 'chaplain's room') back to the hall. It is worth looking finally from outside at the undercroft of this, which was the W monastic range. Towards its E end a window to the chaplain's room is preserved behind an oddly contrived arch, while in the opposite direction the monastic kitchen is indicated by (restored) Gothic windows, and beyond can be seen (just inside the 'Gothick' entrance arch of 1755) the blocked arch of a store room.

Laleham Greater London: TQ 052683
700 yards S of Laleham church on B376, and 2½ miles SE of Staines

Anglican Benedictine nunnery of St Peter of Westminster founded
  1858; moved to Laleham c.1950. Dissolved c.1978

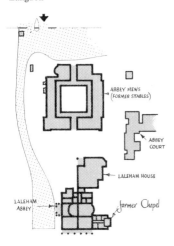

ABBEY MEWS
(FORMER STABLES)

ABBEY
COURT

LALEHAM HOUSE

LALEHAM
ABBEY

former Chapel

In multiple ownership. Exterior (only) partly accessible to public

The abbey's principal work was the care of old people. It occupied
Laleham House, the former home of the Earl of Lucan, a
distinguished two-storey white stuccoed house of *c*.1805 in Greek
Revival style, with a Doric portico facing the Thames. A chapel was
added to its rear. The yellow brick stable block, in the form of a
hollow square with a bellcote, formed a kind of cloister, a pantiled
inner walk being added.

The entire estate was converted to housing by Barratt
Developments, the house and chapel being split into flats, and the
'mews' into terrace cottages, and a separate new block of flats built
behind. Though the privacy of individual dwellings is maintained it
is still possible to see much of the exterior from the roadway within
the former precinct wall.

Langdon Kent: TR 327470
½ mile SE of West Langdon and 3½ miles N of Dover

Premonstratensian abbey of St Mary and St Thomas of Canterbury,
founded 1189 by William de Auberville, a daughter house of
Leiston. Dissolved 1535 (the first abbey confiscated by Henry
VIII) and granted to Archbishop Cranmer

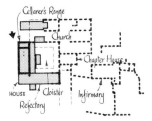

Owned by Kinderman family. Site accessible to public subject to
  permission from house

The history is only scantily recorded but limited evidence from a dig
in 1882 confirmed a building period c.1200. Probably the quire
aisles and single nave aisle were added early on, and any subsequent
additions were only minor. It is likely that much of the stone went at
the Dissolution for strengthening Dover castle, but the W and S
monastic ranges were converted to domestic use; although the
former was later given a typically Georgian modest red brick façade
it has some 16th or 17th c. brickwork at the rear, as well as the walls
and some vault corbels of its undercroft (now cellar) of c.1200 –
entered under the S end of the house. A small chamber at the N end
is still tunnel-vaulted. The E wall of the refectory stands in altered
form, the rear lawn approximately represents the cloister, and the
flattish area behind, terminating in a bank, was the church site. The
N aisle stood roughly where the big brick outbuilding is. Traces of a
gatehouse exist beside the approach lane.

Langley Norfolk: TG 362028
3 miles N of Loddon, close to road between Langley Street and
Langley Green

Premonstratensian abbey of the Assumption of the Blessed Virgin
  Mary founded 1195 by Robert fitzRoger, a daughter house of
  Alnwick. Dissolved 1536 and given to John Berney

Owned by Allhusen family. Accessible during normal hours subject
  to permission from farmhouse adjacent

The original, early 13th c. buildings seem to have been little altered
subsequently. However a S aisle was quickly added to the church
(so making the cloister no longer square), and in the 14th c. a W

tower and adjoining gatehouse, and an outer chapel beyond the N
transept. By the Dissolution the buildings were already called
ruinous and, as so often happened, the church was probably taken
down first (though the base of some of its walls stood till last
century), and the rest went to domestic and farm use by the Berney
and then the Beauchamp families. So it remains, an interesting
group of which detailed knowledge was increased by temporary
excavation in 1921.

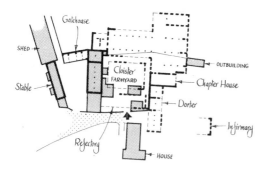

The biggest gable on the left of the approach drive is the end of
the cellarer's or W cloister range. On its left is the outer court, its
further end closed by a modern brick building on the site of the
gatehouse. Left of that is the high pointed gable of the thatched
16th c. stable block (probably pre-Dissolution).

To the right of the cellarer's range a gap in the wall leads to a yard
which occupies the cloister. Within the left-hand garage against the
W range is an arched washplace. The interior of the range has
remains of ground-stage vaulting and of upper-stage roof, but has
been extensively altered. It is thought that the dorter was
transferred to this building at a late stage in the abbey's existence.
Facing it and still with its trefoil-headed doorway and a window
each side is the 13th c. chapter house; within are considerable
remains of wall-arcading and vault corbels. On the further side of
the yard a gate leads into a field where the church was. Just inside
on the left is the W end of the S aisle with the crumbling base of a
spiral stair. The lumps beyond are the bases of the tower arch piers,
and further W was found that of the 13th c. main entrance,
apparently reset when the tower was added.

From inside the field one can look back at the N end of the

cellarer's range (the chimney on the gable possibly served a
fireplace in the tower), continuing with the inner façade of the 14th
c. gatehouse which has modern brickwork across the main arch.
Undulations in the field 300 yards further N represent fishponds.

Lastingham North Yorkshire: in village   SE 728905

Monastery founded between 654 and 664 by St Cedd; probably
    destroyed by Danes *c*.870; recolonised 1078 by Benedictines from
    Whitby. Dissolved before 1086 and moved to York

Parish church. Open during normal hours

An unusual instance of an abbey church commenced in the 11th c.
(the 7th and 8th c. remains are fragmentary), abandoned when only
partly built, and converted in the 13th c. into a parish church. The
crypt was retained, and the upper arcades reduced in scale by
subdividing each arch. The tower is 15th c., the vaults of the
remainder 1880 (by J.L. Pearson). Nothing is known of the
monastic buildings.

    The **nave** as it stands is two squares in plan and has to be imagined
without the quatrefoil-shaped columns and early 13th c. arches. The
square nearer the present tower was meant to be the crossing.
Further outwards probably than the present aisles, transepts were
planned to project from it. The other square (where the crypt
begins) was to have formed the presbytery, with the apse beyond.
Looking the other way, the W wall blocking off the intended nave is
13th c., and the tower arch (without piers) 15th c. The piers at the
corners of the squares are easily recognised as early Norman, some
with primitive volute capitals and some with simple imposts. The
clerestory and vaults (barrel to the chancel, groined to the nave) are
of 1880, much lower of course than would have been meant
originally.

    The crypt, reached by 19th c. central steps, is awesomely low with
astonishingly stumpy columns and seemingly giant capitals, a
Canterbury in miniature and in fact almost contemporary with it

(*c.*1080). It has its own nave and three-bay aisles (adding up to the width of the nave above) and groin vaulting. Carved stones ranged around the aisles include the broken head of a Saxon cross which when complete must have been larger than any other known, as well as pieces of other crosses, door jambs, etc. These are of the 7th to 11th cc. and some (in particular a 'hog-back' tombstone) show Danish influence, from the period between St Cedd's monastery and the refoundation. A moorland cross (the 'Ainhowe Cross') is preserved here too, a new one having taken its place. There is also a medieval bier; the date and origin of the carved pieces of wood on it are unknown.

Back in the church, the **N aisle** has a window by Charles Kempe, a few 18th c. memorials and an early 19th c. copy of a Correggio, by J. Jackson.

In the **chancel** the little volute capitals of the late 11th c. window shafts should be noticed; the glass is Florentine of 1880. The pulpit is also 19th c., and on the E side of one of the columns opposite is a 17th c. Spanish Calvary taken from a ship which surrendered to the *Victory* at Cape St Vincent in 1797. At the W end of the **S aisle** (which was widened in the 14th c.) are a pillar stoup and another Kempe window. The font, within the tower arch, may be 11th c.

Sheep fences make a circuit of the **exterior** difficult, but it is important to see the E and W ends. At the W, on either side of the tower, are Norman responds with big scalloped capitals. They show where the nave was to have started. At the E, the apse has shallow buttresses, a band of billet ornament at sill level, and a corbel-table with grotesque heads at the eaves. Under the sides of the chancel, big arches made possible the little windows into the ends of the crypt aisles, an unusual and ingenious arrangement.

Lavendon Buckinghamshire: ¾ mile WSW of village   SP 903535

Premonstratensian abbey of St John the Baptist founded *c.*1155–8 by John de Bidun, a daughter house of Sulby; dissolved 1536 and given to Sir Edmund Peckham.

Owned by Capel family. Accessible at all times

The site (marked merely by tumbled earthworks) can be reached through a gate at the end of the farmyard of Abbey Farm (Capel family) and is between there and the Rookery, a prominent group of trees to the E; the public footpath towards the village passes its S

side. Lavendon Grange, 100 yards N of the farm buildings, was
rebuilt in 1623, presumably on the site of a house of the abbey.

Leicester Leicestershire: 1 mile N of city centre   SK 584061

Augustinian abbey of the Assumption of the Blessed Virgin Mary
  founded 1143 by Robert le Bossu, Earl of Leicester. Dissolved
  1538 and leased to Francis Cave

Owned by City of Leicester. Open without charge at all times

Also known as St Mary de Pré, de Pratis, or of the Meadows.
Practically nothing is known of the building history. The one event
for which the abbey is famous is the death of Cardinal Wolsey there
in 1530.
  Henry Hastings, Earl of Huntingdon built a house (Cavendish
House) out of some of the remains. This in its turn was ruined in the
Civil War. What is left seems to include part of the abbey inner
gatehouse. Much of the precinct wall also survives. The abbey itself
was excavated about 1930 and low walls built on the foundations.
The church layout so marked may be authentic, but the remainder
was partly based on analogy with other abbeys and is not wholly
trustworthy.

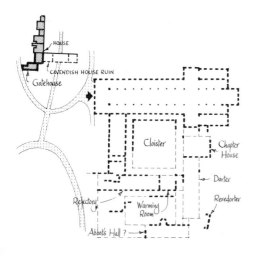

From the Abbey Park Road entrance, the shell of Cavendish House is prominent. The abbey lies to the left. From its W end walk along the **nave** and into the NE chapel where a plain modern stone commemorates Cardinal Wolsey. The **cloister** is conventionally arranged and readily identified, with the chapter house and dorter undercroft along the E walk. In the S range the warming house and refectory seem well authenticated, but the layout behind is based on very scanty evidence; the semicircular piece of wall is thought to have been a bay of the abbot's hall. The layout of the W or cellarer's range however has a sounder basis.

The mass of walling adjoining Cavendish House on its SW almost certainly contains parts of the medieval inner **gatehouse**; the domestic building to its N is 19th c.

The E **precinct** wall which can be followed along the bank of the river Soar (separately approached from Abbey Park Road) is 14th c. at least in its S part, whilst the brick wall on the W side (along Abbey Lane) is attributed to Abbot Penny, c.1500.

Leiston Suffolk: TM 445642
1 mile N of town and 200 yards W of Yoxford road B1122

Premonstratensian abbey of the Blessed Virgin Mary founded 1183 by Sir Ranulph de Glanvil, Lord Chief Justice of England, at Old Leiston; moved to new site 1365. Dissolved 1537 and given to Charles Brandon, Duke of Suffolk

Owned by Diocese of St Edmundsbury and Ipswich; ruins in care of Department of the Environment. Open at all times (except house and NE chapel) without charge

A small chapel near the coast at Minsmere (TM 473659), converted into a house, may have a connection with the original buildings. When resited the abbey must either have incorporated existing structures or made use of 12th and 13th c. worked stones transferred the 2 miles – or both. Rebuilding after a fire in 1382 is recorded, so there is mid- and later 14th c. work. A big brick porch was added c.1510 to the W range.

After the Dissolution the S aisle was made into a farmhouse and the N chapel into a barn. In the 18th c. a new wing of the house was built across the W end of the church; bought by Ellen Wrightson in 1918, it was bequeathed in 1946 to the diocese and is used for retreats and conferences, the still impressive ruins being taken into state guardianship.

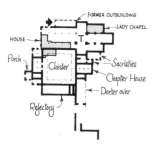

The approach is along the N side of the N aisle (its wall much altered by being built against) into the N transept and **crossing**. Here the E piers stand quite high and contain late 12th c. work, but of the other two there is little or nothing. The nave has completely

Leiston: Abbey ruin from N, with 16th c. gatehouse turret

gone too; the further side of the house marks its W front. Of the E arm much more survives. Its blocked two-bay N arcade is partly 14th c. but also incorporates earlier work. Long used as a granary, it is now a Lady chapel (not usually open). The **presbytery** end has remains of three big traceried windows, also rough holes where the piscina and sedilia were. The S chapel has another piscina recess; two doorways led to a sacristy. A still intact arch leads to the S transept, the most complete part of the church, with remains of clerestory windows. Another sacristy, reduced to low walls, is on its S side, close to a broken spiral stair; at its cloister end is broken vaulting.

The square **cloister**, now all grassed, is broken at the NW by the intrusion of the house. At the NE next to the sacristy are the three arches of the chapter house; here and elsewhere most of the dressed stone has been robbed. The W half stands quite high but the rest is no more than foundation. Then a doorway to what was a passage, followed by the dorter undercroft – wholly gone except for a distant lump marking the SE angle. At this corner of the cloister is the fairly complete day stair, with another passage alongside. Then the refectory; its floor has gone, so there is a sudden view into its undercroft – thought to have been the kitchen. A rough recess alongside the cloister marks the washplace; the refectory doorway just beyond is blocked.

The **W range** comprised the usual series of cellarer's rooms; walls of various heights are left, and some remains of vaulting. It is best to leave the cloister at the NW corner where it merges into the house with some work of c.1950, and to return anti-clockwise outside the ruins. The way passes the 16th c. brick porch (of which one half has gone) and leads down to the big refectory gable with its once fine window now devoid of tracery. The refectory undercroft can be entered; in its SE corner is the pulpit stair within the wall thickness.

The detached walling away to the SE was the reredorter, once linked with the dorter. From here the way back passes the chapter house, the E end of the presbytery with its fine flint flushwork, and the E wall of the N chapel which has the most complete remaining window of curvilinear Decorated tracery. To the right of the way out is a 13th or 14th c. granite crucifix from Brittany, while straight ahead is an ancient barn of monastic origin.

Lesnes Greater London: TQ 479788
between Plumstead and Erith, 100 yards S of B213

Arrouasian abbey of St Mary and St Thomas the Martyr, founded
   1178 by Richard de Luci; become Augustinian. Dissolved 1525
   and granted to Cardinal Wolsey's college at Oxford

Owned by Greater London Council. Open at all times without
   charge

Also known as Westwood. The foundation is thought to have been
a penance for implication in Becket's murder in 1170. It was never
large. The buildings were mostly complete by about 1200, the
church plan being more Cistercian in character than Augustinian.
The Lady chapel (S of the presbytery) was added c.1370.
   Following Wolsey's fall the property passed through many hands.
The abbot's house became a manor house and then a farmhouse,
and the rest was soon destroyed. In 1632 the estate was given to
Christ's Hospital, which in 1930 sold it to the London County
Council. Excavations were done in 1909, 1939 and the 1950s, and
the abbey remains (in parts artificially 'improved') are now a
feature of a public park; the abbot's house has not been dug for.

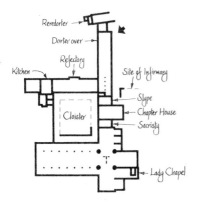

The steep slope meant that the drainage, and hence the cloister,
lay N of the church. Thus the first walls encountered on the way up
from Abbey Road are those of the reredorter, followed by the
dorter undercroft which on its W side still stands about 12 feet high.
Steps at its further end lead to the slype and thence into the **cloister**
at its NE corner. Here turn left along the E walk; on the left is the
chapter house with the reassembled base of its doorway and
reconstructed stepped wall seats. Next (seen over the wall) is the

sacristy, then a book cupboard and an opening into the N transept. Ahead is a three-order doorway to the N aisle, with some medieval tiles in the steps beneath.

Turn left into the **church** transept. All the buildings are systematically labelled. The three E chapels are well defined: the first contains a slab with the clear indent of a brass, the second is marked as the heart burial place of the benefactress Roesia of Dover, and the third has a plain grave slab. Next is the presbytery, with the altar site marked, and another grave slab on the N side; beyond it stood the big late 14th c. Lady chapel, the only substantial addition to the original church. At its E end is a curious sunken chamber with tiled floor, thought to have been a repository for relics. A 14th c. effigy found in the chapel is now in the Victoria and Albert Museum.

Because of the insertion of the Lady chapel the S transept finished up with only one other chapel. The two W crossing-piers stand 3 or 4 feet high; those of the nave are indicated by modern stonework. More old tiles can be seen at the entrance to the S aisle; also a grave slab in the easternmost bay of the nave. At the W end the main doorway is marked by a gap in the reconstructed wall. Mere traces survive of a spiral stair at the W end of the N aisle, but past the doorway on the N side are two and a half substantial bays of original wall with attached shafts.

Go through the doorway into the SW angle of the **cloister** and straight ahead along the W walk. On the left is a remarkably complete doorway with unusual mouldings, probably 14th c.; at the end is a rough recess, then various rooms of which that with the cobbled floor was probably the kitchen.

The refectory occupied the N range. At its NW corner is a small opening possibly used for serving dole to the poor. The N wall, still about 8 feet high, has clear remains of the customary pulpit, with a stairway lit by two small lancet windows. Finally the slype again, leading out to a small detached angle of walling, probably part of the infirmary.

An external circuit will add little to one's understanding; far better is to go up the steep steps into the edge of the wood for a bird's eye view.

Lilleshall Shropshire: SJ 737143
1 mile SSE of village and 3 miles SSW of Newport

Arrouasian abbey of the Blessed Virgin Mary founded *c*.1143 at
Lizard (2 miles to SE) by Philip de Belmeis and colonised from
Dorchester; moved to Donnington Wood *c*.1144; refounded at
Lilleshall by 1148 by Philip's brother Richard, dean of the
collegiate church of St Alkmund, Shrewsbury and later bishop of
London; became Augustinian. Dissolved 1538 and passed to
Cavendish family

In care of Department of the Environment. Open to the public
during normal hours as repair works permit

Permanent buildings seem to have been commenced after the
middle of the 12th c. and to have been mostly completed about the
beginning of the 13th c. The W cloister range was a century later;
foundations were also laid then for a bigger quire but funds were
lacking for its completion. The church, like many of those of
canons, was aisleless.

The usual story of partial unroofing and partial retention for
domestic purposes followed the Dissolution but in the Civil War Sir
Richard Leveson fortified the abbey for the king and the resultant
siege caused a good deal of damage. The ruin passed to the Ministry
of Public Building and Works in 1950 and subsequent repairs have
been bedevilled by coal extraction beneath the site, causing it to
sink bodily several feet. For this reason some parts may be found
closed off for safety and some foundations.discovered in an 1891 dig
have not yet been re-exposed.

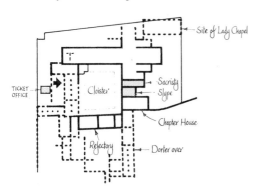

First and foremost is the magnificent shafted W doorway of three
orders, Romanesque in form but with Early English detail in its

Lilleshall: Early 19th c. engraving

capitals and its delicate outermost ring. The big pier on its left with pure Early English detail was a buttress base of a tower over the W bay of the nave. Though the long nave may be closed and its N wall still shored up, its interior may be seen through the doorway.

The W monastic range has practically gone, so its site can be crossed to reach the **cloister** with its central yew. The cloister walks have gone too; the projection into the NW corner is of a post-Dissolution porch. At the NE corner are a splendid and unusual twin book-locker with segmental Romanesque arch, and the rich processional doorway into the church, its arches, shafts and piers carved with a wide variety of bold Norman ornament.

Within the **nave** are the bases of three transverse screens. Westward of the middle one is early 13th c. building, eastward late 12th c. All was vaulted. Opposite the S doorway is a big semi-circular arch evidently intended for an aisle. E of this are remains of the N transept with its E arch also shored. The 12th c. **quire** has four round-headed windows each side, some of them blocked, and the remains of a big early 14th c. E window. The tomb recesses in the side walls contain damaged figures of an unknown abbot (N) and knight (S). The S crossing arch (to the transept) has gone except for its piers, which have fat attached shafts on corbels, but the twin transept chapel arches stand, and parts of the chapels themselves. The sacristy, reached from the transept, is still barrel-vaulted.

Back in the **cloister**, next to the sacristy is a slype, rib-vaulted in two bays and with another 12th c. doorway. Then the chapter house: the base only of its doorway and E wall, but the side walls to a fair height. The grave slabs in the floor are, as usual, of abbots. From here southwards the dorter undercroft has been traced for an unusually long distance, but nothing of it can be seen now. The S range, surviving fairly high again, starts with another 12th c. doorway and passage; the remainder was the refectory, its E half partitioned off in the 14th c. as a warming house with fireplace. The kitchen area at the other end seems to have been altered in the 14th c. in connection with the abbot's hall, which is now represented only by some blocks of masonry projecting from the site of the W range towards the ticket office.

Passing the W front again, the circuit can continue along the N side of the church, round the E end (crossing the site of the buried NE Lady chapel foundation) to the E side of the chapter house and slype. Just past the chapter house the way is barred by a part of the precinct wall, so it is necessary to return by the same route.

The 15th c. choir stalls in Wolverhampton church are believed to have come from here.

Llantarnam Gwent: ST 312929
½ mile E of Llanvihangel Llantarnam and of Newport–Pontypool road A4042

Cistercian abbey of the Blessed Virgin Mary founded 1179 by
Hywel ap Iorwerth, a daughter house of Strata Florida; dissolved 1536 and leased to John Parker. A change of name from Caerleon decreed in 1273 may indicate that there was a move to a new site. The name, perhaps from Nant-teyrnon (valley of Teyrnon) was corrupted to Lanterna. The names Vallium and Dewma were also used. The building history is very uncertain, but the Morgan family, noted Catholics, later made a house around the cloister. Rebuilt c.1830 (probably under Sir Thomas Wyatt), it contains some delicate almost rococo plasterwork and some inside walls may still be medieval. Excavations have been inconclusive; a

grotto by the lakeside is made up of medieval stones. The Sisters
of St Joseph (a non-enclosed order) took possession in 1946 and
built a separate chapel. A roofless 14th c. tithe barn stands a
short distance from the house.

London (St Mary of Graces) Greater London: TQ 339806
200 yards NE of Tower of London

Cistercian abbey of the Blessed Virgin Mary founded 1350 by
Edward III, a daughter house of Beaulieu; became mitred 1415.
Dissolved 1538 and granted to Sir Arthur Darcy

Owned by the Crown; site not open to the public

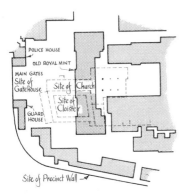

Actually in Stepney, and not to be confused with the nearby
Minoresses' abbey dedicated to the Grace of the Virgin Mary and St
Francis. A very late foundation, and hence called New Abbey, it
had its church practically complete in 1391, with the infirmary and
abbot's house still being built. By the end of the 16th c. the site had
become a naval victualling yard. In 1799 it was used for tobacco
warehousing; in 1810 it was cleared for erection of the Royal Mint
under Sir Robert Smirke. The main mint building, now disused, has
been shown to cross the site of the church, the outer wall represents
the precinct wall, and the formal gateway almost certainly coincides
with the abbey gatehouse. Excavations in progress at the time of
writing will produce a more accurate plan.

Louth Park Lincolnshire: TF 354885
1½ miles NE of Louth, near road to Cockeringtons

Cistercian abbey of the Blessed Virgin Mary founded at
   Haverholme 1137 by Bishop Alexander of Lincoln, a daughter
   house of Fountains; moved to Louth Park 1139. Dissolved 1536

Owned by Dixon family. Accessible at all times subject to
   permission from Abbey House, preferably prearranged

The site is interesting for its waterworks, the Monks' Dyke and the
now dry great fishpond being more impressive than the scanty bits
of masonry visible. Excavations in 1873 confirmed a 12th c.
character, merging into the Early English style by the time the W
front was built.

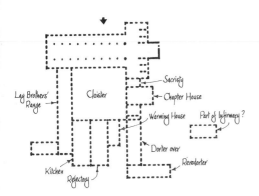

   The two shapeless lumps of wall seen as one climbs the rise from
Abbey House are parts of the sides of the presbytery. The deep
depression in front (i.e. to their N) was the fishpond, with an island
in it. A flattish area represents the church itself, with a maple
somewhere near the W doorway and various moulded stones lying
about on the site of the nave. To its S the cloister shape can be
picked out, a hillock in the central round depression marking where
the washplace was. The general ground irregularity is partly due to
excavations and partly to the rather complex system of moat and
watercourses that was fed by the Monks' Dyke about 200 yards S of
the church, bringing water from St Helen's spring in Louth. A
mound 200 yards to the W marks the gatehouse site.

Lulworth Dorset: ¾ mile SE of West Lulworth   SY 830798

Cistercian abbey of the Blessed Virgin Mary founded 1149 by
   William of Glastonia, a daughter house of Forde; moved to Wool
   1172 (see Bindon). Also called Little Bindon. The only relics are
   two 12th c. stones – a king's head and a monster – in the E gable
   of a 13th c. joined cottage and chapel near the E end of Lulworth
   Cove, part of the Weld Estate.

A ruined house 1 mile SE of East Lulworth at SY 861810 was
from 1794 the Trappist monastery of the Most Holy Trinity and
ranked as an abbey from 1813 until 1817 (see Mount St Bernard).

Lyminge Kent: TR 161409
in village on B2065, 4 miles N of Hythe

Benedictine abbey for monks and nuns founded c.633 by
   Ethelburga, wife of King Edwin. Dissolved after 964

Parish church of St Mary and St Ethelburga (or St Eadburga?).
   Open during normal hours

An early building alongside the parish church was partially
excavated in 1874. The three-apsed plan then drawn, though largely
conjectural, may approximate to the abbey church of 633. St
Ethelburga's tomb is recorded to have been in its N porticus, which
is believed to have survived a Danish invasion in 840 and to have
become part of the S wall of a new church built beside it c.965 under
St Dunstan, archbishop of Canterbury. Of his building much of the
chancel survives too. It became parochial and the N aisle and tower
are late 15th c. and early 16th c.; the two-storeyed N vestry was
added in 1971.

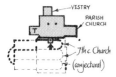

At first sight medieval, the **nave** has a tall Perpendicular N
arcade, tower arch and plain low-pitched roof. But the chancel arch
is 14th c. (on very much older piers) and the S wall undoubtedly

Saxon – with herring-bone walling in the lower parts and a
triangular-headed opening near the chancel arch. This is all part of
the 965 church, which probably had abbey status. The chancel is of
the same date and has original windows – two on the S and one on
the N. The priest's stall contains part of a 15th c. screen, the pulpit
is 17th c., and there is a medieval cross-slab by the N chancel arch
pier. The font, in the N aisle, is probably of the 1660s, with an 18th
c. bowl superimposed.

Outside, the 19th c. timber S porch spans the N wall-base of the
7th c. church – an apse of which is represented by bits of foundation
just E of it and by the line of the curved retaining wall to its S. To
the W of the porch in the outer face of the nave wall is the supposed
reliquary recess of St Ethelburga (but also ascribed to St Eadburga
or St Mildred), with a rough arch in Roman tiles (a stone to the E of
the porch marks an alternative position). The 10th c. origin of most
of this wall and of the chancel is evident from the nature of the
stonework, much of it of herring-bone pattern. The flying buttress
at the SE corner was a medieval addition.

Maenan Gwynedd: SH 790657
7½ miles S of Conwy on Llanrwst road A496

Cistercian abbey of St Mary and All Saints founded 1283 by Edward
I for the community displaced by his fortification of Conwy.
Dissolved c.1538 and passed to Wynne family

Owned by William Frederick. Site accessible at all times with
permission from adjacent hotel

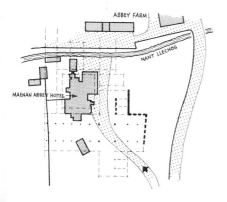

This is Aberconwy abbey on its later site, well removed from the
military operations of Edward I. Even less survives than of its
predecessor, and only in recent years have excavations tentatively
established its general layout in relation to the house formerly
called The Abbey and now Maenan Abbey Hotel. This was rebuilt
in 1848–52 but retains some cellars of its 17th c. predecessor. The
principal survival to be seen is a length of wall-base beside a box
hedge parallel to the hotel front. A spiral stair marks a turn in this
wall, at the N presbytery aisle/N transept junction. It is hoped that
more comprehensive marking out can be done. Any outbuildings to
the E must lie buried under the bank of the main valley road –
which probably did not exist in the Middle Ages. The stream on the
E was evidently bridged at several points but nothing of the
buildings beyond it has been found.

Malling Kent: TQ 682577
200 yards E of West Malling town centre

Benedictine nunnery of St Mary founded 1090 by Gundulf, Bishop
   of Rochester. Dissolved 1538 and granted to Archbishop of
   Canterbury. Given 1893 to an Anglican Benedictine community
   of nuns founded 1868 (moved to Milford Haven 1911: see
   Talacre); became St Mary's abbey of the present community 1916

Owned by Diocese of Rochester. Exterior (except nuns' enclosure)
   open during normal hours

The S wall of the church (thought by some to have been dedicated
in 1106) is a remarkable survival, and the W front (mid-12th c. and
possibly inspired by Rochester cathedral) even more so. The rest of
the church was mostly rebuilt after a fire in 1190, but only its S
transept remains. From then till after 1300 nothing is documented,
and indeed only on evidence of style can additions of c.1380–1420
be dated: the octagonal top of the W tower, gatehouse with chapel,
guest house, and improvements to cloister and chapter house. The
original E end was square with a projecting chapel, as also was
Rochester's.
   After passing through the hands of the Crown, the Brooke and
Brett families, the Crown again, and John Rayney, the abbey was
bought by the Honeywoods who built a mansion around the S
cloister walk and refectory, reusing much old material. This S walk
is within the main block of the house so that its arcade, early 13th c.

with trefoil-headed arches, supports the outer N wall. Much of the E range (with reroofed chapter house) survives, but the W range disappeared and in its place is one of the 1960s by Robert Maguire and Keith Murray. By them also are the cloister, re-formed in timber (with a new S walk parallel to the surviving one, so enabling the arcade to be unblocked) and the new church of concrete and brown tiles within the site of the medieval E end. A big tile-hung residential block to the SE had been built in 1935 under Sir Charles Nicholson, and Laurence King made minor changes to the Honeywoods' house in 1961.

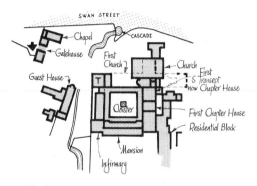

Limited access is allowed on application alongside the **gatehouse** in Swan Street. This is a 14th and 15th c. building with the customary large and small arches. At the back it turns out to be prettily timbered and creepered, with jettied upper floor; attached is a little chapel with W window of 'Kentish' tracery and simple waggon-roofed interior. The exceptionally well kept grounds, with a stream dancing through, are dominated by the venerable W front of the **medieval church** – five tiers of late Norman arches rising to two low corner turrets, behind which looms the octagonal stump of the late 14th c. upper part. The centre lower part of this façade, like a stage-set on the green lawn, was brought forward in the 18th c. The nave N wall peters out; so one can enter on this side and look up at the E face of the tower. Against it now is a lean-to structure incorporating Perpendicular windows. The S wall is original late 11th c. work with herring-bone masonry of Saxon character. On its other side lies the cloister. The N transept has long gone; the S, now the chapter house, was used by the nuns as a chapel until the present **church**, rather to the N of the former presbytery, was built

(1966). Concrete blockwork and pantiles contrast agreeably with the mature textures of the medieval work. The high clerestory, apsed both ends, that rises within the outer rectangle was daringly intended to be without internal supports, but a series of slender columns was inserted later. The visitors' entrance is from the further side where the great Norman S transept block can be seen again with two big arches on its E side, built to serve chapels but now glazed.

From further down the footpath Nicholson's 1935 residential block can be seen, three and four storeys and tile-hung. Finally the other monastic buildings – or such as can be seen – starting back by the W front. First is Maguire & Murray's **W range**, with a great tiled roof and continuous first-floor window, terminating round the corner in the infirmary, of which the three S gables can just be glimpsed, with the Honeywood mansion beyond. The dwarf wall in front is modern but defines the position of the outer wall of the original W range.

Over the stream is the 15th c. **guest house**, restored as such and with a W extension of the early 20th c. The continuous upper window here is like a Tudor version of modern 'curtain walling'. In the hall on the ground floor postcards, and cards and books written by the nuns, can be bought, while to the W extends the beautiful garden and beyond that (but private) the kitchen garden. At the far end of that and visible from Water Lane is an abbey barn, now used by a community of Anglican Cistercian monks. The picturesque cascade by which the abbey or Ewell stream emerges into Swan Street was formed in 1810.

Malmesbury Wiltshire: in centre of town   ST 933874

Nunnery said to have existed by 603; succeeded later in 7th c. by monastery of Our Saviour and St Peter and St Paul, under St Aldhelm; became Benedictine abbey of St Mary the Virgin c.965. Dissolved 1539 and granted to Sir Edward Baynton and William Stumpe

Part of church parochial; remainder in various ownerships. Church open during normal hours

Of the pre-Conquest buildings, including those burnt in 1042, there are no traces. Everything was rebuilt c.1160–70, the church with a chevet – the latter being replaced by a square E end and Lady chapel later in the 13th c.; the monastic buildings were also largely rebuilt about that time. In the 14th c. the central tower was given a very tall wood and lead spire, and another tower was erected over the W part of the nave; the nave and transepts also received a new clerestory and vault.

The central tower fell in 1479, damaging the presbytery and transepts, and was never rebuilt. At the Dissolution William Stumpe built a house on top of the reredorter, used some of the other buildings for cloth manufacture, and gave the church nave to the parish in place of that of St Paul which had also collapsed. In the 17th c. the abbey W tower fell down too, reducing the church still further in size. The principal remains are of the church nave and crossing, and Stumpe's house (Abbey House) and the Old Bell inn; excavations under Sir Harold Brakspear established the general form of the remainder, and he directed a restoration in 1900–3.

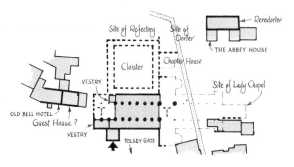

This is a fragment of an abbey. That something has been spared and preserved in Malmesbury's good fortune. That it includes the superb Norman **S porch** seems a miracle, considering the destruction and neglect that followed the Dissolution. It is this that one sees first and last. The 14th c. monks evidently treasured it, for they encased it in an extra layer of stone and built a protective extra outer arch. They also built the wavy parapet. The vault is a reconstruction of 1905. There are three separate and splendid groups of sculpture. First, in the outer archway of eight orders there are three containing Biblical pictures, the inner being from Genesis, the middle from the stories of Noah, Abraham, Moses and David, and the outer from the New Testament; the other five rings are of foliage. Secondly, the tympana over the wall-arcading inside represent the Apostles, six seated each side with an angel over, powerful draped figures which have even been compared with those of Autun cathedral in France. Last, the inner doorway, of three orders only, has unusual scrolly patterns in all of them, and a beautiful little tympanum of Christ in Majesty flanked by angels.

Now the interior, i.e. what is left of the **nave**, starting at the W end of the S aisle (the extreme W end is partitioned off as a vestry). The inclusion of pointed arches in a church of otherwise Norman character suggests the date of 1160–70 – there is no documentary evidence. Of that period are the large round piers with scalloped capitals, and the triforium with four little arches within each big one (these are all semi-circular with plenty of zigzag). The clerestory is completely replaced by a taller 14th c. one, with a lierne vault of unusual pattern forming (on plan) a hexagon in each bay. The rib vaults of the aisles are original Norman.

Along the W end are some minor wall-tablets (the church is poor in memorials) and the 17th or 18th c. font. On the N side the sixth bay is walled off as another vestry. From here can be seen the curious stone box (probably a watching chamber) added into the S gallery. The **N aisle** has simple 12th c. wall-arcading and near the end the 15th c. tomb-chest and effigy of King Athelstan (d. 940). The 15th c. stone screens are said to have come from St Paul's church in the town.

Across into what is now the **chancel**, the pulpit, stalls and side screens are of 1928, but the communion rail with twisted balusters is of c.1700. Behind the altar still stands the early 16th c. embattled stone pulpitum, bearing the Tudor royal arms in the centre; the sacred monogram in the blocked middle doorway is of course modern.

In the S aisle are two medieval stalls, another stone screen to St Aldhelm's chapel (the principal shrine in the abbey was his), an octagonal 15th c. font from St Mary's church, a chest dated 1639, and many minor monuments. The 12th c. wall-arcading has been broken into by the 14th c. windows; on the stone seat below are four medieval roof bosses. Other relics, including an early 15th c. Flemish bible, are in the little porch room reached by a stair from the aisle, but this is not normally open.

Now the **outside**, and first the E parts of the church. Turn left outside the porch, beside which is a medieval stone coffin. The aisle parapet and windows are largely 14th c., and (together with the nave clerestory and flying buttresses) disguise the Norman structure. But curious medallions surrounded the Norman clerestory windows and many of them remain. At a lower level most

Malmesbury: Late 12th c. sculpture of Apostles in S porch: W side

of the wall-arcading survives, and it continues along the remaining wall of the S transept. One can walk round this into the **crossing**, of which the 12th c. N arch still stands, as well as that to the nave. The 14th c. vaulting line above them is clear, and the beginning of the N presbytery arcade. Evidently the presbytery design was very like the nave; the 13th c. additions further E have altogether gone.

Return now to the W end. The two W bays of the clerestory were restored by Brakspear, its blind openings adding to the 'ruin' effect (it was a tower over these two bays that fell in the 17th c.). The end of the S aisle is relatively undamaged; the Norman main arcade can be seen continuing on its inner side, and the big window-wall closing off the nave. The Old Bell hotel to the W contains 13th c. walling thought to have been part of the guest house. Go between it and the church to the site of the cloister, now a public garden with a loggia (1980). Beyond it is a terrace with a rather uninspiring view over the valley. Follow the top of the bank eastwards and go through a small gate; this is private but leads to the river flank of the reredorter, a (probably much altered) medieval wall on which the 16th c. Abbey

House stands; within is an undercroft once vaulted. Continuing south along the main path, one passes the site of the vanished chapter house and crosses the presbytery site, back to the S side again.

The gatehouse called Tolsey Gate leading from the churchyard back to the Market Cross is late 18th c. and probably unrelated to the original; on the left of the path towards it is the headstone of Hannah Twynnoy, killed in 1703 by an escaped circus tiger. The stone steeple nearby is that of St Paul's church which, being itself ruinous, caused the abbey church to be saved.

Margam West Glamorgan: SS 802863
3½ miles SE of Port Talbot and ¼ mile E of A48 and of M4 at junction 38

Cistercian abbey of the Blessed Virgin Mary founded 1147 by
    Robert, Earl of Gloucester, a daughter house of Clairvaux.
    Dissolved 1536 and sold to Sir Rice Mansel

Part parish church, part owned by West Glamorgan County
    Council. Church open during normal hours, but museum only
    occasionally at times of most demand; monastic ruins normally
    only accessible through Margam Country Park (admission
    charge)

The 12th c. nave is, apart from Holm Cultram, the only medieval Cistercian one still in use in Britain. The rest of the abbey, to judge from surviving remains, was 13th and early 14th c. and is distinguished for its twelve-sided chapter house.

At the Dissolution the nave (excepting its two E bays which were of *c*.1200) went to the parish and the remainder to Sir Rice Mansel who demolished most of it and built a mansion in place of the S range. The chapter house was kept, but so maltreated (latterly as a coal store) that in 1799 its vault collapsed. Yet a splendid orangery, the longest in Britain, was built in 1787 S of the refectory site, under Anthony Keck. The house had already been demolished (1782) and was replaced (though not till 1830–5) by a 'castle' on higher ground which was burnt out in 1977, four years after Margam Park with all its buildings had been bought by the then Glamorgan County Council. It too remains a ruin.

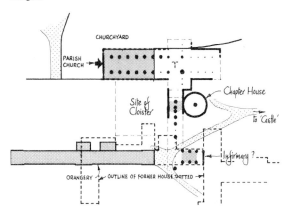

Parish church and abbey ruins have to be seen quite separately.
Sometimes the gate in the intervening wall is left unlocked;
otherwise it is necessary to go more than a mile round from the
church forecourt via the main park entrance.

The church aisles with their S walls were rebuilt on old
foundations *c.*1805, so of the W front only the centre part is
Norman – in fact only up to the base of the three windows. The roof
profile and added twin turrets produce a deliberately Italianate
effect. Over the three-ringed doorway are roof lines of a vanished
(but post-Norman) porch. The **nave** arcades are Norman too, of
great simplicity with the plainest of imposts. The plaster vaults of
the aisles are of *c.*1805, the main timber roof with big deep panels
later 19th c. The W chapel of the **N aisle**, with early 19th c. screen,
and modern hanging triptych and stained glass by Frank Roper, was
formed in 1977. At the other end, beyond the organ, is the chapel of
the Talbots, who succeeded the Mansels. Their numerous
memorials and hatchments include a big multiple one on the E wall
(a post-Dissolution blocking of the abbey aisle). The canopied
Gothic tomb is of Theodore Talbot (d. 1876).

The E window, somewhat in Burne-Jones style, is by Sir William
Lawrence, *c.*1910; the W windows, well seen from the chancel end,
are by William Morris. The **S chapel** is notable for the Mansell
monuments, chief of which are those of four successive generations,
Sir Rice, Sir Edward (d. 1585), Sir Thomas, and Sir Lewis (d. 1638)
– table tombs with effigies of themselves and their wives. Sir Lewis's
stands apart. Each of the other three, closely packed at the E end, is

coupled with a nearby tablet. Sir Thomas's (with two wives) is at the chancel end, Sir Edward's in the centre (his tablet is on the first arcade pier) and Sir Rice's on the outer side. Evidently the three were all made at one time, *c*.1610. In the centre of the E wall is a tablet to Sir Rauleigh Bussye (d. 1623), and on the S wall one to Katherine Bussy (d. 1625) with a delicate kneeling figure.

Outside the church is little of interest, thanks to the early 19th c. changes. At the old schoolhouse at the NW corner of the large churchyard, which slopes away up to the N towards the ruin of St Mary's chapel on the hill, is a small museum which houses the famous 10th c. Wheel Cross of Cynfelyn and several tomb slabs from the abbey, the best being that of Robert, abbot of Rievaulx (d. 1307).

The orangery is prominent in the approach through **Margam Park**. To its right stand arches of the infirmary or, more likely, of a passage leading towards it under the reredorter. They are of *c*.1200. Nothing is left of the cloister, but much of the chapter house vestibule survives, rib-vaulted on slender columns, and it leads into the marvellous chapter house – roofless but still with its central column and the start of its vault. Further on is the base of the S transept with two recognisable column bases of its arcade and a bigger one of the former central tower. The 15th c. NE processional doorway from cloister to S aisle also stands; so do parts of the outer walls both sides of the E end of the church. Lastly the outside of the chapter house, with noble shafted lancets and, low in the E face, a traceried circular window brought from some other part of the abbey.

Marham Norfolk: TF 707098
in village, 8 miles SE of King's Lynn and 2 miles N of A1122

Cistercian nunnery of St Mary, St Barbara and St Edmund founded
    by 1249 by Isabel, Countess of Arundel; incorporated into
    Waverley Abbey 1252. Dissolved 1536 and granted to Sir
    Nicholas and John Hare

Owned by Palgrave-Brown family. Not open to the public

Little is known of the building history. What remains is evidently 13th to 14th c. and can mostly be seen from the road – within the field rough outlines of the S half of the cloister and the adjoining ranges, and beyond the fence a considerable standing length of the

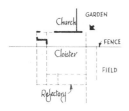

S wall of the nave. The latter, in the garden of Abbey House, contains two unusual round window openings, one sexfoiled and the other quatrefoiled. Attached to its far end the ruined parlour at the N end of the cellarer's range is identifiable, with the bases of vaulting shafts now very close to the (risen) ground level.

Meaux Humberside: TA 092395
6½ miles N of Hull and 200 yards W of Wawne–Routh road

Cistercian abbey of the Blessed Virgin Mary founded 1150 by
   William le Gros, Count of Aumale, a daughter house of
   Fountains. Dissolved 1539 and granted to Lancelot Alford

Owned by The Chamberlain Trust. Site accessible at all times
   subject to permission from Meaux Abbey Farm, ¼ mile to N (on
   Wawne–Routh road)

As Meaux (pronounced to rhyme with 'deuce') was a sister house of
Kirkstall (both were daughters of Fountains within three years) it is
safe to assume close resemblances of style and plan, which have
been confirmed by digging and deduction though here hardly
anything remains above ground. However the presbytery of Meaux
was aisled and there seems to have been no lay brothers' lane. As at
Fountains and Kirkstall the final abbot's lodging lay to the SE,
though here it was of brick and 15th c.
   The entire site was rapidly cleared in 1542 for stone for the King's
fortifications at Hull, and the only surviving building today is a
'cottage' which may have been part of the mill. The usual tradition
of underground passages led to the discovery in the 1920s of a
54-foot length of stone drain about 8 feet deep leading from the
reredorter site. The abbey well also exists. Earlier excavations
(from 1760 onwards) produced some circular patterned tile paving,
some of which with other fragments is at Meaux Abbey Farm.

Further relics are at Hull Museum, while at the cottage but not accessible to the public is a 15th c. effigy of a monk; this is to be put in Wawne church.

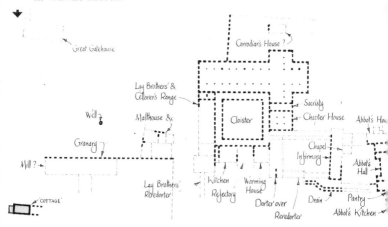

The lane to the abbey is that to Crown Farm, marked 'Private'. Past a small bungalow and just before the second cattle grid is a field gate on the left. This is on the site of the great gatehouse. At the far end of the field is the 'cottage', and on the right a hedge and a deep ditch which was the abbey millpond. The cottage has much 13th c. evidence in its stonework. The actual abbey site lies away from the millpond towards the public road, and with the aid of the plan the ground undulations can be fairly readily identified once one's general bearings have been established.

Medmenham Buckinghamshire: SU 806838
in village, 600 yards S of Henley–Marlow road A4155

Cistercian abbey of the Blessed Virgin Mary founded 1201 by Hugh de Bolebec, a daughter house of Woburn. Dissolved 1204 and recolonised 1212; dissolved 1223 but reoccupied 1230; dissolved 1536

In multiple ownership. Not open to the public

Following a chequered early history (in the course of which the founder became a monk but his son turned the community out) the abbey never achieved size or fame and at the end it had only an abbot and one monk. Apart from a piece of 13th c. column, no architectural detail survives, and the exact plan is unknown.

As so often, the church probably quickly disappeared and the cloister buildings (which were on its N side) were converted to domestic use. The E range with chapter house gave way in 1595 to an E-shaped block with central porch and projecting wings. To the S end of this (i.e. on the N transept site) a mock ruined tower was added in the 18th c. and then an open arcade facing the Thames. These were associated with Sir Francis Dashwood's notorious Hell-Fire Club. In the 19th c. the arcade was made to look more authentic; the picturesquely irregular extensions westwards from it (on the site of the nave) are of 1898 and 1911. The house is now divided into three dwellings.

Though little can be seen from its own side of the river, a good view of the S side and a glimpse of the E can be obtained from opposite. Three miles E of Henley on the Maidenhead road A423 is the Black Boy inn. Beside this a lane leads to the river bank which can be followed on foot for 500 yards upstream to a point where a passenger ferry once plied. But nothing can be seen that is monastic, or even medieval.

Merevale Warwickshire: SP 292977
1 mile W of Atherstone and ½ mile S of A5

Cistercian abbey of the Blessed Virgin Mary founded 1148 by

Robert Ferrers, Earl of Derby, a daughter house of Bordesley.
Dissolved 1538 and granted to Sir Walter Devereux, Lord Ferrers

Owned by Dugdale family. Accessible at all times subject to
permission from the Estate Office, Merevale Hall

Excavations in 1849 determined the church layout, but the resulting
published plan was wanting in accuracy. Evidently the whole layout
was of standard Cistercian type and although plenty of evidence of
13th c. work was found, nothing was identified as original 12th c.
The refectory, almost the only part above ground, is 13th c., and
when rebuilt at that time was not made to conform with the by then
more usual Cistercian N–S arrangement. The former gate-chapel
continued in use as an ordinary church and probably contains items
saved from the abbey.

The buildings went to farm uses, the mansion of the estate,
Merevale Hall, being erected ¼ mile to the SE on a hill. More
extensive walling evidently still stood up to the 18th c., when ashlar
stone was being advertised for sale.

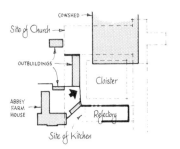

From the rear courtyard of the farmhouse adjoining the ruins a
small gateway leads straight into the W side of the cloister; the
outhouse wall running to the left represents the face of the W range,
ending with a featureless gable which was actually a part of the S
aisle wall of the church. In the other direction, however, are two
13th c. doorways; the right-hand one led to the kitchen and the left
(with traces of the washing trough beside it) into the **refectory**.
Further along is an impressive part of the N wall of the refectory,
embellished unusually with little buttresses closely spaced. Inside,
the same wall has attached wall shafts, curiously not aligned with

the buttresses. Opposite is the pulpit stair, almost complete, with two little quatrefoil openings near the bottom.

Nothing else survives. A big cowshed covers much of the church site, and ground undulations all round indicate the fishponds and other waterworks. On the W they stretch up towards **Merevale church**, which should be visited for its own sake and for its abbey relics. The key is obtainable at the gaunt stone gatehouse – designed by the same Henry Clutton who supervised the 1849 excavations.

Without doubt the big 13th c. figure of an unknown knight is from the abbey, for its right leg was found during the digging. So almost certainly is the splendid 14th c. Jesse window, which is cut down to fit the space above the altar. On the other hand the screen and other glass and memorials are likely to have been part of the original fittings of the building as a gate-chapel.

A 14th c. abbot's effigy (probably from the abbey) is at Orton-on-the-Hill church (4 miles NNE).

Milton Dorset: ST 798023
½ mile NW of Milton Abbas and 6 miles WSW of Blandford Forum

Benedictine abbey of St Mary the Virgin, St Michael, St Sampson and St Branwalader founded 964 on site of previous collegiate church by King Edgar and St Dunstan. Dissolved 1539 and sold to Sir John Tregonwell

Church owned by Diocese of Salisbury; remainder by Milton Abbey School. Church open during normal hours and historic parts of Abbey House open during school Easter and summer vacations only, 10.0 a.m. to 7.30 p.m. (admission charge)

The abbey originated in a foundation for secular canons made by King Athelstan c.937 in expiation for complicity in the death of his brother Edwin. Only one pre-Conquest stone is preserved, but many 12th c. ones are built into the existing church walls. Lightning striking the steeple caused a serious fire in 1309 and made complete rebuilding of the church necessary; it was however never finished. Very little is discoverable about the monastic buildings, almost the only survivor of which is the fine late 15th c. abbot's hall.

This hall was incorporated by Sir John Tregonwell into a mansion. That with its subsequent accretions gave way in 1771–4 to a house by Sir William Chambers whose client was Joseph Damer, later Earl of Dorchester. Damer also swept away the town which had grown up around the abbey and appropriated the abbey church (which had become parochial). Instead he built for his tenantry at a discreet distance a new village of Milton Abbas complete with church. James Wyatt and Sir George Gilbert Scott also worked on both house and church, and Capability Brown designed the landscaping. After 80 years of ownership by the Hambro family the church was bought in 1933 by the Ecclesiastical Commissioners and in 1954 the house became the nucleus of a boys' public school.

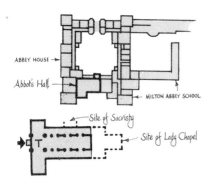

For lack of a nave the W entrance leads straight into the **crossing**. The church is almost wholly 14th c., but the crossing tower is 15th c. The architecture is particularly pure and clear, clean and light, with clustered piers and moulded capitals, and vaults throughout. That of the crossing is a fan vault. The N transept, shorter than the S, has high side windows nearly down to the floor and a great Perpendicular N window which would have made a dorter range in the normal position impossible. The S transept in contrast has a clerestory and walkway, the latter dropping to cross the reticulated Decorated main window, the Jesse Tree glass of which is by Augustus Pugin, 1847.

A heavy stone pulpitum separates the **quire**. It contains stairs to what is now the organ loft, and has a big central boss in its vault. A showcase within contains various treasures. An unusual feature of the quire is the alternation of arches and solid walls; refinement of the proportions of these has made the bay spacing irregular. The later reredos against the E wall (c.1500 but much restored by Wyatt) is little more than three tiers of empty niches. As in the S transept there is a clerestory but no triforium; the vaulting is plain quadripartite. The seating in the W part contains a dozen old misericords but is mostly 19th c., as is the low arcaded screen behind. The stone pulpit is of 1912. Turning back now towards the pulpitum, on the E side is coving with heraldry that probably formed part of the chantry of Abbot Middleton (d. 1525). The paintings of King Athelstan and his mother Egwynna on either side came from a 15th c. screen.

Through the pulpitum next, and into the **N transept** where stands the white marble tomb chest of Lady Milton (d. 1775), wife of Joseph Damer, designed by Robert Adam. Their effigies are by Agostino Carlini. The big brass behind is to Capt. Henry Dawson (d. 1841) and the shell font with figures of Faith and Victory is by a Dane, J.A. Jerichau. On the E side is a broken tomb slab of an abbot of c.1300.

The **N aisle** has vaulting like the quire, and an outer wall mostly – and unusually – flint-faced within, and some interesting ledger stones. The memorial at the end with reclining effigy is to Mary Bancks (d. 1704). To its right is the canopied tomb of Sir John Tregonwell (d. 1565) with a brass at the back; another brass in the floor nearby is to a 15th c. monk. Between the aisle and chancel is the high canopied tomb of Baron Hambro (d. 1877) designed by Scott.

In the **chancel** floor is the Purbeck marble matrix of a big brass of a 14th c. abbot. A closer look at the delicate but monotonous reredos may be had; traces of colour are visible, and the window above has pieces of 15th and 17th c. glass. On its right, the piscina and stepped sedilia are 14th c. but rather spurious, having been made from the chantry of Abbot Middleton, dismantled by Wyatt. On the opposite wall is a rare survival, a late 15th c. canopied oak tabernacle formerly in front of the reredos. The **S chapel** altar was designed by Wyatt, also for the chancel. At the back of the sedilia are a 17th c. chest and part of a medieval statue of St James the Greater. Photographs of stonework moved to other churches are displayed: the font at Milton Abbas, the pulpit at Winterbourne Whitechurch, and part of the cloister arcade at Hilton. The **S transept** has a patch of medieval tiles in the centre, and in the SE corner the surviving part of the Middleton chantry. The former organ is displayed, as well as a number of carved stones.

Now the **outside**, and first the W front, which is really the start of the unfulfilled nave: a big blocked arch to that and smaller ones to the aisles, and the completed flanks of the transepts. The porch was tacked on by Scott in 1865. Along the N end of the N transept are

remains of a vaulted passage which may have been a cloister walk –
but, if so, it could not have fitted any orthodox cloister plan. Two
further bays of former vaulting against the N aisle belonged to a
sacristy. A left turn leads into the house, into the screen passage of
the former **abbot's hall**, completed in 1498 by Abbot Middleton.
Much restored outside, it has most to show inside: a richly moulded,
richly carved hammer-beam roof with angel corbels, big windows
containing 16th and 17th c. heraldic glass, the 16th c. screen now of
rather fragmented appearance, a fireplace added late in the 17th c.,
and a big flat-ceilinged oriel bay. Some of the other fine rooms of
Abbey House may also be visited but all are post-monastic
excepting the two-storeyed porch which Chambers made into a
central feature of the inner courtyard.

Reverting to the circuit of the church, its E front next claims
attention. Five equal blocked arches here show where the Lady
chapel and other eastern chapels were joined on by an ambulatory.
Flying buttresses and a quatrefoiled parapet rise from the quire aisle
walls, and the unequal bay spacing is noticeable.

At a turn in the path somewhat E of the church is the base of the
market cross of the former town.

Minster-in-Sheppey Kent: in village   TQ 956730

Benedictine nunnery of St Mary founded *c*.670 by Sexburga;
   refounded 1130 as Augustinian priory of St Mary and St
   Sexburga; became Benedictine again 1186 and Augustinian again
   1396. Dissolved 1536; church became parochial; remainder
   granted to Sir Thomas Cheyne

Gatehouse owned by Swale District Council. Church key
   obtainable from Vicarage immediately to NE. Gatehouse open
   end of May to end of October only (except Thursdays) 2.0 p.m.
   to 5.0 p.m. (admission charge)

Not to be confused with Minster-in-Thanet where another abbey
was founded in 669 but has left no remains (the present 'Minster
abbey' there is a priory established in 1937 in a medieval grange of
St Augustine's abbey, Canterbury). The hilltop community of
Sheppey was driven out by Danes in 835 and again by Earl
Godwin's men in 1052. Re-established in 1130 as a priory, it made
use of the shell of the former church as a nave, a chancel being
added (or rebuilt) later. In the 13th c. a parish church was added on

the S, as was frequent with nuns' churches, and in the 15th c. a new tower was begun and the gatehouse rebuilt.

Apart from church and gatehouse the monastic buildings – abbey and later priory – have quite gone; it is presumed they stood to the N. The double church was restored by Ewan Christian in 1879–81. The gatehouse, long used as a dwelling, became local council property in 1967 and is leased as a museum of island history.

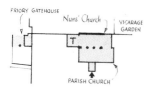

The wide S or **parish nave** is divided from the nuns' by a modest 13th c. arcade. Beneath it stands a 15th c. font with scrolled Jacobean cover. A cusped arch in the S wall of the chancel covers the tomb and mailed effigy of Sir Robert de Shurland (d. *c.*1310); on either side of the E window are niches with medieval paintings. A rood-loft opening above the arcade comes out in the N nave to the W of a wide 13th c. chancel arch. This N chancel is furnished as **St Sexburga's chapel**; on its S side under a 14th c. arch is the tomb chest of Sir Thomas Cheyne (d. 1559) and on the N a late 15th c. tomb with effigy supposedly of George Plantagenet, the Duke of Clarence executed by being drowned in a butt of malmsey. Numerous stone fragments nearby include another 15th c. knight. The E wall has a 14th c. doorway with an amusing head stop, three niches which formed a reredos (these show outside), and a window high above. As the sedilia touch the E wall, it may be that the chancel has been shortened.

The **nuns' nave**, entered through a late 14th c. screen, has evidence of the 7th c. abbey in the form of two tile-arched windows high above the arcade, blocked and hidden when the wall was pierced; one of them was only rediscovered in 1977. That the N wall is 7th c. too is only evident outside. Against it stands the organ; on either side are replicas of the famous Northwode brasses (the originals are in the chancel floor): a knight and lady of *c.*1330.

Outside, the porch is of 1881 but its inner doorway is Norman, probably resited when the parish nave was added. Building of the tower, begun on a big scale, was abandoned at the Dissolution; hence the odd timber belfry. However the most interesting part is the nuns' original N wall, overlooking waste ground and best reached from the E end. Two more blocked 7th c. windows, towards the E end and again quite high, are just traceable by their stone jambs and tile arches; E of them is the upper part of the original NE angle.

The plain solid **gatehouse** is mostly 15th c. but with 13th c. work at the NE corner of its three-storey domestic side.

Missenden Buckinghamshire:
in Great Missenden village 200 yards W of A413

SP 897010

Arrouasian abbey of St Mary founded 1133 by William de
  Missenden, a daughter house of St Mary de Bosco, Ruisseauville,
  Picardy. Dissolved 1538 and forfeited to the Crown

Owned by Buckinghamshire County Council. Not open to the
  public unless attending courses or functions, except on rare open
  days as advertised

Of the abbey buildings very little is known, save that the plan of the present house evidently perpetuates part of their layout and that the timber roof of the E or dorter range is 15th c., much later than the foundation date; so there must have been a prolonged period of development from the 12th c. onwards.

The church must have been soon demolished. The house, following several short occupations, was owned by the Fleetwood family from 1574 until 1774. A later owner, James Oldham Oldham, made alterations *c*.1790, and *c*.1810 his successor John Ayton remodelled it more drastically in the fashionable 'Gothick' style. Their architects are not recorded. Shortly afterwards the Carrington family bought the estate and it was they who sold it to the County Council in 1946. It became an adult education college, and at the time of writing is about to be developed as a management education centre.

Though a close view is not normally possible, some appreciation of the house can be gained from, for example, a vantage point near the parish church and the road to Chesham. The embattled show front facing S down the valley is on the refectory site and the E range (centred round the present kitchen on the site of the chapter house) is the part which beneath its slate roof still contains 15th c.

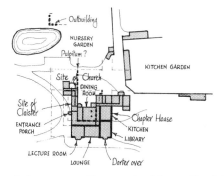

timber trusses. How much of the walling is in part medieval is impossible to tell. Parts of the cloister walks are perpetuated in the present corridors, the garth area is occupied by the dining room, and the W range is Gothick like the S; only the N side has totally changed, there being nothing above ground to indicate the exact position or extent of the church. Limited excavation in 1983 did however produce some information in the form of two N–S wall foundations. Traces of an unidentified medieval building to the N of the pond were also revealed.

Monkwearmouth Tyne and Wear: NZ 403578
½ mile NE of Sunderland town centre on Roker and Whitburn road A183

Benedictine abbey of St Peter founded 674 by Benedict Biscop; refounded as cell *c*.1075; became subservient to Durham 1083. Dissolved 1536 and granted (except church) to Thomas Whitehead

Parish church. Open 10.0 a.m. to 5.0 p.m.

Monkwearmouth's early history runs parallel with that of Jarrow. Bede writes of the 'monastery of St Peter and St Paul which is at Wearmouth and Jarrow'. Jarrow however never ranked as an abbey. Of the 7th c. church the W wall remains, with its porch raised to form a tower early in the 11th c. following a period of Viking raids. Subsequently both monasteries were refounded by monks of Evesham and Winchcombe. Nothing of the monastery is left above ground, though a little has been traced by recent excavation; parts of the buildings became the vicarage, and were burnt down in 1790. There were two other churches, of which St Mary's may have stood on the site of the present chancel, which is 14th c. The N aisle was added in 1874. The tall narrow nave repeats its 7th c. predecessor in general form but is substantially rebuilt. A 'chapter house' was built in 1973, as an exhibition and meeting room.

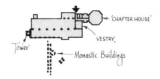

Visitors enter by the NE (vestry) doorway and are encouraged to see the displays in the chapter house before passing into the **church**. Architecturally this has little to offer except the 7th c. W wall of the nave. The doorway at the base leads into the porch, and on that side are shafts and dragon-like carvings. The next stage, supported by a barrel vault, was once reached by an opening in the N wall, but later by an enlargement of that facing the nave. Above are two 7th c. windows, originally external, blocked in the 11th c. when the top stages were added, and now partly reopened.

The chancel arch is mostly 14th c. Near the pulpit is a pier base probably of the 11th c., and beside it a damaged 14th c. priest's effigy. The piscina is 14th c. too. Another effigy under a canopy on the N side of the chancel is believed to depict William, Baron Hilton (d. 1435). Under the N chancel arcade are display cases with Saxon carved stones, including two lions (probably chair arm rests) and a possibly 8th c. cross slab to 'Herbert the Priest'. In the entrance lobby some later cross slabs are set into the wall.

Outside, the tower is by far the most interesting feature. Its unforeseen upward growth (on top of a surprisingly slender porch) has produced a rather ungainly appearance. In the churchyard to the S the excavated monastery remains are marked by stones let into the grass.

Mount St Bernard Leicestershire:
SK 458162

4 miles NE of Coalville and 2 miles W of M1 near junction 23.

Cistercian (Trappist) monastery of St Bernard founded 1835 by
    Ambrose Phillipps (later Phillipps de Lisle); became abbey 1848

Church (only) open during normal hours

The (English) colonising monks mostly came from Melleray
(Brittany), having gone there from the short-lived (1794–1817)
monastery at Lulworth in Dorset (with the exception of which,
Mount St Bernard was the first abbey in England since the
Reformation). Others went to a newly established house at Mount
Melleray in Ireland. Temporary buildings were opened in 1837;
permanent ones and a new site were given by the Earl of
Shrewsbury and first used in 1844. They were designed by Augustus
Pugin – at first, typically, on a far grander scale. Building of the
church did not commence till 1843. The chapter house (by E.W.
Pugin) was added in 1860, the original one becoming a sacristy. The
clock tower was added in 1870–1 and there were other additions
later. The church was radically altered by the addition of its tower in
1934–9 under Albert Herbert, and of a lay nave following Pugin's
design under Abbot Brasil's guidance.

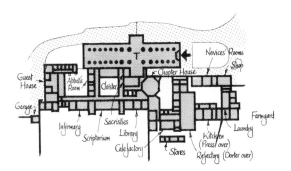

The church is double-ended, with altar beneath the crossing-
tower, the **lay nave** being at the E end. This was modelled closely on
Pugin's monastic nave and is approached through a severely Early
English W front (with date plaque of 1935). All the windows are
lancets, including those of the aisles and clerestory. Round columns
with moulded caps and bases support equilateral arches, and the
typically Puginesque roof has thin 'scissor' trusses. Herbert's
crossing is vaulted, and ingeniously includes short transition bays on
all four sides, those to N and S being in effect junction bays between

old and new aisles. Over the internal entrance lobby stands an exquisite white early 16th c. Flemish wood Madonna.

The **monastic nave** and the stalls by Eric Gill can be seen across the crossing, but this part is not open to the public. Nor can the **monastery** itself be visited (except the men's guest house), but a rewarding general view can be gained by going along the N side and following the path up to the Calvary, set up on a natural rock outcrop. The buildings are mostly two-storeyed, of the same slaty rocky stone as the church and with wide lancet windows in pairs. Below the Calvary is a tiny apsidal chapel of 1837 by Pugin, transferred here in 1955 to house a Pietà carved in 1836 by Petz of Munich for Grace Dieu Manor.

On the N side of the forecourt is the abbey shop, formed from an outbuilding. A side passage leads towards the S transept, with Pugin's octagonal chapter house of 1860 on the left – with four dormers on its slated pyramidal roof – but both are private.

Muchelney Somerset: ST 429249
in village, 1½ miles SSE of Langport

Monastery probably founded *c*.700 by Ine, King of Wessex; destroyed by Danes *c*.878; refounded as Benedictine priory of St Peter and St Paul by King Athelstan 939; became abbey *c*.950; became mitred. Dissolved 1538 and granted to Edward Seymour

In care of Department of the Environment. Open during standard hours, but only from 1 April to 30 September (admission charge)

On ground only a little above the Sedgemoor marshes. Its known building history begins with a pre-Norman apsed church followed by a bigger one of *c*.1100 with five apsidal chapels. The transept chapels and eastern Lady chapel were later extended in rectangular form and so was the apse-ended chapter house. The S walk (at least) of the cloister was lavishly rebuilt *c*.1510, together with the refectory and adjoining abbot's house.

The abbot's house survived as a farmhouse almost complete, together with a part of the cloister because there were rooms above it. The remainder (apart from a small piece of church projecting into the parish churchyard) became lost under an orchard, and the cloister was used for cider making. It was partly excavated in 1873, but more fully in the 1940s, having become Crown property in 1927.

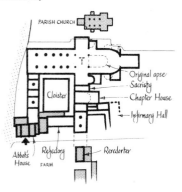

The 16th c. **abbot's house** is seen first; a few of its features date from the farmhouse occupation. The original kitchen is now the entrance hall with ticket counter. A modern wooden stair leads to a guest room with a fine panelled wood ceiling and a stone fireplace with recess for spices. The room beneath is a museum of carved stonework. The big kitchen fireplace backs on to another in the next room. Beyond that is the abbot's stair, with worn skewed stone treads. It goes up to the splendid abbot's parlour which still has a long wooden settle with linenfold panelling, some original blue and red glass, a simple panelled ceiling, and an elaborate (but incomplete) fireplace topped by lions. Off the far corner is a trio of rooms over the S cloister walk, with a variety of ceilings: one boarded barrel, one flat, and the last open to the wind-braced roof. In two are traces of wall paintings. The windows offer an easily understood view of the excavated church and W and E cloister ranges; the sunken area represents the small pre-Norman apsed chancel.

Return down the main stair and turn left into the big ante-room where more stones, tiles etc. are displayed. The end doorway leads out into the surviving six bays of **cloister** walk, a shadow of its original self but still with late Perpendicular tracery in abundance, springers of the former fan vaults, and the washing trough against the refectory wall.

Outside, the embattled S front of the house is typically Tudor; the tall transomed windows and gable of the abbot's parlour should be noticed. Beyond was the **refectory**, the rich internal stone panelling of its N wall preserved where it backs on to the cloister. Reached through a gate opposite is the monks' **reredorter**, now become a detached building and in use as a farm store. The upper floor with one side open to the drainage channel beneath has been reconstructed.

Finally the remaining foundations can be explored, starting with the E cloister range: warming house, parlour and chapter house, to the SE of which are fragments of a second cloister and infirmary hall. The original apse of the chapter house is indicated. The **church** plan, also clearly laid out, shows several chapel apses later replaced by square ends. From its W end the foundation of the W cloister range is visible, and beyond it the picturesque outside face of the S range with its big windows and upper storey.

Nashdom Buckinghamshire: SU 920842

1¼ miles NNE of Taplow church and ½ mile E of Bourne End road B476. Anglican Benedictine priory founded 1914 at Pershore; became abbey 1922; moved to Nashdom 1926

Chapel and bookshop (only) open during normal hours

Nashdom in Russian means 'our house' and this was the house of Prince Dolgorouki and his English wife, built for them in 1908–10 by Sir Edwin Lutyens and regarded as one of his masterpieces; they died, he in 1915 and she in 1919. Following in many ways the typical style of gentlemen's houses of the Thames valley, its formally classical lines challenge an adversely sloping site, and its whitened brick with red tiled parapeted roofs and cheerful green shutters are far away from the usual concept of an abbey. The community broke away from that of Caldy in 1913 when the latter became Roman Catholic, and Nashdom itself became the mother house of St Gregory's abbey, Three Rivers, Michigan.

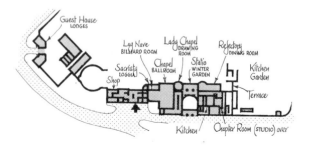

Nashdom: Abbey in a Lutyens country house: 1910

A new brick wing to the design of Norman Davey was erected at the upper end in 1967–8 and the public entrance is into this, up a flight of open concrete steps. Its ground storey containing a concourse with sitting area, office and shop connects by a lobby with the old house. Here the public or lay 'nave' is the top-lit former billiard room, opening off the main chapel which was the 'Big Room' or ballroom. The hexagonal central altar is by Christopher Firmstone, and the hanging corona by David Nye. At one end are three big windows to the garden, at the other a former music gallery housing the organ. Behind the altar is the principal celebrant's seat, with a curtain where the fireplace was; the opening back into the concourse was formed within another fireplace. The former loggia alongside the 'nave' has been enclosed to serve as a sacristy.

No other parts are open to the public, though permission may be given to walk in the rear garden. From the road the lower (kitchen) garden may be glimpsed, with its dramatic wall and steps to the upper terrace. Most of the house is three storeyed but at this end Lutyens tucked in an ample basement of servants' rooms. Further up the lane is the guest house formed out of a pair of lodges intriguingly planned on a corner site to guard the entrance to the stable yard.

Neath West Glamorgan: SS 738973
1 mile W of Neath and 250 yards S of Swansea road A465

Savigniac abbey of St Mary founded 1130 by Sir Richard de
  Granville, a daughter house of Savigny; became Cistercian 1147.
  Dissolved 1539 and passed to Sir Richard Williams

In care of Welsh Office. Open during standard hours (admission
  charge)

The date of the W or lay brothers' range, *c*.1170–1220, supports a
theory that the abbey stood first on a different site, perhaps at
Cwrt-y-Bettws nearer the river Neath. The rest of the monastic
buildings were mainly 13th c. and have survived to varying degrees;
the church underwent a complete rebuilding *c*.1280–1330 and
enough of that remains to give a good idea of its size and scale.
   At the end of the 16th c. the abbot's house, which had been
formed in the 15th c. out of the S end of the E range, was made into
a mansion by Sir John Herbert. Abbey stone went into this and
neighbouring houses and into St Thomas's church in the town.
Smelting, mainly of copper, was introduced into the area, and by
the 1720s into the ruins themselves, with workmen living in the by
then abandoned Herbert house. Encircled by canal and railway,
and buried in industrial waste up to 17 feet high, the abbey became
a daunting subject for antiquaries. From being the 'fairest building
in all Wales' it had descended to utter ignominy. Nevertheless it was
eventually cleared in the 1920s and 30s and passed into state
guardianship (1944) and then ownership (1949); its dignity and, to
some extent, its setting are restored.

   The approach is towards the mansion, which is best inspected
last. Bearing left, a path leads to the well defined cloister, beyond
which is the **church**, uniformly early Decorated in style – standing at
the W end almost to full height but at the E much more
fragmentary. The **nave** aisle walls are fairly complete, but
unfortunately the arcades are reduced to mere column bases. Wall
shafts and springers of white limestone show that the aisles were
vaulted, and at the W end are slight remains of the clerestory. The
monks' quire, extending into the crossing, is marked by screen walls
each side and has unusually extensive areas of tiled paving, mostly
with Gothic tracery patterns; with one exception the crossing piers
are also only stumps.

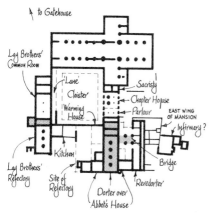

In the N transept are more old tiles and clear remains of two
chapels, one with its altar base. The N **presbytery** aisle has one bay
surviving to full height, but not much else. A block of masonry
marks the high altar site; behind runs an ambulatory across to the S
aisle where there are more tiles, an unidentified cross slab and the
base of a shafted external doorway. The **S transept** retains the base
of the main respond pier of its E arcade, as well as altar bases in
both chapels, the base of the night stair (still with its wrought stone
wall handrail) and, as in the N transept, an unusual amount of
original plaster. A tablet commemorates Glen Taylor who led the
20th c. clearance of débris; red tiles set into several walls show how
high it had stood.

Openings lead into the sacristy/library and thence back to the
cloister. To the right is the base of the processional doorway into the
nave, to the left the site of the chapter house and parlour – both
practically disappeared. Next, the slype, more complete because
here the Herbert mansion began. A rough mass of stonework at the
corner indicates the day stair, its top broken into by early 17th c.
walling. Continuing next along the S walk: the warming house has
gone and so has most of the refectory except the base of a fine
shafted doorway and on each side part of a washing trough. Of the
kitchen, subdivided in the 18th c., only wall bases survive, but it
leads into the lay brothers' refectory which is much more complete
(though without its vault) and has a fireplace in the W wall. Above,
lit by the three lancets in the S gable, was the lay brothers' dorter.
This range is the earliest part of the abbey, c.1170–1220.

Next off the W walk – or rather off the 'lane' running parallel –
are a tunnel-vaulted passage leading to a 14th c. rib-vaulted porch,
then the common-room, also fairly complete with its vault
springers, and finally two smaller rooms. Back now into the church
at its SW corner, and out again to look at the W front. The blind
tracery at its base was originally protected by a galilee porch. The
great W window has all gone and only the base is left of the doorway
below. Continuing round the **outside**, the N aisle wall shows clearly
how the best ashlar stone has been nibbled away for use elsewhere.
Further on are many spectacular masses of fallen masonry, some of
them complete with parts of vault ribs and window arches.

The circuit leads back to the **mansion**, formed mainly from the
monks' reredorter block and the end of their dorter. But the N
façade is an Elizabethan addition. From its centre one can look
down into the main drain, running between close-set walls the
length of the block. To the left is a four-storey gable; to the right,
nearer the cloister, a doorway through which is a striking view along
the length of the reredorter. Entering here: on the left is the drain
and on the right two complete rib-vaulted bays that originally
formed the access bridge and were later the basis of a first-floor long
gallery. Beyond is an open court with high domestic chimneys
around it. The Herberts' work can be readily identified by its big
rectangular windows and bold string courses. The bridge leads to a
round-arched doorway and into the 13th c. dorter undercroft
(probably a novices' room) – with its quadripartite vaulting on
round columns, the most complete surviving part of the abbey. The
tiled floor is modern; the windows were enlarged in the 16th c.
when it became a servants' hall. The fireplace with overmantel
brackets is original and in a corner some carved stones from various
parts of the abbey have been assembled. They include some bosses
and a 14th c. abbot's effigy.

Adjoining this room to the N (i.e. nearer the cloister) are two
smaller tunnel-vaulted rooms, one with an Early English two-light
window over the doorway. Next it is best to continue the **outside**
circuit, following the N side of the mansion to its E end, which is a
wholly Elizabethan addition. Beyond it are some excavations for
the infirmary, and at the far corner the ends of the drain and
reredorter, followed by a two-storey block put in in the 15th c. to fill
the gap before the dorter so as to form a suite of rooms for the
abbot; this became the Herberts' main front. Beyond that and past
the refectory site the outside of the W or lay brothers' range can be
followed back to the W end of the church, passing the big severe
porch.

Finally the **gatehouse**, reached by returning along Monastery Lane to the main road and there turning left. The lower part of one side stands on the right just past the Hope and Anchor public house. The pavement now runs where the passage was, and the other side has been swept away by the road.

Netley Hampshire: SU 453089
2¾ miles SE of Southampton city centre

Cistercian abbey of the Blessed Virgin Mary and St Edward the Confessor founded 1239 by Peter des Roches, Bishop of Winchester and, after the bishop's death, by Henry III, a daughter house of Beaulieu. Dissolved 1536 and granted to Sir William Paulet, later Marquis of Winchester

In care of Department of the Environment. Open at all times without charge

Originally Letley, incorrectly explained as *laetus locus* = glad place. The buildings, substantial parts of which remain, date mostly from the middle of the 13th c.; however the church nave is of *c.*1290–1320.

After the Dissolution Sir William Paulet created a mansion here. He rebuilt the S range, keeping its cloister wall but destroying the refectory. He also made a hall in the nave, removing the arcades to do so. The cloister garth remained as an open court, its E and W ranges being turned to domestic uses. Early in the 18th c. the house in its turn was abandoned and dismantled. Some materials of the church went for the rebuilding of St Mary's Southampton and in 1770 a portion of the N transept was re-erected at Cranbury Park. Otherwise the whole abbey, though roofless and overgrown, remained very recognisably complete and became the focal point of the fashionable cult of the romantic and picturesque, the subject of poems and fiction which dwelt on various combinations of 'ruins, ivy, owls, moonlight, musing melancholy and life's passing pageant'. Even in its present secure and lawned state it still has few equals in beauty.

From the entrance gate one sees on the right the dorter range, and on the left the purely domestic façade grafted on to the **S range** in the 16th c. The entrance porch stands on the site of the frater.

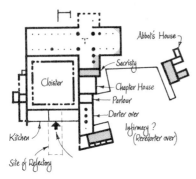

That lay N to S and has totally gone; its doorway to the cloister is
replaced by a Tudor one, and on either side are rooms adapted in
brick to domestic uses – on the right the warming house, on the left
(separated by a wall with pointed doorway and three lancets) the
kitchen.

The **cloister** has quite high walls all round, but the walks have all
gone. A central fountain was put in in the 16th c. and part can still
be seen. Beyond stands the church with an unbroken line of eight
triple lancet aisle windows, their sills above cloister roof level. The
S transept survives even higher, with two complete triple lancet
windows on the W, and on the S gable the dorter roof line showing
clearly. Centrally in the E walk is the triple opening to the chapter
house. In the S walk, just E of the refectory position, are remains of
the monks' washplace. The W or lay brothers' range is smaller than
was usual in Cistercian houses for this was a late foundation made at
a time when their numbers were dwindling; one room of it is fairly
complete. All this is 13th c., but the single central opening from
cloister to S aisle was a Paulet insertion.

As a shell, the **church** is remarkably complete. The aisles have
most of their windows, wall shafting and vault springers (especially
on the S side). The once fine W window tracery has gone, leaving
the main arch shape. On either side of it are effective cross-sections
through the vanished arcades, showing that in each bay a single big
arch spanned the triforium walkway and the clerestory. This end of
the church was not built till early in the 14th c. Few main pier bases
are left except at the crossing, where inscriptions relating to Henry
III are preserved on three.

Though the N transept is gone, the S is almost complete. As at
the W end the main arcade piers have attached shafts on their four

sides and combined arches over clerestory and triforium. The vault
here was rebuilt early in the 16th c. and has curious panelled
springer stones with embattled tops. Over the chapels the (earlier)
vaults are intact.

The great E window was of four lights and put in after the
remainder. The aisle windows at this end are lancets, mostly in
pairs, and here too some parts of the vaults still stand.

From the transept a doorway leads to the sacristy (with a piscina)
and library, a three-bay compartment with quadripartite vaulting;
the old floor tiles have been reset. Beyond it as usual is the **chapter
house** – here rather small and square with three two-light windows
in the E wall, each with a sexfoil over – but above on the E and W

Netley: Early 19th c. engraving

sides is Tudor brickwork. From here can be seen another vaulted storey over the sacristy, probably a treasury. The ground-level connecting openings between all these rooms are post-Dissolution: next was a parlour, and then a continuation of undercroft beneath the dorter, with vault springers but more Tudor brickwork above. The fireplace in the E wall is a 16th c. insertion too. At the far end is a room of uncertain purpose with a drain at the far end 10 feet or more below floor level. Adjoining this is an impressive vaulted room with a continuation of the same drain, thought to have been an infirmary; above was the reredorter. It contains a big original fireplace, the corbels of which also carry brackets for lamps; at the far end is a good Early English two-light window.

From here a way out on the N side enables the outside of the E range (chapter house etc.) to be seen. Facing it is the 13th c. **abbot's house** which still has most of the vaulting of its ground storey. The brick terrace walls between are 16th c.

Now the **exterior** of the church, starting at the E end with the fine main window. Cross the N transept site and look across at the S transept again, and pass the N nave aisle. The foundations outside it are probably post-monastic. The W front had three doorways; the S one, taken diagonally through a buttress, led from the lay brothers' quarters via a covered way which has disappeared.

Newbo Lincolnshire: SK 862379
¼ mile E of Sedgebrook and 200 yards N of Nottingham–Grantham road A52

Premonstratensian abbey of the Assumption of the Blessed Virgin Mary founded 1198 by Richard de Malebisse, a daughter house of Newsham; dissolved 1536. Going E from Sedgebrook, the modern Abbey House (Wade family) stands in a farm lane on the left. A superb traceried 14th c. piscina in the front garden came from the site, which was roughly in the centre of the large field beyond the big group of barns further E. Almost nothing is known of the buildings, such traces as there were having been bulldozed away in 1959.

Newenham Devon: SY 287973
1 mile SW of Axminster and ¼ mile E of Seaton road A358

Cistercian abbey of the Blessed Virgin Mary founded 1246 or 47 by
   Reginald de Mohun, Earl of Somerset, a daughter house of
   Beaulieu. Dissolved 1539 and leased to Duke of Suffolk

Owned by Burrough family. Accessible at all times subject to
   permission from Lower Abbey Farm

The church was partly in use by 1270 and its main altar was
consecrated in 1277. It can be assumed that all the main buildings
were likewise of the second half of the 13th c., the domestic ones
being no doubt the earliest.
   Most of the stone was quarried away after the Dissolution and the
site passed to farm use, as at present. Destruction has unfortunately
continued, even in 1977 when a barn was built on the site of the
church, and in 1980 when a late medieval barn 100 yards to the S,
possibly a monastic tithe barn, was demolished.

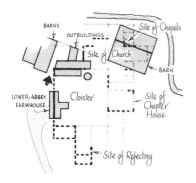

So much has gone that the layout is not easy to grasp. Lower
Abbey Farm House is built around part of the W wall of the
cloister, which thus lay behind it as seen from the lane. Part of its N
wall, which was the S wall of the church, is within the old block of
outbuildings beyond the house. Arched recesses and some cloister
roof corbels are visible. A short exposed ruined wall on the further
side of these buildings may have been part of a pulpitum across the
church nave; much of the church site however now lies beneath the
concreted cow-yard and barn. Fragments of the refectory and
kitchen chronicled as recently as 1938 have gone; so has a supposed
chapel against the S end of the refectory which in 1843 stood almost
entire. Some indistinct bumps show where the chapter house was.

The 13th c. doorway of a shop just S of Axminster church came
from the abbey. Some decorated floor tiles are kept at the
farmhouse, but the best are at Rougemont House Museum, Exeter.

Newminster Northumberland: NZ 189858
½ mile W of Morpeth, near Cambo road B6343

Cistercian abbey of the Blessed Virgin Mary founded 1138 by
    Ranulf de Merlay, a daughter house of Fountains. Dissolved 1537
    and granted to Henry Grey

Owned by Errington family. Open at all times without charge
    subject to permission from Abbey House, adjoining

The first buildings, of which St Robert was abbot, are said to have
been destroyed by the Scots within a year. But then the abbey
prospered and soon established daughter houses at Sawley,
Pipewell and Roche. Most of the eventual buildings were probably
late 12th c., the reredorter and E end of chapter house 13th c., and
the galilee and probably other parts of the church 15th c.

    Parts were occupied as a house by Sir Henry Chillingham late in
the 16th c., but subsequently almost all the stone was quarried
away. Since 1900 numerous partial excavations have left the site in a
successively more chaotic state; the last, more ordered one was in
1961–3, since when undergrowth has again taken hold.

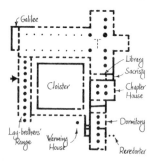

Past the western outskirts of Morpeth, just beyond the narrow
bridge over the Wansbeck, is a lane on the left marked 'Private
Road Public Footpath'. After 200 yards this path leads through a
wicket gate. A path signposted 'Kirkhill ½ m.' should be followed

to a second wicket gate, where a left turn along the fence leads to the abbey site.

What is then visible – and accessible – will depend very much on the season, the weather and one's apparel. It is best to take bearings from the **cloister**, of which short lengths of arcading were re-erected in 1924. Just inside the upper gate, the W (lay brothers') range lay parallel to the fence. Thus the first view is across this and across the cloister towards the E, so the two examples of arcading in the foreground belonged to the W walk; they are of delicate and unusual design with twin shafts and waterleaf capitals, clearly late 12th c. Immediately to the left are column bases of the lay brothers' undercroft, and on the right the base of a doorway in its outer wall.

Go forward now into the cloister. To the left lay the church, of which very little remains. To the right is another substantial length of cloister arcade (part of the S walk), and straight ahead two shorter pieces, one of them propped by steel rods. Go between them; the round-headed doorway ahead, of four orders with more waterleaf (also re-erected), leads into the **chapter house**, the left (N) wall of which is readily traceable. Various tumbled columns belonged to this room, which was extended eastwards into a squarer form in the 13th c. To the right, i.e. SE of the cloister, another prominent wall marks the side of a slype, and the column stumps beyond belonged to the reredorter undercroft. Further round to the right are fragments of the warming house at the E end of the S range. The mounds beyond are merely excavated soil.

Return to the cloister. The **church** (on the right as one looks back towards the gate) hardly merits a visit. The only substantial fragment, fairly easily found, is some tracery re-erected in the N transept, not *in situ* but possibly belonging to a main N window enlarged in the 15th c. Close to this it should be possible to locate one or two of the pier bases of the transept arcades. To the W there remains an arch, apparently of the nave N wall but probably re-erected as a folly in the 18th c.

Newsham Lincolnshire: TA 128134
1½ miles SE of Ulceby and ¼ mile NE of B1211

Premonstratensian abbey of St Mary and St Martial founded 1143 by Peter of Goxhill, a daughter house of Licques, Artois; dissolved 1536. 1½ miles NW of Brocklesby Hall (Earl of Yarborough), built from its stone. From a point ¼ mile E of the

N lodge of the park a farm track leads to an 18th c. stone bridge. An overgrown footpath branching left beyond it leads after 500 yards or so to the site, marked by hillocks and old hawthorns amongst pasture. Now totally vanished, it was the first abbey of the order in England and in its first 50 years sent out over 100 canons to colonise others.

Northampton Northamptonshire: SP 737606 approx.
½ mile W of town centre near Weedon road A45

Augustinian abbey of St James founded early in 12th c. by William Peverel; dissolved 1538 and granted to Nicholas Giffard who converted it into a mansion. Though the history is well recorded hardly a trace remains apart from the name of the suburb St James. The tomb slab of Abbot de Flore (d. 1334) is in the vestry floor of Duston church.

Norton Cheshire: SJ 548831
2 miles E of Runcorn and ½ mile S of Warrington road A558

Augustinian priory of St Mary founded at Runcorn c.1115 by William fitzNigel; moved to Norton 1134; became abbey 1422. Dissolved 1536 and sold to Richard Broke

Owned by Cheshire County Council. Open to the public from 12 noon every day till 4.0 p.m. (November to March), 5.0 p.m. (remainder of year, but 6.0 p.m. weekends and bank holidays); admission charge

The church was consecrated in 1157, and by c.1200 all the main buildings were complete. Following a fire in 1236 the church was lengthened at both ends and its transept chapels extended; the chapter house was also enlarged. An eastern Lady chapel was added c.1280, and the side chapels further enlarged. In the 15th c. a N nave aisle was added, and early in the 16th c. the cloister walks rebuilt.
   The suppression in 1536 was resisted, the abbot being captured and condemned to death but afterwards released. The Brokes made the W range into a house and demolished most of the remainder. About 1730 a classical house was built on the site of the W and S ranges, and even when it was remodelled c.1790 under James Wyatt

the undercroft of the medieval W range was retained. Happily it was still left when the house was demolished in 1928 – together with a fine Norman doorway, a 19th c. replica of it, and a protective porch around the two. Excavation in the 1970s revealed the entire plan; the undercroft was restored, an ambitious museum built (1982), and the surrounding park transformed into a tourist resort, with well signposted approaches. The name Norton priory is invariably used.

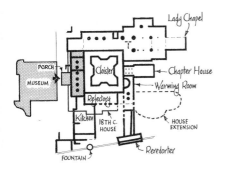

Entry is via the **museum**, which provides an automatic slide show on the abbey, some splendid models, numerous exhibits of tiles, worked stones, grave slabs etc., and a reconstructed length of cloister arcade. Visitors then pass into the 19th c. porch with its twin doorways to the late 12th c. W range **undercroft** – one genuine Norman and the other a competent copy. The genuine is the right-hand one; possibly it was the processional doorway from the E cloister walk into the church, and reset here when that was demolished. The undercroft itself has heavy ribbed vaults on low round columns with scalloped capitals, and some 18th c. brick wine bins. It leads through to the cloister, lawned in the centre and punctuated on each side by angled bays formed during its early 16th c. reconstruction. The W wall stands to undercroft height; a viewing gallery has been built above, reached by an outside stair at the back. First, however, the passageway at the N end of the undercroft: its wall-arcading was long forgotten behind brickwork and it now houses a remarkable 11-foot high 14th c. statue of St Christopher which survived the Dissolution and was for some years in Liverpool Museum.

The **church** plan, no more than foundations but understandable either from the gallery or by walking round, is unusually long and narrow; the added portions at W and E are clearly demarcated (the final eastern one being the Lady chapel) but the various extensions of the transept chapels are less easy to follow. Many stone coffins are left *in situ*, mainly in the chapels N of the presbytery and in the **chapter house** vestibule. The chapter house itself is not yet fully exposed owing to a tree. From there the long dorter undercroft runs to the reredorter, past an oblique drain connected to the main channel along the S end of the site. The circular fountain basin directly over the channel is a relic of the 18th c. house, the base of the façade of which can be seen starting at the SW corner of the undercroft, turning in the medieval kitchen area and going parallel to the refectory, the S wall of which has been lost.

Notley Buckinghamshire: SP 716092
2 miles NNE of Thame and ½ mile SE of Long Crendon–Chearsley road

Augustinian abbey of St Mary the Virgin and St John the Baptist
   founded *c*.1162 by Walter Giffard, Earl of Buckingham.
   Dissolved 1538

Owned by Danny family. Not open to the public

A first presbytery, crossing and transepts were built late in the 12th c., and the nave and aisles and cloister ranges in the 13th c. The E end was reconstructed on a bigger scale early in the 14th c., and the crossing tower in the 15th c. The two-storeyed abbot's (or guest) house, 15th and early 16th c., is the only part of which very much survives, except for a big square stone dovecote on the hill above.
   After the Dissolution the abbot's house remained a dwelling while the rest was turned to farm uses or fell gradually to ruin. The refectory, at least, stood as a shell early in the 18th c. The E part of the church foundation was quarried away for road-mending as late as *c*.1890. Digging in 1932–3 and 1937 revealed enough to compile a moderately complete plan and the above tentative datings. Some linenfold panelling from the house is at Weston Manor Hotel, Weston-on-the-Green, Oxfordshire; also a timber roof.

   Though the house and grounds are private, a public footpath is thoughtfully routed so as to afford interesting views from W and

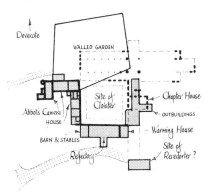

SW. The lane marked 'Notley Farm' continues past the farmyard
and past the big dovecote on the left, downhill to a gate. The path
begins here at a stile and runs beside the house drive. The nearer
end of the house, with prominent hexagonal turret, is 16th c., and
the further part of the wing 15th c. – but with many alterations. The
rest of the house, the other arm of an L, represents the 13th c. W or
cellarer's range of the cloister; what is left of the original walling is
however out of sight on the cloister side. From further down, the
barn and stable on the site of the S (refectory) range can be seen;
here too the wall facing the cloister is 13th c., and so are those at its
E end, defining the warming room. The church stood on the other
side of the whole group; of it very little indeed is above ground.

Osney Oxfordshire: SP 504060
½ mile WSW of Oxford city centre

Augustinian priory of St Mary founded 1129; became abbey 1154.
   Dissolved 1539. Became a cathedral 1542 (till 1545 only). Passed
   to Stumpe family

Site largely occupied by St Mary's Cemetery. Open at all times
   without charge

The 12th c. buildings are known to have been extended in the 13th
c., and by the time of the Dissolution the church was one of the
most magnificent in the whole country, boasting a tall central tower
and one even higher at the W end.
   The cathedral establishment set up by Henry VIII stayed here

only a few years before moving to the smaller Christ Church. After the usual period of decay the abbey's final destruction was wrought by Charles I, who used its stone to complete the city's defences in the Civil War. The extent of the church (but not the monastic buildings) has been found by partial excavation; the only actual structure left is part of a 15th c. barn at Osney Mill.

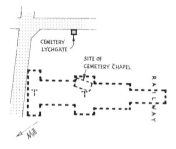

The site is now St Mary's Cemetery, but the Lady chapel extended into what is now railway land. The mill barn can be reached across the yard at the end of Mill Street, just beyond a very rough flat late Gothic arch. Through its broken window a fine 15th c. roof truss is visible.

Oulton Staffordshire: in village, 1 mile NE of Stone   SJ 908356

Benedictine nunnery of the Immaculate Conception founded at Gent 1624; moved to Preston 1795, to Caverswall castle 1811, and to Oulton 1853

Church (only) open during normal hours

The buildings are basically by Edward Pugin, 1853–4. He was then only nineteen. The slated grey stone church is Decorated in general style, with hints of Perpendicular. The sacristy and chapter house, as well as the presbytery attached to the (ritual) NE corner date from 1892. All this was added to an earlier 19th c. Tudor-style red brick house with stone mullions and quoins which forms the actual monastery.

The entrance drive leads past the presbytery on the right to a

small court with a gatehouse into the enclosed part of the abbey straight ahead and the **church** on the right. An unobtrusive porch reached down steps beside the presbytery leads into the N transept, the only part open to visitors. The sanctuary is visible from here, and part of the tall impressive high-windowed nave which forms the nuns' quire. A wrought iron screen separates the two. The sanctuary has a fully coloured panelled roof, lower than the nave, and a big original E window with large areas of raw colours.

Outside, little of the abbey itself can be seen except the N side of the church, standing high above the garden.

Owston Leicestershire: SK 774080
in village, 5¼ miles W of Oakham

Augustinian priory of St Andrew founded by 1161 by Robert
    Grimbald; became abbey. Dissolved 1536 and given to Ratcliffe
    family (except church)

Parish church. Open during normal hours: key at The Priory
    immediately to E

Pronounced 'Ooston'. What remains here is the E end of a church
of somewhat unusual plan, originally 12th c. but given a N chapel in

the 13th c. and a N tower-porch in the 14th c. The nave, probably aisleless, stood till the 18th c. The monastic buildings are presumed to have been to the S, and The Priory to the E may be a relic of the infirmary.

Site of Nave

There is a right-of-way across the front garden of The Priory to the churchyard gate. The **tower** is 14th c., built separately against the N aisle so that its inner arch encloses an earlier shafted doorway. **Inside**, the arcade is of two giant arches on round columns. Nave and chancel together formed the presbytery of the abbey church; their present roofs are 19th c. On the S side is a Norman doorway. The font may be 17th c., and in the N chapel is a tomb recess with clumsily crocketed arch. Other memorials are minor.

Outside is a miscellany of buttresses and windows suggesting continual change. Some 15th c. stone panelling on the SW corner may denote the beginning of the E cloister range; certainly the nave began at this point, the present main W wall probably being an 18th c. blocking following its demolition. Further W the ground falls away towards various earthworks, of no obvious significance.

The Priory (former vicarage) is an essentially 17th c. house incorporating (at front and back) two 15th c. doorways which may have been part of the infirmary.

Pershore Hereford & Worcester: in town centre   SO 947457

Monastery for secular canons probably founded c.689 by Oswald, nephew of King Aethelred; refounded as Benedictine abbey of St Mary the Virgin, St Peter and St Paul by King Edgar 972 after destruction by Danes; dedication changed to St Mary, St Eadburga and (parochial portion) Holy Cross; became mitred 1401. Dissolved 1539; nave granted to parish and remainder to William and Francis Sheldon

Parish church. Open during normal hours

A general rebuilding took place c.1100. The church presbytery was again rebuilt and newly consecrated in 1239, and extensive repairs to it followed a fire in 1288; it is an outstanding example of early and late 13th c. work.

After the Dissolution the nave and Lady chapel were taken down, leaving the presbytery and central tower for the use of the parish who had elected to exchange them for the nave. Subsequently the N transept collapsed. The E apse (a shortened replacement of the Lady chapel) is of 1847, and subsequent restorations were done under Sir George Gilbert Scott in 1862–5 and Sir Harold Brakspear in 1912–14. Excavations in 1929–30 revealed only a little of the monastic buildings, which stood to the S.

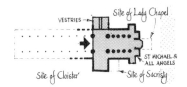

What is left of the **nave** against the outer W face of the tower closely resembles Norman Gloucester and Tewkesbury. The arcades had big round columns, and the start of the clerestory can just be seen, as well as evidence of aisle vaults. All that remains of the outer walls is a short length at the E end of the S nave aisle, with a Decorated doorway that led to the cloister. Of the **crossing** arches, that from the nave is rebuilt (and of course blocked). The other three are like Tewkesbury too – big Norman, each on pairs of shafts at each stout pier. But above the arches the tower rises as an open lantern with lavish 14th c. stone panelling and double-traceried windows. Within the top hangs a curious 'cat's cradle' ringers' gallery inserted by Scott; most of the eight bells are 18th c. The N transept was rebuilt in the 19th c. in shortened form with a lean-to roof. The S transept however is of c.1100 or earlier, with Norman details – in some cases looking almost Saxon in their lack of refinement. But the vault is 14th c.

The presbytery, which is Pershore's glory, is low; it replaced a Norman one with triforium gallery. Gallery and clerestory are combined here in an unusual way with a shafted three-lancet opening in each bay screening both the true clerestory of single windows and the walkway below. The richly moulded main arches rest on piers with sixteen shafts and beautiful stiff-leaf capitals; the E arch is wider and higher, causing awkwardness higher up. All that is of c.1210–39, but the vault was rebuilt c.1290 with a beautiful pattern of lierne ribs and large leafy bosses.

A walk round the interior begins with the **N transept**. The arcaded font with figures of Christ and the Apostles is 12th c. The big monument of the W side to Fulk Haselwood (d. 1595) has lost the main effigies; the plain tomb in the NE angle is unidentified. At the opening into the **N presbytery aisle** are an interesting benefaction board and a fragment of wooden screen dated 1435. The aisle itself, neither wide nor high, has a quadripartite vault and lancet windows; from it one can admire at close quarters the splendid main column bases and capitals.

The little E transepts are an uncommon feature, particularly in combination with the standard Lady chapel, destroyed and replaced by the stumpy **apse** of 1847, which is creditable Early English by an unknown designer. Traces of wall paintings can be seen within the triple lancet at clerestory level above the altar. The SE chapel (St Michael and All Angels', reserved for private prayer) was rebuilt by Scott and has an E window by C.E. Kempe; the rather similar 'historical' aisle windows are a memorial of 1870 and tell the story of Pershore.

In the centre of the **S transept** stands a war memorial with winged *Victory* by Alfred Drury. On the E wall are a number of hatchments and wall tablets, also the top part of a 15th c. stone reredos. On the right, and continuing along the S wall, is quite primitive early Norman wall-arcading from which the shafts are missing. Higher up is more arcading, either part of a clerestory or the gallery below a clerestory that has disappeared. The sadly damaged effigies are of a 13th c. knight (on a later chest) and a cleric, possibly Abbot Hert (d. 1479). The twelve seats nearby were 19th c. choir stalls. On the W wall is the biggest monument in the church, to Thomas Haselwood (d. 1624), portraying his wife and son kneeling and himself lying. The chest is 14th or 15th c.

From the W door the nave stretched to the iron gates. The big buttresses against the tower were added in 1913; the vestry against its N side was built in 1936 alongside another giant buttress put up in 1686 after the transept collapsed. Past this are the older flying buttresses of the presbytery, and then the curtailed and much rebuilt E end.

The church across the road served St Andrew's parish and is used as a parish centre. On the S side of the abbey, the blocked doorway to the former late 13th c. sacristy should be noted, also the nearby base and steps of a churchyard cross. The arches on the E face of the S transept were also part of the sacristy and there are traces of the earlier opening into an E chapel which it replaced. The area clear of trees to the SW of the tower represents the cloister but there is nothing of it left. From here is a good view of the 14th c. tower top, blossoming out with four sets of two-light gabled windows and with tall pinnacles of 1870, and of the early Norman transept with its corbelled parapets. On its S side are the blocked doorway of the night stair, a 19th c. three-lancet window breaking the dorter roof line, and above that some more elaborate Norman arcading. Of the 'clerestory' arcading visible inside there is no sign.

The 12th c. lectern at Crowle (7 miles to the N) is said to have come from the abbey.

The Anglican community now at Nashdom (*q.v.*) used a nearby house as their own Abbey House in 1914–26.

Peterborough Cambridgeshire: in city centre   TL 194985

Benedictine abbey of St Peter founded 655–6 by Saxulf, the first abbot; destroyed by Danes 870; refounded 972 by Bishop Ethelwold of Winchester; became mitred *c.*1400. Dissolved 1539 and became cathedral

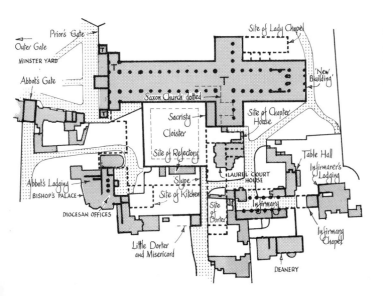

Cathedral church (only) open during normal hours; remainder
   private

For a full description see *A Guide to the Cathedrals of Britain*,
pp.304–11

Pipewell Northamptonshire: on E side of village   SP 840857

Cistercian abbey founded 1143 by William Bouteveleyne, a
   daughter house of Newminster. Dissolved 1538 and granted to Sir
   William Parre

Owned by Comerford family. Site accessible at any time without
   charge

Pronounced 'Pipwell'. By an odd misunderstanding, rival colonising
parties arrived from both Newminster and Garendon; the latter had
to withdraw. The buildings were reconstructed late in the 13th c.
and rededicated in 1311.
   No walling remains above ground, and little below. Parts of the
plan were established by excavation in 1909.

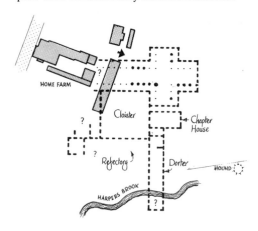

Access is by the track alongside Home Farm on the E side of the
Cottingham road (the modern so-called 'Abbey church' further N is
misleading) and permission should be sought from the house
nearest the road. Irregularities in the field behind the farmstead

give a rough idea of the siting; one of the small mounds bears a stone inscribed ABBAS R.I.P. marking the point in the chapter house where a burial was found. The U-shaped sinking to the SW was probably a fishpond; the steep little mound to the SE is likely to be prehistoric and may have been used for a windmill by the abbey.

Polesworth Warwickshire: SK 263024
in village on B5000, 3½ miles ESE of Tamworth

Benedictine nunnery of St Mary the Virgin probably founded by
   839 by King Egbert at 'Trensall' in Forest of Arden; moved to
   Polesworth; refounded as abbey of St Editha *c*.980; moved to
   Oldbury (Warwickshire) *c*.1100 and refounded at Polesworth
   c.1130 by Robert Marmion. Dissolved 1539 and granted to
   Francis Goodere

Parish church. Open during normal hours (key at vicarage
   adjoining)

Early histories, the usual amalgam of fact and fantasy, assert (probably in error) that St Editha was the daughter of Egbert. They then describe how the Marmions of Tamworth displaced the nuns but in the 12th c. reinstated them and improved their buildings. The church, double-naved as is frequent with nuns' churches, has an arcade and S wall to support this date, but most is 14th and 19th c. and the E end and claustral buildings have left little trace. The gatehouse survives, much weathered and patched.
   It seems likely that the Gooderes made a house out of the W range after the Dissolution, which in due course became the vicarage. When it was rebuilt in 1868 part of a medieval roof was preserved, presumably not *in situ*.

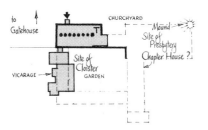

The low Norman arcade dividing the **church** interior is really largely 19th c.; the original portions at the ends are easily distinguishable. The round piers have scalloped capitals; the splays of the clerestory, now a row of unglazed openings, show that the S part was the nuns' nave and the N the lower parish aisle, widened in the 14th c. Moreover the sill heights on the other side seem to confirm that the cloister walk ran below the S wall.

At the W end of the N aisle is the 14th c. font, big with plain ogee-headed panels. Stone fragments nearby include a coffin and two grotesque corbels, and in the nave is a medieval 'dug-out' wooden chest. The marble pulpit, brass eagle lectern and oak screen are Victorian, as is the entire chancel, rebuilt in 1869 in place of what was probably the nuns' quire – which had long disappeared except for a part of the S wall still to be seen outside.

Of the tower, N of the chancel, one is hardly conscious inside. Against its W face towards the aisle are some old floor tiles. The two tombs under the arcade are attributed to Sir Richard Herthull and his daughter Isabel Cockayne (d. 1447). The former however bears the flat effigy of an abbess of *c.*1200 (a rare survival); the latter lady is a much more lifelike figure in alabaster. On the N wall is a 14th c. stone Crucifixion.

The porch is 19th c., the tower a strange mixture: its big N window appears to be 14th c. but the odd-shaped belfry stage with irregular windows is probably 17th c. The abbey presbytery is thought to have extended as far as the mysterious grassy mound – which may well have been here before the nuns; it was heightened in the 19th c. with excavated soil from the new chancel which left part of the nuns' S wall still standing, with a Norman doorway facing the vicarage lawn. The W end expresses the twin naves; an unusual feature is the small 14th c. doorway into what was the parish part. The Victorian brick vicarage stands more or less on the site of the W claustral range, and it is the part next to the church which contains old arch-braced roof timbers and an Elizabethan fireplace.

The **gatehouse**, some way to the N, is a modest affair with separate openings for foot-passengers and carriages, but little architectural detail. Parts are probably 12th c., of decayed stone patched with tiles, but the added brick and half-timbering is 14th c. The black-and-white house against the E part is specially picturesque.

Prinknash Gloucestershire: SO 879138
5½ miles NNE of Stroud, close to A46

Anglican Benedictine community of Our Lady and St Peter
  founded 1896 by Benjamin Carlyle in the Isle of Dogs, London;
  moved to Caldey 1906; became Roman Catholic 1913, abbey
  1914; moved to Prinknash Park 1928; became abbey 1937; moved
  to new site 1972

Crypt chapel open during normal hours; cafeteria 9.30 a.m. to
  5.30 p.m. daily; shop 9.0 a.m. to 6.0 p.m. daily (to 5.30 p.m. in
  winter); pottery 2.0 to 5.0 p.m. Sundays and 10.0 a.m. to
  12.30 p.m. and 1.30 to 5.0 p.m. other days

Pronounced to rhyme (approximately) with 'spinach'. A new
church and monastery to replace the old abbey were designed by
H.S. Goodhart-Rendel and begun in 1939. The foundations were
used for the severely modified design by F.G. Broadbent built in
1968–72, but the church remains unbuilt. In shape and style totally
different from the usual concept of a monastery, it makes careful
use of an unusually steep site with superb views over the Vale of
Gloucester.

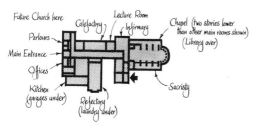

    From the car park the way to the 'crypt' chapel is clearly marked.
It is not underground but lies under the far end of the main
building, the hotel- or college-like appearance of which is
accentuated by rectangular windows and large plain areas of
unweathered creamy Cotswold stone.
    Not surprisingly, the **chapel** lacks height inside. There is little
enrichment except a reticulated ironwork motif appearing in the
communion rail and in the grilles over the side chapels, resin-
mounted glass patterns in the entrance lobby and apse, and a rather
mannered 'sounding board' over the quire altar. The piers either
side have a rather restless chamfered form. The N aisle (with more

Prinknash: Modern Benedictine abbey in the Cotswolds

coloured glass) is really an arched ambulatory, while the S side is occupied by the sacristy. In the entrance lobby is an oval stone tablet to H.S. Goodhart-Rendel (d. 1959).

Outside, the windows of the apse are particularly unlovely at close quarters; beyond it are private grounds. Returning up the hill, one can pick out some of the principal monastic features in their modern guise: above the chapel the library, and above them the monks' cells; further up and projecting forward the refectory, with laundry beneath; beyond it (over a range of garages) the kitchen, and facing up the hill the entrance front with a single roundel of sculpture, Our Lady and St Peter. The church will occupy the adjoining ground below the car park and will have a big 'laity chapel' accessible from it.

Prinknash pottery, on sale in the nearby shop, is made of clay dug from the estate, in fact from the abbey foundations.

Prinknash (old) Gloucestershire: SO 880135
5½ miles NNE of Stroud, close to A46

See under Prinknash for summary of history; ceased to be abbey
   1972 and became St Peter's Grange. Passed on suppression of
   Gloucester abbey to Sir Anthony Kingston

Owned by Prinknash abbey. Not open to the public but may be seen
   outside at any time

By 1339 Prinknash, already extra-parochial, was a grange of
Gloucester abbey. The SW part of the present house is a survival of
it. Much of the remainder, making an H form, is 16th c., though the
NW wing was rebuilt *c*.1780 and the adjoining porch on the W
façade is 17th c. Prince Rupert made his headquarters here during
the Royalist siege of Gloucester in 1643. Having passed through
several family ownerships, it was bought by Thomas Dyer
Edwardes who extended the chapel *c*.1890 and whose grandson
Lord Rothes gave it to the Benedictines from Caldey in 1928. They
erected a prefabricated overflow building on the W approach in
1945 and enlarged the chapel again in 1954. The house received
abbey status in 1937 but became a retreat house when the new
buildings were opened in 1972.

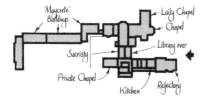

   Approaching from the direction of the new abbey, one sees first
the E court; both wings received extensions in the 19th c. – on the
right the polygonal chapel apse and on the left what was to become
the refectory. The remainder, typically Cotswold Tudor, is early
16th c., the most prominent room being the first-floor library with a
pair of tall three-light windows. On the left wall is a carved head
said to be that of Henry VIII, who was entertained here by the
abbot in 1535. Of the chapel the most valuable feature is some 16th
c. glass of the Nine Choirs of Angels. The laity chapel added in 1954
forms a transept on its far side. Following the drive up the other side
of the house, one comes to the W façade with its Jacobean porch,

now so unhappily enclosed with 'temporary' buildings put up after the end of World War II when the new abbey was still no more than a vision.

Quarr Isle of Wight: SZ 562928
2 miles W of Ryde and ¼ mile N of Newport road A3054

French Benedictine abbey of Our Lady founded 1833 at Solesmes by Dom Prosper Guéranger; moved to Appuldurcombe House, Isle of Wight 1901, to Quarr 1907 and back to Solesmes 1922, leaving cell which became a priory 1925, an abbey 1937 (the community is now in majority English)

Church (only) open during normal hours

Quarr House was built for the Cochrane family in the 19th c., 200 yards W of the ruins of the medieval Cistercian abbey. To this nucleus the new abbey was added in 1907–12 under the monk-architect Dom Paul Bellot. The church is his masterpiece, all in hard Belgian brick in a highly individual manner reminiscent of Berlage and de Klerk in Holland and of Gaudi and Moorish buildings in Catalonia.

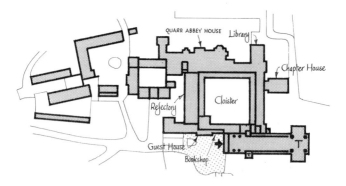

A tree-lined drive leads towards the guest house, which hides the cloister garth. The church, to the right, stands almost clear of other buildings. Its unusual plan comprises a short nave of three bays (defined by great transverse brick arches), a long quire at much higher level separated by two more arches, and a sanctuary crowned

by a massive tower criss-crossed with an ingenious system of still
more arches supporting its roof as though they were ribs of a vault.
That cannot be seen, since only the nave is open to visitors. Under
the quire is a crypt.

The limitations of plain unmoulded brick imposed a rigid design
discipline. Big curves were possible. Little ones give way to
triangles and steppings, and Gothic forms and mouldings to simple
interplays of reds and yellows or to the plainest of rebates and
corbellings. Above the big nave arches the brickwork is lightened
by rows of vertical slits; at the sides by very small arches from the
narrowest of aisles – which continue alongside the quire as hidden
corridors. The stalls stand in double ranks in front of bare walls but
above are very tall triple arches.

Outside, only the W front and the guest house façade may be seen
– the former given a somewhat sunken appearance by its deep but
low-springing arch but enabling the massive Spanish-looking
campanile at the corner of the quire to dominate. Its spire is a good
deal higher than the pinnacles of the big sanctuary tower, and
prominent in distant views and as a sea-mark.

Quarr (old) Isle of Wight: SZ 566927
1¾ miles W of Ryde and ¼ mile N of Newport road A3054

Savigniac abbey of St Mary founded 1132 by Baldwin de Redvers;
  became Cistercian 1147. Dissolved 1536

Owned by the present Quarr abbey. Open at all times subject to
  permission from the present abbey

Not much is known of the buildings, but little work on them seems
to have occurred after the early 13th c. The abbey never became
rich, partly because its position on the N coast of the Isle of Wight
involved it in the French raids of the 14th c.

In the 16th c. much of its stone went to build Yarmouth castle.
The W monastic range was converted into a barn and became the
nucleus of a small farmstead, while a public right of way developed
through the church site. A few other scattered bits of wall survive;
excavations in 1891 established the general plan, some years before
the new Benedictine abbey was set up in the 19th c. house on the
hill to the W.

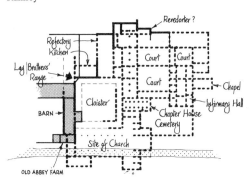

The bridle path from Fishbourne to Binstead passes lengthwise through the church site. Beside it stands Old Abbey Farm, a small, partly early 19th c. stone house containing a doorway and triple lancet window probably recovered from the church. Behind (and attached to it) is the barn which represents the cellarer's or W cloister range. Entry to the monastic site is by the track on the left – beside Quarr Abbey Lodge, across the yard behind the farmhouse and through a re-erected arch across the NW angle of the cloister. From here the N walk can be followed, with the kitchen ruin on the left (S and E walls only). A low-arched hatch to the refectory is visible, and a recess to the N of it. Of the refectory itself only a bit of the SW corner survives.

Away to the NE are arches of the end of the dorter undercroft, and further round, at the extreme E, a short length of wall with a 13th c. window ascribed to the infirmary chapel.

Of the barn, much is altered. An Early English triple lancet has been reused in the bay added on its E side, but the main E wall with its various windows is mostly original and faced into the cloister. A rough arch just N of the house suggests an entrance into the church N aisle.

Considerable parts of the precinct wall survive, the most noticeable being on either side of the (modern) arch over the bridle path where it leads W. One of the abbey bells is in Binstead church nearby.

Ramsey Cambridgeshire: on E side of town   TL 292851

Benedictine abbey of St Mary and St Benedict founded *c*.969 by

Ailwine = Æthelwine; became mitred. Dissolved 1539 and
passed to Cromwell family

Owned by Lord de Ramsey, but gatehouse National Trust.
Gatehouse open 10.0 a.m. to 5.0 p.m. (or dusk if earlier) without
charge; remainder not open to the public

Of the main abbey buildings little is known. The 13th c. Lady
chapel, the base of which is the one survival, is thought to have
stood almost detached to the N of the quire, as at Ely. The
'gatehouse' of c.1500 is in fact only a part, the remainder having
been re-erected at the Cromwells' other house, Hinchingbrooke.

The Cromwells used the Lady chapel (preserved only at
basement level) as the nucleus of an E-shaped house of c.1600,
much of the stone of the remainder being taken for Cambridge
colleges. Sir John Soane designed additions in 1804–6, and Edward
Blore some more extensive ones (the entire top storey and W wing)
not long after. The house is now used by the mixed comprehensive
Abbey School.

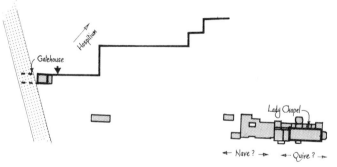

The gatehouse, standing back from the green, originally extended
over the road alongside. The half that remains can be entered from
inside the grounds. Its S doorway was originally a window; above it
is a pretty two-light oriel window, a detail repeated on the N face.

In the main room is a 13th c. monument with recumbent effigy,
supposed to represent Ailwine the founder. The gallery above is not
open, but in the adjoining (added) room are some carved stones
including five fine bosses.

The parish church (nearby) is extremely unusual in having been
built as a hospice of the abbey. It only became a church later, and
was probably not parochial till the abbey church was dismembered;

its tower, built of abbey stone, is of 1672.

Ramsgate Kent: at S end of town TR 377643

Benedictine priory of St Augustine founded 1856 by Bishop Grant of Southwark; became abbey 1896

Church (only) open 7.0 a.m. to 12 noon and 5.45 to 7.0 p.m.

The foundation history is unparalleled. The architect Augustus Pugin built the church for himself in 1847–51, with a small cloister and extensive sacristies on one side and a house (The Grange) also for himself on the other – with no intention of there ever being a monastery. He died a year later, aged 40. Monks came in 1856 and his son Edward designed their abbey on the other side of the road (1860–1). Edward also added St John the Evangelist's chapel off the cloister (1857) and his brother Peter Paul built St Joseph's (1893). In the richness of its Pugin fittings the church is unique, though in recent reordering a few have been sacrificed.

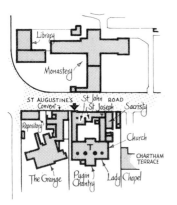

The unassuming doorway on the street opens into the two-sided **cloister**. To the left is a long row of Stations of the Cross by the brothers de Beule of Gent (1893); modern Disneyesque paintwork conceals their sculptural merit. Within the grille opposite is the Digby chantry (St John the Evangelist's) added by Edward Pugin in 1857; it has a patterned painted vault, marble columns with foliage caps, and rich glass and floor tiles. The smaller St Joseph's chapel

(1893) and the Sacred Heart altarpiece at the further end (1884) are by Peter Paul Pugin; in front of the latter is a floor brass to Abbot Alcock (d. 1882). Virtually all the glass here and in the cloister walk and in the church itself is by John Hardman.

Just before the **church** door is another brass, to a founder priest Alfred Luck (d. 1864). The church is not large, but perfectly proportioned and of exquisite craftsmanship in brownish Whitby stone. The foliage capitals of the short single S arcade are almost of Southwell quality. Massive tower arch piers dominate the interior, which has lost a number of its original fittings – yet to modern eyes still appears over-furnished. The magnificent 'Te Deum' E window is one of Hardman's first and finest. The W window (Life of St Benedict) and the N in greys and purples with three abbesses are also specially good.

The roofs are mostly quite plain and open, without trusses. That of the crossing is flat; the chancel's panelled and lightly gilded. Reordering has meant the loss of the pulpit (not by Augustus Pugin) from the crossing N wall, the resiting of the stalls around the E end, and the removal of the chancel screen to enclose the now overcrowded **Lady chapel**. There the E window and the blue and gilt gates by John Powell were memorials to Augustus Pugin.

The S transept chapel is the **Pugin chantry**. Behind the elaborate oak screen are the canopied tomb-chest of Pugin himself, a splendid St Augustine window above (as well as two others), a richly carved, painted and gilt altar from his private chapel in The Grange, a 16th c. Flemish Pietà as reredos, brasses to the Pugin and Powell families, and a beautiful heraldic floor of Minton tiles. The **S aisle** has a window depicting SS Bede, Wilfrid and Cuthbert, and at the W end the font and towering canopy designed by Pugin for the far bigger St George's cathedral, Southwark; the font is based on the Seven Sacraments font at Walsingham.

A nearby door leads to the walled churchyard. From here the church **exterior** can be studied. In contrast to the interior, it is faced with flints and bands of stone. The tower was meant to have a spire. To the W is the brown brick tower of Pugin's house The Grange.

The road front is dominated by the long cloister wall of black flint; at its W end are a smaller tower and the gable of the chapter house (at first a temporary church, and now a sacristy), while at the W is St Edward's House, a lodge of 1849, followed by the gate piers of The Grange. All this is part of the abbey precinct, and not open to the public. The abbey itself, through a gabled porch on the other side of the road, is private too. A T-shaped building of two and three storeys, of flint with bands of brick, it has fussy saw-tooth arches over some windows and is only vaguely Gothic.

Reading Berkshire: SU 720735
in town centre, ¼ mile SE of railway station

Cluniac abbey of St Mary and St John the Evangelist founded 1121, a daughter house of Lewes priory. Became Benedictine in 13th c., became mitred. Dissolved 1539 and granted to Lord Somerset

Owned mostly by Reading Corporation, the Roman Catholic Church and the Home Office. Open during normal hours without charge

Henry I followed his benefactions to Cluny abbey by endowing that of Reading where he was buried in 1136; the final consecration of the church was in 1164. It remained little altered but for the Lady chapel added in the 14th c.

Not much is known of the monastic buildings, but some kind of palace was made of them by Henry VIII, the materials of the quire went to repair St Mary's church, those of the Lady chapel were taken to Windsor, and those of the nave were used up in Civil War defences. Apart from the gatehouse, little remains but great masses of flint rubble, mostly of the E monastic range.

The inner **gatehouse** or Abbey Gate is 13th c., extensively restored in 1879 under Sir George Gilbert Scott. E of it is Abbot's House, a prefabricated office building; its car park behind is on the site of the cloister, with a piece of Perpendicular tracery re-erected in the middle. The rear (S) wall is part of the refectory, and the shapeless lumps to the E are the chapter house etc. These are reached by going back across Abbot's Walk (which corresponds with the S nave aisle) and through Forbury Gardens. A subway leads into what was the **S transept**, close to the recognisable base of the SW crossing pier.

The two chapel apses can be made out, and a decayed tomb canopy. The high brick wall beyond bounds the county gaol. Next to the transept is the slype, once barrel-vaulted; then the **chapter house**, an enormous room now open to the sky, where Parliament sat on occasion. On its N wall is a modern tablet recording the writing of 'Sumer icumen in' at the abbey, c.1226; two others on

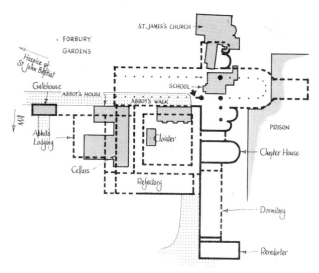

the E wall commemorate the first and last abbots.

Next down the slope is a lawn enclosed by the dormitory walls, and at the bottom (past another cross-passage) the reredorter, now used as a tip.

One can then follow the river along Chestnut Walk, skirt the prison and come to some minor remains by the Catholic church: bits of the N transept apses standing to the S of its chancel and (visible by walking up the path on its W side) two enormous collapsed lumps of masonry left where they fell. The church font is made of a carved stone from the abbey. The path leads back to Abbot's Walk.

Two other brief tours may be made, one to the three arches of the abbey mill which stand in a state of arrested decay behind Abbey Mill House (through Abbey Gate, down Abbey Street and past the White Lion), and the other to the former Hospice of St John Baptist, founded c.1190, a largely 15th c. building to be seen either from the churchyard of St Laurence which was itself the gate-chapel of the abbey, or from Valpy Street behind.

Fragments of 12th c. abbey sculpture can be seen in the Reading and Victoria and Albert Museums.

Reculver Kent: on coast, 3 miles E of Herne Bay   TR 227694

Benedictine abbey of St Mary founded 669 by King Egbert.
  Annexed to St Augustine's abbey, Canterbury 949

In care of Department of the Environment. Open during standard
  hours (admission charge)

The church ruin stands in the middle of a Roman fort, a third of
which is now under the sea. Its 7th c. plan was apsidal, with nave
and chancel separated by three arches, and a porticus like a transept
each side. In the 8th c. these porticūs were extended along the sides
and round the W end. Danish raids probably drove the monks out
in the 10th c.; thereafter the church was parochial, but it had a dean
till c.1030. In the 12th c. the W towers were added, and in the 13th
c. a bigger E end. By 1805 it was on the brink of the sea, as it still is,
and was scandalously abandoned for a new church safely inland and
largely destroyed; Trinity House then repaired the towers as a
sea-mark. The two 7th c. chancel arch columns and parts of a cross
are preserved in Canterbury cathedral crypt. Excavations in 1927,
following transfer to state guardianship, enabled the remains to be
analysed.

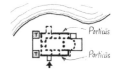

Apart from the twin W towers, which are round-arched at the
base and pointed-arched at the top and which have a weatherworn
Norman doorway between, the first impression is of a rather
ordinary parish church ruin. The original 7th c. plan is however
distinctively marked out inside, and parts of its actual walls remain,
particularly on the N side where there are sills of early windows.
The NW tower may be ascended, offering views of the ruin, of the
coast, and of the appalling caravan park nearby.

Repton Derbyshire: in village, 6½ miles SW of Derby   SK 302271

Benedictine abbey founded c.660 by Diuma, Bishop of Mercia.
  Dissolved 874

Parish church. Open during normal hours

Repton was the capital of Mercia. The abbey was for monks and nuns under an abbess. It was abandoned during the Danish invasion but the church was later salvaged, became parochial and underwent numerous changes. In it there survives the sanctuary crypt, thought to have been built as a mausoleum for King Ethelbald in 757; also the sanctuary itself, probably of *c.*840. Nave aisles were added in the 13th c. and rebuilt with their arcades in the 14th c.; the tower, porch and S chapel were also added. The side walls of the chancel, probably also 9th c., were pierced with round arches in 1792, altered in 1854 to match the 14th c. work.

In 1172 an Augustinian priory was founded close by; parts of it were converted into Repton School in 1556. Of the monastic buildings of the Saxon abbey nothing is known.

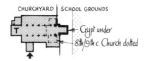

The uniformity of the arcades disguises the fact that the two E bays of the **nave**, those which mark the chancel of the three-cell Saxon church, have 9th c. walling and 19th c. arches. The clerestory and roof are 15th c. overall. The chancel arch is 14th c.; it too supports Saxon walling, with quite a wide upper opening partially blocked. At the E end of each arcade is a round column base. These columns supported 9th c. arches that probably remained until the sides of the chancel were further opened up in 1792, and their upper parts are preserved in the S porch.

The **crypt** is accessible either side, but preferably from the N where a light switch will illuminate one of the two steep stairs cut late in the 9th c. through earlier walling, probably for pilgrims' use. The outer walls of the crypt are now ascribed to 757 and the columns and vault to the early 9th c. Whether or not this was the mausoleum of Kings Ethelbald (d. 757) and Wiglaf (d. 840) and the shrine of the latter's grandson St Wystan (d. 850) there can be no doubt of its special sanctity.

The **sanctuary** is almost wholly Saxon, i.e. of *c.*840. The wall plaster was stripped in 1940, exposing walling stones like the E part of the nave. In the rest of the church the main features, taken clockwise and starting at the E end of the S aisle, are: a memorial with kneeling figures of George Waklin (d. 1617) and wife; an incised alabaster slab to Gilbert Thacker (d. 1563); royal arms of George III over the S doorway; some medieval tracery incorporated into the organ case; and at the E end of the N aisle a tablet with bust of Francis Thacker (d. 1710) and a knight's effigy of *c*.1400.

The 14th c. S **porch** is two-storeyed and contains the columns already referred to, as well as a Saxon cross-shaft and other fragments. An **external** circuit shows mostly 14th c. work, including tower and tall spire, but the W walls of the aisles are partly 13th c. Along the N side is a way through into the school grounds, from which the 9th c. E end can be well seen, with irregular stonework and massive quoins. The building sequence as analysed in recent years seems to have been quite complex; suffice it here to point out that the base of the E wall of what is now the N aisle is also Saxon, together with the projecting NE angle of the nave, but that of the S aisle was rebuilt further E when the bigger 14th c. S chapel was formed. The rectangular windows of the crypt are of *c*.1500.

Revesby Lincolnshire: ½ mile S of village and A155   TF 297607

Cistercian abbey of St Mary and St Laurence founded 1143 by
   William de Romara, Earl of Lincoln, a daughter house of
   Rievaulx. Dissolved 1538 and given to Duke of Suffolk

Owned by Lee family. Site accessible at all times without charge

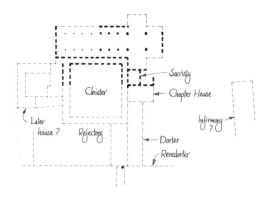

What little is known of the building history was deduced from 19th c. excavations. Some 13th c. fragments found on the site are built

into the inner walls of the tower of the 19th c. parish church, and some specimens of a fine tiled pavement also uncovered are in its floor.

The site is an open pasture field separated from a farm lane on two sides by a deep ditch. About 250 yards SE of the gate is a granite slab of 1890 marked 'Site of the high altar'. Here was found the reputed tomb of the founder and his two sons; two other graves (one 14th, one 15th c.) were in the cloister walk. Nothing else is now obvious, though parts of the layout not disturbed by excavation are roughly traceable by air photography, including a square courtyard against the W side of the cloister, probably a relic of a post-Dissolution house.

Rewley Oxfordshire: 600 yards NW of Oxford city centre   SP 506064

Cistercian 'studium' founded *c*.1272 by Richard, King of the Romans, a daughter house of Thame: became abbey 1281; dissolved 1536 and granted to Dr George Owen. Little is known of the buildings, but the refectory stood as a malthouse till the 18th c. Railway coal sidings swept away the last remnants in 1850 – except a piece of precinct wall with a 15th c. doorway, visible from the canal path N of Hythe Bridge.

Rievaulx North Yorkshire: SE 577850
2¼ miles WNW of Helmsley and ¼ mile S of Stokesley road B1257

Cistercian abbey of St Mary founded 1132 by Walter l'Espec, a daughter house of Clairvaux. Dissolved 1538 and passed to Thomas, Earl of Rutland

In care of Department of the Environment. Open during standard hours (admission charge)

Founded directly from Clairvaux as the first Cistercian house in northern England, it quickly became very large and sent out colonies. Rievaulx = Rye vale. The splendid buildings in the valley (including the big church) were practically complete by *c*.1180, but reconstruction of the refectory and S cloister range was soon undertaken, followed *c*.1225 by ambitious rebuilding of the whole of the church from the crossing eastwards. Apart from the 15th c. formation of a new abbot's house little was built later; from about

140 monks the numbers dwindled to 22, a decline reflected in
reductions in size of the chapter house, dorter, etc. Because of the
steep slope, the church actually lies almost N–S instead of W–E;
descriptions always assume normal orientation.

Much was quarried away following the Dissolution – particularly
the nave – but the ruin as it stands now is amongst the most
complete Cistercian ones in England. It was taken over by the
Commissioners of Works in 1918. Its picturesqueness was
recognized in the mid-18th c. when Thomas Duncombe laid out the
Rievaulx Terrace on the hill above and used a series of views from it
as a part of the landscaping of his park.

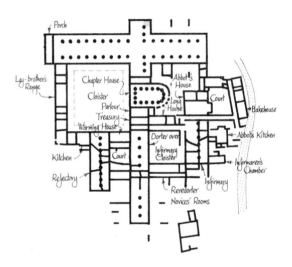

Visitors come past the SE outbuildings to the E end of the
church, so – exceptionally – the tour starts there. This is the part
rebuilt early in the 13th c., and is thus fully developed Early
English. The E wall has two tiers of three shafted lancets with
dog-tooth ornament, and had a third tier to light the roof space. The
N wall has broken away (leaving two spectacular 14th c. flying
buttresses), so one can look across to the S arcade, to the triforium
with its pairs of double openings (once two-light but now lacking
their shafts) and to the stepped lancets of the clerestory. Triforium
and clerestory both have dog-tooth, and the triforium bay nearest

the crossing has a round, instead of pointed, super-arch. There was a vault, and the great crossing arch still stands.

The transepts, rebuilt a little before the quire, resemble it on their E side, though the upper stages differ. They also differ a little from one another. Moreover they were never vaulted, though their E chapels were, and the most northerly still is. At both ends are three more great lancets, but in the W side the earlier work commences – the Transitional of half a century before, with round arches in the bottom stage. The base of the end walls is part of the earlier work too – identifiable also by the rough brown stone contrasting with the later cleanly worked white. At the S end is the high-level night doorway to the dorter.

The nave is wholly earlier, much more decayed but also much more austere in design, with big square pier bases. Latterly the aisles had subdivisions into chapels. Though their outer walls only survive to a height of 6 feet or so, there is evidence on the S side that they had transverse tunnel vaults; that is most unusual. In one S chapel is the 15th c. tomb slab of Abbot Burton, while centrally near the crossing are the indent of a brass and some old tiles echoing Ave Marias. More tiles – plain ones – survive at the W end, while in the galilee or W porch are numerous grave-slabs, one of 1262.

Now the **cloister**, reached from the S aisle. A piece of arcading with twin colonnettes and round arches has been re-erected at the NW corner. From it one looks across at the refectory. The W (lay brothers') range is on the right (now low walls only but evidently curiously inadequate for the 500 or more lay brothers the abbey is believed to have had in its heyday), and at the end of the W walk the kitchen – also curiously small, with fireplace, hearth and rough hatch into the refectory.

This S range is the part reconstructed *c*.1225; disregarding subdividings and demolitions, the rest of the domestic buildings may be taken as original work of *c*.1180. Through the kitchen, outside steps lead into the **refectory** basement, with columns down the centre but split up by later partitions. Note the lancet windows at upper and lower levels, remains of floor vaulting, and the relics of the pulpit on the W side, its stair continuing down to the undercroft.

Back in the cloister, the refectory doorway is trefoil-headed, with washing recesses on each side. Next is the warming house, with big double fireplace against the refectory wall, and a former 'aisle' blocked off in the 15th c. At the start of the E walk is the curved base of the day stair. Under it was the treasury. Then comes a parlour with seats along the sides, and then the **chapter house** – once

Rievaulx: 'View no. 5' from the Terrace

with vaulted aisles and apsidal ambulatory, the latter being blocked off in the 15th c. This is a very uncommon plan. Of five tomb slabs, three are of identifiable 13th and 14th c. abbots; more important is the 13th c. shrine of St William, the first abbot (d. 1148), set into the W wall.

Beyond the chapter house is the library/vestry, and past that in the cloister wall a book recess. The vestry leads out into an irregular court. On the left of this against the church is the sacristy foundation, and on the right the big curve of the chapter house end. At the far corner wooden steps lead down to the **abbot's house**, formed in the 15th c. out of the original infirmary. Its N end, marked by a tall cliff of masonry, contains two small rooms and a bigger one with fireplace and bay window; it can then be traced southwards by the line of stumpy columns with scalloped caps that ran down the centre. When the upper part became the abbot's hall the windows were altered and stairs added – one flight on the E side and one within the infirmary cloister. The latter leads to an upper doorway bearing a relief of the Annunciation. As in the main cloister, a short length of arcade has been reconstructed. Along the S side is the reredorter – its further wall standing high but the rest largely gone, so exposing the drain channel – and on the W a day room (the undercroft of the dorter), accessible from a little passage leading to the corner of the main cloister. This has more column bases down the middle, and two fireplaces; at the end is the drain again.

Back now into the infirmary cloister. On the left at higher level is the domestic range called the Long House, from which is an interesting view of the presbytery – looking into its triforium from the wrong side – and of the S transept from which nearly all the adjoining structures have gone.

Now a look at the low walls alongside the entrance path. The extreme SE building between the path and the old infirmary was the infirmarer's chamber. Below this, a path leads round and down into the drain channel again, and there is an unidentified isolated building on the lawn beneath. Up the hill is the abbot's kitchen, with fireplaces, washing trough and drain, and above it another small court. Between that and the path are various outbuildings, including a bakehouse identifiable by its hearth.

The village church of St Mary was the chapel outside the abbey gate and retains a little 13th c. work. To its NW are a few stones of the gatehouse itself. Much more rewarding are the views from Rievaulx Terrace down to the abbey through cleared openings in the wood.

Robertsbridge Sussex: TQ 755238
1 mile E of Robertsbridge village on A21

Cistercian abbey of the Blessed Virgin Mary founded at Salehurst 1176 by Alured de St Martin, a daughter house of Boxley. Moved to Robertsbridge (on opposite side of river Rother) c.1250. Dissolved 1538 and passed to Sir William Sydney

Owned by Heath family. Not open to the public

The scanty evidence (largely based on aerial photography of crop markings) suggests that most or all of the buildings were 13th c., with few if any later additions. The supposed abbot's house became a farmhouse and, much altered, is now called The Abbey; in its lowest storey is a 13th c. vaulted undercroft. The monastic S range, comprising refectory and warming house, though now in an advancing state of decay, survived through conversion into barn and oast house; at its E end are traces of the commencement of the dorter undercroft vault.

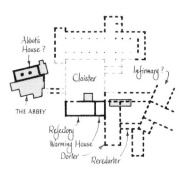

The present white weather-boarded house and its garden are strictly private, but parts can be discreetly seen from the lane (marked 'Private Road' for its last ½ mile). The gable end containing remnants of a traceried window is conspicuous enough to be seen from Salehurst churchyard, away to the NW. Further on, the crumbling outline of the refectory can be glimpsed; that is all.

Rocester Staffordshire: in village   SK 112393

Augustinian abbey of the Blessed Virgin Mary founded 1141–6 by Richard Bacon; dissolved 1538. Abbey and parish church stood separately within a Roman fort. Earthworks in the hayfield (Atkins family, owners) S of the church are probably relics of the abbey; so are some medieval tiles in the church.

Roche South Yorkshire: SK 544898
1½ miles SE of Maltby, and ¼ mile S of East Retford road A634

Cistercian abbey of the Blessed Virgin Mary founded 1147 by Richard de Builli and Richard fitzTurgis, a daughter house of Newminster. Dissolved 1538 and given to William Ramsden and Thomas Vavasour

In care of Department of the Environment. Open during standard
   hours (admission charge)

Historically the church is important in that the standard Cistercian
plan was, perhaps for the first time, developed by linking the E
chapels of the transepts to form transverse aisles. Moreover the
transepts and presbytery (the only parts surviving to any degree of
completeness) indicate a more decisive transition from
Romanesque to Gothic than almost any known building hitherto.
The suggested date of *c.*1170 applies to the whole church and to the
lay brothers' (W) cloister range. The remaining cloister buildings
and the supposed lay brothers' infirmary were 13th c., the abbot's
house and kitchen 14th c.

   Capability Brown landscaped the grounds and ruins in their rocky
limestone valley in the 18th c. for the then owner the Earl of
Scarbrough of Sandbeck Hall, whose descendant passed them to the
Office of Works in 1921. Roche building stone is still quarried
nearby.

   The early 14th c. gatehouse is encountered first – low, vaulted,
and with an inner wall separating pedestrians and vehicles. Close by
is a pretty 18th c. Gothick lodge with papery window tracery,
through which visitors enter the abbey site.

   The prominent parts of the **church** ruin are the E sides of the
transepts; nothing else stands so high. From the W end of the nave
their blend of Romanesque and Gothic is well seen, the main arches

Roche: Late 12th c. church, looking E

being pointed but on clustered piers of Norman type, the blind triforium of plain twin arches pointed too, but the clerestory of large single lights round-headed. The bases of the three W doorways stand, also the foundation of a long 13th c. narthex built to protect them. The nave columns, in design like those of the transepts, stand several feet high, and much original paving remains. Though not at once obvious, many medieval grave-slabs lie amongst it, mainly in the five W bays where lay burials were allowed. Parts of the foundations of the dividing pulpitum and of the four chapels that stood against its W face can be seen.

Next the crossing, and a closer look at the E parts. Of the N transept, the southern chapel has a large piscina, and half of its vault survives. The presbytery has lost its E wall and most of the detail on its side walls, which were refaced with stone canopy-work in the 14th c. but which originally resembled the transepts. The 14th c. sedilia and piscina should be noticed, also the altar dais. The S transept chapels have their vaults complete, with carved bosses; the left one has traces of a later window, the right one a piscina. Along the S side of the transept, from right to left, are foundations of the night stair and of a circular stair, and a doorway into the sacristy.

From the last one can look over into the chapter house and then pass into the **cloister**, noting the curved steps and doorway base back into the aisle, the two projections into the N side of the garth indicating big 15th c. buttresses, and traces close to them of a tub and a drain for laundering.

Following the E walk past the chapter house (all this is 13th c. work) one comes to the parlour and then the **dorter** undercroft with octagonal column bases. The foundations running off to the E are probably those of a passage to the infirmary. Another feature of special interest at Roche – though by no means unique – is the running water that still flows under the dorter and beneath a series of bridges in both directions, draining the reredorter to the E and the kitchen and lay brothers' range to the W. The land on either bank of this stream was separately donated by agreement by the abbey's two founders. The small rooms at the end of the dorter range may have been a meat kitchen (the one with tiled fireplace) and misericord.

Beside the reredorter is another small court or cloister, its N side broken away where a branch drain from the abbot's house enters the stream. The tall mass beyond this court belonged to a 13th c. house attributed to the infirmarer, while the S side was closed by that of the abbot (14th c.). To the W (i.e. also on the S bank of the stream) another high wall-angle marks the abbot's square kitchen, with a big fireplace on one side; a range of stores lies beyond, and in the corner of the site what was probably the lay brothers' infirmary, showing several fireplaces and round column bases. The stream at this point has a waterfall and yet another branch drain, coming out of the lay brothers' range. Return now downstream, round the buttressed end of the **refectory**, and into it near the dais. Probably at first planned wholly on the N bank in an E–W direction, the refectory had to bridge the stream to conform with the then newly adopted Cistercian manner of building it N–S. Looking towards the cloister, on the right is the warming house with two hearths, on the left the kitchen with the base of a great double fireplace (with burnt stones at the back), and the remains of smaller ones on the other three sides.

The whole W range was the **lay brothers' wing**: refectory and stores below, dorter above. Unlike the remainder, this is of the same period as the church. A small addition on the further side was the checker's office. Unusually, there was no doorway into the

church from the NW angle of the cloister; however, by going over
the wall base or walking round, one can see the base of the lay
brothers' night stair which led to the aisle from their dorter.

Romsey Hampshire: in town centre   SU 351212

Benedictine nunnery founded *c*.907 by King Edward the Elder;
   refounded as abbey of St Mary and St Elfleda 967 by King Edgar.
   Dissolved 1539; church became parochial; remainder granted to
   J. Bellow and R. Bigot

Parish church, but S part of site in multiple ownership. Open to
   public during normal hours

Foundations of an apse found under the central tower are probably
of the 967 church, dedicated to abbess Elfleda, daughter of King
Edward; so possibly is part of the S wall. Otherwise the building
sequence is readily grasped, an E to W progression from *c*.1120 to
c.1230. The Lady chapel was rebuilt *c*.1275. Of the monastic
buildings little is known; the chapter house seems to have been
polygonal and part of the refectory survives in houses to the S.
   At the Dissolution the town bought the church for £100, only its
Lady chapel and the additional N aisle being demolished. Apart
from the N porch of 1908, it is an outstanding example of
Romanesque and the change to Early English.

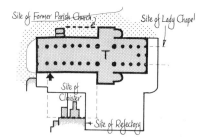

The NW cloister doorway forms the visitors' entrance on the S.
As is often the case, one sees the last building work first – the two W
bays of the nave, Early English of *c*.1220. The next bay is
Transitional, the main arch being pointed but plainer, and the rest
Norman. The crossing arches are Norman too and so is the
presbytery, the prominent Geometric E windows being insertions.

A closer look at the **nave** should start at the earliest bay, next to
the crossing. Its unusual design, with the main lower arches running
into columns of triforium height, is paralleled at Jedburgh and at
what is now Oxford cathedral. Even odder is the triforium itself,
with the spaces above its twin arches bisected by single little shafts.
One bay is like this; the second and third, obviously a little later,
dispense with the giant columns. The fourth has rich zigzag on the N
side only, and a plainer triforium. The fifth is the Transitional bay,
in which both the triforium arch and the lower are pointed; the
capitals become more elaborate, with a hint of foliage instead of
scallops, and the triforium shows trefoil heads and plate tracery.
The last two bays, fully Early English, still respect the general
system of arches and sub-arches, and on the N the main capitals
have stiff-leaf carving. Of the clerestory the first bay, evidently
completed at the same time as the tower to provide stability, is
Norman, three bays with central window; the rest, fairly uniform
Early English, must have proceeded at a slower pace than the stages
below. The three big clear-glazed lancets in the W wall may be of
original design but the barrel roof is of 1850, by Benjamin Ferrey.
Below are three tablets to the Palmerston family, 1769–1856. The
two flags were Earl Mountbatten's when in command in Singapore
and as Viceroy in Delhi. The font is by W.D. Caröe, 1912.

The **N aisle** echoes the styles of the nave. Bays 1 to 3 have 13th c.
vaults with moulded ribs. Bay 4, the first of the Norman, has
enriched vault ribs – alongside the most ornamented of the main
arches; the others are plainer. The intricately traceried chest at the
W end is 16th c. Flemish. In bay 2, the late 19th c. figure of a
sleeping child, Alice Taylor, was carved by her doctor father; in bay
3 is a 19th c. font, and by bay 7 the large pulpit, 1891.

The **N transept**'s E wall is like the E bay of the nave, its clerestory
being wholly Norman; in one triforium bay the odd motif of the
little shaft appears over a trio of arches instead of two. In the 15th c.
this transept was made the chancel of the parish church, the nave of
which stood outside the present N aisle; the 'chancel arch' cut
through the earlier triple window was later replaced by the one now
containing St Swithun glass of 1951. Opposite this is a reredos of
1525 painted on wooden boards, a rare survival. The apsed chapel
behind, now a choir room, can be glimpsed from the **N presbytery
aisle**. Its vault has traces of painting and there is a monument to
Robert Brackley (d. 1628).

The aisles continue the design of the nave aisles, and have some
fascinating capitals. In bay 2 is a 15th c. embroidered cope, and at

the end another apsidal chapel, with wall-arcading each side of its window; the glass is by Charles Kempe, 1897. The two-bay E ambulatory is very like the aisles and has blocked openings to the Lady chapel. The monument to Maud Ashley (d. 1911) is by Emil Fuchs; one of the daughters portrayed became Countess Mountbatten; opposite is a framed 16th c. painting. The first chapel, now St Mary's, has a good 18th c. cartouche and, as an altar, the tomb-chest of a late 15th c. abbess. The window-jamb painting is 13th c. The second is St Ethelfleda's (Elfleda's). Both have glass by Clayton & Bell, c.1880. St Anne's, the chapel at the end of the **S presbytery aisle**, has another Kempe E window with, below it, a stone Crucifix carving of c.1000 set beneath a piece of 15th c. screenwork.

Moving now W, opposite the memorial to John Storke (d. 1711) turn right into the **presbytery**. The splendid Norman design repeats that of the transepts, i.e. like the E bay of the nave, but without the giant columns afterwards tried there and found satisfactory. The glass in the twin Geometric E windows (insertions of c.1275) is by Powell, 1888, and the Madonna below by Martin Travers.

The **S transept** differs from the N mainly in its W wall. Its apse chapel, now another vestry, is blocked off by the recoloured 17th c. memorial of John St Barbe. To its left is a tablet to John Kent (d. 1694) and in front the grave slab of Earl Mountbatten (d. 1979). On the S side a rich early 14th c. canopy covers a 13th c. lady's effigy (possibly an abbess). The **crossing** with its four great Norman arches and flat, panelled ceiling is impressive. The organ is 19th c., and the stalls too with their Mount Temple and Mountbatten associations and inscriptions; their back cresting is older.

Over the arch from S transept to **S nave aisle** is a strange triforium bay with a ridiculously fat column. The aisle windows are higher because of the cloister. On the left, the abbess's doorway is curtained with embroidered saints by Maureen Helsdon, 1961. At the W end is the 1868 tomb chest of Sir William Petty (d. 1687).

The **exterior** adds little to what has been already seen. The SW doorway is renewed 13th c. The bay to its W was where the monastic W range abutted, while over the garden wall to the S are houses which embody bits of the refectory. Bays 4 and 5 of the S wall are those which may contain masonry of the 967 church, and the end bay has the fine abbess's doorway. On the transept wall adjacent is the famous 11th c. stone Rood. On the further side of the transept, a conical roof emphasises the apse. At the E end, where the Lady chapel abutted, two Norman arches gave way to two of *c*.1275 and these in turn to two windows of *c*.1275 set back when the chapel was taken down.

On the N side, the gargoyles around the NE corner should be noticed, and the mixture of window types; those of the nave aisle owe their late date to the fact that the former parish church lay alongside, though two have been made 'Norman' again. The best general view is from this direction and demonstrates the differences between the Norman quire clerestory and the Early English one of the nave. Even here, the stumpy central tower does not assert itself; its wooden turret put on in 1625 has eight bells.

Rufford Nottinghamshire: SK 646647
close to A614, 7 miles ENE of Mansfield

Cistercian abbey of St Mary founded *c*.1147, a daughter house of
   Rievaulx. Dissolved 1536 and passed to Earl of Shrewsbury

Owned by Department of the Environment. Not accessible, but
   visible through perimeter fence at any time without charge

The founder was Gilbert of Gaunt, Earl of Lincoln. Of the buildings little is known but their plan, determined mostly by excavation.

Bess of Hardwick is associated with the W range's conversion into a mansion. The Savile family owned this from the early 17th c. till 1938 and made numerous additions. The only recognisable monastic survival is a 13th c. vaulted basement room, probably the lay brothers' refectory. After World War II the house became largely derelict. In recent years Nottinghamshire County Council acquired the estate, now called Rufford Country Park, and handed the historic buildings to the Department of the Environment, which is undertaking their drastic reduction and gradual restoration.

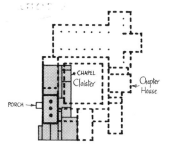

The main building lies within a temporary barbed wire fence but can be seen from all sides. The monastic undercroft is behind and beneath the barley-sugar columned Jacobean porch, and can hardly be seen. The high-windowed wing on the left is attributed to Bess of Hardwick. Till recently there was an imposing 18th c. continuation – now demolished and leaving a rugged end with a rough arch near the bottom which seems to represent the line of the cloister walk. The fenced enclosure has been extended sufficiently beyond it to skirt the church foundations, which are to be marked out.

Round on the E side the back of the 17th c. wing is reduced to ruin; in front of it lay the cloister. The tall S wing with added 19th c. turret (built clear of the monastic ranges) can be best seen by continuing along the path and turning up the steps into the stable yard; a grassed area with a well then leads back to the W front.

Rushen Isle of Man: SC 278703
at Ballasalla, 2 miles NE of Castletown

Savigniac abbey of the Blessed Virgin Mary founded 1134 by Olaf, king of Man, a daughter house of Furness; became Cistercian 1147. Dissolved 1540 and granted to Earl of Derby

Owned by Chellean Ltd. Open to the public daily without charge

Written evidence and finds of graves point to the existence of an earlier church and perhaps monastery. The plan was of small but normal Cistercian type and probably little altered though the nave may have been rebuilt prior to a reconsecration in 1257. In 1316 (during Scottish overlordship) severe damage was caused by Irish pirates led by Richard de Mandeville, and it was possibly a risk of similar raids, coupled with a diminution in the size of the community, which then prompted the building of a semi-defensive belfry tower in a strange position over the N transept, its S and E walls being built upon pre-existing arches. The cloister may also have been rebuilt at that time.

The tower, the slype S of the S transept, and walls to the SE thought to be of the infirmary and associated buildings are the only important survivals above ground. The adjoining house, built in 1773, became a school in 1800 and an hotel in 1846. It and the abbey grounds have kept in step with the times as a tourist and leisure centre.

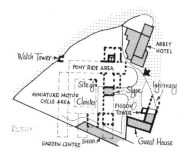

In season, the church area is taken up with pony rides and the cloister with miniature motor cycles. The low ivy-clad ruin near the centre was the slype and the modern dwarf wall running from it towards the 'garden centre' shop marks the E side of the cloister. The prominent 14th c. tower to the N, the other side of the riding area, was over the N transept; its blocked late 12th c. lower arches, S into quire and E into chapel, survive. The much lower 14th c. 'watch tower' close to the W end of the nave is entirely hidden by vegetation; it formed part of a defensive precinct wall.

On the E side of the site, backing on to the Silver Burn, are the Pigeon Tower (probably part of the infirmarer's lodging), to its right the abbot's lodging, and behind them the infirmary. All have been greatly altered; two of the rooms now form a museum and 'relic room'. About ¼ mile upstream is a well preserved 14th c. packhorse bridge built by the abbey.

Ryde Isle of Wight: ¾ mile E of town centre   SZ 603925

Benedictine nuns' priory of the Peace of the Heart of Jesus founded at Ventnor 1882, a daughter house of Liège; became abbey 1926

Church (only) open during normal hours on request

The foundation at a house called Steephill View, Ventnor (since demolished) resulted from anti-religious laws in Belgium. The move to Appley House, Ryde came about from the buildings here being vacated by a similarly expatriate community. This had left Solesmes, France (see Quarr) in 1901, was at Northwood, Isle of Wight till 1906, and then took over what was at first a square stone mansion which had become the nucleus of the short-lived Isle of

Wight Proprietary College. The Solesmes nuns converted the
college 'gymnasium' into a block with monastic cells, retained the
house (it has since lost its tower) and in between built the yellow
brick cloister and church in an effectively simplified Gothic style.
The Benedictines of Ventnor kept the name of the church's titular
saint and the whole abbey is still called St Cecilia's today.

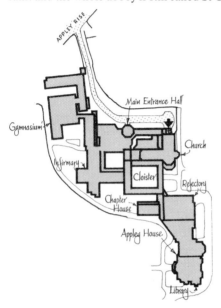

The church entrance is beneath the tower at the end of the public
drive; if it is locked enquiry may be made at the main door further
back. Only the N transept may be entered, but from it most of the
brick interior can be seen. An unaisled cross with unequal arms, it
has plain plaster vaults with ribs continued down as wall-shafts with
simple stone capitals, high lancet windows with patterned glass
enlivened with plum-coloured squares, and an attractive coloured
tiled floor. A wrought-iron screen divides the now central sanctuary
from the nuns' quire, which has two rows of stalls each side.

Comparatively little lies outside the nuns' enclosure except the
long N front and the plain tower with louvred and slated top which
is a landmark at this end of the town. In front as one returns to the

main gate is a glimpse of the high so-called 'gymnasium'.

St Albans Hertfordshire: in city centre TL.145070

Dual monastery of St Alban for men and women founded or
refounded 793 by Offa, King of Mercia; became Benedictine
*c.*970; nuns moved to Sopwell 1077; became mitred in 12th c.
Dissolved 1539; church sold to town and remainder to Sir Richard
Lee; church became cathedral 1877

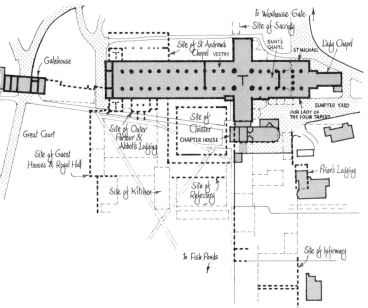

Cathedral church open during normal hours

For a full description see *A Guide to the Cathedrals of Britain*,
pp.332–9.

St Benet of Holme Norfolk: 1¾ miles SSW of Ludham TG 383156

Monastery of St Benedict founded *c.*800 by Suneman. Refounded as Benedictine abbey 1019 by King Canute. Annexed to see of Norwich 1536 and never suppressed

Owned by see of Norwich. Accessible at all times without charge

Records of building work on the riverside site, now as always difficult of access by the marshland roads, indicate much building activity in the 12th c. and the existence of both a central and a W tower, the former apparently being circular. The E end of the church was rebuilt in the 13th c., and an aisle or aisles added to the quire in the 15th c. After the Dissolution almost all was quarried away, but the Perpendicular gatehouse largely survived through the odd misfortune of being built into a windmill in the 18th c. This was the only medieval English abbey not actually suppressed: the Bishop of Norwich is still Abbot of Holme and receives its revenues.

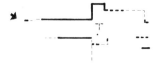

The gatehouse, approached by an often dauntingly muddy track, stands near the bank of the Bure, its inner face towards the river and its outer visible only from inside the circular brick shell of the windmill that straddles it. Part of its ribbed tunnel vault remains, and in the outer arch spandrels the figures of a rampant lion and a man with a sword – their significance unknown.

Of the church, some 400 yards to the E, the general form of the nave (possibly with narrow S aisle) is clear from the low fragments surviving, but that of the E end rather less so. Undulations towards the river suggest only roughly where the monastic buildings stood, while bigger, more regular ones towards the gatehouse and the approach track indicate the fishponds.

St Dogmael's Dyfed:
in village on B4546, 1 mile W of Cardigan

SN 162460

Tironensian priory founded *c.*1113–15 by Robert fitzMartin, a daughter house of Tiron, Normandy; became abbey 1120. Dissolved 1536 and granted to John Bradshaw

In care of Welsh Office. Open at all times without charge

Or Cemais; one of the very few abbeys of the (Benedictine) Order
of Tiron in Britain. Its nucleus was the church at Llandudoch (still
adjoining in rebuilt form) on which had been based an earlier
monastery destroyed in 987 by Vikings. The early 12th c. building
work stopped short of completion of an aisled nave; the W and N
walls and the cloister are 13th c., the N walk of the latter having
been rebuilt further N on the site of the intended S aisle. The E end
of the church and its crypt were a later 13th c. improvement while
much reconstruction of the cloister ranges and a new guest house,
chapter house and infirmary were completed in the 14th c. The N
transept was lavishly rebuilt early in the 16th c.

   The church continued for a time to be used by the parish, while
the rector apparently lived in the W range, and the rest went into
decay. Eventually all was abandoned when a new church and house
were built; the ruins were put into state care in 1934 and began to be
investigated in 1947.

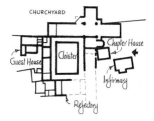

   The approach from the road below is towards the centre of the
group, the apse end of the 12th c. S transept chapel being readily
picked out. To its right is the **church** itself, with numerous areas of
old floor tiles exposed, and on the right of that the presbytery from
which steps lead down into the 13th c. crypt – no longer vaulted but
retaining wall shafts all round.

   The crossing pier bases, all standing to about 3 feet, are 12th c.
The N transept, however, probably rebuilt as a chapel for the Lords
of Cemais, is Tudor and retains springers of a surprisingly elaborate
vault with carved corbels, as well as two big tomb recesses. The
angled enclosing wall of the passage across to the nave is not
medieval, though the start of a stair which led up into the tower is
13th c. This passage was actually the first bay of a projected 12th c.
aisle. There would have been a solid wall by the monks' quire, and

then three more arches; on the S side these were built (and so was
an aisle) but not on the N, where the walling is 13th c. and contains
two more tomb recesses. The extensive plain floor tiling is 14th or
15th c. and there is a nice 14th c. N doorway with ballflower
ornament outside. The W wall, 13th c. too, stands high with a big
empty window arch and a stair at the SW angle. Various cross-walls,
particularly one near the W end, are mostly connected with
parochial use of the church after the Dissolution.

Now the **cloister** ranges, small and rather complex especially on
the W side which underwent much domestic conversion in the 16th
and 17th cc. The walk wall-bases are nearly complete, 12th c. to the
building ranges and 13th c. against the garth, and the W walk has its
slate paving. Working anti-clockwise, first and extending up the
slope was perhaps a guest house, while the main W range probably
latterly housed the abbot on the first floor. The uses of most of the
rooms can only by surmised, but at the junction with the S range are
three circular ovens of the 16th or 17th c. The monastic kitchen
must have been close by, followed by the refectory and warming
room along the S range, all quite small in scale and marked by
foundations only. The E range too has all but gone; towards the end
of the E walk is another patch of old tiles. The 14th c. chapter
house, off to the right and almost detached, looks almost like an
afterthought. Only its S wall stands to any height, but there are
tomb recesses on three sides and traces of an upper-level fireplace
showing later domestic use.

Much of the **infirmary**, detached to the SE, stands to full height
and was clearly tunnel-vaulted. A collection of carved stones inside
includes many roof bosses, capitals, turned shafts (from the cloister
arcades), a cadaver effigy of *c.*1500 from the N transept, and in the
recess on the S side an abbot's effigy and a cross slab.

St Osyth Essex: TM 120156
in village, 3½ miles W of Clacton-on-Sea

Nunnery founded in 7th c. by St Osyth; refounded 1121 as
    Augustinian canons' priory of St Peter, St Paul and St Osyth by
    Richard Belmeis, Bishop of London, and colonised from Holy
    Trinity Aldgate, London; became abbey before 1261, mitred
    1397. Dissolved 1539 and granted to Thomas Cromwell

Owned by de Chair family. Grounds, with monastic remains and
    parts of gatehouse, usually open 10.0 a.m. to 5.0 p.m. May to

September. Admission charge

St Osyth, daughter of Frithwald, first King of the East Angles, was
martyred in 653 by Danes invading her own nunnery, and her name
is associated with subsequent miracles. Of the 12th c. priory a little
is left, of 13th c. work slightly more – in the N parts of the cloister
buildings which here were N of the church. Of the church itself,
little is known beyond some foundations met when the gardens
were formed. Much more important are the late 15th c. gatehouse
(one of the best in England) and the early 16th c. façade of the
so-called Bishop's (really abbot's) Lodging.

In 1553 the estate was bought by Lord D'Arcy, who demolished
the church and built a brick mansion (now mostly gone) around the
N range, adding a big Gothic flint and stone tower to the E and
probably using the refectory as a hall. His son and grandson
continued the work. Their 18th c. descendant Lord Rochford built a
more up-to-date house (since curtailed) to the W of the abbot's
lodging, and in the grounds he planted the first Lombardy poplars
in England. Since 1948 the main house (much altered c.1865) has
been a convalescent home; the gatehouse is a private residence
partly shown to the public.

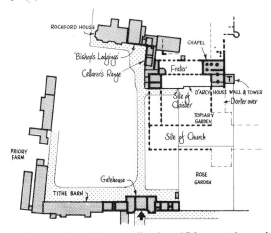

The comfortably spreading late 15th c. **gatehouse** has East
Anglian flint 'flushwork' and carvings in the main arch spandrels of
St Michael (or St George?) and a dragon. Over the roadway is a

splendid lierne vault, and for symmetry there are two footways. Its right (E) wing only is shown to the public: a small sitting-room with fireplace and traces of medieval frescoes, a suite of upper rooms, and lastly the rest of the lower floor ending with a bigger room at higher level with tiled floor, big brick fireplace and open ceiling. This is outside the gatehouse proper, the pointed arch in its S wall being 13th c. – much earlier than the flanking ranges seem from outside.

The rear door opens to a small court. Keeping right, a path goes into the rose garden and the topiary garden beyond it. The sunken part of the latter roughly represents the vanished **church** nave. The **tower** dominating it is Lord D'Arcy's, post-Dissolution; the brick wall that divides the former cloister garth was also part of his house. Through the carved wooden gate and to the right is part of the 12th c. groin-vaulted undercroft of the dorter, now leading to the tower stair. The view justifies the climb: S are the gatehouse and gardens; below is another piece of undercroft and passage (13th c. and now roofed as a chapel) which continued westward as the refectory range (where the courtyard now is); beyond that stands the cellarer's range, also added to by the D'Arcys (but the turret is 18th c.), and to its right a 19th c. wing; to the N the monastic E range (the dorter undercroft) terminates in its own ruin and in that of other pieces of 16th c. D'Arcy building, with twisted brick chimneys.

Below again, fine 13th c. arcading of the internal end wall of the refectory is exposed behind what is now the **chapel**. Entered round on the N side, this has a 'nave' of six 13th c. vaulted bays on slender round columns, and a largely 12th c. three-celled E end with groin-vaulted right-hand bay. The dado arcading is 19th c.

Next, the ruins to the N can be looked at from ground level, and then the path followed right round the **main house**, passing the 19th c. wing, the back of the 'Bishop's Lodging' (rebuilt 1865) and the 18th c. Rochford house. The pedestal on the rear lawn was once a gate-pier. Facing the gatehouse is the splendid front of the 'Bishop's Lodging' built by Abbot Vintoner for himself, c.1525. The big oriel window of the hall above has been rebuilt. The 13th c. cellarer's range is disguised on this side by early and mid-16th c. additions, but its S end (facing the gatehouse) shows its original cross-section. Lord D'Arcy truncated it. His brick wall (already seen) has a Tudor arch leading back into the courtyard. There the ivy-covered walling in the centre is the N side of the refectory.

The other buildings facing the lawn of the great **outer court**

include two of the 16th c. – one of unknown purpose on the W, and
a splendid tithe barn next to the gatehouse. Outside, facing the
green, is another medieval wall with a 14th c. arch.

St Radegund's Kent: 2½ miles W of Dover   TR 275419

Premonstratensian abbey of St Radegund founded 1193 by Hugh,
the first abbot, a daughter house of Prémontré. Dissolved 1536
and granted to Archbishop Cranmer

Owned by Moynan family. Open to the public subject to permission
from the house

Also known as Bradsole. All the surviving buildings seem to be not
later than *c*.1220, in spite of some initial indecision about the
suitability of the site. Their unusual feature is the three-part tower,
probably defensive, in the angle between nave and N transept.
Some parts still stand high, but elsewhere the flint rubble, robbed of
ashlar, has crumbled badly or gone altogether. Excavations in 1830
enabled the plan to be completed.

Abbey stone was used in building Sandgate castle in 1539–40.
After a succession of owners, Simon Edolph made a house of the
refectory in 1590; this still stands and is privately occupied. The
church itself being by then mostly demolished, he made the tower
into a gatehouse, simply by forming an archway in each face, and so
effectively that it was long thought to be the real gatehouse. That in
fact is traceable beside the approach drive within one of the still
distinguishable lengths of precinct wall.

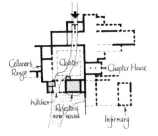

The mysterious **tower** still guards the entrance. Its triangles of
flint flushwork were added by Edolph. Previously the only access to
it from the church seems to have been through the side chambers –

spanned now by a dramatic tangle of crumbling arches. The nave site is immediately beyond. To the right is its W end, with flint rubble walls still quite high. Ahead is the refectory, now the house; the **cloister** lay between and can be followed anti-clockwise, starting at its NW doorway into the church nave. Of the two-storeyed W range the inner side has nearly gone but the gabled N wall stands nearly to full height, and the W wall with its lancet windows tapers down to a low stump at the S end. Little is left of the kitchen, but the main **refectory** walls still stand. This has seen many changes, from Edolph's porch and triangle patterns (again) to the tile-hung W flank and the quite recent mullioned timber windows. The undercroft has lost its vault and the upper floors are modernised. On the S of the farmyard, facing the house, is a big tithe barn, and about 200 yards to the SE are slight remains of a second gatehouse.

Back now into the cloister. In its E wall are a blocked doorway to the parlour, with an isolated piece of the infirmary visible beyond, and then the **chapter house** doorway with a once shafted opening each side. The church adjoins immediately, without an intervening sacristy, and is much less well defined this side, though the position of the E wall can be recognised by banks and bits of rubble some 30 yards away.

Salley Lancashire: SD 777465
in Sawley village, ¼ mile N of Clitheroe–Skipton road A59

Cistercian abbey of the Blessed Virgin Mary founded 1147 by
    William de Percy, Earl of Northampton, a daughter house of
    Newminster. Suppressed 1536 but restored under Pilgrimage of
    Grace for brief period

In care of Department of the Environment. Open during standard
    hours without charge

Or Sallay. The church at first had an unaisled Cistercian square end but big transepts each with three chapels – all late 12th to early 13th c. The nave was never built beyond the first few feet, though in the 14th c. a start was made with a N aisle. The elongated cloister shape suggests that a S aisle was also intended. The quire was lengthened and given aisles in the 16th c.

The reinstated abbot was executed in 1537. The buildings fell to ruin. They were investigated in 1848 by Earl de Grey and again in more recent years after passing into state ownership.

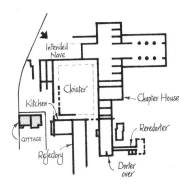

The prominent mass of walling seen first is the 'temporary' W wall of the **nave**. Over to its S (to get one's bearings) is the cloister garth. The intended nave size is marked out by stone strips. Go through the wall into the **crossing**. Steps ahead mark the pulpitum; on either side are the transepts, their shaly walling in parts as high as 15 feet. Each had three chapels; the inner ones became passages to the quire aisles – as will be seen by going into the **quire** which had solid walls each side, extended by four-bay 16th c. arcades of which merely the column positions survive. In the S quire aisle a 13th c. arch and shaft have been found embedded in the solid part of the quire wall, which was at first external. In the S transept the right-hand chapel has its original floor tiles. Opposite it is the gentle night stair that led to the dorter, and an arch which would have led into the S aisle if one had been built, but which now goes to the **cloister**.

In the E range is the former sacristy, and next to it the chapter house, with the base of a clustered doorway. The other cloister buildings, or rather their foundations, can now be recognised clockwise, in their usual sequence: on the E the long dorter undercroft, with reredorter at right angles at the end of its E side: on the S the warming room, the refectory (set N–S) and kitchen: and on the W the lay brothers' range, with projecting reredorter now forming part of a (private) cottage. After the lay brothers went, this range probably served for the abbot and guests; the high building with a big chimney at its N end is thought to be post-monastic.

Many carved stones are set out to the N of the nave and others may be seen in house walls of the village. The archway about 100 yards further N lacks satisfactory credentials and was probably put up by Earl de Grey.

Sawtry Cambridgeshire: TL 197825
2 miles ESE of village and ¾ mile N of St Ives road B1090

Cistercian abbey of the Blessed Virgin Mary founded 1147 by
  Simon, Earl of Northampton, a daughter house of Warden.
  Dissolved 1536

Owned by St John's College, Cambridge. Accessible at all times
  subject to permission from Abbey Farm house

A dedication of the church in 1238 suggests that the E end had then just been rebuilt. Most of the known fragments, in or near buildings in the neighbourhood, indicate a mid-12th c. date for most of the abbey. The last remaining stones seem to have been dug out in the 1850s for road-making, but a plan was compiled in 1907–12. It shows extensive earthworks and ponds within the precinct, of which many still exist.

An ancient rhyme runs:

> Ramsey the rich of gold and of fee,
> Thorney the bane of many a fair tree,
> Croyland the courteous of their meat and their drink,
> Spalding the gluttons as all men do think,
> Peterborough the proud as all men do say,
> Sawtry by the way *that* poor abbaye
> Gave more alms in one day than all they.

Past the farm the lane bears right (with a big drainage channel on the left) and leads to an iron gate. The field beyond is the abbey precinct. Continue in the same direction along the cart track. The church site lies on its right-hand side about three-quarters of the way to the next field, its W and E ends being marked by obvious depressions. With the aid of the plan the cloister with its E, S and W ranges can be roughly identified. Another small depression within the cloister garth was probably a well. Over to the E, three parallel fishponds join a bigger one along the field boundary. The reredorter drain from the SE corner of the buildings can be traced downhill to a much wider ditch. A right turn at this point leads

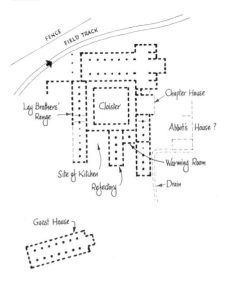

towards a bigger fenced-in pond, on the abbey side of which a large aisled building has been traced, believed to have been the guest house or hospice (like that at Ramsey). No stonework of any of these buildings can be seen on the site; a few pieces and some tiles are in the parish church.

Sclerder Cornwall: SX 222530
2 miles W of Looe and 300 yards S of Polperro road A387

Nunnery of Our Lady of Light founded for 'Dames de la Retraite'
   c.1843 by Anne Trelawny; dissolved 1852. Franciscan friary
   founded 1858; dissolved 1862 and replaced 1864 by Carmelite
   nunnery; dissolved 1871. Nunnery of the Sisters of the Sacred
   Heart of Jesus and Mary founded 1904; became Franciscan again
   c.1925 and an abbey; became Carmelite again 1981 and no longer
   an abbey

Secular chapel (only) of church open during normal hours

Sclerder = 'light' in Cornish. The first priest's house and church,
   consecrated in 1843, are believed to have been designed by A.W.N.

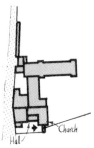

Pugin. The main house was enlarged in 1858 for the Franciscans and again altered in the 1860s for the Carmelites. From 1878 to 1891 it was a private residence. In 1904 it was enlarged for a sisterhood from France, and in the 1920s again for the Franciscans or Poor Clares, who built the extern or secular chapel, a new priest's house and a new nuns' wing.

Of the largely Gothic building of warm grey stone with slate roofs very little is visible to the public. The extern chapel however serves as a Catholic church, in a plain lancet style with varnished wood ceilings. An iron grille separates the main chapel, which has a carved oak reredos and similar roof. A small hall adjoins its S side. Of the main building a glimpse of the 1920s wing can be had from the parish graveyard to the E (liturgical N) down a side lane.

Selby North Yorkshire: in town centre   SE 615324

Benedictine abbey of Our Lord Jesus Christ, St Mary the Virgin and St Germain founded 1070 by William I. Dissolved 1539 and sold to Sir Ralph Sadler; church made parochial 1618

Parish church. Open during normal hours without charge

At the time of the foundation there existed on the site a hut built a year earlier by one Benedict, an absentee monk of Auxerre. The church was started c.1100 – the transepts and nave being Norman but the latter merging into Early English. The E end is of c.1280–c.1340, replacing a shorter, apse-ended one.

Except for two outlying fragments, the monastic buildings have utterly gone; they stood to the S. A wall was built to divide off the nave, which became a store for market stalls, and even a drill hall,

for the quire sufficed for the parish. The central tower fell on the S
transept in 1690 and was patched up in 1702. Restorations were
done in 1871–3 under Sir George Gilbert Scott and in 1889–90
under his son J. Oldrid Scott, who had to repeat much of his work
after a serious fire in 1906. The central tower was rebuilt in 1908,
the S transept in 1912 and the W tower tops in 1935.

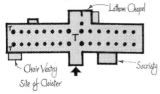

From the S transept doorway (not of course a monastic feature) it
is best to go straight into the **nave**, begun c.1100 at its E end. The
architectural system was intended to be the normal Romanesque
one of double bays with alternate round and clustered piers, like
Durham. There is zigzag on the arches, and on one pier an incised
pattern. But changes occurred as work progressed, and the four W
bays (c.1170) have clustered piers only, with water-leaf capitals. Of
the triforium, the first bay was evidently built at once to help
buttress the tower. It starts off with twin round-headed openings
within a single big arch (the first is more solid). Then matters
become more complicated. On the N side, keeping the double-bay
idea and the single big arches, each alternate clustered pier gives
way instead to a dumpy column encircled by little free-standing
shafts – an unusual design of c.1190. But the S gallery is later still
(c.1225) and there the main arches (still round, even at that date)
enclose two pointed ones with more orthodox Early English
enrichments – except for the curious hexagonal shafts that run twice
per bay right up to the roof forward of all the others and create their
own rhythm. In the clerestory, the general imbalance is accentuated
by a repetition on the N side of the dog-tooth enrichment of the S
triforium – whereas its S side is a more modest design controlled by
the grid of shafts. On the S are two windows per bay, on the N only
one. Apart from the flat timber roof, reconstructed after the fire
with some old bosses, the whole nave is a fascinating history of
development from Norman to Early English. The aisles have
quadripartite ribbed vaults, of more refined design as one moves W.

In the **S aisle**, starting from the E, bay 4 contains a floor slab to

Richard Field (d. 1694) made to look like an abbot's, and bay 6 an early 14th c. knight (probably Hugh de Pickworth) in chain mail. At the W end the bay system is varied to take account of the twin towers – never actually completed till 1935. These are vaulted too. The glass of the great W window is by Heaton, Butler & Bayne. The **N aisle**, starting at the W, has the mutilated tomb of John, Lord d'Arcy (d. 1411), the plain round font with spiky 15th c. cover (rescued from the fire), in bay 6 the damaged effigy of a woman, and by the N doorway a square heraldic tablet to Richard Spencer (d. 1690) surmounted by skull and cross bones.

A pointed arch leads into the **N transept**. This part with the crossing arches is essentially of *c.*1100. But its E side – a foretaste of the presbytery – is early 14th c., with clustered columns and foliage capitals and big clerestory windows with walkway and pierced balustrade below. The Lathom chapel (now vestry) beyond was founded by the archbishop of that name in 1476; a long 'squint' looks from it into the sanctuary. The big inserted N window is 15th c. too and has German glass of *c.*1910 on the subject of St Germain. Transept and crossing both have flat wood ceilings.

From here eastwards all is early 14th c., and a look into the **presbytery** shows its similarity to the transept – except for its wooden vaulting. The E window is regarded as one of the finest of all examples of flowing Decorated tracery. The N aisle has octopartite vaulting and a beautiful wall-arcade on shafts with compact foliage caps. More foliage is on the window and vault shafts. In bay 1 (on the organ console) is a well lettered brass plaque to Walter Hartley (d. 1962); further on is a musical 'serpent' in a glass case, facing some raw-coloured mid-19th c. windows by William Wailes; then the back of the chancel screen, partly wooden of *c.*1910 and partly 14th c. stone continuing round the other side of the reredos. Of the pleasantly greyish E window glass nearly a quarter is early 14th c.: tier upon tier of figures forming a Jesse Tree. The walkway below it continues across the aisles too.

In the E bay of the S presbytery aisle are incised ledger stones of three abbots, the finest being of Abbot Barwic (d. 1526). Through a door in the S wall is the vaulted former sacristy, now a War Memorial chapel with furnishings by George Pace, 1955, and a 15th c. Nottingham alabaster Deposition. The **S transept** is of 1912, on the site of the original; in it is a model of the church and an old chest used as a collection box. In the crossing, the wood and stone pulpit and the rich coved **quire** screen are by Oldrid Scott, *c.*1910. So are the choir stalls with their canopied rear screen, the wrought iron communion rail and the over-large reredos with Oberammergau carving by Peter Rendl. But the four splendid pinnacled stone sedilia are restored 14th c. work. Perched on the walkway parapet above the organ on the N side are playful stone figures of a man and a boy and dog, a medieval feature probably unique in Britain.

The **outside** is as fine as many a cathedral. Turn left outside the S transept. The former sacristy has a scriptorium above, long used as a school and with its own stair from outside. Like the rest of the 14th c. E end, it has a pierced parapet and gargoyles and big crocketed pinnacles. Its upper windows are curvilinear, and so are those of the S aisle and the great E window; above the last is a smaller five-light window of reticulated pattern, while those of the N aisle beyond are Geometric and thus a decade or two earlier. The N transept with its shallow buttresses is obviously Norman, but the clerestory is curvilinear again, and the great N window Perpendicular. Similarly the nave and aisles commence by being Norman, but have later windows; the clerestory is Transitional throughout, with plain pointed windows.

The vaulted **N porch**, the original lay people's entrance, is an imposing one, Transitional rather than pure Norman, with pointed wall-arcading inside and out though both inner and outer doorways are round-headed; the top stage is probably in fact a little later, and the battlements are 15th c. One Norman aisle window remains in the last bay before the NW tower. This, with its twin, is Norman at the base, but the upper parts above the main windows are wholly by Oldrid Scott, 1935 – hence the statues on the **W front** depicting King George V and Queen Mary. The main W window is 15th c., within a 13th c. framework in the same Early English style as the W parts of the interior. But the doorway below is lavish Norman, of five orders; evidently the lower part of the walls was built long before the rest.

The S side is like the N, with differences necessitated by the one-time cloister: instead of a porch, the two former doorways to the cloister walk, and instead of full-length aisle windows, shorter ones (actually Decorated replacements) that started above the cloister roof. Finally the main tower, solid Norman work up to clock level, but above that by Oldrid Scott, 1908; he replaced the squatter 18th c. makeshift with something more worthily resembling the likely medieval form of the top which fell in 1690.

The gatehouse, 30 yards W of the church, was demolished in 1806. The only other monastic remains are part of a 12th c. building called Abbot Staith's Buildings in The Quay, N of the bridge.

Shaftesbury Dorset: in town centre   ST 862229

Benedictine nunnery of St Mary founded or refounded *c*.875 by
King Alfred; from 1001 dedicated also to St Edward King and
Martyr. Dissolved 1539 and sold to Sir Thomas Arundel

Church site owned by Taylor family. Open to the public 10.0 a.m.
to 6.30 p.m. April to October (admission charge)

There is a record of an abbot *c*.670 whose community may have
preceded the nuns'. King Alfred's own daughter was abbess but the
nunnery's fame grew with the translation of the bones of King
Edward to a shrine here in 1001 and it became the richest in
England. Though a few earlier stones have been found, the
originally five-apsed church was mostly of *c*.1100. A NE chapel with
crypt was added early in the 14th c. (possibly to contain St Edward's
shrine) and later in the century a SE Lady chapel in place of one of
the apses. Not much is known of the monastic buildings.

The property passed from Sir Thomas Arundel to the Earl of
Pembroke. The buildings were quarried away and eventually lost
under houses and gardens. Excavations in 1816, 1861, 1902–5 and
1930–2 revealed the church layout and a little more.

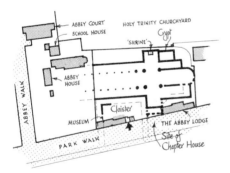

The broad cliff-top Park Walk obliterates the S half of the cloister
site; the present entrance leads into the centre of the N half, but the
greater part of what is now in effect a garden represents – by
foundations – the actual church.

Within the garth is a stone coffin. The **church** nave is entered close to the garden wall on the left. It extended beyond the wall, though how far has not been proved by digging, and the column bases throughout are little more than rubble indicators. Scattered patches of tiled paving survive, as well as traces of the pulpitum and nave altar. The positions of the crossing pier bases are clear. To their N a small stone hut houses a lead casket; some bones thought to be relics of St Edward were found in this in 1931 within the recess in the floor on the E side of the transept, close to the curving steps into the NE chapel crypt. This crypt is 13th c., and corbels of its vault survive. Alongside is the N presbytery chapel with remains of its apse end and of altar steps and tiles.

The chancel also was apsidal but the curved walling on the S side is a restoration. A wayside cross of *c.*1400 (moved in 1931 from Angel Square) marks the high altar site; it very unusually contains four alabaster plaques. The wall recesses were tombs. The original apse of the S chapel (before its 14th c. enlargement) is marked out by bricks. Further W, the chapel/transept junction is somewhat confused by piles of stone; nearby are a stone grave and the head of a coffin. A gritted path alongside represents the slype between transept and chapter house, the wall of the latter being marked inside the present boundary. Within the transept is another sunk coffin in which remains probably of an abbess were found. Finally, the transept W wall and the S aisle wall are clearly defined and so is the extent of the cloister N walk.

Carved stones, tiles and other remains of considerable interest are housed in the museum alongside the entrance.

Shap Cumbria: 1 mile W of A6 at Shap village   NY 548153

Premonstratensian abbey of St Mary Magdalene founded at Preston
    Patrick after 1192 by Thomas, son of Gospatrick, a daughter
    house of Cockersand. Moved to Shap by 1201. Dissolved 1540
    and granted to Sir Thomas Wharton

In care of Department of the Environment. Open at all times
    without charge

The centre parts of the church and the E cloister range were built first. Later in the 13th c. the nave and north aisle were completed with their four W bays, and the S and W ranges of cloister buildings, as well as the reredorter, were added. The infirmary was built *c*.1420. In the 15th c. the presbytery and the adjoining chapel on the S were extended, and about 1500 the W tower was built and then the upper part of the nave reconstructed.

The S and W ranges were put to farm uses and the remainder fell to ruin. After being owned for two centuries by the Lowthers, Earls of Lonsdale, the buildings were taken over in 1948 by the Ministry of Works.

The **tower** of *c*.1500 dominates the site and has lost very little but its parapet. The W window and doorway seem to have been opened out as a 'picturesque improvement' in the 18th c.; above them is an empty niche. Tower and **nave** both retain much of their stone paving, the latter with some unusual incised circles considered to be procession markers. A S aisle was never intended. Some column bases of the N aisle have been reconstructed with stones recovered from Lowther Castle where they had lain for many years; slight differences in them and in the outer walls indicate where work broke off in the 13th c. The W bay of the arcade is partly engulfed by a modern tower buttress. On the E face of the tower are marks of the steep late 13th c. roof and of the later one with clerestory.

The **presbytery**, and the transepts with their chapels, are clearly distinguishable, though reduced to low wall bases only. Here and elsewhere are a number of monastic graves. Various inconsistencies in the piers of the crossing suggest an unsuccessful attempt to build a central tower. On the ground N of the presbytery a miscellany of carved and moulded stones is set out.

Next the **cloister**, reached through the S transept. The E walk passes the usual sacristy, chapter house (evidently divided by two arches into a vestibule and the chapter house proper) and warming house (with fireplace), all early 13th c. The dorter ran over all these. Structurally, the chapter house vestibule and warming house were a single unit with continuous vaulting and central columns, but separated by a wall just thick enough to conceal a column; this is most unusual. At the end, running at right angles towards the river, was the later 13th c. reredorter. At its drain outlet a well preserved stone channel against the bank is still flushed by the stream. Over the wooden steps, mostly where the sheep pens now are, stood the 14th c. infirmary.

Now pass round the outside of the warming house and back to the S walk of the cloister. On the left at an upper level was the late 13th c. refectory (now partly cut off by the lane). The W range, of similar date, was altered in the 14th c., probably to accommodate guests on the upper floor; vaults over two of the store rooms survive, and at the end beneath a grid is a garderobe pit.

Across the field on the abbey side of the bridge, below the lane, is a bank which represents part of the precinct wall; other parts are also traceable.

Sherborne Dorset: in town centre   ST 638165

Monastery of St Mary the Virgin founded before 672, possibly by King Kenwalc; became cathedral 705; became Benedictine 998; ceased to be cathedral 1075. Dissolved 1539 and granted to Sir John Horsey who sold church to parish

Church owned by parish; monastic buildings by Sherborne School. Church open during normal hours; school (exterior only) subject to permission from porter's lodge

The recorded history begins with the forming of a bishopric out of that of Winchester in 705. Its secular canons were replaced in 998 by Benedictine monks. In 1075 the see was moved to Old Sarum, where the bishop continued to be abbot of Sherborne until 1122; thereafter the abbey was independent.

Parts of the Saxon cathedral still exist not only at the W end of the church but also in the cores of the nave and crossing piers and in the N transept. Otherwise the nave, aisles, porch and transepts are substantially Norman (*c*.1110–70) in their lower parts and late 15th c. in their upper. The presbytery and aisles are earlier 15th c. Hardly any Decorated work exists in the church, but there is Early English in the Lady chapel and in Bishop Roger's chapel on the N side. Of the monastic buildings the abbot's hall and house (N range) have Norman and 15th c. work, and there is 14th c. in the guests' hall (W range) and in the almost disappeared cloister. The main N range with refectory has gone, and so has most of the E except for a few 13th c. bits.

Sherborne School was the abbey's, was refounded by Edward VI, and continued to use some of the abbey buildings including the eastern chapels. In 1852–86 it grew and overflowed out of them towards the N. The church was sold in the 16th c. almost entire to the parish, which proceeded to demolish its former church of All Hallows standing against the W wall. In more modern times it was restored *c.*1850–1884 in an exemplary manner by William Slater and R.C. and R.H. Carpenter (father and son) and the Lady chapel was rebuilt by W.D. Caröe in 1921–34.

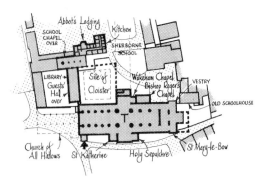

A start in the centre of the **nave** is instructive. The main piers, apparently Perpendicular, are believed to encase the Saxon (early 11th c.) ones of the cathedral, and to perpetuate their irregular spacing. The stone panelling added to them *c.*1510 continues up and round as Gothic arches. Above them begins the purely Perpendicular work of the high clerestory and the splendid fan vault. In place of a triforium is merely a blind continuation of the clerestory; below this are prominent angels with shields which help to disguise the irregularities of bay spacing. The crossing arch is Norman, almost unaltered. At the opposite end, the great W window has garish glass attributed to A.W.N. Pugin; it originally lacked its lower half because All Hallows' church abutted it outside.

In a little protective lobby at the W end of the **N nave aisle** is a Saxon doorway which led into a W transept long disappeared; its tympanum is Norman. The small window by Frederick Cole (1962) commemorates St Stephen Harding, Abbot of Cîteaux and

Sherborne: Early 16th c. nave vault

legislator of the Cistercian Order, who was born in or near
Sherborne. A clock mechanism nearby is dated 1740. The N aisle
itself has a 15th c. lierne vault but its main wall is 12th c. (or even
earlier) at its base. All along are colours of the Dorsetshire
Regiment, including the famous 'Sarah Sands' colour, and poor
19th c. glass; the renewed ogee-headed opening at the end led into
the corner of the cloister.

The **N transept**, largely occupied by the organ, is also fan vaulted,
with unusually large bosses (so is the crossing). From here both N
and S arches of the crossing can be seen, on enormous piers which,
it is thought, are largely Saxon – particularly in the fat shafts which
project into both transepts and seem unrelated to the rest. To the
nave aisle is a Norman arch, to the presbytery aisle another but
altered to Perpendicular. Beside the latter is another altered
opening leading to the otherwise mostly Norman Wykeham chapel.
But it too has been given a little fan vault and it is occupied by the
big four-poster tomb of the abbey's impropriator Sir John Horsey
(d. 1546), originally in the N transept. A modern brass
commemorates Sir Thomas Wyatt, 'father of the English sonnet'.

In the **crossing** the octagonal oak pulpit with marble base and
stair is by B. Ingelow (1889) and the brass eagle by R.H. Carpenter
(1869). Unlike the nave, the **presbytery** was rebuilt from its
foundation in the 15th c. though its panelled piers running right up
to the clerestory and its fan vault are a richer variation on the same
theme. The vault itself is earlier, indeed the earliest such vault on a
large scale, and of less sound design (it had to be rebuilt in 1856)
while the overall grid of the clerestory extends down to the main
arches. The wall decoration and the clerestory glass are by Clayton
& Bell. The reredos is an 1858 conjectural reconstruction of the
original. The oak stalls are 19th c. too but incorporate ten 15th c.
misericords. The credence table in the sanctuary was the altar table
of the chapel of Leweston Manor and is 17th c.

Next, the **N presbytery aisle**, separated by a high stone screen of
1856. A door in bay 1 leads to the 13th c. Bishop Roger's chapel,
now the choir vestry. It has a triple lancet E window but high on its
S wall is Norman interlaced arcading which was formerly external.
Opposite are assembled numerous memorials tidied away from the
rest of the church and dominated by that to Carew Mildmay (d.
1784). In bay 2 of the aisle is the head only of an effigy of Abbot
Clement, *c.*1160, set in a canopy, and in bay 3 another abbot's,
more complete, 13th c. The two stone coffins a little further on were
once believed to have held the bones of Kings Ethelbald and

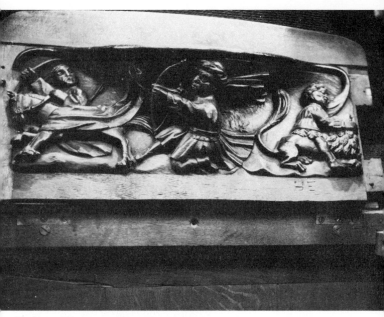

Sherborne: Miserere seat with archer and animals

Ethelbert; a brass commemorates them. Through a screen is the
retro-quire at the back of the main reredos, fan vaulted again and
with some medieval tiles. Here are more colours of the Dorsetshire
Regiment, also rolls of honour and memorial screens and other
furniture. The finely moulded 13th c. arch to the **Lady chapel** rests
on three orders of dark 'marble' shafts with white foliage caps. The
single quadripartite vaulted bay is Early English too, but beyond is
Caröe's work of 1921, a war memorial replacement of what had in
1560 become partially absorbed into the school headmaster's house
(along with the chapels on both sides). The E window is by
Christopher Webb, 1957, and the engraved glass reredos panel by
Laurence Whistler, 1968. The brass chandelier, given in 1657, is the
earliest dated 'Dutch' one in England.

Beside the Lady chapel is that of **St Mary-le-Bow**, now a
baptistry. Originally 14th c., it was remodelled in Perpendicular
style with another fan vault, but the 1560 alterations deprived it of
its two E bays. Finally in 1921 it was restored to its present form,
leaving the fireplace and other signs of its one-time domestic use.

The rough font has a 15th c. base and an earlier bowl. The corresponding chapel at the E end of the N presbytery aisle now forms a clergy vestry with two library floors over, and is private.

The **S presbytery aisle**, entered through a partly 15th c. stone screen, contains a slate memorial of a flood of 1709, an effigy thought to be Abbot Bradford (d. 1260), and an early 17th c. pulpit tester made into a table. On the left is the lierne vaulted Holy Sepulchre chapel, balancing the Wykeham one but mostly 15th c. in its present form. The wooden statue of St James is 15th c. Spanish.

The **S transept** is plainer than the N and has an open timber roof on corbels, and a raised black and white chequered floor associated with the giant memorial by John Nost to John Digby, 3rd Earl of Bristol (d. 1698) and his two wives. To the Holy Sepulchre chapel is a 15th c. arch, to the S nave aisle an early Norman one. The great S ('Te Deum') window is Pugin's, of 1851–2. The stone screen to the Holy Sepulchre chapel is a memorial to John Wingfield Digby (d. 1904) and a tablet on the S wall is to Robert and Mary Digby (d. 1726 and 1729). On the SE tower pier is a coin-operated switch for floodlighting the main vaults.

Off the **S nave aisle** is the 15th c. St Katherine's chapel, also fan vaulted, dominated by the six-poster tomb of John Leweston (d. 1584). With its two recumbent effigies, this is thought to have been carved by Allen Maynard who worked at Longleat. A tablet in the SW corner to Johanna Walcot (d. 1630 and sister of a Churchill ancestor) and four neat gadrooned ones on the E wall are also worth noting. 15th c. glass, mostly heraldry and prophets with some very unusual lattice backgrounds, has been collected into the windows. In the aisle itself is more recent glass, and another font which is 19th c. In the W wall is a doorway of which one jamb is 11th c. long-and-short work while the other indicates a Norman widening. Subsequently (c.1437) it was narrowed again with a pointed arch to restrict access to All Hallows' church, touching off a quarrel between abbey and parish that culminated in a serious fire in the abbey church. The painted board on the W wall bears the 'feathers' of Henry, Prince of Wales who held the castle in 1610–12.

Now the **outside**, commencing with the S porch of c.1170, rebuilt in 1849. It reproduced the Norman ground stage but replaced with imitation Norman the upper storey that had been added in the 15th c. The big inner doorway is segmental headed and there is a rib vault. The W front is complex. Obvious features are the 15th c. central window and doorway, the partly Saxon SW doorway, and the E responds of the arcades of All Hallows' church. Less evident is that the whole wall below clerestory level is Saxon too. Excavations have shown that a tower stood against the centre of the wall and transepts against its sides. On the N is the S gable of the late 14th c. guest hall forming the upper storey of the W range of the cloister and now the school library; further Saxon work has been traced inside its lower parts.

After the interior, the S side of the church will be readily understood, being mostly Perpendicular excepting the Norman transept and base of the nave aisle; traces of Norman windows are visible in the transept E wall. The tower top is 15th c., resting on a Norman base. It contains the heaviest peal of eight bells in the world, including one believed to have been made in Tournai and presented by Cardinal Wolsey in 1514. The 16th c. domestic changes to the SE or Bow chapel can hardly be missed; behind and beyond it is the 17th c. Old Schoolroom. The wrought iron gates are of 1723. A little further on stands the conduit house, which is actually the early 16th c. hexagonal washplace transplanted from the abbey cloister after the Dissolution – a rare survival.

Finally the parts within the school precinct, reached by going up Cheap Street and along Abbey Road. Entry should be requested at the porter's lodge. The **cloister** site lies straight ahead and the blank wall against the S transept is the stump of the 13th c. E range, stopping short of the chapter house site. The lower half of the transept wall (the part hidden by the later building) is Saxon and contains pre-Conquest wall-arcading within the bottom storey. Higher up are marks of 12th and 13th c. dorter roofs, progressively higher than the Saxon.

The S range (against the church) seems to have been two-storeyed; the aisle was called the Dark aisle and its present windows are 19th c. In the W range is the guest hall already seen – much restored in 1850 but with a 15th c. roof – while across the N end of it ran the former abbot's hall now (on the upper floor) formed into the school chapel and with some 15th c. roof timbers. On the other side of this block are 15th c. survivals from the abbot's house: a projecting wing which was the kitchen, an oriel, and a pretty ogee-headed blocked arch. Then follows an imitation 'Norman' cloister of 1855, built around an undercroft which in part is genuinely Norman. Over this is the abbot's hall, and from a court on its other side it is possible to see the W face of the guest hall.

The famous Sherborne Missal, a splendid illuminated manuscript of *c.*1400, is now in the British Library.

Shrewsbury Shropshire: ½ mile E of town centre   SJ 498124

Benedictine abbey of St Peter and St Paul (nave Holy Cross)
   founded 1083 by Earl Roger de Montgomery, a daughter house
   of Séez, Normandy; became mitred. Dissolved 1540; church
   given to Holy Cross parish and remainder to William Langley

Parish church; remainder of site largely public roadway. Church
   open Easter–October 10.0 a.m. to noon and 2.0 to 4.0 p.m.; at
   other times by arrangement at the Vicarage

The parish church is the abbey nave, much of it original work of the
late 11th and early 12th cc., though the galleries, W end and tower
and other parts were altered in the 14th c. The N porch is 15th c.,
built for the parish. Of the E end and the monastic buildings very
little is known, but Parliament met in the chapter house on two
occasions.

   The crossing and transepts, presbytery and Lady chapel were
taken down after the Dissolution. Of the monastic buildings most of
what was still left by 1836 was swept away when Telford drove his
London–Holyhead road clean through the site so as to bypass the
loop of Abbey Foregate N of the church, and the rest went in 1865
'for railway purposes'. The only survival, high and dry on the wrong
side of the road, was the 14th c. refectory pulpit. The church was
'restored' in 1855–63 under S. Pountney Smith, and provided with a
complete new E end in 1886–7 under J.L. Pearson.

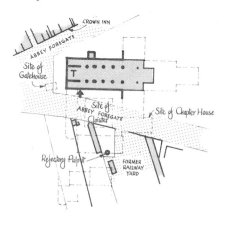

The **nave**, entered via the S aisle door, is Gothic (late 14th c.) in its two W bays, with a tall clerestory and no triforium. Beyond these are three Norman bays (*c*.1090) with big round piers and plainly moulded arches on shallow caps of typical West Midlands type. Their triforium storey, originally similar, was filled with tracery in the 14th c. but again altered in 1862; the true clerestory and high timber roof were a restoration by Pearson to their likely original appearance. Looking W into the **tower**, the heraldic W window glass is mostly of 1814; its stonework and that of the tower arch are late 14th c. though the W wall was still Norman at its base. The giant round font is said to be a Roman column base, reversed.

At the W end of the **N aisle** is another font bowl of 1653, disused. On the left is a wall tablet to John Loyd (d. 1647) with a bust. The three tomb chests come from demolished churches: from left to right, William Charlton (d. 1544) with alabaster effigies, from Wellington; Richard Onslow (d. 1571) from St Chad's; and William Jones (d. 1612) from St Alkmund's. The Norman pillar piscina was found in a local garden. Wall shafts and arch springers show that the aisle itself was (or was meant to be) vaulted; the flat ceiling at the W end and the gabled form of the remainder are 17th or 18th c. The N doorway (seen from within the barrel-vaulted porch) is 12th c. Above it hang royal arms of 1736; the re-erected stonework opposite is believed to be part of St Winifred's shrine. The effigy nearby is of a lawyer of *c*.1300.

The arch from aisle into transept is part of the 11th c. building, bold and primitive. The figures on the nearby 19th c. stone pulpit could hardly provide a greater contrast. The present **crossing** is by Pearson, using the Norman piers of its W arch; the Crucifixion painting on the N pier is by Richard Burley, early 18th c. The **chancel** is Pearson's too, square-ended to hold his triptych reredos but with a radiating vault. The S or Lady chapel is reserved for private prayer; in the centre of its E window is a little Crucifixion of medieval Flemish glass.

Now across the truncated S transept into the **S aisle**, gabled like the N. On the left are a cartouche to Thomas Rock (d. 1678) and a late 13th c. knight once thought to be the founder Earl Roger; the garish heraldic window is of 1820. Then a florid tablet to Richard Prynce (d. 1690) and two better windows, of 1883 and 1896. Several hatchments and small memorials are of minor interest; then on the floor by the S wall are two 14th c. figures from St Alkmund's and a cross-legged knight from Wombridge, and opposite them a restored coffin lid of a priest, *c*.1300, with a tiny effigy and 'bell, book and

Shrewsbury: Early 19th c. engraving of 14th c. refectory pulpit

candle'. The standing figure of Faith at the W end is by Peter
Hollins in memory of Mary Anne Burd (d. 1859).

Looking now into the nave again: on the N side at the junction of
the Gothic and Norman work has been set a 14th c. stone Madonna.

On the **outside** perhaps the most impressive feature is the great
Perpendicular W window of the tower, its hood mould continuing
nearly to the top, between the twin belfry openings. The Norman
doorway below is somewhat altered. On the S side the entrance
doorway (originally the NW one from the cloister) is also Norman;
but the aisle windows are post-monastic. On the other side of the
main road (which cuts right across the cloister site) is the 14th c.
refectory pulpit standing high in a railed garden, still with its central
vault boss of the Crucifixion – a remarkable survival.

The ruined bit of wall projecting from the curtailed S transept
contains what may be book recesses. To the E of that, all is Pearson
work with lancet windows, till one gets round to the N transept with
another piece of ruined wall. Then the three gabled bays of the N
aisle: behind them rises the triforium, cruelly made into a clerestory
in 1862 but later capped with Pearson's properly restored
clerestory. The N porch was once three-storeyed; the two upper
floors are combined and can still be warmed by an open fire on the
hearth; the very large 15th c. outer doorway contains remains of a
pedimented wooden doorcase of 1640.

Sibton Suffolk   TM 365698
4¼ miles NNW of Saxmundham and 300 yards N of A1120

Cistercian abbey of the Blessed Virgin Mary founded 1150 by
   William de Cheyney, a daughter house of Warden. Dissolved
   1536 and sold by abbot to Duke of Norfolk

Owned by Scrivener family. Accessible at all times (dogs
   prohibited)

The building history is undocumented. However the plan appears to
have followed general Cistercian practice except that the refectory
was never in a N–S position. That and the S aisle wall are the chief
parts remaining, late Norman and Transitional in character.

The survival of the refectory walls and the traces of a later
structure against its N side suggest that it was retained, no doubt for
farm use, after the Dissolution. But it was totally abandoned at least
a century ago.

The ruin is clearly visible from the main road, across the valley from Sibton church. Access is by a lane (marked 'Private') leading off it to the N, ¼ mile further W. In wet weather this is a morass of mud. The ruins are thoroughly overgrown and only accessible with difficulty. Pheasants abound; hence the ban on dogs.

The **refectory** walls stand quite high, but for a gap in its N side, and many of the shafted round-headed windows are reasonably complete; across the E end is a big round arch, and in the outer face of the N wall are remains of the double arch of the washplace, rather later in date. Further E, this wall was evidently built against, blocking the lower parts of the windows. On the opposite side of the cloister is the S wall of the **church**, of plain rubble standing to about 15 feet. The only other remains – difficult to find and not at all informative – are broken fragments of the kitchen and of the W or cellarer's range.

Stanbrook Hereford & Worcester: SO 835498
at Callow End, 3 miles SSW of Worcester

Benedictine nunnery of Our Lady of Consolation founded at
    Cambrai 1625; moved to Woolton 1808, then to Abbots Salford
    (Warwickshire), and to Stanbrook 1838

S transept of church (only) opened to public on request (at NE door
    of monastery) during normal hours

The so-called Old House, already existing by 1838, was the nucleus
and served till 1871 when the present church, designed by E.W.
Pugin, was finished; the first chapel then became a chapter room.
The remainder of the complete new monastery, forming two sides
of a square, was complete by 1880. The other two sides that Pugin
had intended were outlined c.1965 by covered ways added in a
different style by Martin Fisher.

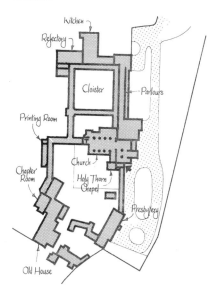

The only parts of the exterior really visible to the public are the three and four-storey **E façade** and (from a distance for it is quite a landmark) Pugin's thin round tower, horizontally striped in brick and stone and with a tapering turret. The rest is hidden in the enclosure but is mostly similar and mostly brick, with slated roofs and big pointed-arched sash windows. At the S end of the E range the rose window of the church chancel looks out over a connecting corridor; the public entrance to the church is just round the corner. Beyond that is a low connecting wing to the presbytery, a curiously austere 18th c. house.

The **church** interior was redecorated and the sanctuary was reordered under Anthony Thompson in 1971, losing its Pugin chancel fittings in favour of a plain square altar and tabernacle, white stone walls and quarry tiled floor, all of which can be seen from the public ('extern') chapel through a black and aluminium folding screen. The rest is only partially visible; its main features are the heavily ribbed painted roof, New Zealand pine stalls, and emphatically patterned Minton Tile floor. There is Hardman glass in the E rose and other windows. The extern chapel has similarly ribbed roofs, smaller in scale, and a central column of brown marble.

Stanley Wiltshire: ST 963722
1¼ miles WSW of Bremhill and ¾ mile N of Calne–Chippenham
road A4

Cistercian abbey of the Blessed Virgin Mary founded 1151 at
   Loxwell (1½ miles SSW) by Matilda and her chamberlain Drogo,
   a daughter house of Quarr; moved to Stanley 1154. Dissolved
   1536 and granted to Sir Edward Baynton

Owned by Harding family. Accessible at all times subject to
   permission from farmhouse

The first site at Loxwell was called Drownfont (Drogo's spring);
when it was abandoned water was ducted from it all the way to the
new one. The first (late 12th c.) buildings at Stanley gave way after
half a century to new – excepting probably the W monastic range
(separated from the cloister by a 'lane') and the N transept. The
rebuilt church was consecrated in 1266. The cloister walks were
rebuilt in the 14th c. and an unusual series of small chapels added
against the S aisle.
   Sir Edward Baynton pulled down most of the buildings (it is
thought that a workman was killed in the process) to build a
mansion at Bromham but the W range was probably kept as a
house. By the 1660s however hardly anything was left. The railway
(now disused) was cut through the precinct in 1860–3. Excavations
in 1906 revealed the plan, and some well preserved tile paving of the
W cloister walk was protected by a permanent building; unhappily
that has since decayed and the tiles have gone.

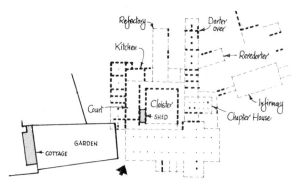

The lane from the road turns quickly right to the farmhouse. Straight ahead however it goes on as a cart track through a gate (the 'trespassers' sign refers only to fishing) and over the railway cutting. Ahead are derelict cottages. Behind them in the field to the right is the pantiled building meant to protect the 14th c. paving but now merely an indicator of the cloister position – the garth being still a well defined flat square beside it. Given the plan and a good deal of imagination one can place the main buildings – the refectory towards the river and the church up the hill and roughly parallel with the railway. But the irregular humps bear no particular relationship to them. A few bits of moulded stone lie around the farmhouse and some more are at Bremhill Court.

Stapehill Dorset: SU 054003
in village on A31, 2½ miles E of Wimborne Minster

Cistercian nunnery of Our Lady of the Holy Cross founded 1802 by
    Mère Augustin de Chabannes, a daughter house of Bas-Valais
    (Switzerland)

Church (except nuns' quire) open during normal hours

Perhaps more than any other, the community endured years of hardship in its first decades – including privations as refugees through Bavaria, Austria and Russia and inadequate quarters at Hammersmith, and at first at Stapehill itself where a few farm cottages and a barn had been a Jesuit centre since the 17th c. Gutted by fire in 1818, the buildings were restored, and by 1822 a dorter and workroom had been added. A dorter for lay sisters was built in 1843, and in 1847–51 the two-naved church under Charles Hansom. The chapel then became refectory and kitchen. The cloister and the W range were completed in 1860–1, while the guest house was added and other alterations made in 1882–5.

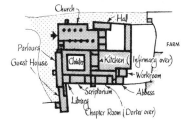

The drive leads past the public cemetery to the modest red brick **church**, which has a small slate-spired tower at the W end of the S nave (nuns' quire), and an aisle to the N or secular nave. The general style is Early English, with low arcades on octagonal columns, and open high-pitched roofs. The W and E windows, rather worn, are attributed to John Hardman. High panelling screens the nuns' quire, which can nevertheless be partly seen through the modernistic 'sunray' grilles that separate the two sanctuaries.

The rest is private. **Outside**, the cottagey guest house continues the line of the W end of the church, while the lane past the N side leads on past a small church hall (former school room) to the farm and offers limited views of the E and S ranges with their battlements and 'Gothick' sashes of c.1820. The original buildings, those at the far SE corner, are out of sight.

Stepney (Abbey of the Minoresses) Greater London: TQ 338811
¼ mile N of Tower of London

Franciscan nunnery of the Grace of the Blessed Virgin Mary and St Francis founded 1293 by Edmund, Earl of Lancaster; dissolved 1539. Part of the church survived until World War II as the N side of the one-time parish church of Holy Trinity Minories. Its site at the NE corner of St Clare Street (the nuns were nicknamed 'Poor Clares') is now occupied by offices.

Stoneleigh Warwickshire: SP 318712
1 mile SW of village and ½ mile E of Warwick road B4115

Cistercian abbey of the Blessed Virgin Mary founded c.1135–47 at Redmore, Staffordshire by Stephen and Matilda, a daughter house of Bordesley; refounded by Henry II at Stoneleigh 1155. Dissolved 1536 and granted to Charles Brandon, Duke of Suffolk

Owned by Lord Leigh. Parts of grounds open to public at advertised times May to September; parts of house also open from 1984

Evidence suggests that the first buildings were mid-12th c. and of standard Cistercian plan, probably without any later rebuilding of the church. However the E cloister range, partly embedded in the present house, has work of c.1300. The gatehouse and attached guest house, standing complete, are 14th c.

The dukedom of Suffolk quickly died out and the buildings were sold jointly to a London merchant, Sir Rowland Hill, and his one-time apprentice, Sir Thomas Leigh; they are still in the latter's family and succeeding generations made a mansion of them – preserving the cloister garth as an inner court, and the base of the E range, all the way from S transept to base of dorter undercroft, as the foundation of a domestic block of *c*.1600. The N range stands on the base of the S nave aisle and preserves parts of it, but was much altered in the 1830s. The W range gave way to a grand Baroque building of 1714–26 by Francis Smith, while the S is a mixture of later 18th and early 19th c. work. The fine conservatory (now visitors' tea-room) between house and river is of *c*.1760; the extensive Tudoresque stables and riding school to the NE are of 1814–20.

From the W (Grecian Lodges) entrance the drive leads over the river to the abbey **gatehouse**, whose domestic scale and character are emphasised by 16th c. dormers and other windows added to the guest house alongside. Both are essentially 14th c.

The following description assumes limited access, and none at all to the interior – as a result of a serious fire in the W range in 1960. Visitors will in due course be able to see more, though not all of the medieval parts which are mostly in the private E wing. From the gatehouse one looks across the site of the nave to the N side of the **house**, built into remains of the S aisle, and in its outer wall are traces of four high arches of the Norman arcade. Within there exist also the Norman arch between aisle and transept and the doorways from both aisle and transept into the cloister (the latter still opening into the inner court). However, much of the N side, with porch, is

Stoneleigh: 14th c. gatehouse with 16th c. additions

of the 1830s. It meets the grand W range, which extends down towards the Avon.

The S front, starting with the other end of the W range, is another miscellany, and its further end is swallowed up in the more rambling private regions of the house, which cannot be seen by the public. An abbreviated view of the E front is however possible from the NE, from its other end, by following the main drive eastwards from the gatehouse towards the stables; its regiment of seven Elizabethan gables quite disguises the underlying plan of chapter house etc. The two bigger gables at the N end represent the church transept.

A fine general view can be obtained from the top of the hill on the other side of the river; it too emphasises the splendid Renaissance buildings at the expense of the monastic. A big model railway adds to the attractions of the riverside grounds.

Stow Lincolnshire: SK 882820
in Stow village, 6 miles SE of Gainsborough

Benedictine abbey of St Mary moved from Eynsham, Oxfordshire
by Remigius, Bishop of Lincoln 1091, using pre-existing
collegiate church. Transferred back to Eynsham *c.*1094–5 (or
1109?)

Parish church. Open during normal hours

Of abbey status for only a brief spell after the Conquest, Stow is
very remarkable for having retained substantial remains of a pre-
Conquest church which served as a kind of sub-cathedral in the
diocese of Dorchester from *c.*975 until the see was moved to
Lincoln in 1073. Its actual dating has been the subject of a
succession of theories. That normally accepted identifies six main
building phases, of which three existed at the time of the monastery:
late 10th c. the lower parts of the transepts, mid-11th c. the upper,
and *c.*1070 the aisleless nave.

Later changes happily left its scale and nobility unaffected. The
chancel is mid-12th c., the tower *c.*1400, and the roofs (including
the rebuilt chancel vault) by J.L. Pearson, 1853–64. After the
monks returned to Eynsham it became an ordinary parish church.
Nothing is known of the monastic buildings.

The splendid four-order main S doorway is a late Norman (mid-
12th c.) insertion into an earlier Norman wall. The interior is famed
for its four giant Saxon crossing arches, within which in the 14th c.
were fitted more ordinary arches and piers for a new tower – the old
one having been dismantled only to about nave-roof level. The high
nave roof (with 17th c. tie-beams), W windows and tiled floor are
19th c., but the nine-shafted font with dragons is 13th c. and the
tracery-ended pews 15th c.; also there are two old chests. The brass
lectern is 19th c. by Hardman. A plaque beside the W crossing arch
attributes damage to the attached shafts to the Danish raid of 870
and calls Stow the former bishopric of Sidnacester; neither is now
thought possible. The N transept, 10th c. at the base and early 11th
c. above, has a primitive W doorway (now to a vestry), inserted
12th and 13th c. windows, a Jacobean chest, a wall painting of St
Thomas à Becket (*c.*1200) and a rood loft stair.

The chancel was much restored by Pearson to its supposed late Norman form; the Saxon one may not have been as big. Rich wall-arcading runs all round, and the window surrounds have zigzag and Greek key. There is even a clerestory, but the lavishly zigzagged rib vault and most of the E wall are 19th c. Two 13th c. floor slabs have women's heads in roundels, one with an unusual inscription in Old English instead of Latin. 15th c. screen panels are reused in the stalls. The S transept, Saxon again, has inserted windows like the N.

Partial fencing of the churchyard means that a circuit is best made outside it. The W doorway is another fine Norman one, with a simple Gothic niche added alongside; a third, smaller one on the N leads into a new vestry extension approximately on the site of a 10th c. porticus. The steep roofs are a restoration by Pearson to their original form, and the tower top is 15th c. The stair turret, now within the 19th c. vestry on the N side, was moved from inside the nave by Pearson, reusing two tiny Saxon windows.

From the SE, however, is the most instructive view: the comparatively unrestored mid-12th c. wall of the chancel, the S transept with its 10th c. lower and 11th c. upper parts, and (as in the other re-entrant angles) an outer corner of the Saxon tower base showing through. The transept gable wall nicely sums up the variety of styles with its three windows: big round Norman, two-light Geometric, and Saxon slit – the last being enriched with rare 'palmette' ornament.

Strata Florida Dyfed: SN 746656
1 mile SE of Pontrhydfendigaid and Tregaron–Devil's Bridge road B4343

Cistercian abbey of the Blessed Virgin Mary founded 1164 by
     Robert fitzStephen, a daughter house of Whitland; refounded on
     new site 1184 by Rhys ap Gruffydd. Dissolved 1539 and passed to
     Stedman family

In care of Welsh Office. Open during standard hours (admission
     charge)

The first buildings were near Old Abbey Farm 2 miles to the SW in a field called Yr Hen Fynachlog (the old monastery); foundations were found there and dug out in the 19th c. Of the second abbey, low walls of which survive, the presbytery, crossing and transepts were of 1184–1201, and the nave and chapter house slightly later. The cloister was rebuilt about the end of the 15th c. Though of Norman origins the abbey became a great centre of Welsh culture.

The W cloister range and walk became a house, but then went to ruin with the rest; but by good fortune the unique main W doorway has survived. Excavations were done in 1847 and 1887 and after the site passed into state care in 1931. The southern part is however still in private hands, a farmhouse being on the refectory site.

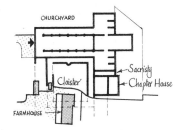

The round-headed sandstone W doorway, early 13th c., is most unusual in the continuing of the shafted treatment of all five jambs right round the head, interrupted only by ring mouldings 'tied' to the wall face with volutes of curiously primitive character.

Much of the remainder is no more than foundations of slaty stone though the E parts stand to 5 or 6 feet. The **nave** aisles were separated by solid screen walls (except in the W bay) on which the arcades stood, the actual column bases being about 5 feet above the floor, resting on piers projecting into the aisles only. This unusual arrangement occurs elsewhere only in Ireland. The N aisle wall, the churchyard boundary, is modern but on an old foundation.

The three E chapels of the **N transept** are clear, each with its altar and the bases of shafted piers that carried vaults. Many old floor tiles are preserved (reset) and there is a memorial slab of 1951 to the medieval poet Dafydd ap Gwilym. The presbytery (extended one bay eastward c.1250) also retains its altar base, and traces of sedilia in the right-hand wall. In the **S transept** the three chapels are more complete and roofed over for protection, and the outer one has two tomb recesses. S of them is a long sacristy, through which the E walk of the cloister can be reached. Next is the chapter house, originally of c.1250 but rebuilt to half the size in the 14th c. and possibly used thereafter for a different purpose. Near the N wall is a plain 13th c. grave slab.

Strata Florida: W doorway of *c*.1200

The other monastic remains lie unexcavated beyond. So the route continues over the chapter house, past the monastic cemetery outside the S transept, to the E end of the church where the added end bay is marked by a change in the outside plinth; from here the simple 19th c. parish church is well seen.

Finally double back through the presbytery and along the S nave aisle or the N walk of the cloister. The alcove in the outer wall of the latter is believed to have housed a lectern. At the end of the walk is a mass of stone filling the N end of the W range, which has not yet been fully investigated, and in the corner of the aisle is the start of a stair to the lay brothers' quarters on the upper floor.

The small museum at the ticket office contains some interesting carved stones.

Strata Marcella Powys: SJ 251104
2 miles NE of Welshpool on Oswestry road A483

Cistercian abbey of the Blessed Virgin Mary founded 1170 by
  Owain Cyfeiliog, a daughter house of Whitland; moved to new
  site 1172. Dissolved 1536

Owned by Earl of Powis. Site accessible at all times

Or Ystrad Farchel. It gained a reputation for dissolute living. For example Enoch, the first abbot, founded a short-lived nunnery at Llansaintfraed in Elvel and eloped with a nun – but came back repentant to be abbot again. Later it became subject to Buildwas. Possibly the four W bays of the church (one of the biggest in Wales) were built later, thus extending the building period to *c.*1240.

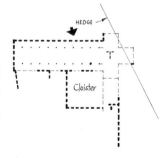

Probably too it was sacked by Owain Glyndwr. No buildings remain above ground; excavations in 1890 recovered some carved stones, some of them now scattered in museums etc., but failed to establish the full plan.

A modern commemorative tablet is in a lay-by on the W side of A483. The abbey site is on the other side of the road, one field nearer Welshpool. Some posts near the left side of the field and half-way to the Severn bank roughly demarcate the church, and there is a heap of carved stones under a hawthorn in the centre. A second, less definite depression marks the cloister site further down the slope.

The font in Buttington church is said to be a 13th c. capital from the abbey chapter house.

Stratford Langthorne Greater London: TQ 390834
600 yards SW of West Ham church

Cistercian abbey of the Blessed Virgin Mary founded 1135 by William de Mountfichet; dissolved 1538. Much of the site now lies under railway tracks. A small two-light window and a skull carving at West Ham church were formerly near the Adam and Eve public house – which probably grew out of a monastic building.

Sulby Northamptonshire: SP 658801
1 mile E of Welford on Naseby road

Premonstratensian abbey of the Blessed Virgin Mary founded at Welford 1155 by William de Wideville, a daughter house of Newsham; moved to Sulby shortly afterwards. Dissolved 1538 and given to Sir Christopher Hatton

Owned by Chambers family. Site accessible with permission from house at head of drive

Also sometimes called Welford. Nothing is known of the abbey plan but the few known remains confirm a 12th–13th c. building period. The Hattons built a house on the site, probably incorporating parts of the abbey, and the present Abbey Farm may also do so in its foundations.

Site of Abbey

ABBEY FARM

The gravelled drive to the farm is not public, although a bridle way crosses it diagonally. The main abbey buildings lay on its left (E) side before the farm. No excavation has ever been done. At the bottom of the drive can be found a pointed arch built to display three carved stones, one with Norman chevron ornament. All around are extensive earthworks of the precinct, and below the farm a complex system of fishponds and channels connecting with the river Avon.

Swineshead Lincolnshire: TF 250407
on A52, ¾ mile NE of town and 5 miles WSW of Boston

Savigniac abbey of the Blessed Virgin Mary founded 1135 by
  Robert de Gresley, a daughter house of Furness; became
  Cistercian 1147; dissolved 1536

The traditional refuge of King John after losing his jewels in the Wash. The modest house called Swineshead Abbey (Emmitt family), basically of 1607, almost certainly contains abbey stone. Against a corner is a 13th c. knight's effigy (to be seen with permission from house).

Syon Devon: SX 724611
1¾ miles ENE of South Brent and 200 yards E of A38

Bridgettine abbey of St Saviour (and later Our Blessed Lady and St
  Bridget of Syon) founded at Twickenham 1415 by Henry V;

settled at South Brent 1925 after repeated moves (see Syon, Greater London)

Chapel open to the public during normal hours; entrance hall and parlour on application

After the final dissolution at Isleworth in 1558 the community went to Antwerp. Hounded by political upheavals, they moved about Flanders, then to Rouen, and in 1594 to Lisbon. From 1695 when the last brother died, there have only been sisters. A group that returned to England in 1809 died out; in 1861 the Lisbon house closed and the community came to Spettisbury, Dorset, then to Chudleigh (1887), and finally to their present home, the 18th c. grey stone Marley House, former home of the Carews. Wings containing priest's house and nuns' quarters were at once added under the architect Father Benedict Williamson.

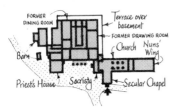

The imposing Greek Doric porticoed entrance leads into a spacious stair hall with Ionic marble columns, stone floor with black marble diamonds, and simple curving wooden stair. Behind the main front (within the private enclosure) the house is square, seven bays by seven, with a small open court. Above the two main floors are a dormered attic; below them a terrace and a basement (containing the kitchen and refectory) with arched façade continued along the garden front of Williamson's extension. Many fine doors, ceilings and chimneypieces remain in the principal rooms.

Visitors enter the 1925 chapel separately, by the customary secular transept. Its chief treasures are a beautiful 15th c. octagonal stone pinnacle with figure sculpture which came from the gatehouse of Isleworth, an iron cross from its church roof, and an ancient figure of St Bridget – all of which went with the sisters on their enforced travels through Europe. The famous Syon cope, however, passed into private hands and is now in the Victoria and Albert Museum.

Syon (old) Greater London: TQ 173767
in Isleworth, ¼ mile S of A315

Bridgettine abbey of St Saviour (and later St Mary and St Bridget of
   Syon) founded 1415 at Twickenham by Henry V; moved to
   Isleworth 1431. Dissolved 1539 and granted to Duke of Somerset.
   Refounded 1557. Dissolved again 1558 and granted to Earl of
   Northumberland

Owned by Duke of Northumberland. Open to the public 10.0 a.m.
   to 5.0 p.m. most days (admission charge)

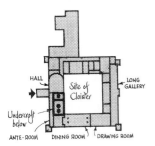

Henry V's foundation, made in expiation of his father's connivance
in Richard II's murder, was for separate nuns and priests with an
abbess. Surprisingly little is known of the buildings, the site of
which was used for a house by the Duke of Somerset c.1550. After
his execution it was given to the Duke of Northumberland. He was
himself executed, the abbey reverted to the Crown, and the nuns
briefly returned. After many wanderings the community settled in
Lisbon in 1594, and in 1861 returned to England (see Syon, Devon).
The Earldom of Northumberland was twice revived, for the Percys
and then for the Smithsons who virtually rebuilt the house c.1765–
1830, primarily to Robert Adam's designs.
   The only medieval work still exposed is part of a 15th c.
undercroft – one vaulted compartment of two bays and one of
three. If it is accepted that the square inner court round which the
house is built is the site of the cloister, these represent part of the W
monastic range. No proof however exists. They extend now beneath
the S end of the entrance hall and part of the ante-room beyond and
are not open to the public, whose visits are limited to the
magnificent principal rooms of the ground floor. In 1823 two late

Gothic doorways were found embedded in the W wall on either side of the porch; probably they had been reset during Somerset's remodelling and hidden again in Adam's. They are no longer visible.

Talacre Clwyd: SJ 104833
1 mile E of Gronant and 2¼ miles E of Prestatyn

Anglican Benedictine nunnery of Our Lady Help of Christians founded 1868 at Feltham, Middlesex by Hilda Stewart; moved to Twickenham 1889, to West Malling 1893 and to St Bride's 1911; became Roman Catholic 1913; moved to Talacre 1920

Church and shop only, open during normal hours (remainder within enclosure)

The community is unusual in having begun within the Church of England and entered the Roman Catholic Church many years afterwards. Its history is further complicated by the numerous moves outlined above. Its present home, Talacre Hall, had belonged to the Catholic Mostyn family since the 15th c., but as it stands is an embattled Tudor-style house of two and three storeys rebuilt *c.*1830 and later. The drawing room and library served as a chapel till 1932 when the church was finished. The bell tower is of 1952, replacing a temporary one of 1938.

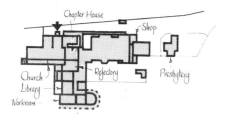

Visitors arrive at the shop, on the corner of the main building, of which little can be seen. The church is at the further end, reached by the narrowing path that continues from the main drive. Its orientation is reversed; that is, the altar is at the W end. Only the N transept may be entered, alongside the sanctuary – from which the nuns' quire is screened by a lattice. Low arch-trusses and plastered walls with slightly Tudoresque windows do not make the interior in

any way remarkable. Near the transept/quire junction a stone from
Basingwerk abbey is preserved.

The brick tower is just visible from outside the porch. The
octagonal building on the right of the hill on the way out was a
stable block but is now a generator house.

Talley Dyfed: SN 632327
in village, ¼ mile W of Llandilo–Lampeter road B4302

Premonstratensian abbey of the Blessed Virgin Mary and St John
the Baptist founded *c.*1184–9, probably in place of an earlier
community, by Rhys ap Gruffydd, a daughter house of St Jean,
Amiens, Picardy. Dissolved 1536 (?) and retained by the Crown

In care of Welsh Office. Open during standard hours (admission
charge)

Or Talyllychau (two lakes). Rhys ap Tewdwr is credited with a
foundation a century earlier on the same site. As refounded, it was
the only Premonstratensian house in Wales; its 'parenthood' was
transferred in 1285 to Welbeck. Such walling as remains is mostly of
*c.*1200 and suggests a church of eight bays on which work was soon
curtailed. The four bays actually built and used were blocked off
from the rest. Similarly any ambitions for a big cloister were
unfulfilled.

The E end was adapted as a parish church and the remainder
allowed to go to ruin. But it too was abandoned when a new church
was built just to the N in 1772. The remains passed into state care in
1933.

Of the **nave** only foundations remain, but it seems clear that the
four W bays were never proceeded with and that the part actually

used was enclosed by the cross-wall (looking now like a pulpitum) and by another wall blocking the N arcade – in fact the area now gravelled. The lean in one of the S arcade piers may have been connected with the last major collapse that occurred in 1845. The E and N walls and arches of the crossing tower are however still a landmark, and though devoid of much detail still retain stairs within the thickness of their upper walls. **Transept** and presbytery walls stand to a few feet only, but on the N side the plain arch into the nave aisle survives, also the bases of two altars; the third chapel was extended further E subsequently to the original work. Some old tiles survive too. S of the sanctuary are wall-bases of two small sacristies.

The S transept has remains of all three chapel altars, and in its SW corner a mass of masonry that supported the night stair. The **cloister**, reached through the S aisle, has lost its S part and all its surrounding buildings to the adjoining farmyard, but parts of the walks are indicated by dwarf walls. From here a circuit round the E end of the church and the N side is possible but not particularly profitable.

Tarrant Dorset: ST 921033
at Tarrant Crawford (3 miles SE of Blandford Forum), probably about 400 yards W of church

Nunnery, possibly of St Mary Magdalen and possibly of no
  recognised order, founded *c*.1186 by Ralph de Kahaynes;
  refounded by 1228 as Cistercian abbey of St Mary and All Saints;
  dissolved 1539 and given to Wyatt family. Tarrant Abbey Farm
  (Tory family) may be on the site, or it may have been opposite,
  nearer the stream. The windowless side wall of the parish church
  suggests too that either the nuns' or an anchoresses' building may
  have adjoined.

Tavistock Devon: in town centre on A386   SX 482744

Benedictine abbey of St Mary and (later) St Rumon founded by 971
  by Ordulf, son of Ordgar, Earl of Devon; became mitred 1458.
  Dissolved 1539 and granted to John Russell, Earl of Bedford

In multiple ownership. Site accessible at all times except where
  stated, without charge

After being ravaged by Danes in 997 the abbey was at once rebuilt, still under Ordulf as founder and abbot. A later rebuilding was dedicated in 1318, but work on the church tower and claustral buildings went on at least till the end of the century, and quite extensively on the outer buildings into the 15th and 16th cc. The abbey is said to have had the second printing press in England.

St Rumon's shrine and the abbey church itself (which remained remarkably narrow) were soon pulled down. The abbot's hall (adjoined by a big porch and long thought to be the refectory) became a chapel, later nonconformist and since 1701 Unitarian. The actual refectory gave way to Abbey House, rebuilt c.1720 and now the nucleus of the Bedford Hotel; its last medieval walls above ground went c.1810. The present Tavy bridge and approach road were built in 1762, obliterating much else. The Town Gate or Higher Abbey Gate has survived (latterly as a library) and is 12th c. to 15th c. So have parts of the precinct wall and the ruined 15th c. southern gatehouse known as Betsy Grimbal's Tower. The parish church tower, arched on all sides, formed the Cemetery Gate. Of the abbey church, part of the tower stood till c.1670, and there is still a remnant of the nave.

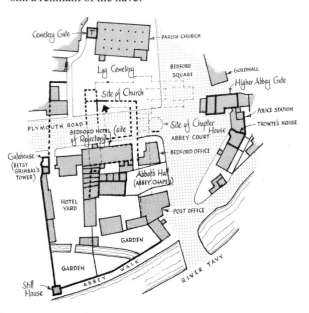

A tour, necessarily piecemeal, is best begun with the ruin in the parish churchyard: the NW angle of the cloister with the top part of a 13th c. arch into the W end of the abbey **nave**. Digging in 1914 and 1920 revealed a good deal more of this S wall of the church, as well as part of the N wall nearer the parish church.

Opposite the E end of the churchyard alongside the Guildhall of 1848 is the two-storeyed **Town Gate**, 12th and 15th cc. but repaired and somewhat altered. S of it is Abbey Court, where **Trowte's House** (three-storeyed with projecting turret) is medieval; the original range here was all monastic and continued right across the present bridge approach. W of that, a stretch of precinct wall faces the Tavy. Next to the Post Office, set well back, is the abbot's hall (now the Unitarian **Abbey Chapel**) curtailed and given a new end doorway in 1845. The early 16th c. pinnacled building alongside was its porch, and is still vaulted. These are not normally open to the public.

Round the corner now into Plymouth Road. The Bedford Hotel was formerly Abbey House and stands on the refectory site. Beyond, beside the old vicarage, is the 15th c. **Betsy Grimbal's Tower**, which was the main gatehouse. Several fanciful tales surround the name. Under its barrel vault are a big stone coffin and part of a roof truss from the Abbey Chapel. Between the tower and the hotel a yard runs down to a garden where part of the precinct wall can again be seen; the embattled corner tower is called the Still House.

The names Bedford, Russell and Tavistock (as well as Woburn) were used for London squares developed by the Russells.

Teignmouth Devon: SX 945741
¾ mile N of town centre on Dawlish road A379

Benedictine nunnery of St Scholastica founded at Dunkirk, Flanders 1662 with the secret authorisation of Charles II, a daughter house of Ghent; became an abbey 1663; moved to Hammersmith 1795 and to Teignmouth 1862

Chapel open to public during normal hours

Like many other present-day communities, Teignmouth began its history on the Continent, being driven home by the French Revolution after the English Penal Laws were repealed. After 60 years at the former Mary Ward convent at Hammersmith (London) the nuns moved to a house called Dun Esk high on the N side of Teignmouth and built a complete new abbey beside it, under the architect George Goldie. The church was consecrated in 1864. Additions and alterations were made in 1871–2 under Charles Hansom.

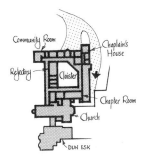

Three-storeyed and slate-roofed, of grey stone and darker bands and softened by relieving arches over the first floor windows, it is one of the nuns' wings that greets the visitor. The church is reached by continuing along the upper (left) end past the long 'washroom' wing and the chapter house gable, and entered at the N or secular chapel. The interior, in many ways typical of its date, has pink marble columns to the sanctuary and side chapel arches, and stencilled patterns on the sanctuary ceiling, but has been generally enhanced with lighter, fresh paintwork. The chapel on the other side, 'Miss English's', was for the use of the benefactress owner of Dun Esk.

Tewkesbury Gloucestershire: in town centre   SO 891324

Benedictine monastery of the Blessed Virgin Mary founded 715 (?) by Duke Doddo on site of hermitage; refounded c.980 as cell to Cranborne, Dorset; refounded as abbey by Robert fitzHamon c.1102 on interchange with Cranborne. Dissolved 1540 and given to T. Strowde, W. Erle and J. Paget; church bought by parish

Owned by parish. Open 7.30 a.m. to 6.0 p.m. (summer) or 5.0 p.m. (winter, but 4.30 on Saturdays); but till 7.0 p.m. on Sundays

The church is substantially that consecrated in 1121; its great central tower was finished a decade or two later. In the 13th c. two chapels were added to the N transept. Early in the 14th c. the apsidal E ambulatory was rebuilt and provided with a ring of little chapels including a Lady chapel no longer standing. Then the whole upper part of the quire was rebuilt, with new clerestory and vault, and (still in the 14th c.) the timber roofs of tower and nave were replaced by vaults. The series of still-surviving medieval tombs and chantries is second only to those at Westminster. The last decisive battle of the Wars of the Roses took place nearby in 1471.

The nave had long been used by the townspeople but after the Dissolution they moved to the quire (which they had bought for £453, the value of the lead and bells); the nave went into partial disuse and the chapel E of the N transept became a school. The Lady chapel and most of the monastic buildings were taken down, but the abbot's house and gatehouse and a barn were kept and still exist. Till 1817 a detached bell tower also stood to the NE. The church was restored by Sir George Gilbert Scott in 1875–9.

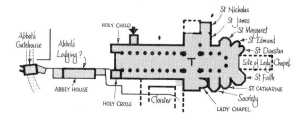

The overwhelming external impression of Romanesque is reinforced inside by the giant cylindrical columns and round arches of the **nave**. Unlike similar additions in other great churches, its 14th c. lierne vault has a distinctly oppressive effect, springing low from the tops of the pier caps, hiding the small triforium, and smothering the clerestory. The vault panels are painted and the splendidly carved bosses gilded; these continue in great variety throughout the church, and in the nave can be viewed by a trolley-mirror and coin-operated lights. The W end is spanned by a big pointed arch on luxuriant corbels with heads and foliage, and it seems that corner towers were planned at the aisle ends. The W window tracery – unusually – is of 1686, and its glass (by Hardman) of 1886. Below hangs the Garter banner of Lord Ismay (d. 1965).

The high octopartite **N aisle** vault is of *c*.1300 and springs also from the Norman pier caps. At its W end the Holy Child chapel has a 16th c. altar painting and seven 18th c. benefaction boards. Further along are two splendid black Gurney stoves, an ornate oak doorcase by W.D. Caröe (1913), and in the fifth bay a little 17th c. brass. Then on the right the nave pulpit (1892) and in the end bay the canopied tomb of a 14th c. knight. The aisle glass (S as well as N) is by Hardman, 1892.

The **N transept**, closed off by an oak screen of 1982, is over-filled with an organ of 1887, and thus difficult to appreciate. To its right can be seen a wall memorial with ruffed bust of John Roberts (d. 1631). The E apse of this transept gave way to the bigger, rectangular 13th c. chapel of St James, now the abbey shop and approached from the ambulatory through a 14th c. stone screen. Beyond it is the chapel of St Nicholas (now the choir room) – 13th c. but with 14th c. vault; its nave has gone, as will be seen outside, but what remains is fine Early English work with wall-arcading.

The vaulted **ambulatory**, essentially 14th c. but built against Norman columns, is punctuated with noble tombs and little chantries which alternately hide and reveal the presbytery and polygonal chapels as one walks round. On the presbytery side is, first, the chantry of Richard Beauchamp, Earl of Worcester (d. 1421) built by his wife, later Isabel Despencer, Countess of Warwick. Both storeys are vaulted, the upper perhaps having been meant for kneeling effigies. Next to it is the fan-vaulted chantry of Robert fitzHamon (d. 1107), regarded as the abbey's founder; built *c*.1395, it is beautifully detailed Perpendicular in miniature.

Now the ambulatory opens out and the outer chapel, St Margaret's, is guarded by the canopied tomb of Sir Guy de Brien (d. 1390). Reserved for private prayer, it has good heraldic ledger stones on the floor and some ancient glass in one window. Opposite is another richly canopied tomb, of Hugh, Baron Despencer (d. 1348), with alabaster effigies of him and his wife. Next are the twin chapels of St Edmund and St Dunstan, the latter (with a 15th c. Flemish altar painting) being partly hidden by a graceful 15th c. canopied screen used a century later to display the horrific effigy of John Wakeman (d. 1549), the last abbot. On the decaying cadaver are carved a mouse, a worm and other vermin.

The E end of the presbytery, facing the blocked Lady chapel arch, is closed by another traceried 14th c. stone screen; the floor grating leads to the burial vault of George, Duke of Clarence (brother of Edward IV) and his wife. The next chapel, St Faith's,

has windows by Geoffrey Webb, 1941, and Charles Kempe, 1896.
The monument at its entrance, in the form of a table tomb, is to
Archdeacon Robeson (d. 1912). Opposite, against the presbytery,
are two tombs smashed by Puritans in the 17th c.; the left-hand one
is of Hugh le Despencer (hanged 1325) but confusingly covers the
effigy of Abbot Cotes (d. 1347), moved from the nave. Yet another
canopied tomb, opposite, is that of Abbot Cheltenham (d. 1509).
The chapel behind, now called St Catharine's, contains a number of
stone fragments and an Italian-looking wardrobe of 1818.

Continuing W: on the right is the chantry of Edward, Baron le
Despencer (d. 1375), known also as Trinity chapel – remarkable not
only for having a very early fan vault but also for the spirelet on its
roof containing an effigy kneeling towards the altar (this can only be
seen from a distance). It also retains traces of colouring, including
the remains on the E wall of a 14th c. painting of the Holy Trinity.
On the left is a tomb believed to be of Abbot Forthington (d. 1254),
its canopy rich with ball-flowers. The doorway beyond leads to the
vaulted sacristy, two-storeyed and private; on request the inner face
of the door may be seen, strengthened with strips of armour metal
retrieved from the 1471 battlefield. Then come two more tombs: the
trefoil-headed canopied one of Abbot Alan (d. 1202) and another
unidentified within which some medieval tiles have been assembled.

Now the **quire**, entered through another stone screen. Around
the E end, looking clockwise from the N side, the tombs and
chantries are of: Richard Beauchamp, Robert fitzHamon, Hugh
Baron Despencer, and (S, after the 14th c. sedilia) Hugh le
Despencer and Edward le Despencer. The 'Milton' organ,
originally built c.1580 for Magdalen College, Oxford, has tin pipes
of fine workmanship. The front stalls are of 1875–9, but at the back
(especially on the N side) some are 14th c. with misericords. The N
screenwork is 14th c. too, but that to the nave is by J. Oldrid Scott,
1892.

The quire has big round piers like the nave, but here they were
halved in height in the 14th c. and given new capitals and richly
moulded arches, a big clerestory and an ambitious lierne vault –
altogether a more satisfactory remodelling than the nave. The seven
windows contain glass of 1340–4, as is proved by the heraldry; they
were given by Eleanor de Clare in memory of her husband Hugh.
The subject of the E window is the Last Judgment; the two next to it
on either side show Old Testament kings and prophets, while on
each side the westernmost has armoured figures of the abbey's
noble patrons. Though typical of this period, the greens and the

Tewkesbury: Early 12th c. W front with inserted Perpendicular window

yellows and whites have a special quality.

The altar slab, one of the longest in England as well as one of the oldest, has undergone many vicissitudes since being consecrated in 1239. Modern brasses near the communion step mark the graves of de Clares and Despencers, and another beneath the tower that of Edward, Prince of Wales (killed 1471). The **crossing** (tower) vault is also 14th c.

Next the **S transept** where on the N wall is a tablet to the novelist Mrs Craik (d. 1887) by H.H. Armstead. Tall plain Norman arches support another 14th c. lierne vault like that of the N transept. On the E side the Norman apsidal chapel survives, with its ribbed vault. The mosaic in its window recess is by Antonio Salviati, 1893.

At the entry to the **S nave aisle** can be seen the beginning of a half-barrel vault (12th c.) over the aisle which, if it had been proceeded with, would have been unique in England. On the left is another tomb with cinquefoil arch, then the cloister doorway: on the right the eagle lectern, 1878. Minor tablets line the outer wall. The step (now a ramp) two bays along marks where the monastic wooden pulpitum went across the church. Traces of its rood-loft stairs and of paintings on the columns correspond with it. The font, under the main arcade, is an amalgam of 19th c. canopy and bowl (by Scott), 14th c. clustered stem, and a possibly older base.

Lastly the **exterior**, starting with the unusually tall two-storeyed N porch, early 12th c. A curious feature is the chevron-ornamented inner door lintel. The statue over the outer doorway is by Darsie Rawlins. The aisle windows are all Decorated enlargements – except that the first towards the W is Perpendicular. The great W window, as already noticed, is a 17th c. renewal; it is interesting to speculate on the original infill of the six great concentric arches which with their flanking turrets and (later) pinnacles form one of the finest Norman façades in England. Past it stands Abb y House – possibly the guest house, possibly the abbot's – on this side 15th c. with an early 16th c. oriel. Further along the path is the much restored gatehouse, of similar date; the barn and cottages beyond may represent the abbey almonry.

Now one must turn back, repassing the porch and looking up at the Norman clerestory with its added 14th c. windows. The great tower is well seen from this side; probably the finest of its period in England, it is enlivened with rows of arcading and once had a spire. The roofs, the old lines of which are evident, were lowered in 1593. Then the N transept, Norman too but with a big off-centre Early English shafted doorway which led to the 'nave' of the partly destroyed outer chapel. The 'chancel arch' of this chapel retains part of a 14th c. stone screen which makes it resemble a window.

From the now public lawns at the E end the chevet with its 14th c. windows is impressive. The clerestory above, enriched with ball-flower, is capped by a pierced parapet and punctuated by flying buttresses. Round on the S and beyond the Norman transept a stretch of 15th c. stone panelling marks the cloister; one bay with its fan vault has been reconstructed.

Last of all, the intricate 18th c. wrought iron N churchyard gates should be noticed, and in Mill Street (not far to their N) part of another abbey barn with traces of the precinct wall adjoining it.

Thame Oxfordshire: SP 717038
1½ miles SSE of Thame and ½ mile E of Postcombe road B4012

Cistercian abbey of the Blessed Virgin Mary founded 1137 at
   Oddington, Oxfordshire, by Bishop Alexander of Lincoln;
   moved to Thame 1139–41. Dissolved 1539 and granted to John
   (later Lord) Williams and Robert Lee

Owned by Bowden family. Not open to the public

The church was consecrated in 1145, and its presbytery rebuilt early in the 13th c. Excavation c.1840 suggested a size of 230 feet by 70 feet, with a Lady chapel extending 45 feet further. Not much is known of the abbey buildings but they were partly ruinous by 1525 and were mostly demolished c.1561, leaving the cloister (now disappeared) as stables and two parallel blocks – one mainly 13th c., the other, which was the abbot's lodging, largely 16th c. How they stood in relation to the remainder seems to be forgotten. Joining them on their W side and undoubtedly on the site of another abbey range which had survived till then is the grand classical house called Thame Park built for William Wenman in 1745, probably by Francis Smith. The abbot's range contains a small upper and lower hall with bay windows, a larger hall added on its E side, and a low tower containing on its first floor a room with rich plasterwork and panelling in early Renaissance style, done c.1535 for the last abbot. Some distance to the NW, within the park, is an early 14th c. gate-chapel in which are some abbey tiles.

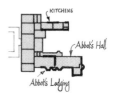

Site of Church?

KITCHENS

Abbot's Hall

Abbot's Lodging

Notwithstanding the 'Private' signs, a public footpath passes through the park and gives a glimpse (but no more) of the abbey. From the lodge gate nearer Thame, continue some 150 yards along the main road to a stile. From here a right-of-way footpath runs parallel to the house drive and in due course gives a view of the broad drive on the axis of the house, with stone piers and wrought iron gates. It then passes (undefined) across the field to the right, parallel to the ha-ha and towards a wooden footbridge. From this field the monastic oriels and roofs of the right-hand return wing are just visible. The chapel stands on the opposite (N) side of the house.

Thorney Cambridgeshire: .TF 283042
in village, on A47 and B1040

Benedictine abbey of the Holy Trinity, the Blessed Virgin Mary, St
   Peter and St Benedict (later St Mary and St Botolph) founded
   972–3 by St Ethelwold; became mitred. Dissolved 1539 and given
   to John Russell, Earl of Bedford

Parish church. Open during normal hours

An anchorite settlement was founded here c.662 by Saxulf, first
abbot of Peterborough, and destroyed by Danes in 870. Refounded
a century later as an abbey, it was rebuilt from 1085 onwards, the
church being consecrated in 1128. The chapter house was rebuilt
c.1300.
   Stone from the buildings went in the 16th c. to Trinity College,
Cambridge and the chapel of Corpus Christi College. Part of the
church nave was repaired in 1638 for parish use under Inigo Jones –
though it remained (until 1910) in effect a private chapel of the
Dukes of Bedford. The present transepted E end was added under

Edward Blore in 1840–1 and internal alterations were made in 1888.
The house to the W called Thorney Abbey contains a little medieval
work and may be on the site of the guest house; it is not open to the
public.

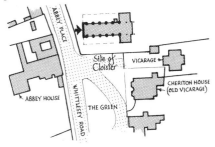

The **nave**, though a fragment without clerestory or aisles, still
impresses with its Norman strength. The main arcades are partly
swallowed up in masonry blocking off the aisles, but clearly show
the alternating pier system and retain their heavy attached shafts
rising through the triforium but there finishing at a simple cornice
and nearly flat ceiling put in by Inigo Jones. The single round arches
of the triforium are filled with 15th c. windows, probably those of
the clerestory lowered to this level. What has happened to the W
window is best seen outside.

A little medieval glass is preserved in windows on both sides, that
in the easternmost probably being 16th c. German. The rich red and
blue E window is a 19th c. copy of work of *c.*1200 at Canterbury
cathedral. The 'crossing' arches and the groin-vaulted chancel and
barrel-vaulted transepts are all by Blore. The font too is 19th c.
Memorials are of minor interest – a few small wall-tablets and on
the N wall a 17th c. brass.

Outside, the W front is a curious amalgam of several periods. The
corner turrets are Norman but with 15th c. tops. The round-arched
window between was replaced with a Perpendicular one and this in
its turn in 1638 by a similar smaller one. Judging by its weak shafts
and the four shallow niches each side, the doorway below may be
entirely of 1638 – Gothic survival as distinct from revival.

On the N side, against the NW turret, is a surviving piece of
Norman clerestory – a big blind arch with billet moulding. Probably
such panels alternated with actual windows. The churchyard has
innumerable well carved headstones. The outside of the main

arcade shows through; where it stops and Blore's work starts is painfully obvious. The S side virtually repeats the N, even to the stub of clerestory – which here however has a plain surround.

The 'village green' to the S approximately occupies the cloister area; the old vicarage is believed to stand roughly where the chapter house was.

Thornton Humberside: TA 118190
2 miles ENE of Thornton Curtis, close to East Halton road

Augustinian priory of the Blessed Virgin Mary founded 1139 by William le Gros, Count of Albermarle, colonised from Kirkham priory. Became abbey 1148; mitred 1518. Dissolved 1539; refounded 1541 as secular college of Holy Trinity; suppressed 1547 and granted to Bishop Randes of Lincoln

Mainly in care of Department of the Environment. Open during standard hours (admission charge)

The original buildings have left no record; the S end of the dorter range, the earliest part of the ruin, is early 13th c. A general rebuilding began about 1264, commencing with the church. The chapter house was finished c.1308 and the new cloister with refectory and kitchen by 1330. St Thomas's chapel on the N side was added in the 14th c., and the Lady chapel c.1410. The exceptional fortified gatehouse, its full purpose a mystery, is late 14th c. The college founded by Henry VIII included an almshouse that survived till the 17th c. The remainder, after passing through various hands, was demolished by Sir Vincent Skinner who built a house between church and gatehouse; this, it is said, promptly 'fell quite down'. The abbey site was taken over by the Office of Works from the Earl of Yarborough in 1938.

The very impressive **gatehouse** was extended outwards across the moat with a 125-foot long barbican of two thick parallel brick walls some time in the 16th c. – probably long after the Dissolution and probably merely for show. It forms an approach 'avenue', lined with blind arches. The gatehouse, itself largely of brick, seems to have been designed as much from pride as for strength. Its crenellation was however licensed in 1382. The abbot may have lived in it – yet it has inadequate service facilities, and no kitchen. Throughout there

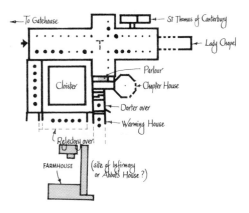

is much ornament to enjoy: on the outer face, carved corbels, brackets, niches over niches, and a rich segmental cusped arch with portcullis groove. Formerly there were standing figures all along the battlements and turrets. Inside are many large bosses on the unusual lattice vault. The wooden gates are decrepit but original, and the branching footway has its own vault with a fine lion boss. The inner face, with four upstanding turrets and a fine oriel and other windows, is more domestic. A turret stair leads to the spacious first-floor hall, now used for an expert display of carved stones. The oriel is vaulted inside; the rest has a ceiling on fine corbels, and the narrow perimeter passages are vaulted in brick. They contain garderobes, and the turrets have arrow slits. The second floor has a similar large room with a fireplace and at the top of the stair is a delicate vault with open traceried ribs, sadly defaced.

The undulations near the path to the **church** show where the 17th c. Skinner house stood. Of the abbey itself the highest standing walls are of and near the chapter house; little else survives above foundations. The approach is to the W end. Amongst the octagonal pier bases are many medieval grave slabs, some with indents of brasses; some on the N side, found in pier foundations, had been sacrificed as hardcore. That even the new church begun in 1264 had no S aisle is shown by the excavated remains, at the E end of the arcade, of the first doorway to its cloister and of buttress bases and stone benching of the cloister walk alongside.

In the crossing is the grave slab of Abbot Medeley (d. 1473); many others are in the N transept, of which the two E chapels are well defined. The presbytery has square pier bases and traces of its reredos two bays from the end but little else to show; to its E lay the Lady chapel, to its N (probably) that of St Thomas à Becket. The S transept alone provides an indication of architectural detail – typical

Thornton: Late 13th c. chapter house

of *c*.1280 – and here one chapel has its piscina.

Benching and buttresses in the **cloister** exactly repeat the superseded remains in the S aisle. Off the E walk is first the narrow parlour, vaulted still and with arcaded seating. Behind it is a room thought to have been the treasury and only approachable from above, in which (so legend says) a canon was found entombed seated at a table. A vestibule leads through a fairly complete arch to the chapter house – with typical Geometric wall-arcading of *c*.1290, the W and NW sides of the octagon standing almost to full height.

Next is the dorter undercroft, older (early 13th c.) than anything else but with rather complex subsequent alterations. More buildings lay under the lane, and indeed the farmhouse beyond (not open to the public) may contain masonry of the infirmary or abbot's house. The warming house at the corner of the cloister has a 13th c. fireplace; another is in the undercroft of the S (refectory) range, which shows evidence of extensive 15th c. alterations. The W (cellarer's) range (fully marked out on the ground) has no special features. The W walk however has old brick and tile paving and steps at the end to a second doorway into the church. Some of the cloister window stonework can be seen in the gatehouse.

Tilty Essex: TL 600266
200 yards N of parish church and 3 miles NW of Great Dunmow

Cistercian abbey of the Blessed Virgin Mary founded *c*.1153 by
    Maurice fitzGeoffrey, a daughter house of Warden. Dissolved
    1535 and passed to Marchioness of Dorset and Medeley family

Owned by Waring family. Accessible at any time without charge

Not very much is known of either the history or the buildings (other than the gate chapel) which were mostly 13th c., though it seems that the abbey's prosperity was a result of trading wool to Italy.

The gate chapel became a parish church. The guest house was lived in for some years; all the abbey buildings passed through various hands to the Maynards (1590) who demolished them and dispersed the materials.

What little is left of the abbey can be seen from the gate at the end of the lane beside the church. The surviving rubble walling is the E side of the W range of cloister buildings, cellars with

dormitory over. On their W face can just be detected traces of two bays of vaulting. The roughly square depression to their E was the cloister garth; the church occupied the flattish area S of that. Nothing remains of any of it above ground.

Another ground irregularity about three-quarters of the way back to the gate marks the gatehouse site. The pretty gate chapel, now St Mary's church, has a 13th c. nave and a much grander 14th c. chancel and has on the S wall a brass to Abbot de Takeley, 1475.

Tintern Gwent: ST 532998
in village on Chepstow–Monmouth road A466

Cistercian abbey of the Blessed Virgin Mary founded 1131 by
    Walter fitzRichard, a daughter house of l'Aumône (Eleemosina),
    Normandy. Dissolved 1536 and given to Earl of Worcester

In care of Welsh Office. Open during standard hours (admission
    charge)

Only a little is left of the 12th c. buildings, mostly in the chapter house and dorter undercroft. A complete reconstruction began in 1220, with the cloister ranges first. The new, much bigger church was started c.1270, the E parts (including two bays of the nave) being complete by 1287 but the remainder not till 1301. It is unusually wide in proportion to its length, and its siting with axis much further S than its predecessor resulted in the asymmetrical relationship of chapter house to cloister. The only substantial works of later date were the 14th c. abbot's hall and the 15th c. alterations to the infirmary.

After the Dissolution Tintern became noted for its brass and iron works, and cottages sprang up around the ruins. The church remained quite well preserved, but the remainder degenerated to low walls. Much later, Tintern became a centre of the cult of the picturesque and attracted Wordsworth and Turner. In 1901 the Duke of Beaufort sold the abbey to the Crown; it passed into Office of Works care in 1914 and has since been tidied up. Till quite recent years the sites of the main kitchen and the abbot's hall were occupied by cottages.

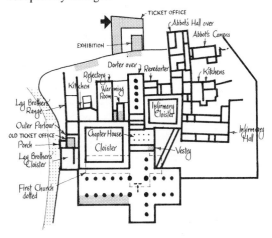

A new entrance building and exhibition hall stand near the bank of the Wye, and from them the church is approached towards its N side. The low ruin straight ahead is the base of the reredorter. To its left, steps go up to the small infirmary cloister; from the further right corner of this a slype leads to the main cloister, the inner wall and arcades of which have almost gone. Going now up the left (E) walk, on the left is a small parlour, then the **chapter house** – in its original 12th c. position but reconstructed in the 13th c. The base of the triple entrance with clustered shafts exists, also those of the columns that supported its vault. Several grave slabs lie in the paving of the walk outside; further on is a book room leading into a vestry, the latter still vaulted and with its own doorway into the transept. Then comes a short length of original wall of *c*.1230 containing two book recesses (one blocked), and ahead is the 14th c. multifoiled processional doorway into the church.

The **nave** has lost its N arcade, but by way of recompense the S aisle vault survives complete. The design is without triforium; some of the shafts of the clustered columns branch out at clerestory sill level to support what must have been an unusually wide vault. The clerestory is the main distinction between the mid- and late 13th c. work; in the former the window shafts are detached. The great W window, with tracery almost intact, belongs to the latter phase.

At the crossing the shafts of the two W piers stop on corbels, which allowed the monks' stalls to stand against the wall. The central tower has gone, but the four big arches remain. The S transept of the first church extended just to the centre of the present crossing, though the N transept end coincided with the present one and consequently its walls contain some earlier work. The earlier plan, which overlapped the present cloister, is marked by thin concrete strips. The **N transept** is similar to the nave but has only one aisle. Also, unlike the rest of the church, it has an upper walkway. The end window is blanked off at the bottom where the dorter adjoined, and below it is the stone night stair.

The **E arm** is wholly mid-13th c., similar again to the nave but with both arcades standing, and with the skeleton of a great Geometrical E window. The **S transept** matches the N, without the complexities of the dorter junction; both transepts had two E chapels.

Back now to the W end of the nave, where in the 15th c. there was a porch over the twin trefoil-headed doorways; this had a chapel on an upper floor. The doorways are united by a single hood mould and on either side are traceried panels. Above is the great W window; alongside that the aisle windows are insignificant, and only the S has its own doorway. Continuing round the **outside**, the S aisle (still roofed) and transept retain some Geometric window tracery, while the transept front is a dramatic design with the window sill, nearly at ground level, broken into by a single gabled portal. Next come the transept chapels, the presbytery aisle, and the E gable with its window strutted by cross-bars.

The foundation straight ahead towards the N is of the late 13th c. **infirmary**, a hall with small rooms along each side which were divided off in the 15th c. and given their own fireplaces. A diagonal passage linked it with the church. Adjoining its left side (against the E walk of the infirmary cloister) is a reredorter with drain beside it. Beyond are kitchens with some original stone flooring, and past them and standing rather higher than the rest the abbot's camera. Linked to that and extending towards the N boundary is the foundation of the 14th c. **abbot's hall**.

Tintern: Late 13th c. church interior, looking E

Back now to the infirmary cloister. Its N walk leads past a conspicuous drain (above which was the monks' reredorter) to the novices' lodging, the 12th c. undercroft of the monks' **dorter**. Of this the three bays nearest the church are amongst the earliest work that survives here, and there is ample evidence of the former vaults and supporting columns. Next, the N range of cloister buildings, starting with the warming house near its E end – early 13th c. with quite spectacular remains of vaulting and central fireplace. Alongside is a pantry, also vaulted. Then the **refectory**, the opening to which is sadly decayed. Here only the E side wall remains to any height, but the bottom part of the pulpit stair can be seen in the opposite wall, as well as cupboard recesses just inside the main entrance. A hatch opens into the kitchen, the next room beyond.

The W or cellarer's range has a parlour in the centre equipped in the 15th c. with an outer porch to the lane. The modern structure inside was formerly the ticket office. Adjoining it on the side away from the church is the lay brothers' refectory/dorter range, still standing fairly high and with 13th c. lancet windows. The drains running beneath can be followed past the rear parts of the kitchen, whence it is a short distance back to the exhibition room and exit.

Opposite the W end, on the other side of the approach lane, are partially excavated foundations, not yet fully analysed but probably of guest houses and a mill. A nearby house called St Ann's incorporates some remains of the gatehouse chapel.

Titchfield Hampshire: SU 542067
¾ mile N of village and 500 yards N of A27

Premonstratensian abbey of St Mary and St John the Evangelist founded 1232 by Peter des Roches, Bishop of Winchester, a daughter house of Halesowen. Dissolved 1537 and granted to Thomas Wriothesley, later Earl of Southampton

In care of Department of the Environment. Open during standard hours (admission charge)

A relatively small abbey with cloister on the N side, its buildings were completed before the end of the 13th c. and little altered subsequently.

After the Dissolution Thomas Wriothesley converted them into a dwelling (Place House), demolishing the whole E end, using the unaisled nave as a gatehouse and building an assertive three-

storeyed tower in its centre. The cloister garth became his courtyard
and the refectory his hall, the W and E ranges being adapted to
domestic purposes. In 1781 the house was itself partly demolished,
fortunately retaining the main 'nave' block. Part of the abbey plan
was recovered by excavation c.1900, and the remainder when the
ruins were taken over by the Office of Works in 1923.

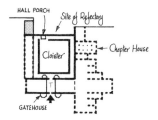

The first impression is of a Tudor house with a show of strength in
its sham arrow slits and embattled corner turrets – big ones at the
corners of the four-square gate-tower and lesser at the ends of its
wings – and in the original (i.e. Wriothesley's) strong outer wooden
doors with their two oriel windows above. That this is the nave of
the abbey church is at first hard to conceive. But inside the wings, a
few abbey details can be identified – a vault shaft in the SW corner,
the spiral stairs in the W corner turrets (their tops altered), the
outer jambs of the former triple-lancet W window. The roofs have
all gone.

Behind the gate-tower everything falls better into monastic
shape, with a familiar square cloister marked by low wall-bases. To
the left, the cellarer's range was adapted to later purposes and
shows three inserted fireplaces. At both ends of the W walk are
patches of old floor tiles. The N walk is interrupted by a porch built
on to the refectory when it became Wriothesley's hall. Some of the
medieval tiles exposed beneath it have ornamental letters. The
nearer hall wall still stands about 10 feet high but the further one
(on private ground) has gone altogether. In the NE corner of the
cloister is a 16th c. wall.

What is left of the wall of the E range is largely 16th c. but the
outer face is still visibly earlier and the chapter house arches can be
identified, as well as the grave slabs of two abbots in front. Beyond,
and across the whole E end of the church, is nothing but
foundations marked in the grass. From the site of the crossing the

bases of the W piers of both transept arches can be seen, and
between them one can look into the shell of the E part of the nave,
very similar to the W part. Finally it is worth passing along the S
side to the former W front – mostly replaced in the 16th c. by
brickwork (including an ornamental double chimney) except at the
base of each end. The outside of the W range shows a similar
mixture of 13th c. brick and 16th c. stone.

Torre Devon: ¼ mile NE of Torquay station   SX 907638

Premonstratensian abbey of St Saviour or Holy Trinity founded
    1196 by William Briwere, a daughter house of Welbeck.
    Dissolved 1539 and granted to John St Leger

Owned by Torbay Corporation. Open most days 10.0 a.m. to
    1.0 p.m. and 2.0 to 5.0 p.m. (admission charge)

Parts of the original buildings of *c*.1200 and the 13th c. remain,
though little of the church. Chief are the undercrofts of the W and S
ranges, chapter house doorway, and tithe barn. The inner
gatehouse is 14th c., and additions to the W range to form the
abbot's lodging 15th c. At the Dissolution Torre was the richest
Premonstratensian house in Britain.
    It passed through several families, and most of the church and the
E range were quarried away. The Ridgeways made it habitable
c.1600. The Carys, owners from 1662 until 1930, converted the S
(refectory) range into a Georgian mansion, built flanking wings,
and adapted the W range to include a private Roman Catholic
chapel. The house is now used as an art gallery, standing in an
extensive public park.

    When the house is not open the monastic ruins can be well seen
from the rear gardens; the following route however assumes entry
through the house, and starts with the outside of the **W range**,
altered late in the life of the abbey to form guests' and abbot's
quarters and punctuated by the embattled Abbot's Tower. The
lower block in front and to the right is modern; the higher building
behind contains the Carys' chapel on an original undercroft.
Further to the right is the **gatehouse**, round-arched though of
c.1320, with separate foot and carriage openings; its grey walling
and red sandstone dressings lack fine detail, and the vault bosses

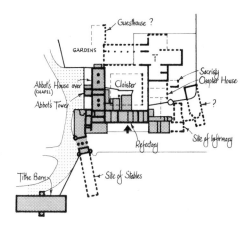

and corbels are plain and flat. Against the further (S) side are marks
of the vanished Fawden or stables.

Through the gatehouse on the left is the Georgian mansion, its
main block standing on the base of the S claustral range and the side
wings corresponding less exactly with the ends of the W and E
ranges. The cloister garth is entered through the house, where
payment is made. The rich Norman **chapter house** doorway will be
seen at once, with a window each side in normal Cistercian style and
a criss-cross of later dove-holes above; beyond is a doorway that led
to the S transept. The upper side of the garth is defined by the line
of the S wall of the nave.

Through the Norman doorway is a wilderness of gravel and stone
mounds; the chapter house walls have gone, but a dig in the far
corner of the enclosure revealed foundations earlier than the abbey,
perhaps of a manor house (re-covered). Of the **church**, the S
transept chapels are traceable (each with a stone coffin), also the
crossing (full of great tumbled masses of masonry from the
collapsed tower), and the presbytery S wall to a height of 10 feet
and more. The coffin nearby is attributed to William Briwere, son
of the founder. The N transept is merely marked out, and the nave
has to be imagined.

Across the garth is a doorway leading into the **undercroft** of the
W range, and thence to part of that of the S. This is the least altered
part of the abbey, and not all of one date, judging by the vault and
column details which are much rougher in the part nearer the

church. Some carved stone fragments are displayed, and there is the start of a stair that led to the abbot's lodging above. The Abbot's Tower forms a kind of porch to this undercroft.

Within the **house** nothing medieval is on view to the public. The galleried chapel formed in 1779 from the abbot's or guest hall is however well worth a visit. It contains marble tablets to the Carys.

Finally there is the **tithe barn**, with big plain porch and heavy buttresses, early 13th c. Called the Spanish Barn from its use for Armada prisoners, it now serves as a theatre and is not normally open to visitors.

Tupholme Lincolnshire: TF 145682
mid-way between Bardney and Bucknall, close to B1190

Premonstratensian abbey of the Blessed Virgin Mary founded
    between 1155 and 1166 by Gilbert and Alan de Neville, a
    daughter house of Newsham. Dissolved 1536 and given to Sir
    Thomas Heneage

Owned by Strawson family. Open to the public at all times

The buildings appear to have been of the 12th and 13th cc. and not to have been subsequently altered. The S wall of the refectory has survived, initially perhaps through being incorporated into a dwelling for Heneage's daughter. The now deserted farm buildings around it are no older than the late 18th c.

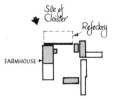

The gatehouse stood near where the now disused drive joins the road. The refectory wall (its inside face) is seen prominently to the left of the farmhouse, with lancet windows all along and the start of the undercroft vaults beneath. Its main feature is the surprisingly well preserved pulpit and stair, finished at the top with a pair of beautiful trefoil-headed arches. At the end is an earlier, round-headed window – then a short, more recent wall incorporating pieces of worked stone. An opening leads to the farmyard from which the other side of the wall may be seen, with the pulpit corbelled out.

The cloister and church sites can be detected from depressions on the N side of the refectory, towards the road; others may represent water channels and fishponds.

Vale Royal Cheshire: 2½ miles NW of Winsford   SJ 639699

Cistercian abbey of St Mary the Virgin, St Nicholas and St Nicasius founded at Darnhall by Edward I in 1266 and moved here 1281. Dissolved 1539 and granted to Sir Thomas Holcroft

Owned by the Michaelmas Trust. Open on Sundays from 2.0 to 5.0 p.m. (subject to change: see below)

This was the largest Cistercian abbey in England, and in 1277 one of the last to be begun. Enlargement of the E end of the church, started in 1359, was on a unique plan with thirteen radiating chapels.

After the Dissolution the church was soon demolished and the W monastic ranges converted into a mansion of 'E' type, the S range being allowed to remain. Much alteration took place after damage in the Civil War and again in the 18th and 19th cc. The S range, now the SE wing of the house, was rebuilt in 1833, still apparently on the medieval base. The clock tower is of 1861. The buildings were bought by the Michaelmas Trust in 1977 and became an education centre for mentally handicapped young people, but at the time of writing are about to be divided into residential flats.

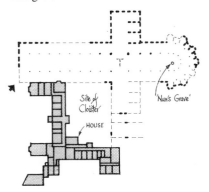

The church plan as partly excavated in 1911–12 is no longer visible; it lay along the left side of the house (as seen from the front), corresponding roughly with the side driveway. At the far end, supposedly on the site of the high altar, is the so-called Nun's grave, really a medieval churchyard cross head erected on a 17th c. column and pieces of 13th c. column bases. There is an explanatory notice nearby. Documentary evidence of the E chapels was substantiated by an excavation in 1958.

In the house itself the only convincingly medieval survival is the main door. There is little doubt that some of the walls rest on monastic foundations, but such features as the Gothic vaults of the ground-floor passage are introductions of much later date.

Valle Crucis Clwyd: SJ 203443
1½ miles NNW of Llangollen on Ruthin road A542

Cistercian abbey of the Blessed Virgin Mary founded 1201 by
   Madog ap Gruffydd, a daughter house of Strata Marcella.
   Dissolved 1538 and passed to Sir William Pickering

In care of Welsh Office. Open during standard hours

Valle Crucis = The Vale of the Cross, that was set up on the 9th c. Pillar of Eliseg, ¼ mile to the N. The abbey church is mostly 13th c., the base of the E parts being earliest. The nave and aisles and the upper parts of the remainder (including the crossing) were apparently not completed till after a serious fire towards the middle of the century – a fact deduced from the redness of some of the earlier stonework. The E range, from chapter house southwards, is late 14th or early 15th c.; the first-floor dorter is unusual in having been subdivided and altered for the abbot's private use late in the 15th c.

After the Dissolution this E range survived as a private dwelling. It fell to ruin but c.1800 was restored as a farmhouse. In the middle of the 19th c. the farm was removed and some repairs done to the church under Sir George Gilbert Scott. The Ministry of Works assumed ownership in 1950.

The **W front** is seen first. Its base is of the first phase of work; the rest is mid-13th c. except at the top where 14th c. work of different character contains a small wheel window, and above it a band of

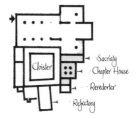

Latin inscription: 'Abbot Adam did this work. May he rest in peace. Amen.' The three two-light Geometric main windows closely set under a single arch are distinctive; beneath them is a once fine shafted doorway with four enriched arches; its doors were put in by Scott.

The modest-sized **nave** retains the bases of most of its columns, and aisle walls up to about sill level (higher on the S side where the cloister abutted). At the crossing the two S piers stand up to their capitals, the others less high. Several blocking walls need explanation. That in the E arch of the S arcade strengthened the SW pier of the crossing when it was rebuilt in the mid-13th c., and formed a backing to the stalls. That across the W arch of the crossing is part of the pulpitum, moved from one bay further W in the 14th c.; others across the N and S arches of the crossing formed a backing to the stalls in their final position and suggest a diminishing community.

What is left of the **N transept** is early 13th c., except for the modern inserted doorway from the aisle. On the N side are the base of a doorway and circular stair; on the E, the bases of two altars and the start of vaults. The tomb lids ranged across the **presbytery** were collected there in the 19th c. The E windows, three lancets and two more above, are later 13th c. and form an unusual group; the centre one has foliage capitals. There was a sixth at the top centre, and it can just be seen that there was a vault here too. The tomb recesses on the N side and the single sedile on the S are original.

The **S transept** is more complete than the N, and in its upper part is later 13th c. Its chapels are vaulted and one has a piscina. The night stair position is marked by the doorway at the top which led into the dorter. Below it, the early 13th c. sacristy is entered through another doorway; it has a rough barrel vault and a round-headed opening with volute caps into the **cloister**. To the right is a large three-order doorway to the S aisle; to the left, the chapter

Valle Crucis: Half-destroyed 13th c. vault over S transept chapel

house, rebuilt *c*.1400. First however is an elaborate traceried stone screen facing the cloister; this enclosed a book cupboard. The low thick-ribbed chapter house vault survives, resting on four columns without capitals. Its centre window is a modern restoration.

Next, the narrow day stair still leads up to the dorter, the roof of which has been reconstructed. A doorway at its S end led to the reredorter. Seven coffin lids laid out on the floor include the splendid late 13th c. one of the founder's grandson, also Madog ap Gruffydd. The N end of the dorter is the part subdivided in later years for the abbot; his camera (not now open to the public) was added on top of the sacristy.

Near the corner of the cloister garth is a square water basin that supplied the washplace for the refectory. Past the day stair is a rib-vaulted passage, and next to it the base of the reredorter with its flushing stream. Both refectory and kitchen have nearly gone, but the first four steps of the pulpit stair survive. The whole W range is marked only by low wall-bases. From there one can look back at the small windows of the dorter, and at its N end at the four-light Tudor window and now blocked doorway inserted when the abbot took it over; his outside stair must have been of wood. The corbelled parapet on the S transept and the tracery in the head of the window below were additions of *c*.1400.

Finally an **outside** circuit, first passing the W front again and then going along the N side to the E end. A little farm building of 1773 stands isolated, and to its N stretches a long and picturesque fishpond. But the important feature here is the curious modelling of the main E wall, with the second tier of lancet windows set into widened upward extensions of the flat buttresses between the lower. The square-headed (*c*.1500) E window of the abbot's camera can be seen too, and the windows of a post-monastic room over the E end of the chapter house.

Vaudey Lincolnshire: TF 037215
in grounds of Grimsthorpe castle and 3½ miles WNW of Bourne

Cistercian abbey of the Blessed Virgin Mary founded at Castle Bytham 1147 by William le Gros, Count of Albermarle, a daughter house of Fountains; refounded at Vaudey 1149 by Geoffrey de Brachecurt and Gilbert de Gant, Earl of Lincoln; dissolved 1536 and granted to William, Lord Willoughby. Vaudey, rhyming with 'toady', = vallis Dei, valley of God. Owned by the Grimsthorpe and Drummond Castle Trust. Site not open to the public. Nothing remains of the abbey above ground, though the bases of the crossing piers were revealed in 1851. In the present century a wood has been planted over the entire site, adding to its picturesqueness but confounding the archaeologists. The monastic fishpond however still exists to the N, and much abbey stone was used in 1541 by Charles Brandon, Duke of Suffolk (son-in-law of the grantee) in extensions to his nearby Grimsthorpe castle.

Walden Essex: TL 524382
1 mile W of Saffron Walden, close to B1383

Benedictine priory of St Mary and St James founded 1136 (or later) by Geoffrey de Mandeville, later Earl of Essex; became abbey 1190. Dissolved 1538 and granted to Sir Thomas Audley

Owned by the Department of the Environment. Site open during standard hours (admission charge)

Virtually nothing is known of the abbey buildings but it is supposed that the inner court of the mansion called Audley End stands on the site of the cloister, and that the 17th c. stables (now a museum) are on the site of the guest house. A high flint wall beside the latter could perhaps be a part of the precinct wall, and some pieces of medieval glass in the chapel may be from the abbey. The house that replaced the abbey gave way in 1603–16 to a much greater one built by the Earl of Suffolk. About 1721 its entire outer (W) court was demolished and the remainder altered, under Vanbrugh. Later the E range of the inner court (presumably on the chapter house site) was demolished too and an arcaded gallery built on the site of the W walk. During the period 1790–1835 the house was brought more or less to its present state by the Lords Braybrooke from whose successor it passed to public ownership in 1948.

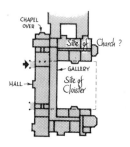

Waltham Essex: in Waltham Abbey town centre   TL 381007

Collegiate church founded c.1030; refounded c.1057 by King Harold; Augustinian priory of the Holy Cross (and St Lawrence from 1242 or earlier) founded 1177 by Henry II, colonised from Cirencester, Osney and St Osyth; became abbey 1184, and later mitred. Dissolved 1540 and leased to Sir Anthony Denny

Parish church. Open 10.0 a.m. to 6.0 p.m. (summer) or 4.0 p.m. (winter)

The nave and aisles of the 11th c. collegiate church were rebuilt *c.*1100–30 and were kept as a kind of narthex for parish use when the E end (which may or may not have been also rebuilt) was demolished to make way for a great 13th c. abbey. The full extent of that was only realised from excavations in the 1930s, for it totally disappeared after the suppression, leaving little but a cloister passage and part of the 14th c. gatehouse. But the collegiate nave and aisles had been partitioned off as early as the 13th c. to serve the parish, and continued to do so. They are amongst the finest Norman work in England. The added S chapel is 14th c. This was the last English abbey to be dissolved.

The present tower was built in 1556–8 following collapse of the old central one. It is the only one in England built in Mary I's reign. Restoration of the church were done in 1859–60 (under William Burges) and, more modestly, in 1964. Abbey House, the Dennys' mansion built and rebuilt on the monastic site, was finally taken down in 1770.

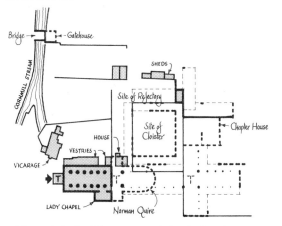

Not only is the W **tower** post-Dissolution, but the wall against which it was built is 14th c. – so most visitors' first impression is not of robust Norman but of Gothic. The inner doorway is a deep one, quite elaborate Decorated with its own little vault and obviously once external, for its surrounds are swallowed by the wall each side. Above are royal arms of 1662, and on the side walls benefaction boards.

The **nave** is somewhat like Durham on a smaller scale – with

massive piers alternately composite and round. The triforium, much
cut about, has single round arches meant to be subdivided, while
the clerestory has threes in a stepped arrangement. Details vary
from side to side and bay to bay; its two E bays are the latest in
character, having probably formed the final link when the monastic
nave and then transepts and presbytery were rebuilt in the 12th c.
The W parts were begun to be remodelled in the 14th c.: one bay is
hidden by the organ, but the next shows the main arch and triforium
opening thrown into one and made pointed, and on the N side the
third bay was started on before confidence (or funds) failed. The
paintings on the flat ceiling (1860) are by Sir Edward Poynter,
modelled on Peterborough; the chief subjects are the months'
labours and signs of the Zodiac. At the E end the big arch is
Norman (the W arch of the collegiate crossing) but its infilling is
partly 12th or 13th c. and the clumsy wheel window and lancets are
by Burges (also 1859–60). The glass is by Burne-Jones, made by
Powell.

The N aisle is open to the curved wooden ceiling of the gallery,
the floor of which has gone. At the W end is a jutting stair turret,
and along the aisle three hatchments, a restored Norman doorway,
a monument to James Spilman (d. 1763) and 19th c. floor tiles. On
the right, the canopied pulpit is late 17th c. The chapel screen with
simple tracery is 14th c. The bust outside is of Francis Wollaston,
17th c., while within are the table tomb of Capt. Robert Smith (d.
1697), with a delicate allegorical carving of a merchant ship
(believed to be by Grinling Gibbons), the indent of the big brass of
an abbot, a memorial urn to Caroline Chinnery (d. 1812) and two
17th c. chests.

Now into the **chancel**, passing close to one of the great helically
incised piers. The glowing E window glass is by Sir Edward Burne-
Jones, 1861. The reredos with four delightful Nativity and
Childhood scenes is by Burges, carved by T. Nicholls (1873); its
frieze depicts two fables of Aesop. Three fine black ledger stones in
the floor should be noticed, also the 19th c. stalls of black walnut.
At the E end of the **S aisle**, an arch now blocked led to the transept;
the window within it is by Henry Holiday, 1864. Nearby are the
effigy of Lady Elizabeth Greville (d. 1619) (the 14th c. tomb
fragments above were found buried), and the resplendent
monument of Sir Edward Denny (d. 1599) and his wife, with effigies
on shelves.

Next, behind a screen of 1886, the 14th c. **Lady chapel**, invitingly
light with its big Decorated windows and long used as a school.

Three have glass of the 1930s by A.K. Nicholson; the threefold one at the W end is unusual for its flat head and elegant inner arcade. The flat roof is 19th c., the Doom painting on the E wall 14th c. The 14th c. Madonna on the (once external) sill below was found in a nearby garden. Further W is another former aisle window, with a round one over that lit the gallery. The painting *The Burial of Harold* is by H.P. Bone, 1815. The chapel **crypt** is entered from the aisle. Beneath two bays of low ribbed vault are numerous relics – including the old clock face and mechanism, and a panel painted by Holiday as a design for the former aisle window mentioned above.

The **S aisle**, resembling the N, has a big, much restored S doorway. On a column nearby are marks of the chains of chained books. Amongst many memorials are three more hatchments, brasses to Edward Stacy (d. 1555) and Thomas Colte (d. 1591), and a Boer War memorial of unusual quality by Harry Hems. The very plain font is of Purbeck marble, perhaps 12th c., and there is another 17th c. chest. From this point is a good view of the uncompleted changes in the N triforium.

Finally the **outside**, starting with the 14th c. W wall of the S aisle and the modern statue of Harold on the buttress. The S wall is 12th c., with two more bays retaining their round gallery windows above the main ones. Next is the Lady chapel, with niched buttresses; in its E wall is a Norman window that faced the opposite way, into the former transept. At the E end can be found remains of the E piers of the former crossing, and markings of the original apse and of Harold's original burial place. The modern wall beyond perpetuates the line of the E side of the cloister and now bounds the Lea Valley Park; meeting it further N is a wall of the chapter house, used by the Dennys in their mansion and continuing (with two brick piers) a long way to the E. The vaulted passage still standing led out of the cloister at its NE corner and is late 12th c.; its key can be obtained (see notice).

Continue N, then W (skirting the lorry depot) to the **gatehouse** ruin – large and small 14th c. outer arches and the base of a turret. Over the bridge, also 14th c., the stream can then be followed, passing on the left a piece of precinct wall and then the picturesque old vicarage.

Warden Bedfordshire: TL 121439
6 miles SE of Bedford, close to Cardington–Old Warden road

Cistercian abbey of the Blessed Virgin Mary founded 1135 by
   Walter Espec, a daughter house of Rievaulx. Dissolved 1537 and
   passed to Gostwick family

Owned by Whitbread family and Landmark Trust. E portion of site
   (except house) accessible at all times without charge

Apart from a rebuilding of the church in the 14th c. little is known
of the buildings, but evidently they were big. They were destroyed
after the Dissolution by the Gostwicks, who built a house alongside.
Of this a small part remains, and it incorporates one 13th c. buttress
of the monastic buildings (possibly part of the chapter house). It
was restored c.1970 by the Landmark Trust and is privately let.

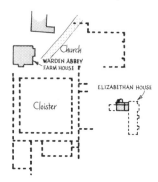

   What is left of the Elizabethan brick house stands prominently
beside the track to Abbey Farm and can be reached over a stile; a
number of moulded stones lie against its W wall. The field between
bears signs of the excavations of c.1839 and of 1960–1, which
located the quire and E cloister walk; the nave lay beneath the
present farmstead.

Waterbeach Cambridgeshire: TL 497650
in village, 200 yards S of parish church

Franciscan nunnery of the Piety of Our Lady (later Our Lady of
   Pity) and St Clare founded 1293 by Denise Munchensey;
   gradually transferred to Denny; dissolved 1351. One of only four
   medieval houses of Minoresses or 'Poor Clares' in England. Their

move to Denny (*q.v.*) was caused by flooding. The side (Badcock family, owners) lies through a farmyard past the parish church, amongst obvious relics of drainage works, and has yielded a few remains.

Waverley Surrey: SU 868453
2 miles E of Farnham, ¼ mile S of Elstead road A3001

Cistercian abbey of the Blessed Virgin Mary founded 1128 by William Giffard, Bishop of Winchester, a daughter house of l'Aumône (Eleemosina), Normandy. Dissolved 1536 and granted to Sir William Fitzwilliam, treasurer of the King's household and later Earl of Southampton

In care of Department of the Environment. Not officially open to the public

The first Cistercian monastery to be founded in England (Furness abbey is older but was originally Savigniac), it is well documented historically and its buildings, though fragmentary, are systematically recorded. The original layout was completed in 1201 with the roofing of the infirmary. A second phase of building continued throughout the 13th c., a new and much bigger church and cloister being built in 1203–78. The original main floors lay about 6 feet below the present grass; in the 12th c. they were raised about 2 feet to avoid flooding, and in the 15th c. another 2 feet.

After passing through various hands the buildings were superseded by the house now called Waverley, begun *c.*1725 on a new site 300 yards to the N. Much of the stone had however already been used on Sir William More's house at Loseley (1562–8). Further demolition was done in 1771–86. The site was thoroughly excavated and measured in 1899–1902, all but the high-standing walls being buried again afterwards. It has since passed into state ownership.

Though at the time of writing the site is indefinitely closed for repair works, responsible visitors are tolerated and can enter by the gate near Waverley Mill, following the left bank of the 18th c. artificial lake called The Canal (beyond which is the house) and turning left by the bridge. The path leads to the N wall of the church, most of which has disappeared. Beyond it, the S wall is more clearly defined; the base of the W doorway of the S aisle still

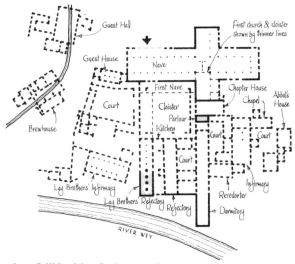

exists. Still looking S, the prominent ruin ahead is the further end of the long vaulted 13th c. cellar beneath the lay brothers' quarters. Though sadly decayed, this is the best thing at Waverley, some of the upper floor being still supported on graceful columns.

A transverse wall links the cellar with the surviving S end of the monks' dorter, originally over 200 feet long. This too is 13th c., with lancet windows of severe Cistercian type.

The third main surviving block of walling lies around the S transept; the way back towards it must be imagined as following the line of the E walk of the cloister. On the right, a room still barrel-vaulted was the parlour. Beside it the outline of the chapter house can be clearly distinguished, and then the S and W walls of the S transept. The excavations revealed that this corner was also the corner of the S transept of the much smaller, aisleless first church, of which the nave coincided with the N walk of the final cloister, and the N wall approximately with the S wall of the final church (this is better understood from the plan). So this rather shapeless lump of transept wall is partly 12th c. and partly 13th c.

Finally back into the nave. Ahead is a low remnant of the N transept, and to the right a few bits of the presbytery. To the right again, i.e. S of the last, another small jagged lump indicates the infirmary chapel.

Welbeck Nottinghamshire: SK 555743
3 miles SW of Worksop and ½ mile E of A60

Premonstratensian abbey of St James founded *c*.1153 by Thomas of
   Cuckney, a daughter house of Newhouse. Dissolved 1538 and
   granted to Richard Whalley

Owned by Lady Anne Cavendish-Bentinck. Not open to public

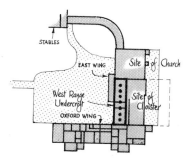

Little is known of the building history, but the abbey was important
enough to become in 1512 the head of the Premonstratensian order
in England, and no fewer than seven others were colonised from it.
   The church, being non-parochial, was soon destroyed after the
Dissolution. The W range of buildings was altered and extended
early in the 17th c. by Sir Charles Cavendish (son of Bess of
Hardwick); its basement is an eight-bay undercroft with mid-13th c.
piers, a doorway of *c*.1200, and vaults redone in the 18th c. Sir
Charles's son, Duke of Newcastle, took down the E monastic range
and built what is now the E wing over the undercroft, as well as the
riding house (later a picture gallery) and stables to the NW. About
1750 the 2nd Duke of Portland demolished the S monastic range
(refectory etc.) and built the Oxford wing, the present S wing,
further W. In 1864–79 the eccentric 5th Duke undertook a vast
programme of ancillary building which included long tunnels (one
of them over a mile), underground rooms, a new riding school 385 x
110 feet, and a glass-covered 'tan-gallop' over 400 yards long; his
successor rationalised all this to some extent. Now many of the
buildings are occupied by an Army college.

Wellow Humberside: TA 268088
¼ mile SSE of Great Grimsby church

Augustinian abbey of St Augustine and St Olaf founded by Henry I,
 probably in 1132; dissolved in 1536 and given to Sir T. Heneage.
 Nothing is left and little is known of the buildings, which are
 remembered by suburban road names like Abbey Drive.

Wendling Norfolk: TF 938128
3 miles W of East Dereham and ½ mile E of village on lane to
Abbey Farm

Premonstratensian abbey of the Blessed Virgin Mary founded by
 1267 by William of Wendling, a daughter house of Langley.
 Dissolved 1536–7 and granted to the Dean and Chapter of Christ
 Church, Oxford.

Owned by Howell family. Accessible at all times without charge

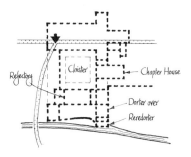

Information on the buildings rests on a plan made in 1810 when the
remaining stone was being carted away for road making. Now there
are only ground irregularities and low lumps of rubble walling, and
the farm lane runs right through the church site. The biggest lump
of wall, close to the road, is the SW angle of the church, and
alongside the stream are considerable traces of the reredorter and
adjacent walling.

Westminster Greater London: TQ 300794

Benedictine abbey of St Peter, of unknown foundation date;
 became mitred c.1170. Dissolved 1540 and became cathedral

establishment. Refounded 1556. Again dissolved 1559 and
became collegiate 1560, with dean and twelve prebends

Owned by Dean and Chapter of Westminster (but chapter house
Crown property). Open during normal hours: eastern parts open
9.20 a.m. to 4.45 p.m. weekdays, 9.20 a.m. to 2.45 and 3.45 to
5.45 p.m. Saturdays (admission charge), also 6.0 to 8.0 p.m.
Wednesdays (free): chapter house 10.30 a.m. to 6.0 p.m., (to
3.30 p.m. only, October to February) (admission charge):
treasury 9.15 a.m. to 5.0 p.m. weekdays (admission charge):
College Garden Thursdays only 10.0 a.m. to 6.0 p.m. (to
4.0 p.m. October to March) (free)

Though undoubted Roman remains have been found here, the story
of a church built in 184 and turned into a temple of Apollo during
the Diocletian persecution is probably pure medieval invention. An
early 7th c. foundation date is rather more likely, and there are
stories too of a grant of land in 785 by King Offa of Mercia to what
was then called Thorney, and of rebuilding after destruction by the
Danes in the 9th c. The abbey's real history and rise to pre-
eminence begins with its refoundation under the Benedictine order
by St Dunstan, c.959, and its endowment and rebuilding under
Edward the Confessor after 1045.
   Though consecration of the E end took place in 1065, just before
Edward's death, and William the Conqueror was crowned in it the
following year, the church lacked its nave – as can be seen on the
Bayeux tapestry; it was indeed probably not finished till nearly
1150. The building layout of that time is known quite fully and a
number of fragments of the monastic parts still remain in the E and
S ranges of the cloister. The infirmary chapel of c.1170 also
remains, in a fragmentary state.
   The Lady chapel at the E end was begun in 1220 and survived
until 1503 when Henry VII replaced it with his chapel. The rest of
the church as it stands, together with the chapter house and the E
side of the cloister, was started in 1245. By 1255 the presbytery,
crossing and transepts, and one bay of the nave had been
completed, in a style much more French than English, for it was
done at royal expense and King Henry III was himself more French
than English: his first master designer and mason is believed to have
been brought from Reims. In the 1260s four more nave bays were
built and in 1269 the body of St Edward (canonised 1161) was

brought to a new shrine. The infirmary, as well as the remainder of
the cloister with the abbot's house at its NW corner, underwent
rebuilding in the middle of the 14th c.

In 1375 the rest of the Norman nave was demolished and work
resumed in the remaining six bays and tower bay, following the 13th
c. design in all but detail – a remarkable early instance of fidelity to
original intentions and of rejection of current fashion, a fashion
which on the analogy of the avant-garde character of the original
would have dictated by then a progression to Perpendicular. This
work went on at least till 1504. The eastern chapel, begun by Henry
VII as a new Lady chapel and completed by Henry VIII as the
chantry chapel of his father, was built c.1503–12.

At the Dissolution the abbey church became a cathedral for a
short period. It then assumed its present collegiate status, and apart
from an enlargement of the school (which had existed in some form
since perhaps the 12th c.) few of the buildings passed to other uses.
Its preservation was due to its unique links with monarch and state,
as the royal coronation and burial church: the chapel of the Pyx was
the royal treasure house and the chapter house was Parliament's
House of Commons from Edward I's reign until 1547.

Preservation however has meant a seemingly unbroken
succession of 'restorations', one effect of which even as early as
1745 was that very little of the visible external stone face was
medieval at all. Sir Christopher Wren became Surveyor in 1698.
The W towers, begun before the Dissolution, were finished to
Nicholas Hawksmoor's design in 1735–45. Henry VII's chapel, the
one part spared till then, was disastrously refaced by James and
then Benjamin Wyatt in 1807–22. Sir George Gilbert Scott
extensively restored the chapter house and virtually redesigned the
N transept front, and his work was completed by J.L. Pearson.
Later surveyors have left less mark.

All these 'restorations' have at least meant well towards
appreciation of the building itself. Not so the insidious introduction
from Elizabethan times onwards of the hundreds of monuments
which have made of the interior a mausoleum, a museum, a
sculpture gallery, a waxworks show, a pageant of the great and
noble, a history lesson in stone, marble, iron, bronze, glass and
gold, which provides a sometimes macabre, sometimes theatrical
background for occasional pomp and pageantry and which would
have amazed and bewildered the Benedictine monks. The pages
that follow cannot possibly do justice to these memorials, very
many of which are the masterpieces of their designers and

craftsmen. Whether or not to include has been dictated by notability, artistic worth or sheer size. In such a tour no more is practicable, but a superb comprehensive guide is available, a model of erudition and clarity and probably the best of its kind available in any church or cathedral.

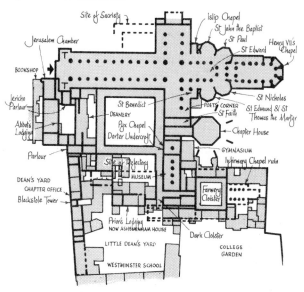

The great W doorway is the main public entrance. The heraldic ornament on the glass doors is by Brian Thomas, 1980. Inside it is best to stand awhile at the extreme W end of the **nave** for a first look at the building design before, inevitably, becoming distracted by the monuments. But historically this is the worst place to start, and a description will be deferred until after seeing the exterior. The architecture can then be examined more nearly in the sequence that it was built. Suffice it for the moment to notice that at 102 feet this is the highest medieval vault in Britain (Reims is 124 feet) and that though largely of the 15th c. the entire nave could well be taken for a 13th c. building.

In the immediate foreground is a floor memorial to Sir Winston Churchill (d. 1965), and beyond it the grave of the Unknown Warrior of World War I. Seen by turning about, the great W window glass is by Joshua Price, 1735, and below it the monument to Sir William Pitt (d. 1806) is by Sir Richard Westmacott. To its left are memorials to Sir Thomas Hardy (d. 1732) by Sir Henry Cheere, and to Franklin D. Roosevelt; to its right Newton's biographer John Conduitt (d. 1737) and the 7th Earl of Shaftesbury (d. 1885) by Sir Edgar Boehm. The two big alms boxes either side of the Churchill stone are early 18th c.

Turn now to the **N side**, and first the vaulted tower bay. Its arch is nearly blocked by the cenotaph of the 3rd Marquis of Salisbury (d. 1903), with bronze effigy by Sir William Goscombe John, and the giant central standing figure is of Capt. James Montagu (killed at Brest 1794) by John Flaxman. Behind on the N wall the 'locked doors' commemorate the 3rd Baron Holland (d. 1840), while the female figure under the arch to the aisle is to the 3rd Viscount Howe (d. 1758) by Peter Scheemakers. Some of the glass in the W window is medieval. The N one is the first of a series lighting the aisle, by Sir Ninian Comper, of 1907–50; they commemorate the kings and abbots who built the abbey, along with (mostly) famous modern engineers.

The big bronze candelabra by the first columns of each arcade are by Benno Elkan, 1939. Next, the **N aisle** with its wall-arcade filled with monuments. In bay 1: on the left, Charles James Fox (d. 1806), a life-size death-bed group by Westmacott; on the wall, Sir Henry Campbell-Bannerman (d. 1908) (a bronze bust) and Maj. Gen. Lawrence (d. 1775); on the floor, slabs to four prominent socialists: Earl Attlee, d. 1967; Sidney Webb (Baron Passfield), d. 1947, and his wife, Beatrice Webb, d. 1943; and Ernest Bevin, d. 1951. In bay 2: the reclining effigy of Anne, Countess of Clanrickarde (d. 1733) and a seated female by Scheemakers with medallioned bust of Dr John Woodward (d. 1728); in the floor (near the second arcade column) a memorial to David, 1st Earl Lloyd George; hanging on the same column but facing the nave, towards the Unknown Warrior, a Congressional Medal of the USA. The Comper window in bay 2 honours the Royal Army Medical Corps.

In bay 3: on the window ledge what is left of a big memorial to two more captains killed at Brest on the 'Glorious First of June', 1794; below, two soldiers killed abroad in 1706–7, also Thomas Banks the sculptor (d. 1805) and at the bottom a tiny stone inscribed O RARE BEN JONSON (d. 1637) (his chief monument is in the S transept); the two big floor brasses are 19th c. In bay 4: on the sill another reduced monument (by Banks) to John Loten (d. 1789); on the wall, Mrs Mary Beaufoy (d. 1705) 'made by Mr Grinling

Westminster: Early 19th c. engraving

Gibbons', Jane Stotevill (d. 1631), the oldest memorial now in the nave aisles, and a double tablet of 1684; a floor stone marks the grave of Sir Ninian Comper (d. 1960). In bay 5: on the sill, Spencer Perceval (assassinated at the House of Commons 1812) by Westmacott, flanked by two nice cartouches; below, two boys of the Cholmondeley family (d. 1679–80) (a single memorial) and Dr Richard Mead (d. 1754) by Scheemakers.

In bay 6 is a doorway which once led to a sacristy, flanked by two admirals' monuments both by Francis Bird (1712/16). The window glass continues as part of the Comper series. In bay 7 the appearance of a continuous passage at sill level marks the change to 13th c. work. The curious memorial to Philip Carteret (d. 1711) with Father Time as a sort of bearded cherub, is by Claude David, and the others are of the same period. In the floor just in front of the gates are the graves of Charles Darwin (d. 1882) and Sir John Herschel (d. 1871).

At this point a charge is usually made to enter the eastern parts, but it is best to reserve the wealth there for a separate visit and so to turn aside into the **nave**, looking next at the early 16th c. hexagonal pulpit with linen-fold panelling. Its size, particularly that of its canopy, is more suited to Henry VII's chapel, where it was. Its stair is modern. In front of the communion rail are graves of several architects: Sir Herbert Baker (d. 1946), J.L. Pearson (d. 1898) (brass by W.D. Caröe), Sir George Gilbert Scott (d. 1878) (brass by G.E. Street), Street himself (d. 1881) (brass by Pearson) and Sir Charles Barry (d. 1860). In the centre of the nave are Admiral Cochrane (d. 1860) and Sir James Outram (d. 1863). Those further on are possibly less notable, so turn briefly down the centre where lie Thomas Telford (d. 1834), Robert Stephenson (d. 1859) (a brass close to Telford's), Thomas Tompion (d. 1713) and David Livingstone (d. 1873).

Back now towards the nave altar. The stalls and altar rail are work of the 1960s and the newly coloured and gilded pulpitum superficially by Edward Blore but probably partly medieval and partly by Hawksmoor. The very prominent, matching memorials left and right are to Sir Isaac Newton (d. 1727) and Lord Stanhope (d. 1721), both designed by William Kent and carved by Michael Rysbrack; Newton's is full of allusions to astronomy and science.

Next the **S nave aisle**, starting by the gate into the choir aisle. Of interest firstly are the painted shields in the wall-arcade spandrels: they are of benefactors in Henry III's reign and occur towards the E end of both aisles. Bay 7 (nearest the iron screen) has a giant-lettered memorial by Cheere to Sir John Chardin (d. 1713) and, at the bottom, one to Sir Palmes Fairborne (d. 1680) flanked by two designed by Robert Adam: one to Maj. John André (hanged as a spy in America in 1780) including a scene with George Washington, the other to Lt. Col. Roger Townshend (d. 1759) with sarcophagus borne by Red Indians.

A double monument to Sir Charles Harbord and Clement Cottrell (killed in Dutch War 1672) dominates bay 6. Above however is a dramatic composition by Roubiliac – the pyramid of Time collapsing at the Last Trumpet – to Lt. Gen. William Hargrave (d. 1751). Beneath are a bust by Francis Bird to Sidney, 1st Earl of Godolphin (d. 1712) and a neat tablet to Diana Temple (d. 1679). High in bay 5 is another big Roubiliac work, to Maj. Gen. James Fleming (d. 1750). In the corners below are two to the wives of Sir Samuel Morland (d. 1674 and 1680) with additional inscriptions in Greek, Hebrew and Amharic; the tablet between, to John Smith (d. 1718), was designed by James Gibbs and carved by Rysbrack.

Bay 4 contains the NW doorway to the cloister. High up is a monument to Field Marshal George Wade (d. 1748), by Roubiliac again; those on the sill are to Lt. Gen. Sir James Outram (d. 1863) and (by John Bacon senior) to Ann Whytell (d. 1788). The busts either side of the doorway are to Col. Charles Herries (d. 1819) by Sir Francis Chantrey and John, 1st Lord Lawrence (d. 1879) by Thomas Woolner. Bay 3 has a taller window (being past the cloister) with glass of 1921 by Dudley Forsyth honouring the YMCA. Below, four monuments with busts are all to deans of Westminster of the period 1756–1856. The central one, to Katherine Bovey (d. 1727) was designed by Gibbs and carved by Rysbrack.

On the sill of bay 2 is a complex theatrical composition to Rear Admiral Richard Tyrrell (d. 1776), full of allegories but less so than before it was reduced in size. Below are tablets to Deans Wilcocks (d. 1756) under whom the W towers were built (hence the bas-relief of the church) and Sprat (d. 1713), and a doorway into the Dean's Verger's office. The next bay has the projecting 'abbot's pew', a much restored early 16th c. gallery. Under it are memorials to John Freind (d. 1728) by Gibbs and Rysbrack, and William Congreve (d. 1728) by Bird, with theatrical masks, and a floor brass to Dean Bradley (d. 1903) by Clayton & Bell.

The stone screen to the **SW tower** space is early 16th c. In front is a stone to Robert, 1st Lord Baden-Powell (d. 1941); above, and continuing on the N side, is a screen by Comper, 1925. On the column between, near the second Elkan candelabrum, is a portrait of Richard II, the earliest surviving one of any English sovereign, c.1398. The chapel of St George (Warriors' chapel), previously the baptistry and consistory court, is used for private prayer and has an extra inner glass screen. The golden altar and canopywork are Comper's. To its right is the bust of William Booth of the Salvation Army (d. 1917) and on the S wall a memorial to James Cragg (d. 1721) with female figure and urn and a curious bronze one to Henry Fawcett (d. 1884) with seven delicate statues by Alfred Gilbert. The W wall is taken up with war memorials; below are the graves of Field Marshals Allenby (d. 1936) and Plumer (d. 1932). The big 15th c. figure in stained glass is believed to be the Black Prince.

Cross back now to the ticket point at the start of the **N choir aisle**. (During nave services tourists use the N transept entrance and cannot enter these three bays. Sometimes, too, entry is on the S side and through the pulpitum. In either case the thread should be picked up on p.000 with the N transept. If in consequence either of the choir aisles has to be missed, a verger may be able to allow entry.)

Bay 8, the first beyond the gate, contains the memorial by John Bacon junior to the 1st Earl of Normanton, Archbishop of Dublin (d. 1809) and, in the floor, stones to the musicians Sir Edward Elgar (d. 1934), Ralph Vaughan Williams (d. 1958), Sir Charles Stanford (d. 1924), William Sterndale Bennett (d. 1875) and (just within the next bay) Benjamin Britten (d. 1976). The canopied marble cenotaph under the organ is of Lord John Thynne (d. 1880) with effigy by H.H. Armstead. Above and beside it are medallions to eight great scientists and a WRVS book of honour. In these bays are more painted shields above the wall-arcade.

In bay 9 the best of the monuments on the wall side are those to Sir Edmund Prideaux (d. 1728) by Cheere, and Admiral Temple West (d. 1761) by Joseph Wilton. Ledger stones below are to more musicians: William Croft (d. 1727), Samuel Arnold (d. 1802) and Henry Purcell (d. 1695). Purcell's wall cartouche is on the extreme left of the inner wall (backing on to the choir stalls). Beneath it is the standing figure of Sir Stamford Raffles (d. 1826) by Sir Francis Chantrey. The big monument with reclining effigy is to Almeric de Courcy, Lord Kingsale (d. 1720); to the right the seated figure is William Wilberforce (d. 1833), by Samuel Joseph.

In bay 10: on the window ledge a modern bust of James Watt; below, the musicians William Croft (d. 1727) and John Blow (d. 1708) and Capt. Philip de Sausmarez (killed at Finisterre 1747), by Cheere; on the opposite wall Hugh Chamberlen, court physician (d. 1731) by Scheemakers and Laurent Delvaux, flanked by more musicians – Michael Balfe (d. 1870), Samuel Arnold (d. 1802) and Orlando Gibbons (d. 1625, but bust of 1907).

The black and gilt gates are of 1764 and lead to the **N transept**. The back wall of the choir stalls continues with one more bay containing the canopied monument and stiff figure of Sir Thomas Hesketh (d. 1605).

Continue forward into the main part of the transept so as to see the whole crossing, the **presbytery** and the S transept. If the monuments can be imagined gone, so much the better. This is the building of 1245–55. There can be no doubt of its main derivation from Reims: its apse and ambulatory and the radiating chevet of chapels that from here can just be glimpsed, bar-traceried windows, big round main columns with four attached shafts, richly moulded arches with (original) tie-rods of iron, tall clerestory, and uncommonly high quadripartite vault are all French. But some

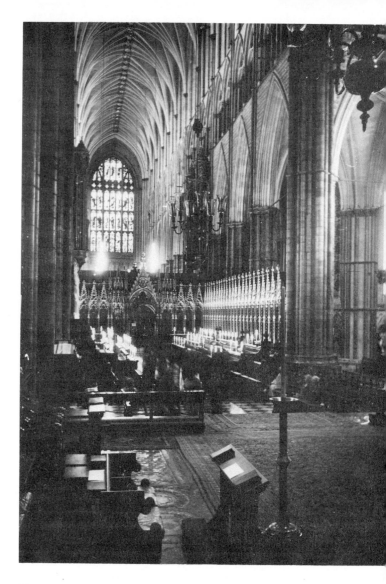

Westminster: Church interior, looking E

features are pure English: the pattern of the vault infilling (the stones not parallel to the ridge, and the inclusion of a ridge rib), the ample triforium galleries (which have doubled pairs of two-light openings) and the use of Purbeck marble. The diaper ornament in the arcade spandrels is possibly derived from Amiens. The foliage and other carving varies greatly in style and will repay detailed study as one goes round.

The **transepts** are similar to the presbytery, their design being strengthened by the uninterrupted continuation of the rich gallery arcade across their ends. Scott's and Pearson's external rebuilding hardly shows inside and much original sculpture remains. The crossing, with its soaring arches, was meant to have a great tower, which was never built; the decoration of its flat ceiling is fairly new.

Now the **N transept** in detail, starting with the outer wall of its W aisle which is effectively of three bays. The sculpture in the wall-arcade spandrels is very varied. In bay 2 (bay 1 being the main aisle 'overlap') are two monuments by Cheere, to Archbishop Boulter of Armagh (d. 1742) and Bishop Bradford of Rochester (d. 1731), and one by Rysbrack to Brig. Gen. Richard Kane (d. 1736). Bay 3 contains two with busts by Scheemakers, to Lt. Gen. Percy Kirk (d. 1741) and Lord Aubrey Beauclerk (d. 1740), and one by Westmacott to Bishop Warren of Bangor (d. 1800); the window glass commemorates the shipwreck of HMS *Captain*, 1870. Another Scheemakers monument, to Admiral Sir John Balchen (d. 1744) is on the left of the end bay; the window above with scenes from *The Pilgrim's Progress* is by Comper (1915). The main memorials on the end wall are to Vice Admiral Charles Watson (d. 1757) by Scheemakers and George, 2nd Earl of Halifax (d. 1771) by John Bacon senior, while the gigantic one in the centre of the bay is by Flaxman to William, 1st Earl of Mansfield (d. 1793).

Now the arcade side of the aisle, and amongst the many more modest tablets in bay 4 (backing the vast memorial to William Pitt) can be found those to Richard Cobden (d. 1865) and Warren Hastings (d. 1818). Bay 3 is taken up with Banks's imposing monument to Lt. Gen. Sir Eyre Coote (d. 1783). By the next column the white marble seated feature of a woman with exquisitely textured garments is by Westmacott and commemorates the widow (d. 1816) of Bishop Warren whose tablet, also by him, is almost opposite.

Next turn left between the columns of bay 2 into the main transept, the so-called **Statesmen's Aisle**. On the column to the right is a small tablet to Herbert Asquith (d. 1928), and on the left John

Thomas's standing figure of Robert, 2nd Marquis of Londonderry
(d. 1822). Bay 3 contains a huge memorial by Joseph Nollekens to
three naval captains killed in the Caribbean in 1782, with Britannia
and Neptune and a lion and sea-horse. By the next column is
Robert Jackson's standing figure of Henry, 3rd Viscount
Palmerston, and then comes another giant monument, to William
Pitt, 1st Earl of Chatham (d. 1778). This, by Bacon senior, initiated
the fashion for honouring statesmen here.

Look up now at the carvings of the N wall, especially the enriched
soffits of the six third-stage windows, the figures at each end (called
Edward the Confessor and Henry III) and the censing angels in the
top end spandrels above the gallery. The rose window glass was
designed by Sir James Thornhill and that of the six lancets by Brian
Thomas. Left and right of the main doorway are memorials to two
18th c. admirals by Scheemakers and Rysbrack.

Move back along the centre aisle and look at the memorials along
the E side: in bay 4 another giant one to John, 1st Duke of
Newcastle (d. 1711) by James Gibbs and Francis Bird; by the
column, three standing figures, of George Canning (d. 1827) by
Chantrey, Charles, 1st Earl Canning (d. 1862) by John Foley, and
Stratford Canning, 1st Viscount Stratford (d. 1880) by Boehm; in
bay 3, William Cavendish, Duke of Newcastle (d. 1677) and his
second wife, with two recumbent figures and an amusing inscription
to the Duchess; by the column, two more standing figures, of Maj.
Gen. Sir John Malcolm (d. 1833) by Chantrey, and Benjamin
Disraeli, Earl of Beaconsfield (d. 1881) by Boehm. Under the seats
nearby is the Cannings' ledger stone. Vice Admiral Sir Peter
Warren's monument (d. 1752) by Lewis Roubiliac in bay 2 has been
reduced so as to reveal the late 15th c. screen of St John the
Evangelist's chapel. In the walkway is the grave of William
Gladstone (d. 1898); his effigy by Sir Thomas Brock and Sir Robert
Peel's (d. 1850) by John Gibson stand against the next column.

At this point one can break off and enter the crossing, passing the
early 17th c. pulpit (base and canopy of 1935), to look first into the
sanctuary and then at the quire. The high altar and reredos as seen
from this side are by Scott (1867), with mosaic Last Supper by
Antonio Salviati; before it the actual ceremonies of Coronation
take place. The sanctuary pavement, of immense artistic
importance, is so-called Cosmati work, done in 1268 by Roman
workmen using Italian porphyry slabs and jasper with marble and
glass mosaic in patterns of circles and squares.

Along the N side of the sanctuary are the three grand canopied

Westminster: Early 15th c. tomb of Lord Bourgchier at entrance to St Paul's Chapel

tombs, each with recumbent figure, of Aveline, Countess of Lancaster (d. 1274), Aymer de Valence, Earl of Pembroke (d. 1324) and Edmund, Earl of Lancaster (d. 1296), the last being triple-arched. On the S side (E to W) are four big sedilia of *c.*1300 (with medieval painted figures) and the plain tomb of Anne of Cleves (d. 1557), above which is a 16th c. tapestry partly hidden by an early 15th c. altarpiece by Bicci di Lorenzo. The lectern is by Sir Albert Richardson, 1949.

Next the **quire** which also cannot usually be entered but can be well seen from the crossing. It is of course within the 'architectural' nave; its first bay was built with the crossing *c.*1250 and the further ones a decade or two later, but it takes a keen eye to detect the differences. The richly pinnacled and gilt stalls date only from 1848 (by Blore), and the organ cases from 1895–7 (by Pearson).

As one returns towards the E aisle of the N transept, Wilton's colossal monument to Maj. Gen. Wolfe (d. 1759) stands ahead. The two real flags are on it at the Canadian government's request. The tomb-chest in front is of Abbot Esteney (d. 1498) and has nearly complete brasses. The **E aisle**'s use as a chair store unfortunately precludes access and only a little can be glimpsed through the gap beside the Wolfe monument. It was originally (from S to N) the chapels of St John the Evangelist, St Michael and St Andrew. In the last (that is, at the far end) the towering eight-columned monument to Henry, 1st Baron Norris (d. 1601) and his wife is prominent. In the centre chapel on the left, the standing figure is Sir William Follett (d. 1845); behind him, with an angel, is the incomplete memorial of Lady Mountrath (d. 1771), while opposite under a big rusticated arch is by far the most theatrical sculpture in the abbey, to Lady Elizabeth Nightingale (d. 1731) by Roubiliac, depicting her terrified husband shielding her from the macabre figure of Death. On its left can be seen part of the 15th c. reredos. Behind Wolfe, against the back wall of St John the Evangelist's chapel, is the odd figure (dressed in 'Roman' armour) of Sir George Holles (d. 1626). In this aisle (familiarly, as a whole, called 'Nightingale') several other important memorials are hidden, including those to Sir Humphrey Davy (d. 1829), Thomas Telford (d. 1834) and Sir John Franklin (d. 1847).

So back to the sanctuary aisle which is the **N ambulatory**. Ahead in its first bay is John Moore's uninspired monument to Field Marshal the 1st Earl Ligonier (d. 1770). The table-tomb (with incomplete brasses) is of Sir John Harpedon (d. 1438); behind and above, Aymer de Valence's can be seen again. Off bay 2, to the left, is the **Islip chapel**; a verger will unlock the door on request, but the lower part can be adequately seen through the 16th c. stone screen. Note the beautiful unworn 18th c. black heraldic ledger stone to the Pulteney family, the window by Hugh Easton (1948) and what is almost a fan vault. The upper chapel is now the Nurses' memorial chapel and uses Abbot Islip's tomb (d. 1532) as an altar. Opposite the chapel is Edmund, Earl of Lancaster's tomb again, with much original painting. The very large ledger stone in front is of Bishop Duppa of Winchester (d. 1662).

Here it is worth looking at the building design. Each main chapel is, as it were, an octagon with two sides (adjoining the ambulatory) left out. So their vaults have seven radiating ribs (those of the aisles are quadripartite). Their windows (four to each) are large Geometric, and beneath is – or was – wall-arcading. All this is very like Reims.

First however is a small bay where the ambulatory curve begins. On the left a doorway leads into the tiny **chapel of Our Lady of the Pew**, now a lobby to that of St John the Baptist but originally opening off it. The alabaster Madonna is by Sister Concordia Scott, 1971.

Central in **St John's chapel** is the great table-tomb of Thomas, Earl of Exeter (d. 1623); space was left for the figure of his second wife who was buried at Winchester. Moving clockwise from the entry, the others commemorated are: Sir Thomas Vaughan (d. 1483), table-tomb with incomplete brasses; Col. Edward Popham (d. 1651), with standing figures; Hugh and Mary de Bohun, children (d. 1305) – in the wall behind is a double aumbry; Henry, 1st Baron Hunsdon (d. 1596), whose vast canopied tomb is taller than any other in the abbey; Abbot Colchester (d. 1420), Bishop Ruthall of Durham (d. 1523) and Abbot Fascet (d. 1500), all under the ambulatory arch; Mary Kendall (d. 1710) with kneeling figure.

The ambulatory continues behind the high altar, so that one can now look up into the Confessor's chapel. Under its first arch is the plain tomb of Edward I, and under the second the once splendid Italianate one of Henry III (d. 1272), rebuilder of the abbey, set with Cosmati work; its wooden canopy is later. Opposite, under St John's chapel arch, is the commanding figure of Rear Admiral Charles Holmes (d. 1761) by Wilton.

The next bay leads to **St Paul's chapel**, with Wilton's giant monument to William, 1st Earl of Bath (d. 1764) usurping the left end of the heavy early 15th c. screen. The right end, fully recoloured and gilded in 1968, contains the tomb of Lewis, Lord Bourgchier (d. 1430). Medieval doors lead into the chapel; near its centre is the tomb-chest of Giles, 1st Baron Daubeny (d. 1508) with alabaster effigies. Going again clockwise and starting behind the Earl of Bath, the main memorials are to: Sir Rowland Hill (d. 1879); Sir Henry Belasyse (d. 1717) by Scheemakers; Sir John Puckering (d. 1596), big canopied tomb with alabaster effigies; Sir James Fullerton (d. 1631), also with alabaster effigies; Sir Thomas Bromley (d. 1587), with effigy and kneeling children; Dudley, 1st Viscount Dorchester (d. 1632), an advanced classical design with reclining effigy by Nicholas Stone; Frances, Countess of Sussex (d. 1589), fully recoloured and gilded, with recumbent effigy and – an amusing touch – a porcupine at her feet; Anne, Baroness Cottington (d. 1634) and her husband whose later effigy lies in front.

Back in the ambulatory, the tomb of Eleanor of Castile (d. 1290) stands high; the painted plinth and original scrolly ironwork by Thomas Leighton can be seen from this angle. Next comes a triple arch where steps go up to Henry VII's chapel. From the top of the steps an ingenious double bridge leads back to the shrine area, just allowing headroom above and below. It eases the ceaseless flow of visitors. Above it, an equally ingenious insertion in its day, is the chantry chapel of Henry V (d. 1422). It is not open to the public but an idea of the intricacy of its stone enrichments can be gained from the walls spanning the ambulatory.

It is worth pausing in the transverse hall at the top of the stairs, though as an architectural space it is hardly enhanced by the criss-cross of barriers. The panelled and coloured four-centred ceiling is a stone barrel vault. The rich doors into **Henry VII's chapel** itself are of wood with bronze cladding and date from its completion *c.*1519. A left turn however takes one through a little fan-vaulted vestibule into the fan-vaulted N aisle. This typifies the final flowering of English Gothic before the Reformation and the Renaissance, with an all-pervading sense of rectangularity, of grids and panelling. Even the arcade rests on panelled piers, not columns. But the structure as a whole is best looked at later, when one comes into the chapel 'nave'.

The monuments are a curious assembly. On the right are Charles, 1st Earl of Halifax (d. 1715) and George, Marquess of Halifax (d. 1695), and then in the centre the eight-columned tomb of Elizabeth I (d. 1603) by Maximilian Colt which contains also the grave of her half-sister Mary I. The richly sculptured end wall of the aisle is typical of the entire chapel, an unusually large proportion of the figures throughout being original. In place of an altar is a small sarcophagus containing the supposed bones of the 'Princes in the Tower', Edward V and his brother Richard (d. 1483?), and put here in 1674. On either side are monuments by Colt to infant daughters of James I: Princess Sophia (d. 1606, aged three days), in a cradle, and Princess Mary (d. 1607, aged two). The tapestry figures on the backs of the stalls are by William Morris.

The chapel proper is reached by going back to the main doorways. Inside, the harmonious contrast of glorious architecture with rich fittings, of blacks and whites and greys with heraldic colours and metals, is utterly breathtaking. Over it all hangs the vault, hard stone fashioned into a soft texture that rises and falls as a veil. Unlike that of the aisles it is not a true fan vault, but a tour-de-force as though to show off what a fan vault would be like with the columns removed. The hanging fans, or rather their bottommost stones – so much is illusion – are really wedges in great cusped arches that form the real bridges from side to side, and all the rest is panelled stonework of the most daring complexity and lightness, leaping from one bridge to the next. The thickness of the vault is only about 3½ inches, probably less than today's steel-

reinforced concrete! That a roof of such ingenuity could be
continued round the polygonal E end is even more miraculous.
Below the vault are conventional plain Perpendicular windows
originally containing magnificent stained glass, pictures on which
those in King's College chapel, Cambridge were later modelled.
Beneath, instead of a triforium, are rows of statues in niches; under
them, hardly noticeable, stand the four-centred main arches, and
then the canopied stalls, mostly early 16th c. but extended into bay
4 in 1725 when the chapel was appropriated to the Order of the
Bath. The banners and the heraldic stall-plates are those of the
Knights of the Order but the carved misericords are of course
monastic.

The black and white chequered floor is 17th c., and many stones
denoting subsequent royal burials will be noticed. The canopied
altar, by Sir Walter Tapper (1935) incorporates several ancient
features, including a late 15th c. Madonna painting by
Bartolommeo Vivarini. The font, if ancient, was completely refaced
in the 19th c.

Now move forward to the centrepiece, the marvellous marble and
bronze monument to Henry VII (d. 1509) and Elizabeth of York –
Renaissance in style but with an intricate bronze screen which was
made first and is still Gothic. The gilt bronze effigies are by Pietro
Torrigiani. James I (d. 1625) was later buried here too.

The little chapel to the N, with a low stone screen, is almost
completely filled by the enormous monument to George Villiers,
1st Duke of Buckingham (d. 1628) by Hubert le Sueur. That in the
next bay, not quite so overwhelming, is to John Sheffield, 1st Duke
of Buckingham (d. 1721) by Scheemakers and Delvaux. The
easternmost chapel was furnished in 1947 under Sir Albert
Richardson as the Royal Air Force chapel, the glass being by Hugh
Easton and the metalwork by J. Seymour Lindsay. Floor stones
record the burials of Air Chief Marshal Baron Dowding (d. 1970),
Marshal of the RAF Viscount Trenchard (d. 1956) and Oliver
Cromwell (d. 1658).

In the SE bay, on the left, is a monument to Antoine, Duke of
Montpensier, a French royal exile (d. 1807) by Westmacott, and in
the centre one by Boehm to Dean Stanley (d. 1881). Finally, behind
another screen in the S bay are the huge canopied tomb of Ludovic,
Duke of Richmond and Lennox (d. 1624) by le Sueur and
memorials to his family. The four caryatids representing Virtues,
and the trumpeting figure of Fame on top are derived more from
Continental than English precedent.

The regulated itinerary now leads back to the chapel entrance (with a glance at the great W window) and over the bridge to **St Edward's chapel**. This means passing under Henry V's chantry and very close to his Purbeck marble tomb. His oak figure lost its silver head and silver gilt plating at the Reformation; the present head is a replacement of 1971. After passing through the iron screen (1431) one can look back at the chantry which on this side has miniature stair turrets ornamented by life-sized figures and connected by sadly damaged canopy work.

St Edward the Confessor's tomb, the most sacred object in the abbey, stands centrally in his chapel. He died in 1066. The shrine of Purbeck marble with mosaic Cosmati work, is mid-13th c. It originally had gilding and precious stones too. The recesses in the sides are for sick persons to kneel in. The wooden upper part (now largely a modern copy) dates only from Mary I's reign when the shrine was temporarily reinstated after spoliation.

The tombs along the N side, moving W, are to the following: Eleanor of Castile again, with her gilt bronze effigy here fully visible; Elizabeth Tudor (d. 1495), infant child of Henry VII, a tiny tomb-chest; Henry III again, also with gilt bronze effigy; Edward I again, exceptionally plain. Then comes the back of the stone high altar screen (15th c. this side), with many empty niches but a fascinating cornice carved with scenes from St Edward's life and relatively undamaged. Against it can be seen some more Cosmatesque flooring (most of which lies hidden beneath the protective boarding), the oak Coronation chair made in 1300–1 and containing the Stone of Scone seized in Scotland by Edward I, and the sword and shield of Edward III. The mysterious Stone has been identified with that used by Jacob as a pillow at Bethel; legend goes on to trace its travels via Egypt, Spain and Ireland to the monastery of Scone and endows it with many powers of augury and blessing.

The tombs along the S side (W to E) are to: Richard II (d. 1400) and Anne of Bohemia, damaged Purbeck marble tomb-chest, splendid gilt bronze effigies and painted canopy; Margaret of York (d. 1472), infant child of Edward IV, another small tomb-chest; Edward III (d. 1377), another gilt bronze effigy on a rather less damaged tomb and with traceried and 'vaulted' canopy; then his queen, Philippa of Hainault (d. 1369), marble effigy on a tomb-chest now plain but once embellished with intricate fretted niches and tracery in alabaster.

The artistic richness and intense historical interest of the chapel ought not to be allowed to distract attention altogether from the building itself, from another look at the vault and clerestory and triforium, before passing back over the bridge and into the **S aisle of Henry VII's chapel**. Central in bay 1, the tomb with corner obelisks is of Margaret, Countess of Lennox (d. 1578), with her recumbent figure and those of her four sons and four daughters kneeling. Bay 2 is occupied by the railed-in tomb of Mary, Queen of Scots (beheaded 1587). With its giant arch on eight Corinthian columns it is even more sumptuous than Elizabeth I's in the N aisle; both were put up by her son James I. In bay 3 within another rail is the gilt bronze figure of Lady Margaret Beaufort, later Countess of Richmond and Derby (d. 1509) by Torrigiani on a tomb with Renaissance detail. The medallion head close by, also by Torrigiani, is of Sir Thomas Lovell (d. 1524); beside it is a tablet to Lady Catherine Walpole (d. 1737). In the end bay this side is an altar, and in front are five royal burials; on its left stands the giant monument (of 1720) to George Monck, 1st Duke of Albemarle (d. 1670) by Kent and Scheemakers.

Back in the vestibule at the W end, a tablet to Cecil Rhodes (d. 1902) can be seen. Now go down into the **S ambulatory**; ahead is the bust of Sir Robert Aiton (d. 1672) and to its left Philippa of Hainault's tomb again with a small piece of restored canopy work and, below, a damaged but valuable 13th c. retable, called by Pevsner 'the finest piece of panel painting of its date in Northern Europe'.

Opposite is the stone screen (*c.*1400) to **St Nicholas's chapel**. Here the central tomb, bearing two white marble figures by Nicholas Stone, is of Sir George Villiers (d. 1605) and his wife. The other memorials, taken clockwise starting at the doors, are to: Lady Elizabeth Cecil (d. 1597), tomb-chest; Lady Jane Clifford (d. 1672), curious square black sarcophagus with scrolls 'nailed on'; Anne, Duchess of Somerset (d. 1587), ostentatious arched tomb; Elizabeth Fane (d. 1618), wall monument of standard village-church kind with kneeling figures but twice normal size; Nicholas Bagenall (d. 1688) aged two months, 'by his Nurs unfortunately overlayd'), a little pyramid; Mildred, Lady Burghley (d. 1589), another giant with figures of her and her daughter, and her husband kneeling. The tomb with lost brasses is of Bishop Dudley of Durham (d. 1483) and the obelisk in front is in memory of a French ambassador's child (d. 1605). The next big one is to Winifred, Marchioness of Winchester (d. 1586); over it is part of the destroyed tomb of Elizabeth, Countess of Exeter (d. 1591). Then, quite different, Elizabeth, Duchess of Northumberland (d. 1776) to

Westminster: N side of nave

Robert Adam's design, with a catalogue of subsequent family burials. Lastly, against the screen is the tomb-chest of Philippa, Duchess of York (d. 1431).

From the ambulatory Edward III's tomb is seen again; on this side the six bronze miniature figures of his children remain. The chapel opposite is **St Edmund's**, with a 15th c. wooden screen and a crowd of tombs. Of the central three, the marble one is to Mary, Countess of Stafford (d. 1694), the middle one (with a magnificent brass) to Eleanor, Duchess of Gloucester (d. 1399), and the third to Archbishop Waldeby of York (d. 1397). The remainder, going clockwise from the doors as before, are to: John Eltham, Earl of Cornwall (d. 1337), alabaster tomb-chest with graceful little figures in niches (the intact ones against the screen are visible from outside); John Howard (d. 1762), characterless tablet; Bishop Monck of Hereford (d. 1661), obelisk of 1723; two children of Edward III (d. 1340), miniature tomb-chest with tiny effigies; Frances, Duchess of Suffolk (d. 1559), tomb-chest with recumbent figure; Francis Holles (d. 1662), figure in Roman armour by Stone; two late 16th c. women, attractive little tablets; Bishop Ferne of Chester (d. 1662), slab with very worn brasses; Elizabeth Russell (d. 1601), seated figure on pedestal; John, Lord Russell (d. 1584), stiff horizontal figure under big arch; Edward Bulwer-Lytton (d. 1873), floor stone; Sir Bernard Brocas (d. 1396), magnificent Gothic canopied tomb with brass and plain effigy in armour; in front, Sir Humphrey Bourgchier (killed 1471 at Barnet), tomb-chest with brasses incomplete; Sir Richard Pecksall (d. 1571), three-arched with him and two wives kneeling; Edward, 8th Earl of Shrewsbury (d. 1618), sumptuous deep-arched with lying effigies of husband and wife, and delightful kneeling daughter; lastly, against screen, William de Valence (d. 1296), wooden chest on a stone one and, on top, an effigy of a type made in Limoges and unique in England, with enamelled copper plates on an oak core.

From the ambulatory Richard II's tomb is next seen again. Opposite is the small arched wall tomb of Katherine (d. 1257, aged five) and four other children of Henry III, showing remains of Cosmatesque mosaic and other ornament. Next, beside St Benedict's chapel, is the alabaster effigy of Cardinal Langham (d. 1376) on a tomb with brass marginal inscription. The window beyond, a World War II memorial, is by Hugh Easton, 1948.

On the other side of the ambulatory the four early 14th c. painted panels with tall figures are the back of the sedilia. Beneath them is the reputed tomb of King Sebert, the abbey's supposed founder (d.

c.616), early 14th c. The iron gates into the **S transept** (like those on the N) are of 1733. Architecturally the big difference from the N transept is the (possibly unique) taking up of the W aisle by part of the cloister, so that one sees a blank wall within the arcade. Above the cloister walk is the muniment room, the intrusion being thus two-storeyed. The rose window here is also different, renewed in 1890 to a 15th c. design.

Reverting briefly to the back of the sanctuary stalls, there are two big marble monuments by Bird, to Dr Busby (d. 1695), Head Master of Westminster School, and to his pupil Archdeacon South (d. 1716). Between them, part of Anne of Cleves's tomb is seen again.

Now the S transept taken clockwise, starting near the ambulatory in front of St Benedict's chapel. On the first column is Armstead's bust of Archbishop Tait (d. 1882), and next to him a bust of John Dryden (d. 1700) by Scheemakers. This is the beginning of **'Poets' Corner'**, but first **St Benedict's chapel** should be looked at (through the gate, which is normally locked). On its far wall is the ostentatious two-arched monument of Frances, Countess of Hertford (d. 1598). The central tomb-chest with two white marble effigies is of Lionel, Earl of Middlesex (d. 1645) and his wife, and the smaller one on the left with brasses (behind Dryden) is to William Bill, first Dean (d. 1561). The kneeling figure in the recoloured wall-arcade on the right is his successor Dean Goodman (d. 1601).

Continue along the E side. The bust of Henry Longfellow (d. 1882) is by Brock. The canopied tomb is of the first poet buried here, Geoffrey Chaucer (d. 1400); it was erected in 1556 by Nicholas Brigham whose name also appears on it. The wall-arcade has been ruthlessly cut away for the sake of the later memorials around it. In the floor in front are stones (all of 1967–76) commemorating Lord Byron (d. 1824), Henry James (d. 1916), Gerard Manley Hopkins (d. 1889), W.H. Auden (d. 1973), John Masefield (d. 1967) and T.S. Eliot (d. 1965). Others are to Alfred, Lord Tennyson (d. 1892) and Robert Browning (d. 1889). In the last bay are the medallioned bust of the actor Barton Booth (d. 1733) and a monument to 'Michaell Draiton' (d. 1631). The bust on the sill above is of Matthew Arnold (d. 1888) and a modern floor slab honours the 7th c. poet Caedmon. The doorway leads out towards the Palace of Westminster.

The end (S) wall has an early 18th c. memorial by James Gibbs to Ben Johnson (so spelt) (d. 1637) with bust by Rysbrack; one of similar date to Samuel Butler (d. 1680); one of 1778 to Edmond Spencer (so spelt) (d. 1599); one of 1737 by Rysbrack to John Milton (d. 1674); and one by Bacon to Thomas Gray (d. 1771).

Still more poets (with one exception) are remembered along the wall facing the doorway; the most prominent is Matthew Prior (d. 1721) by Gibbs and Rysbrack. On the end column are busts of Tennyson (by Woolner) and the Australian Adam Lindsay Gordon (d. 1870) (by Lady Kennet, 1934).

Next, the group round the corner, facing into the main transept area: on a pedestal Thomas Campbell (d. 1844); high up, a bust of Samuel Taylor Coleridge (d. 1834) by Hamo Thorneycroft, 1885; Robert Southey (d. 1843); a bust of Samuel Johnson (d. 1784) by Nollekens; Jane Austen (d. 1817); William Wordsworth (d. 1850); Keats and Shelley, a double tablet of 1954; William Shakespeare (d. 1616) by Kent and Scheemakers, 1740; Robert Burns (d. 1796), tablet of 1885; James Thomson (author of 'Rule Britannia', d. 1748) by Robert Adam; the Brontë sisters, combined tablet of 1947. The inclusion of novelists and others is perhaps 'poetic' licence. In the floor nearby are the graves of the actors Sir Henry Irving (d. 1905) and David Garrick (d. 1779), as well as Dr Johnson.

From the transept S wall Rysbrack's 18th c. memorials to John Gay and Nicholas Rowe have been removed to the triforium, revealing two prominent and important late 13th c. paintings of St Christopher and St Thomas. Over the doorway is Nollekens's memorial to Oliver Goldsmith (d. 1774); to its right a medallion head of John Ruskin (d. 1900) by Onslow Ford and a bust of 1897 to Sir Walter Scott (d. 1832). The biggest monument on this wall is that of John, 2nd Duke of Argyll (d. 1743) by Roubiliac. The doorway (with a 15th c. door) leads to **St Faith's chapel** (reserved for private prayer), a high vaulted plain room with fine corbel heads and many medieval floor tiles. The wall painting of St Faith above the altar is late 13th c. and the teak figures of Christ, St Peter and St Edmund are by Michael Clark, 1967. The gallery at the W end was part of the upper-level access to the dorter.

The W wall of the transept (behind which are the cloister and muniment room) is alive with memorials, of which the following may be picked out. In bay 1: top centre, Gen. Sir Archibald Campbell (d. 1791) by Wilton; top right, George Frederick Handel (d. 1759) by Roubiliac; below, the singer Jenny Lind (d. 1887); on the right a bust of William Thackeray (d. 1863) and, in the floor, stones to Handel, Charles Dickens (d. 1870), Rudyard Kipling (d. 1936) and Thomas Hardy (d. 1928). Against the column are

Westmacott's statue (1809) of Joseph Addison (d. 1719) and a bust of Thomas, 1st Baron Macaulay (d. 1859) whose grave is nearby. Bay 2 has six 17th and 18th c. monuments, the name now best known being perhaps Dr Isaac Barrow (d. 1677), centre bottom; on its extreme right is a bust of John Keble (d. 1866) by Woolner. Here the original wall-arcade has been treated more respectfully. In the centre of the main walkway is a stone to Thomas Parr (d. 1635) whose only claim to fame was his reputed age of 152. Bay 3 has a similar group of memorials, including on the left the architects Sir Robert Taylor (d. 1788) and James Wyatt (d. 1813) and on the right Garrick and the antiquary William Camden (d. 1623). On an arcade column in the direction of the high altar is a bust of William Blake (d. 1827), by Sir Jacob Epstein, 1957.

Now round the corner into the three bays of the **S choir aisle**. The low gates are again of 1764. The sequence here will be anticlockwise – so starting along the S wall where painted shields of medieval benefactors occur as in the opposite aisle (the bay numbers that follow also correspond with the N side).

High in bay 11 is the curious quatrefoiled memorial of Rear Admiral John Harrison (d. 1791); the cloister doorway beneath is flanked by smaller 17th and 18th c. monuments. Bay 10 is dominated by Grinling Gibbons's big commemoration of Admiral Sir Cloudesly Shovell (d. 1707) with naval scene and richly bewigged figure: Horace Walpole wrote of it 'men of honour dread such honour'. Above, Sir Godfrey Kneller (d. 1723) by Rysbrack, to the left Admiral Robert Blake (d. 1657), and to the right Robert Olive (d. 1774), the last two being 20th c. tablets. Bay 9 is a muddled one: at the top John Methuen (d. 1706) and his son, by Rysbrack; at the bottom, but off-centre in spite of its size, George Stepney (d. 1707); on its left John and Charles Wesley (d. 1791 and 1788), put up in 1876. In bay 8 a towering group is crowned by a memorial to Martin Folkes (d. 1754); in the bottom centre is one by Gibbons to Admiral George Churchill (d. 1710); around this are some interesting tablets to soldiers and sailors.

Now the N wall, with the bays numbered as before. Bay 8 under the organ contains the monument to Thomas Thynne ('barbarously murdered' 1683) with a vivid sculpture by Arnold Quellin depicting his assassins attacking his coach in the Haymarket. Bay 9 is dominated by the stiff reclining figure of Thomas Owen (d. 1598), newly coloured and gilded; on its left is a modern tablet to William Tyndale (d. 1536) and on its right Flaxman's bust of Pasquale de Paoli (d. 1807). The best monument in bay 10 is that to Dame Grace

Gethin (d. 1697) with dignified kneeling figure; in the floor is the grave of Dame Sybil Thorndike (d. 1976). Bay 11 contains the sombre black marble memorial of the judge Sir Thomas Richardson (d. 1635) with bronze bust by le Sueur, and the tomb chest of William Thynne (d. 1585) with alabaster effigy in armour.

This concludes the whole of the church, except for the exterior and a final look at the nave interior.

Now go through the doorway opposite the Thynne monument into the **cloister**. This is not all of one date. Work began at this, the NE corner; the N walk and that part of the E walk which is structurally within the transept are of c.1250. The remainder, replacing the Norman work probably ruined by a fire in 1298, is mid-14th c., i.e. more or less contemporary with the W parts of the nave. So what is seen first is 13th c., with the quadripartite vaults and Geometric windows typical of Westminster. The worn doorway behind is of rather different character, with Purbeck shafts and heads each side supposed to be Henry III and Queen Eleanor.

The N walk is given over to a 'brass-rubbing centre', the brasses themselves being replicas from all parts of the country. Many minor monuments line the cloister walls, and only those of particular note will be mentioned. At the end the 14th c. work begins, easily distinguishable by its tierceron vaults and Perpendicular tracery. The W walk was finished last of all. In its 2nd bay is a large plain monument to Charles Godolphin (d. 1720), in the 3rd are tablets to abbey musicians, and in the 6th floor slabs to surveyors to the fabric John Micklethwaite (d. 1906) and Walter Tapper (d. 1935). On the wall nearby, the bronze medallion head of Ian, Baron Fraser (d. 1974) has a well-fingered Braille inscription. Behind this wall lies the Deanery, formerly the abbot's house. The triple memorial to World War II servicemen has statuettes by Gilbert Ledward.

In the S walk ahead is a splendid cinquefoil-headed doorway to what is now the song school. It originally led to the refectory, the wall of which this forms the base being some 35 feet high; the other side (not open to the public) has 11th c. blank arcading and a 14th c. top. The four recesses alongside were towel cupboards, associated with the much altered recess nearby in the W walk which contained the washing trough. The vaulted passage from this corner, with a worn doorway, leads into Dean's Yard. For the present follow the S walk however. In bay 4 is the grave of Muzio Clementi (d. 1832) and in bay 5 a new and colourful marble tablet to the navigators Drake, Cook and Chichester. This is a good point to look out across the garth to the four-tiered S side of the nave with its flying buttresses and to see how the N end of the E walk is swallowed up in the transept. As inside, subtle changes of detail at the fifth nave bay from the crossing mark the junction between mid-13th and late 14th c. work.

Continuing to the SE corner: the three very worn effigies under wall seats in bays 7, 8 and 9 are of Abbots de Humez (d. 1222), Crispin (d. 1117) and Laurence (d. 1173). At the corner is a monument to Daniel Pulteney of Bath (d. 1731) by Rysbrack.

Turn now left up the E walk. On the right, the double doorway to the **chapter house** has sadly decayed canopy work over. It leads to a vaulted vestibule of great dignity at the end of which (this being Crown property) an entrance fee must be paid and (the floors being so precious) special overshoes must be donned. A splendid vaulted stair leads upwards, for there is a crypt (not open to the public) reached from Poets' Corner. The glass on the right (by Clayton & Bell) and a small wall tablet commemorate James Russell Lowell (d. 1891); opposite is a well preserved Roman sarcophagus, probably early 3rd c. Underfoot on both top and bottom landings are medieval tiles.

The big double opening into the chapter house proper was much renewed under Scott, particularly the central column and big circle above with its Majestas. But the jambs and outer arch are largely original, with marvellous carving on both sides, and the top parts are relatively undamaged.

This was not only the monastic meeting room, but also that of the Commons from the reign of Edward I to that of Edward VI. Later it became a record office, full of galleries and stairs, all of which were removed by Scott in 1865. He rebuilt the vault, and the slender central column. The great four-light windows are Geometric and exactly similar to the mid-13th c. work in the church itself. Below, however, the round-headed cusped wall-arcading is not matched elsewhere. The glass includes panels of 1882 by Clayton & Bell, reused in the 1950s in an overall scheme by Joan Howson forming a narrative of the building's history. The floor is mostly of original tiles with fascinating repeating patterns. Many of the paintings in the wall arcade are 14th c., in a variety of styles and scales. In the NW bay is the Apocryphal life of St John, at the base of which a series of animals has been added: 'Reynder', 'Dromedary' and 'Kameyl' are amongst them. The E wall has a Last Judgment, and the S and SW a number of scenes not fully identified but labelled as far as is possible.

If the counter is sufficiently staffed, ask on the way out to be admitted to the Pyx chamber. Its door is on the left past that to the stair leading formerly to the dorter but now to the library and muniment room. This chapel, part of the late 11th c. dorter undercroft, was once the treasury and later housed the Pyx, the box containing standards of gold and silver for testing coinage of the realm. It still has a stone altar and piscina and a 13th c. chest and tiled floor. It too is Crown property. The remainder of the undercroft is used by the Dean and Chapter as a museum, and a separate entrance fee is payable. Here are displayed funeral effigies of wood and wax, robes, uniforms and armour, bells and plate, the second Coronation chair made for Queen Mary II, and other relics. The groined vaults and stumpy columns are eloquent of the early date of this part of the abbey. Above, the dorter itself has given way to the so-called 'School' of Westminster School, now partly 19th c. and much rebuilt after World War II.

Straight ahead, the Dark Cloister leads to Little Dean's Yard, which is private. Around it are the main school buildings, chief of which is the late 17th c. Ashburnham House forming its N side and incorporating parts of the 14th c. prior's house. Another tunnel-vaulted passage to the left leads to the Little Cloister (Farmery or Infirmary Cloister), formed in the 17th c. on the site of the infirmary. On Thursdays one can walk right through to the College Garden; otherwise it is only possible to see its arcading of c.1680, parts of the largely medieval outer walls (which mostly have private residences behind), and the higher brick houses beyond on either side (rebuilt after World War II) framing a view of the Victoria Tower. Behind the left (N) walk are a school gymnasium and classroom and a former chapel of St Dunstan.

When Little Cloister is open the remains of the 12th c. infirmary chapel of St Catherine can be seen through a fine 14th c. doorway in its E side. The figure of St Catherine looking down on its left is a memorial to the architect Lord Mottistone (d. 1963) who rebuilt the houses; to the right was the infirmarer's hall, beside which is the way to the Canons' or **College Garden**. This is bounded on the S by the 14th c. precinct wall and on the W by the school dormitory of 1722, in the design of which both Wren and Lord Burlington had a hand. The four worn stone figures in the garden came from the former Queen's chapel of Whitehall Palace. The Jewel Tower, standing to the SE of the chapter house and visible from here, is mid-14th c. and not really part of the abbey; it was built to house the Crown Jewels.

Return once more to the cloister, turn left along the S walk, and

Westminster: Early 16th c. vault of Henry VII's chapel

go out at the SW corner through a passage in two parts, originally
the parlour, with a high 14th c. vault. A private doorway leads to
the Langham room overhead, which was the abbot's camera, and to
the Litlyngton room. Beyond is a monument to Capt. James
Cornewall (killed 1744 at Toulon) with a naval scene. Then a lower
vaulted passage opens into the **Deanery** courtyard. This is private
too, but the mostly 14th c. College Hall (the abbot's dining hall) can
be seen on its left side, with tall two-light windows, and at the far
end the Jericho parlour, an early 16th c. three-storey addition
against the SW tower. The Jerusalem chamber, not visible from
here, stands between the two in the NW angle and looks out beside
the W front of the church. Not normally open to the public except
on some of the guided tours, it has a beautiful 16th c. interior with
fireplace, panelling and tapestries, 13th c. glass and a fine timber
roof. On the right is the white-walled Deanery itself, the further end
mostly 17th and 18th c., and the nearer parts rebuilt after World
War II.

On now into **Dean's Yard**, site of the abbey granary, bakery and
brewery. Only on the E side do medieval buildings survive, in a
long, largely late 14th c. range starting with the former cellarer's
building and guest house which now contains the chapter offices.
The low gatehouse into a small court is called Blackstole Tower.
The buildings further on were the original home of Westminster
School; another gateway leads into Little Dean's Yard round which
it developed. Through the archway of Church House (1935–9) is
Great College Street where on the left the 14th c. precinct wall
begins – topped at first by inter-war school buildings and then of full
height with a brick capping and a series of medieval openings.
Before Abingdon Street it turns left. At the end of the gardens
there the Jewel Tower can be seen on the left, and just beyond it an
interesting view across the roofs on the N side of Little Cloister
towards the W towers. In between is the turret of the school hall
(called 'School'), occupying the position of the dorter, with a
phoenix weather vane.

Further N, from Old Palace Yard by the George V statue,
another 'back' view takes in the chapter house with the glass roof of
the school gymnasium incongruously beside it. Its great flying
buttresses were a 14th c. addition to the otherwise mid-13th c.
structures, and its roof (which is iron-framed) is 19th c. To the right
are, first the S chapels of the chevet, and then Henry VII's chapel,
panelled overall with a typically English grid embracing walls and
windows and infinitely varied in angle, plane and texture. Here it

can be seen how the thrusts from the astonishing vault inside are
met by flying buttresses lodged on great polygonal piers which,
being so delicately panelled too, merge visually with the zigzagging
leaded windows between. What Wren called 'nice embroidered
work' was, alas, completely refaced a century later.

Round to the N is the other side of the chevet with, on the right,
St Margaret's parish church – then the N transept with its very
French façade. The great portal and side doorways owe much to
Scott and the present rose window design is wholly his. Next is an
opportunity to appreciate the basic external design, on the W side
of the transept and N side of the nave. Above the Geometrical aisle
windows (much renewed, in common with all other external work)
are abbreviated, but similarly traceried, ones lighting the gallery
above the aisle vault. This is the same system as was seen on the S
side, across the cloister, and with changes of detail it continues
(uniquely) around the chevet chapels, as may be seen by looking
back past the transept. Moreover it continues almost unvaried right
along to the W end – although from the fifth bay onwards this is the
building resumed in 1375 at a time when Perpendicular was in
vogue. The slight differences in detail are interesting to pick out.

The **W towers** are best seen from the other side of Victoria Street.
The lower parts are of the time of the W half of the nave, with a
curious continuation of Geometric motifs into the confines of a
Perpendicular framework; from the head of the big W window
upwards is Hawksmoor's work of 1735–40, remarkably pure
Perpendicular but with scrolly Baroque pediments irrepressibly
bursting out in the clock face stage. The porch with statue-niches
and a little vault is early 16th c. Nestling close against it is the
Jerusalem chamber: beside that the modern bookshop, and then the
Scott houses of Broad Sanctuary, 1853.

It will be remembered that a study of the **nave interior** design was
postponed. In any case the temptation to look inside again will be
difficult to resist. Architecturally, the relationship of the W bays as
far as the nave altar is to the remainder exactly similar inside and
out. The design of the E parts has already been examined in the
transepts and the presbytery and quire. As with the exterior, the
quite subtle differences in the W bays are interesting to pick out but
of no great significance to the design; they concern mouldings, and
minutiae of decoration, and not the broad architectural impression
– paradoxically so un-English in a building which above all others is
regarded as essentially English.

Whalley Lancashire: on W side of town   SD 730362

Cistercian abbey of the Blessed Virgin Mary founded 1172 at
  Stanlow, Cheshire by John, Constable of Chester and Baron of
  Halton, a daughter house of Combermere. Dissolved 1537 and
  sold to Richard Assheton and John Braddyll

Owned mostly by Diocese of Blackburn but partly by Roman
  Catholic Diocese of Lancaster. Open to the public, except
  conference house and W range, from 10.0 a.m. (Sundays
  1.0 p.m.) to 9.0 p.m. (or till dusk October to April). Admission
  charge

The move from Stanlow on the Mersey was mainly prompted by
flooding there. Building progress here was slow. The church was
not begun till 1330, nor finished till 1380. The remaining buildings
were mostly of the 14th c., though the inner gatehouse is late 15th
c., and early in the 16th c. a new abbot's house and a Lady chapel
(in a position now unknown) were built.

  At the Dissolution the abbot and two monks were executed for
their part in the Pilgrimage of Grace. Assheton's great-nephew
Ralph converted the abbot's house and infirmary (part of which
seems to be older than the abbey foundation) to his own use and it
was again altered c.1840. The church and most of the remainder
were demolished later in the 17th c. The property was divided in
1922, the W part including the surviving lay brothers' range
becoming a Roman Catholic parish centre and the house (with its
garden containing most of the abbey remains) a conference centre
of Manchester (later Blackburn) Anglican diocese.

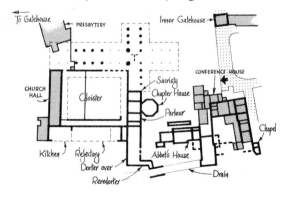

Coming from the town one sees first the embattled inner gatehouse of *c*.1480. The round arch inside, as well as the barrel vault with applied ribs, suggest at least a mid-16th c. completion date. Through it on the left, the adjoining building is post-Dissolution too. Ahead is the Assheton mansion – in origin perhaps a 13th c. manor house, later the infirmary and abbot's lodging, for centuries a private house, and now a conference centre. It is not open to the public. To the right in the spacious garden the **church** walls and columns are marked out on the lawn, the E end with modern altar being nearest the gatehouse. So little is left of the transepts and presbytery that their plan was long in doubt. It seems that the N transept had two aisles but the S (of which some walls survive) only one; both contain several medieval grave slabs. Long 'pits' W of the crossing formed the bases of the quire seating, some of which can still be seen in Whalley parish church. The nave stops short at the present arbitrary boundary but over the wall one can see the W monastic range, now used as a Roman Catholic church hall.

Return now along the S aisle. At its E end some old tiles remain, also the bases of the arch into the transept and of the doorway to the **cloister**. Straight ahead now along the E walk. The three recesses on the left were book cupboards. Beyond is the chapter house doorway with fleuron ornament, flanked by windows in three separate planes. On the left of the vestibule is the sacristy, on the right the parlour, and beyond that the monks' day-room. Above them all was the dorter; traces of its floor and roof supports can be seen. The actual chapter house, no more now than an octagonal footing with some areas of old tiles, lies through another doorway that stands entire.

Back in the cloister, the dorter stair is easily identified at the SE corner. The S range has gone but the doorways to warming house, refectory and kitchen remain, and the washing trough with a big arch over. Another opening by the dorter stair leads across the end of the day-room to the outside. Down to the right from there is the impressive reredorter, with arches over the drain.

Wall foundations on the slope above probably indicate parts of the early 16th c. **abbot's house** not needed by the Asshetons. Alongside, within the main block but roofless, is the abbot's kitchen with three fireplaces; above it the Asshetons had a 'long gallery'. From its lower end one can see the jumbled rear of the house, the most interesting part being the shell of a tiny upper-level chapel at the SE corner (indicated by the traceried three-light window). The

Whalley: 14th c. doorway from cloister to chapter house vestibule

'Avenue' leads round to the front of the house, where some of the walling is 13th c., back to the entrance court.

Finally the parts now outside the main estate. The road called The Sands skirts a length of precinct wall, past which a drive leads to the Catholic church. At the back of the priest's house the whole of the outside of the lay brothers' range (now used for church social purposes) can readily be seen. On its nearer (N) end are traces of the S aisle of the church – two vault springers and part of its W wall. On the cloister side the corbels of the walkway roof are visible, and the row of dorter windows above, while the W side has several original windows and doorways at ground-floor level which led to the cellarer's and lay brothers' rooms.

Further along the road is the spectacular outer gatehouse – early 14th c., long and vaulted. The single big room over the road was a chapel.

Slight traces of the original abbey at Stanlow remain on a small triangle of the Mersey shore (SJ 428775) rendered inaccessible by the Manchester Ship Canal.

Wherwell Hampshire: SU 392407
in village on B3420, 3 miles SE of Andover

Benedictine nunnery of the Holy Cross and St Peter founded *c*.986
   by Elfrida, widow of King Edgar and first abbess. Dissolved 1536
   and sold to Sir Thomas West, Lord Delawarr

Church parochial; remainder owned by Countess of Brecknock.
   Church open during normal hours; remainder private

Elfrida's foundation was in expiation for complicity in the deaths of her first husband and of Edgar's son King Edward. Of the buildings nothing is known and even their siting is conjectural. It is supposed that the parish church was the abbey church, its former twin naves serving nuns and parish as at Minster-in-Sheppey; but it was rebuilt in a different form in 1856 under Henry Woodyer after a fire. The partly 17th c. manor house, though too far S to have been part of a continuous range of buildings, still has a stream running monastic-fashion through an earlier arch beneath its drawing room. Tradition explains this as a relic of a pharmacy established by Abbess Euphemia in the 13th c. Perhaps the pharmacist was prioress, which might explain why her dwelling, set apart from the abbey, retains to this day the name 'priory'.

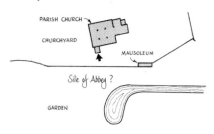

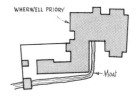

Wherwell priory and its grounds are private, but the house and
water can be glimpsed over the churchyard wall, and in the wall
near the main gate is a stone of 1649 commemorating the abbey.
From its predecessor the church retains some interesting stone
fragments including an early 15th c. nun's effigy (formerly outside),
two late 13th c. sculptures representing an angel and the Harrowing
of Hell, and a curious piece of a Saxon cross-shaft made into a 13th
c. corbel. There is also the tomb-chest of Sir Owen West (d. 1551).
The Iremonger mausoleum at the SE corner of the churchyard has
some grotesque medieval corbel heads built into it.

Whitby North Yorkshire: ¼ mile E of town centre   NZ 903112

Monastery of St Peter founded 657 by King Oswy of Northumbria;
   destroyed by Danes 867; refounded c.1078 by William de Percy,
   and became Benedictine; became abbey by 1109 and mitred by
   14th c. Dissolved 1539 and granted to Richard Cholmley

In care of Department of the Environment. Open during standard
   hours (admission charge)

The foundation is said to have fulfilled a vow made by Oswy before
a victory over the Mercians. It was for men and women and became

famous for the Synod of Whitby at which Celtic ritual gave way to
Roman. Some remains of the cells have been revealed N of the
abbey church and covered again. The refounding after the Danish
invasions was due to the same monks of Winchcombe and Evesham
who revived the monasteries of Jarrow and Monkwearmouth. Of
the late 11th c. buildings the apsed church plan has been found and
marked out, and some small pieces of monastic walling against the S
side of the church still exist. The church was wholly and ambitiously
again rebuilt from c.1220 onwards, the five W bays being a work of
the 14th c. and the W end and clerestory being completed (or
altered) later still. Little is known of the monastic buildings, but the
chapter house is known to have been rebuilt in the 12th c. and
probably other parts were too.

The Cholmleys built Abbey House, supposedly on the site of the
prior's kitchen, from abbey materials and only the church,
unroofed, was allowed to stand – no doubt because of its value as a
sea-mark on the cliff-top. It progressively collapsed from the early
19th c. (the central tower in 1830), and in 1920 was handed over to
the then Office of Works.

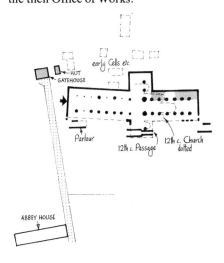

The W front faces the town and is approached first. Now reduced
to its central doorway and the end of the N aisle, its 14th c. detail is
deeply eroded by wind and storm. Inside the doorway, it is evident

Whitby: Abbey ruins from NW

at once that the S and W parts of the whole church have suffered most. Of the five 14th c. bays of the W part of the **nave**, little is left but the N aisle wall, still with a trefoil-headed doorway and considerable remains of four-light windows which had tracery of the type called Kentish; the last three, which are of two lights only, represent the earlier phase, of perhaps *c*.1260. The one entire column of the N arcade was re-erected in 1790, apparently as a result of a bet, and bears an incised inscription.

At the crossing all four pier bases remain, but only the NE pier is complete. The **N transept** is tolerably complete, with three tiers of lancets in its main gable, and once-beautiful trefoil-headed wall-arcading round the base. The window shafts have foliage caps and the arches have both dog-tooth and ball-flower ornament – the former normal in the 13th c., the latter quite a rarity before the 14th. In the right-hand chapel one of the apses of the Norman church has been marked out; similar markings can be followed across the **presbytery**.

Here the finely moulded arcades, triforium and clerestory are complete except at the SW corner and represent the start of the rebuilding, *c*.1220. The triforium, profuse with dog-tooth enrichment, has in each bay a round arch enclosing two double arches, each with a blind quatrefoil over – a typical North of England arrangement. The clerestory is five-arched, the centre arch only being pierced. The quadripartite aisle vault lacks little more than one bay near its centre; the nave roof was never more than timber. The E gable wall is practically complete too, a grand composition with three rows of three big lancets, the top row stepped.

Now along the S side, ravaged so much more by the weather. From the S quire aisle just the foundation of the sacristy can be seen, and in the S transept a column base perched on the side of a Norman apse. Taking advantage of the destruction of the 13th c. work, excavations beneath the end of the **S transept** floor have revealed a late 11th c. passage at a lower level. This is parallel to the presbytery but not to the nave, and it is a matter for speculation, why the two became so greatly out of alignment.

The **cloister** site is just a lawn; the base of the NE doorway into the S aisle can be seen, and the foundation of a parlour by the other end of the aisle. Now turn E, past the splendid E front, to the N side. Numerous remains of the 7th c. monastery, probably mostly nuns' cells, were found in 1924–5 and are now grassed over again. By the N boundary is a shed containing the worked and inscribed stones found, and nearby are three re-erected nave arches, assembled from fallen fragments. From here the mostly round arches of the remaining triforium can be well seen. N of the N nave aisle is a well – also a sunken area with some grave slabs, part of the medieval lay cemetery.

Outside the boundary wall stands a 14th c. cross-shaft on steps, remarkably complete except for the head. The 19th c. gatehouse nearby may be on the abbey gatehouse site; it now leads to Abbey House, which is not open to the public. The gaunt wing visible was a big banqueting hall of c.1680 (dismantled and its windows blocked c.1800). Behind are some 16th and 17th c. bits incorporated into later work, and one or two earlier details support the likelihood that there was an abbey outbuilding here.

Whitland Dyfed: 1¼ miles NNE of village and of A40   SN 208182

Cistercian abbey of the Blessed Virgin Mary founded 1140 at
    Treffgarn (6 miles N of Haverfordwest) by Bishop Norman of St
    David's, a daughter house of Clairvaux, Burgundy; moved to
    Whitland c.1151. Dissolved 1539

Owned by Roman Catholic Bishop of Menevia (Wrexham). Site

accessible at all times subject to permission from farmhouse opposite

Or Albalanda, the first Cistercian house in Wales and the mother of seven others as well as of two in Ireland. So it is ironic that too little is left to reconstruct any building history; past digging seems to have been aimed at recovering building stone rather than the plan.

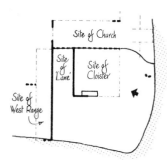

Beyond the mansion called Whitland Abbey, just past a side lane on the left, and opposite a farmhouse, is a field which contains the cloister site near its further end; the wall on the right (with a gabled 19th c. gateway in no significant position) represents the S wall of the church. Along the far side of the field, bounded by the standing wall of the W or lay brothers' range, was the 'lane' separating it from the cloister, while in the centre of the field (actually on the S side of the cloister) around the remnants of a 19th c. garden building, a few old stones have been collected. On the other side of rhe gabled gateway, the church shape is roughly traceable, with a ring of firs at the E end near the road, and clear signs of the W wall. Continuing the line of that, and facing the field beyond, is the further side of the much rebuilt E wall of the W range, with jamb stones of a 12th c. doorway half-way along. The line of its W side can also just be made out, and a shapeless jutting mass of tree-split masonry that may have been part of the reredorter. Lastly, left of the gate back into the road, a rough heap of stones in the NE corner of the first field may be a relic of the chapter house.

Wigmore Hereford & Worcester: SO 410713
1¼ miles N of village and ½ mile E of Leintwardine road A4110

Augustinian (Victorine) abbey of St James founded 1131 by Hugh
   Mortimer, Baron of Wigmore, at Shobdon, a daughter house of
   St Victor, Paris; moved to Eye, near Aymestrey, then to
   Wigmore, then to Byton, then back to Shobdon and finally in
   1172 back to Wigmore; became mitred 1380. Dissolved 1538

Owned by Parry family. Exterior open at all times, subject to
   permission from house; interior by prior appointment only
   (telephone 058 886 454)

What little remains of the aisleless nave and S transept is probably
of *c*.1172. The E end (now gone) was greatly extended late in the
14th c. Of the main claustral ranges nothing survives – only the 14th
c. abbot's lodging and inner gatehouse which were attached end-on
to the W range.
   Though the burial place of the once powerful Mortimer family,
the church seems to have been left to ruin (along with their nearby
castle) after the Dissolution, and the rest mostly turned to farm
uses. The abbot's house however was, and still is, grander than an
ordinary farmhouse and has been discreetly added to at its E end
without in the least impairing its picturesqueness.

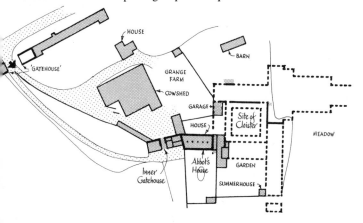

The way into what is now Grange Farm passes between two small
half-ruined blocks, probably a single building broken through to
form lodges after the Dissolution; in each portion is a 14th c.
doorway. The drive forks; the left branch leads between a modern

brick house and a big range of barns into the present main entrance court, beside which is the old house where enquiry should be made.

The upstanding mass of masonry in the adjoining field was part of the 12th c. S transept, and the long grey stretch 12 feet or so high was the S wall of the **nave**, which is considered to have been vaulted. From here it cannot be entered, but from the transept corner one can look into the river-meadow to see a grassy 'platform' marking the quire and aisles, and beyond it the earthworks of fishponds. Access to these is possible via the main entrance court.

The **cloister** occupied the part of the garden nearest the nave, while the E range extended from the transept as far as the little summer house. Nothing is left of either, but the summer house uses two 13th c. half-columns and other fragments. The **abbot's house** was in effect a westward continuation of the refectory range, not a usual arrangement. Its N front clearly shows three periods: W end medieval, centre much altered with Georgian sash windows, and E end more recent. The picturesque S side, heavily buttressed, has 14th and 15th c. windows, and a modern porch incorporating carved stones. Though much altered inside from the 16th c. onwards (to have three storeys instead of two) it retains its 14th c. roof structure.

The adjoining **gatehouse** is picturesque on both sides but only the N, with overhanging timbered upper storey, is original 14th c. work.

Wilton Wiltshire: ¼ mile SE of town centre   SU 099310

Benedictine nunnery founded at pre-existing church of St Mary in 830 by Alburga, sister of King Egbert; new foundation as abbey of St Mary and St Bartholomew (later St Edith too and possibly St Olave) by King Alfred 890. Dissolved 1539 and given to Sir William Herbert, later 1st Earl of Pembroke, with whose descendants it still remains

Owned by Earl of Pembroke and Montgomery. Wilton House and gardens open April to September, Tuesdays to Saturdays, both inclusive, 11.0 a.m. to 6.0 p.m. (admission charge). Almonry may sometimes be seen on request Tuesdays to Fridays

One of the wealthiest medieval nunneries, it had 80 or more nuns in its heyday and possessed the shrine of King Edgar's daughter St Edith; she had rebuilt the church (reconsecrated in 1065) following the ravaging of Wilton by Danes under Swein in 1003.

Little else seems to be known of the buildings, which are

supposed to have been wholly swept away by William Herbert after the Dissolution. The only surviving part attributable to the abbey with reasonable certainty is a low detached once two-storey building, perhaps 13th c., said to have been the almonry, which became the courthouse of the Seignory of Wilton. But it is quite possible that parts of the cloister ranges are embodied in the existing Wilton House. This was rebuilt by Herbert *c*.1560 and partly reconstructed *c*.1650 (S range, under John Webb and Inigo Jones) and again *c*.1805 (W range, under James Wyatt). Wyatt made other changes too, and added or perhaps reinstated the 'cloister' walks in a two-storey version.

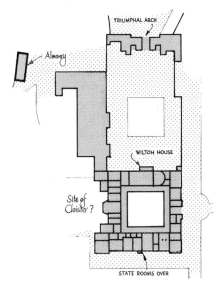

The main entrance gates hang within a triumphal arch of 1759 by Sir William Chambers, transferred here by Wyatt. The almonry, if such it is, lies to the right just off the forecourt; permission to pass the 'Private' notice should be sought at the gate. If the square inner court of the house represents the monastic cloister, then the N range behind the fountain is on the church site. Then the centrepiece of the E front, the four-storey Tudor tower attributed to Holbein, would be where the chapter house was, and the refectory would have been in the centre of the S range. But all that is pure conjecture; tradition says the abbey stood further W, in which case it may be the W range of the house that corresponds with the E monastic range. However the importance of Wilton now lies in the 17th c. State Rooms, particularly the famous Double Cube and Single Cube rooms, and they are outside the scope of this book.

Winchcombe Gloucestershire: in town centre   SP 024283

Nunnery of St Mary founded 787 by King Offa, and abbey for monks 798 by King Kenulf; became Benedictine abbey of St Mary and St Kenelm 969; became mitred 1398. Dissolved 1539 and given to Lord Seymour

In multiple ownership. Site not open to the public

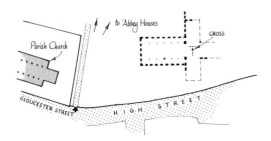

Winchcombe, when its abbey was founded, was capital of the kingdom of Mercia. Kenelm, whose shrine made the abbey famous, was made out to have been Kenulf's son. Following a fire in 1151, rebuilding was still going on in 1206. The abbey was fortified by licence of 1374. Very little is known of the buildings; they were quickly dismantled after the Dissolution and forgotten. Part of the church was found by digging in 1893, and a stone cross set up to mark the centre of the tower. This can be seen from a few yards up the private drive beside the parish church. The two 'Abbey Houses' to which this drive leads are conjectured to have been monastic. The more easterly of them has the greater amount of medieval work, including timber roof. They are not open to the public. Some tiles and two stone coffins are in the parish church.

Winchester (Nuns' Minster) Hampshire: in city centre   SU 483294

Nunnery of St Mary and St Edburga founded late in 9th c. by King
  Alfred and Queen Eahlewith; refounded as Benedictine abbey
  963 by Bishop Ethelwold; dissolved 1539. With the Old Minster
  (Saxon cathedral) and New Minster (moved to Hyde) it occupied
  a single enclosure. Unlike them, its site (somewhere S of the
  Guildhall) is divided and built over, and is undefined. There was
  rebuilding after a fire in 1141.

Woburn Bedfordshire: 1 mile SE of town   SP 965325

Cistercian abbey of the Blessed Virgin Mary founded 1145 by Hugh
  de Bolebec, a daughter house of Fountains. Dissolved 1538 (last
  abbot executed) and passed to John Lord Russell of Chenies,
  later Earl of Bedford

Owned by the Trustees of the Bedford Estate. Park always open;
  abbey grounds at least by 11.0 a.m., and house by 11.30 (times
  vary). Separate charges made for grounds and house

In the absence of helpful documents nothing is known of the abbey
buildings, save that by tradition (and by analogy with similar
houses) the cloister occupied the site of the present main courtyard.
The 4th Earl built the N wing on the site of the monastic N range
c.1630. The W range by Henry Flitcroft is due to the 4th Duke
(1747–61) and the S range by Henry Holland to his successor
(1787–90). An E range, probably corresponding with the E
monastic block which no doubt contained the chapter house, was
also built by Holland but demolished in 1950 when Sir Albert
Richardson designed matching ends for the truncated N and S
wings. There are also very extensive outbuildings by Flitcroft,
Holland and others.

  Visitors go to Woburn to see the game park, the side shows and
the stately house with its precious contents, all outside the scope of
this guide. Nothing monastic survives unless one counts the known
site of the monks' cemetery facing the entrance to the basically 17th
c. N wing, or the name Paternoster Row applied to the corridor
along the other side of the same wing – looking out on to the court
which was the cloister garth and probably perpetuating the actual N

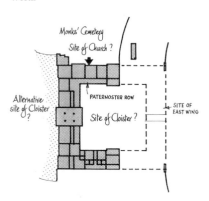

walk. Before the demolitions of 1950 this court was enclosed on
four sides and was more nearly square than it is now.

Worth Sussex: TQ 318343
2½ miles SE of Three Bridges, on B2110

Benedictine priory of Our Lady, Help of Christians founded 1933
  by Downside abbey as a daughter house; became abbey 1965

Church (only) open to the public during normal hours

The foundation was linked with that of a boys' preparatory school
for Downside, set up in the Paddockhurst estate – of which the main
house was begun in 1865 by Anthony Salvin, enlarged in 1881–3 for
Robert Whitehead (inventor of the torpedo) and remodelled after
1894 for the 1st Lord Cowdray by Sir Aston Webb. Additional
school buildings were begun in 1959 and the church in 1966 under
Francis Pollen. The monastery building of the 1930s is to be
replaced by a new one alongside the church.

From a stone lodge the drive leads to a second pair of iron gates
(1932). A left fork just before takes one to the left of the mansion
and towards the concrete-framed **church** beyond. Temporarily this
is entered on the side nearest the house.

As in Liverpool R.C. cathedral, the concept is of 'worship in the
round' with all the congregation facing a central altar. Here,

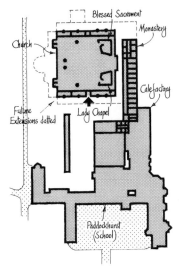

Blessed Sacrament

Monastery

Church

Calefactory

Future
Extensions dotted

Lady Chapel

Paddockhurst
(School)

however, a more definite E–W (really N–S) axis aligns the eventual
narthex on one side with the quire on the other, and the enveloping
ambulatory is square, not round. Crowning the interior is a heavy
circular concrete lantern held aloft by slim umbrella-like spokes on
an outer ring which forms an uninterrupted clerestory. This in its
turn rests irregularly on massive golden-brown brick pylons of
which the two flanking the quire are pierced with tiny niches; the
right-hand one contains a Madonna by Arthur Pollen.

The ambulatory can now be followed to the left, and clockwise
round the church. It has a high flat panelled concrete ceiling. The
'tub' font, close to the future main entrance, is of Portland stone. At
the NE the passage disappears behind the pylon but one can branch
quietly off into its interior, the cave-like chapel of the Blessed
Sacrament, a retreat within a retreat.

The ambulatory goes behind the quire, providing an impressive
westward view, then around the Lady chapel – a second surprisingly
big hidden space. Its big 19th c. Madonna came from Luxembourg.

Outside, the concrete frame is unfinished and unattractive. Below
the church is the 1930s monastery, humdrum red brick, (private)
and between church and mansion a series of utilitarian buildings.
On the upper side of the church a concrete platform with double
flight of steps is ready to support the main narthex; within it will be

found the foundation stone (1968). The buildings on the slopes above are all part of the school and private; so is the main **house** but it is worth going down the narrow steps into the entrance court to see the main front, and to cross to the terrace on the S side. The nearer end of the house is Salvin's and the florid next part by Aston Webb (1895). The single-storey one-time winter garden forms the monks' calefactory and beyond that is the monastery again.

Wymondham Norfolk: in town   TG 107015

Benedictine priory of St Mary and St Alban founded by 1119 by William de Albini, later 1st Earl of Arundel, a daughter house of St Albans; became abbey of St Mary and St Thomas of Canterbury 1449. Dissolved c.1538

Parish church. Open during normal hours

Much of the early 12th c. church survives, though it had a central tower and two western ones which do not. The present W tower, outside the Norman nave, was begun by the parish c.1448; the central one, actually superimposed on the nave and blocking it, by the priory c.1400. In a sense these perpetuate the violent discord between townsfolk and monks (largely concerning bells) that sprang from unclear directions given by the founder and went on for three centuries in spite of the Pope at one stage approving an arrangement whereby the parish had the nave, N aisle and NW tower and the priory the remainder. The N aisle is of the period of the W tower – the Norman NW tower being demolished to make way for it.

After the Dissolution the parish gained rights to parts of the abbey and used the materials to rebuild the S aisle – partly on the site of the N cloister walk. The central tower became an empty shell, and the outermost and domestic buildings vanished. Part of the chapter house still stands however, and the lines of the cloister and other walls have been located.

To the exterior with its two great towers, all essentially Perpendicular, the substantially Romanesque internal character is a marked contrast. The porch and aisles are Perpendicular, it is true, but first one should go to the W end of the **nave**. The Norman bay design is not uniform, and to begin with the westernmost bay each

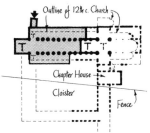

side shows by stouter piers where the towers stood. Then come five bays on square piers with chamfered corners (their form is not original) and in the main arches a variety of zigzag, key and other ornament. The three end bays are plainer, the last two on the S (where the rebuilt aisle stopped short) being blocked; beyond the E wall, now adorned with Sir Ninian Comper's overwhelming reredos (1935), are three more, swallowed up in the substructure of the central tower. The triforium of single shafted arches stops short too in the last two S bays.

The clerestory is a 15th c. rebuilding, and again the last two S bays are different. 15th c. also are the splendid hammer-beam roof with typical East Anglian angels and the tall **tower** arch. The gallery was put in in 1901. The organ is largely of 1793; at ground level its original console and a clock mechanism of 1714 are on view, as well as two stone coffins and a 13th c. font base. The unusually large royal arms over the 'shop' are of George II.

The **N aisle** (Lady chapel) has an even richer hammer-beam roof, with traceried panels and grotesque corbels all along. The font is of standard 15th c. Norfolk type with Evangelists' emblems; its soaring cover is by Cecil Upcher (1962). The many wall memorials are of only minor interest; a line of black marble ledger stones leads the eye towards the great brass candelabrum of 1712 at the altar end. The Madonna is by Comper (1947). The roof here has an extra embellishment of crowned 'M's.

From this point one can look into the sanctuary to see the Comper reredos more closely, and the curious early 16th c. terracotta sedilia, fully Classical and thought by some to be an abbot's monument.

Next cross the E end of the nave, passing the 19th c. brass eagle lectern and oak pulpit and a piece of 'black-letter' text where an earlier pulpit stood, into the **S aisle**. This is of 1544–60 but its roof is of 1903. Behind the vestry partition are two 18th c. Drake family

Wymondham: Church from SE

Wymondham: 15th c. nave roof with hammer-beams and angels

tablets. Of several others, the best is at the W end, to Jeremiah Burroughes (d. 1767), and there are more ledger stones and in one window a few bits of medieval glass. The blank table tomb is of Ann Farmer who gave the organ.

Now the **outside**, starting with another look at the two-storeyed, vaulted 15th c. porch, which has Annunciation carvings in the outer doorway spandrels. Two N aisle windows with 13th c. 'Y' tracery were evidently reused when it was widened. Above, the flint flushwork clerestory has an ornamental parapet at the W end only; its other end finishes against the central tower (c.1400).

With the aid of the plan it is not difficult to unravel the Norman layout and to trace the line of nave arcades through the second tower to the stumps of the first tower piers. The flint wall to their N belonged not to the first transept but to the second N quire aisle. Little else of the E end can now be traced; the prominent arched wall is the E side of the chapter house, c.1400. On the S it is possible to enter the owl-haunted tower shell and to look up at the careful merging of square base into upper octagon. W of it are the two nave bays blocked when the present aisle replaced the Norman one, and at the extreme W one round arch on the clerestory indicates where the Norman SW tower, demolished at the same time, abutted the nave.

Over the fence the line of the S side of the cloister can be made out, and parts of the refectory.

Last, and by no means least, the great W tower – intended, like its ruined rival, to have pinnacles. Now containing ten bells, it impresses more by sheer mass (it is 142 feet high) than by detail and indeed its W face with vertically divided window and original door appears disappointingly flat.

York (St Mary's) North Yorkshire: SE 600523
¼ mile SW of Minster

Benedictine abbey of St Olave founded by 1055; moved to new site by William II 1088; became mitred 1245. Dissolved 1539 and retained by Crown

Owned partly by University of York but mostly by Yorkshire Philosophical Society. Most of the site open in daytime without charge; chapter house etc. 10.0 a.m. (Sundays 1.0 p.m.) to 5.0 p.m. (admission charge); King's Manor 10.0 a.m. to 5.0 p.m. (May to September only)

The late 12th c. church had a seven-apsed E end, proved by excavation. Lavish rebuilding on a much bigger scale began in 1270, the long E arm being complete by 1283 and the W front (by then in the Decorated style) c.1294. Much less is known of the inner monastic buildings; the cloister was late 12th c., and the dorter above 14th c.; the S range was rebuilt in the 14th c. too. Of the outer buildings rather more survives, in the abbot's house forming part of King's Manor, the guest house, the main gatehouse and water gate, and the precinct wall which is the most complete in England.

After the Dissolution the Palace of the Council of the North was set up in the abbot's house, which became King's Manor. That was made in the 19th c. into a National School, then a School for the Blind, and in 1963 a part of the University. The main part of the site was however bought by the Yorkshire Philosophical Society who in 1827–30 built what is now the Yorkshire Museum (housing in its basement important remains of the chapter house and warming room), dug to ascertain the plan of the other buildings, and left the church ruin as the principal feature of gardens accessible to the public.

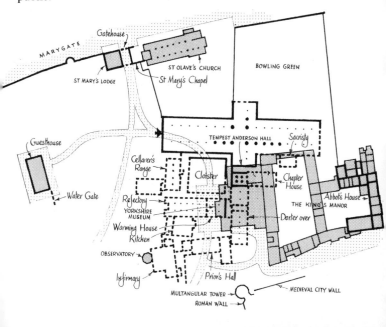

Entry to the Museum Gardens from Marygate is through the 12th c. abbey **gatehouse**, with Norman arch and wall-arcading. The part to the right, now a private house, is late 15th c.; that to the left, now ruined, included a chapel which communicated with St Olave's church tower adjoining. The gatehouse vaulting has gone.

The path bears left up to the **church** W front, an early Decorated, once splendid composition with little now to show but triangular-headed wall-arcading, the W doorway jambs, and part of the N aisle end with a window shell; the date is c.1294. Inside, the N aisle wall, fairly complete, has a similar arcade all along (its shafts all gone), wall shafts with vault springers, and windows that, unusually, were alternately two- and three-light. Of the S aisle wall only the foundation is left; of the arcades merely one column base at the E end of the S arcade, and traces of the next one. But all four crossing pier bases survive, and the arch from aisle to N transept; these are of c.1275. Above the arch, on the transept side, is even a blind bay of triforium with Geometric tracery. Little else survives of this transept, though here the layout of the preceding Norman apses is marked in the turf. More of these can be seen in the quire, as well as its column bases. On the side bank many Early English carved stones are collected together.

To the SE is King's Manor, to be seen later. Its boundary wall overruns the church site, and the museum overlaps the S transept. Some re-erected parts of the chapter house, here visible through a lower window, can also be seen later.

The **cloister** site can be entered from the S nave aisle through a doorway base; here the aisle and S transept walls stand to a height of 5 feet, but of the actual cloister there is nothing above ground. The museum, with Greek Doric portico, is (like the National Gallery, London) by William Wilkins. Apart from other extensive galleries, payment admits visitors to the basement and first to a room built around the great fireplace of the warming room. Another gallery houses not only the excavated remains of the **chapter house** and its vestibule, but also an extensive and important collection of figure and other sculpture, not all of its own period and including some originating from the Minster. The finest figures however are believed to have been Apostles and to have stood between the windows in the eastward extension of the chapter house (c.1200). There is a 14th c. knight's effigy.

Looking left outside the museum portico, one sees the 4th c. Roman Multangular Tower, marking a corner of the city wall. To its left, city wall and precinct wall are one and may be followed up the

side of **King's Manor**. The further end of the flank wall of this
formed part of the abbot's house rebuilt in brick *c*.1480. In it is a
little three-light window of terracotta, one of several here thought
to represent the earliest use of the material in England. The main
front, with two 17th c. doorways inserted to make it face Bootham
Bar and away from the abbey, is 15th c. too as far as the diagonal
buttress just past the centre. But the windows are later and the
brickwork hardly shows its original diapering. The left-hand
doorway leads into the smaller of two courts. On the left of this, at
the end of the present library, is a moulded end of the 13th c. plinth
that underlies much of the 15th c. work. Facing it across the court is
a second return wing of similar length, which itself returns N with
the so-called Huntingdon Room (redone internally *c*.1575). In spite
of such alterations much of the structure of the monastic parts is still
15th c.; public access is however limited. The further and post-
monastic parts are also of considerable interest, with work from the
17th c. to the present day.

Finally the rest of the **precinct wall** (which in 1318 was the subject
of a licence to crenellate or fortify), starting with the square Postern
Tower and the misnamed Queen Margaret's Arch of 1500 facing
Bootham Bar. Along Bootham the wall is visible where houses have
been removed, and the corner of Marygate is marked by a round
tower (blown up in 1644 and rebuilt) strangely called the Hamlet of
St Mary's. Along Marygate is another long stretch, then a
rectangular tower, the church of St Olave, the gatehouse already
seen, then more walling with half-round towers, and at the bottom a
round water tower – beyond which no more survives. From the
esplanade the guest house is well seen – 14th c. stone but with a 15th
c. half-timbered upper floor, all much restored. The two arches on
its S end were part of the abbey water gate.